Winterthur Portfolio 7

Winterthur Portfolio 7

Edited by Ian M. G. Quimby

Published for

The Henry Francis du Pont Winterthur Museum

by the University Press of Virginia

Charlottesville

Statement of Editorial Policy

The objective of The Henry Francis du Pont
Winterthur Museum in publishing *Winterthur
Portfolio* is to make available to the serious student an
authoritative reference for the investigation and
documentation of early American culture.

The publication will present articles about many
aspects of American life. Included will be studies that
will extend current information about objects used
in America in the seventeenth, eighteenth, and
nineteenth centuries; or about the makers, the
manufacture, the distribution, the use, and the settings
of such objects. Scholarly articles contributing to
the knowledge of America's social, cultural, political,
military, and religious heritage, as well as those
offering new approaches or interpretations concerning
research and conservation of art objects, are
welcome.

Ian M. G. Quimby, *Editor*
Polly Jose Scafidi, *Assistant Editor*

Contents

When Wine Turns to Vinegar: The Critics' View of "19th-Century America"

Jay Cantor

WHEN the Metropolitan Museum of Art celebrated the seventy-fifth anniversary of its founding, the United States was just emerging from the dark years of World War II.[1] For the better part of the war years the great treasures of the collection had been hidden away as the threat of German air attacks loomed large and reports of the London blitz underscored the potential danger. With the termination of the war the museum could turn once more to the future, but at the same moment it conjured up the past with an exhibition entitled "The Taste of the Seventies" (Fig. 1). This show included American paintings of the 1870s, their European counterparts, and a group of older European pictures which the Metropolitan had acquired en bloc in 1871 as its first major purchase. Harry B. Wehle noted in the museum's *Bulletin:*

Thus the paintings from the purchase of 1871 remind us that at that time there was a rather well informed taste, which prompted patrons of the Museum to bring to America what they could of European paintings of the seventeenth and eighteenth centuries. But there were also collectors here who went in for the painting of their own day, both European and American. The walls of Gallery A 12, painted in an old-fashioned lees of wine color, are piled high with the contemporary pictures which wealthy New Yorkers cherished in the seventies. Many visitors in 1946 will heave nostalgic sighs upon being reminded of Sunday afternoons long ago when these fair visions first entered into their impressionable consciousness.

Thus, according to Wehle, the museum was still close to the sentiments that had inspired its founding, and nostalgia was an emotion admissable within the precincts of the museum.[2]

Twenty-five years have passed since that exhibition, and another anniversary has come and gone.[3] The Metropolitan is one hundred years old—one hundred years of momentous change in the annals of Western civilization. To celebrate the present anniversary, the museum determined that one of the centennial exhibitions should be devoted to the arts of nineteenth-century America, its first major exhibition surveying the panorama of developments in the fine and decorative arts of the century that gave birth to the museum. When the initial planning for the exhibition began in 1967, the museum had a representative collection of paintings of the period but only scattered objects of decorative art. The American Wing had, since its opening in 1924, boosted the fortunes of colonial and early federal American arts, but its terminal date of 1825 had been keenly observed. The curators felt that the time had come for the museum to extend its consideration of the decorative arts to cover a period consistent with that of the painting collection. As an American museum the Metropolitan has a responsibility to survey American arts in greater detail than might otherwise be required by the museum's general policy.

During the 1960s, in response to the swinging

[1] The Metropolitan Museum of Art was chartered by legislative act of New York State on April 13, 1870. Due to the restrictive conditions of World War II, the celebration of the seventy-fifth anniversary was deferred until 1946. The exhibition commemorating the anniversary, "The Taste of the Seventies," ran from April 2 to September 3, 1946.

[2] Wehle, "Seventy-Five Years Ago," *The Metropolitan Museum of Art Bulletin* 4, no. 8 (Apr. 1946): 202.

[3] Five major and a host of minor exhibitions were created to celebrate the Metropolitan's centennial. "19th-Century America," the third of the major exhibitions, opened during the second week of April 1970 and was thus considered the official birthday exhibition.

FIG. 1. Gallery. "The Taste of the Seventies," Apr. 2–Sept. 3, 1946. (Metropolitan Museum of Art.)

pendulum of taste, there was an inevitable re-awakening of interest in American painting of the nineteenth century, but there was still little serious concern about sorting out the various phases of the decorative arts. A quagmire of stylistic confusion and misread intentions remained to be conquered. The "19th-Century America" exhibition was undertaken with several premises in mind—most of which related to the decorative arts.

1. Nineteenth-century decorative arts represent a serious attempt on the part of American craftsmen to come to terms with both older European cultural conventions and new implications of machine technology, and the resulting products make a significant contribution to the history of American art and culture.

2. Nineteenth-century furniture has suffered in reputation partially because it has suffered in repair; when restored to its original splendor, its intrinsic qualities will become clear (this is even truer of modern furniture, which must be in pristine condition to be of interest).

3. Nineteenth-century arts represent a fast disappearing aspect of our national patrimony, and since they tend to be of urban derivation, it is pressingly important to make a move that will presage the revaluation of the arts and architecture of the period before they are totally obliterated.

Clearly, the main exploratory impulse was in the direction of the decorative arts, where fewer objects were available at the museum or from other public collections and where much essential field research—ferreting out of objects and frequently their acquisition—was requisite to the success of the exhibition. The inclusion of painting was natural at a time when museums are seeking to express the interrelationship of cultural elements and was required in an exhibition that sought to show the best the nineteenth century had to offer. There were, however, two potential conflicts inherent in the premises of the show: (1) adequate guidelines were lacking for distinguishing between a show based on history versus one based on aesthetic criteria, and (2) established principles were deficient for determining whether the aesthetic criteria imposed should represent the taste of our own day or that of the period in question.

Three years of research and planning went into the preparation of the exhibition. The original plan to divide the show into sections devoted to neoclassicism, romanticism, and cosmopolitanism was abandoned because it became clear that the internal history of the century would not support such arbitrary divisions. Although meetings were held between the American Wing and the Department of American Paintings and Sculpture, the two areas of the exhibition were developed separately. Berry Tracy, curator of the American Wing, was responsible for the selection of furniture and other decorative objects, while John Howat, then associate curator in charge of American paintings and sculpture, chose the paintings in consultation with John Wilmerding, chairman of the Department of Art, Darmouth College. Edward Vason Jones, of Albany, Georgia, designed the architecture of the period rooms, provided working drawings, and supervised the construction. The rooms were built by an outside construction firm, and the plaster cornices and centerpieces were run, *in situ,* by plasterers brought from Georgia by Jones. Tracy and Jones selected appropriate wall colors, and Jones provided designs based on period documents for the window hangings, which were made by Brown's of Atlanta. The museum's exhibition design department produced the labels and the Plexiglas cases.

"19th-Century America" was installed in twenty-five galleries normally reserved for the exhibition of European paintings but given over during the museum's centennial to three of the five major exhibitions. In these galleries five period rooms were constructed: New York dining room (Fig. 2), Samuel A. Foot parlor (Fig. 3), Belter parlor (Fig. 4), John Taylor Johnston music room (Fig. 5), and Jedediah Wilcox parlor (Fig. 6). The remaining objects of the more than three hundred works of decorative art in the exhibition were shown either in display areas adjacent to rooms (Figs. 7, 8, 9) or, for many smaller objects, in case-filled galleries (Fig. 10). Nineteen of the twenty-five galleries were utilized in this way, while six were given over to the display of paintings and sculpture with occasional pieces of furniture (Figs. 11, 12, 13). Paintings were also hung in display areas and in period rooms, though those in the rooms were, for the most part, noncatalogued works from the museum's collection included as accessories.

Much energy went into assembling this massive compendium, and it was with dismay that its creators read the first reviews that appeared after the opening of the exhibition. The criticism ranged from the penetrating and provocative to the perverse and petty.[4] A profusion of coy and abusive adjectives was hauled out of the critics' rhetorical storehouse and hurled at the show in general and at specific objects in it. A few of the reviews raised questions that demanded answers, and the following paper represents an attempt to do that, with several asides as to what the museum community might learn from the example of "19th-Century America."

"19th-Century America," wrote Hilton Kramer in the *New York Times,* "is at once an elaborate exercise in cultural nostalgia, a demonstration of museological acquisitiveness, and a celebration of the social class that founded the museum 100 years ago and still presides over its fortunes today. It is only incidentally an art exhibition."[5] Thus early

[4] In addition to those articles quoted below, the following were consulted in the preparation of this paper: "High Style," *Time Magazine* 95, no. 21 (May 25, 1970): 82–83; Emily Genauer, "Art and the Artist," *New York Post,* Apr. 18, 1970; John Gruen, "The Imported Dream, 19th Century America," *New York Magazine* 3, no. 16 (Apr. 20, 1970): 54; J.-B. Hess, "L'Amérique au XIXᵉ siècle," *Le Monde* (Paris), July 2, 1970; Janet Malcom, "On and Off the Avenue, About the House," *The New Yorker* 46 (Aug. 8, 1970): 62–65; Robert Phelps, "The Austere and the Earnestly Ghastly, 19th Century America at the Met," *Life Magazine* 68, no. 23 (June 19, 1970): 10; Henry J. Seldis, "N.Y. Exhibit Surveys U.S. 'Brash Upstart' Period," *Los Angeles Times,* June 14, 1970; Denys Sutton, "American Art," *Financial Times* (London), June 2, 1970; Letters to the Editor, "Art Mailbag —Some Come to Praise . . . ," *New York Times,* May 3, 1970.

[5] Kramer, "Nostalgia Helps Guide Art Choice at Metropolitan's '19th-Century America,'" *New York Times,* Apr.

FIG. 2. New York Dining Room; furniture by Duncan Phyfe for Thomas Cornell Pearsall; details from Williams-Belvin house, Richmond, Virginia, ca. 1811. Period Room; "19-Century America." (Metropolitan Museum of Art.)

in his crusade Kramer fingered the critical distinction between history and aesthetics, and it soon became clear not only that he found little to approve in the selection of paintings and sculpture but that he also found the decorative arts below serious consideration as art. The museum's stated intention was not to create a history exhibition but to produce "a panoramic view of the major decorative and artistic achievements of this country from 1795 to 1910."[6] The elaborateness of their installation suggested that the decorative arts took pride of place; even the poster advertising the show, though reproducing a painting from the exhibition, *The Hatch Family* by Eastman Johnson, illustrates a domestic interior (Fig. 14). To fault the museum for acquisitiveness in an area that is as yet unexplored is extraordinary; to assume that its decisions for acquisition or exhibition were made on a basis other than quality is inconsistent with observable fact. But most critics who wrote about the show seemed to find it difficult to penetrate the basic premises of the exhibi-

14, 1970. Although some allowance should be made for the fact that Kramer was writing under the pressure of a newspaper deadline (the press preview of the exhibition was held on the afternoon of April 12), he repeated many of the same criticisms in a review of an exhibition of American folk art at Hirschl and Adler galleries in May, "Recovering the American Past," *New York Times*, May 10, 1970.

[6] Press release on "19th-Century America," The Metropolitan Museum of Art, Apr. 12, 1970.

FIG. 3. Samuel A. Foot Parlor, New York, 1837; furniture by Duncan Phyfe; columns and door from Matthew Clarkson house, Flatbush, New York, ca. 1835; mantle from Benjamin Halsted house, Rye, New York. Period Room; "19th-Century America." (Metropolitan Museum of Art.)

tion and found it impossible to discuss the show as an entity. Criticisms that might be true of paintings are not necessarily germane to the decorative arts, and the points where the fine and the decorative arts intersected in this exhibition seemed to pass everyone by.

When Kramer claimed that "the history of taste rather than any stringent revaluation of the art of the period has been the guiding principle in the selection of the objects on view," his reference must have been to paintings since a major contribution of the show was the sorting out and appraisal on scholarly and aesthetic grounds of what had previously been an impenetrable morass of cultural miscellany in the decorative arts. The root problem in assembling a coherent exhibition of

painting, sculpture, and decorative arts was the different levels of information available to the curators and what they could assume as general knowledge on the part of the visitor. To have developed specialized theories about painting and to have pushed their selection beyond the scope of a general survey would have been inconsistent with the state of knowledge in the decorative arts. Kramer's arguments against taste fall curiously flat as it becomes evident that what he offers as a substitute is yet another form of taste called the modernist sensibility. He rejects the possibility of judging the nineteenth century by the dynamic intersection of ambition and accomplishment (ideality and reality if you will) and suggests that a penetration of the decision-making process by

FIG. 4. Belter Parlor, ca. 1855; furniture by John Henry Belter, Charles Baudouine, and Alexander Roux; mantle from North Attleboro, Massachusetts. Period Room; "19th-Century America." (Metropolitan Museum of Art.)

which objects are formed would yield nothing, since we are dealing not with artists and craftsmen but with a group of hucksters and pasticheurs groveling at the feet of an elitist company of bourgeoisie. "The true genius of the American decorative arts and crafts in the 19th century," according to this line of thinking, "is to be found in its folk expression—in the kitchen pottery, the wool coverlets, the patchwork quilts, and the humble, plain-style furniture that was created to meet the needs of workaday living. None of this folk art is represented in '19th-Century America,' which, so far as the decorative arts are concerned, might more accurately have been called '19th-Century Bourgeois America.'" Kramer here traverses rocky and indefensible terrain to arrive at

the conclusion that "it isn't until we come to the work of Louis C. Tiffany that we find an American designer of world importance."[7] To reject bourgeois taste and invoke Tiffany, the creator par excellence of the bourgeois precious object, or to suggest that Tiffany sprang full blown from the end of his own pipe is an acrobatic act as daring as it is ethereal. Tiffany belongs to a tradition of innovative manufacture in glass in America that he combined with an outright historicizing interest in ancient glass, which incidentally was being added to the collections of the museum at the same time Tiffany was drawing on it as a resource.

Kramer is a man of his times and knows well

[7] Kramer, "Nostalgia Helps Guide Art Choice."

Fig. 5. John Taylor Johnston Music Room, ca. 1860; furniture by Leon Marcotte; mantle, overmantle, and valance from Jedediah Wilcox house, Meriden, Connecticut, 1869–1871. Period Room; "19th-Century America." Metropolitan Museum of Art.)

the pejorative value of a word like bourgeois, but whether he used it advisedly in this context is an important question. In the nineteenth century, the bourgeois were the makers of America and, whether we like it or not, the shapers of our nation and its culture. The farmers, mechanics, and tradesmen desired nothing so much as to become replicas of the bourgeoisie. Artists were equally bourgeois, and even those who dabbled in the most advanced areas of science and technology, men like Robert Fulton or Samuel F. B. Morse, were company men at heart. As Harold Rosenberg suggested in his review of the show in the *New Yorker:* "The art of new nations is inherently conservative; its primary function is to satisfy the nostalgia or the striving for high culture of artists

and their patrons, and this is best accomplished by imitating the styles favored by the most respectable circles of the home countries. The very notion of art thus becomes identified with 'suitability and decorum.' "[8]

Would Kramer have the museum reject the decorative arts of the High Renaissance in Florence because they were created for the vulgar, self-advertising taste of a group of nouveau riche bankers named Medici? Would he advise us to turn to the countryside to find the true Italian expression in the simpler furniture of the peasants, or should we look at the debased frescoes in village

[8] Rosenberg, "Redmen to Earthworks," *The New Yorker* 46 (July 18, 1970) : 49.

Fɪɢ. 6. Jedediah Wilcox Parlor, Meriden, Connecticut, 1869–1871; furniture from the same house. Period Room; "19th-Century America." (Metropolitan Museum of Art.)

churches instead of at the Sistine ceiling? To invoke coverlets or crude pottery is to summon up an imagery born of the arts and crafts movement and reborn with the vogue for eighteenth-century decorative arts. Because the museum eschewed folk art in favor of the high art aspirations of the period it sought to explore does not mean that it operated out of an inadequate social view. In fact, folk art and country furniture have come to be equated with the nineteenth century as a whole at the expense of the objects that were created by urban craft techniques or machine manufacture. Folk art has gained much of its reputation by priorities other than its own value, either by the very nostalgic longing Kramer condemned, which seeks objects of hand manufacture and idiosyncratic

humanness, or by the promoters of a modernist aesthetic, who find shared values in the style of folk art. These are both fruitful approaches but not when they exclude the other arts of the period for having been produced with the help of machines or for offending our current aesthetic notions.

If material culture is to be of value in reading history, we must use the tools of the present while avoiding the imposition of our own values or prejudices. Patricia Degner's rebuttal of Kramer's assertions appeared in the St. Louis *Sunday Post Dispatch:* "To look at the past through only a modernist's eye is to misread history. Questions of good taste from one generation to the next are always sticky. What the Met show makes clear is

FIG. 7. Display area adjacent to New York Dining Room; federal furniture from Baltimore, New York, and Boston. "19th-Century America." (Metropolitan Museum of Art.)

FIG. 8. Display area adjacent to Foot Parlor; furniture of 1820s and 1830s from Philadelphia, New York, and Boston; paintings and sculpture of same period. "19th-Century America." (Metropolitan Museum of Art.)

Fig. 13. Gallery; paintings of the later nineteenth century including works by Eakins, Homer, Sargent, Whistler, and trompe-l'oeil masters. "19th-Century America." (Metropolitan Museum of Art.)

the tremendous vigor, innocence, inventiveness, confidence, curiosity, craftsmanship and catholicism of the nineteenth century American artists, architects, and artisans."[9] Certainly there is a nostalgic value associated with the taste of the wealthy and their life style, but this does not void the meaning or content of the objects they lived with. These objects were included in the exhibition not for their associational values but because they were considered of aesthetic interest. That folk art has aesthetic merit and might also have been included in the exhibition is a plausible criticism, but to use its absence as the basis for condeming the show as a whole is unfair.

The truth is that the show did not represent a single level of taste within the century, and possible socio-historical reading of the show was kept at a minimum by devices such as the very sketchy

[9] Degner, "Appreciative Look at the 19th Century," *Sunday Post-Dispatch* (St. Louis), May 17, 1970.

treatment of the type of individuals who might have occupied the period rooms. The show presented a dialogue of taste, and for that reason there were regional variations and wide-ranging furniture types. The inclusion of many levels of taste also explains the presence of the work of the craftsmen-reformers, which Kramer professed not to understand. While claiming excellence for the work of Frank Lloyd Wright, Gustav Stickley, or Charles Greene and Henry Greene, he stated: "In the present exhibition, a figure such as Wright remains inexplicable—a sport of fortune—whereas in actuality Wright represents the voice of the American folk spirit raised to a new level of eloquence and power."

Kramer saw the exhibition as a linear ordering rather than as a plastic rendering of influence and counterinfluence (theme, development, and rebuttal). Style changes tended to be revolutionary rather than reactionary, and reforming tendencies were manifest throughout the century. What

Fig. 14. Eastman Johnson, *The Hatch Family*, 1871. Oil on canvas; H. 48″, W. 73⅜″. (Metropolitan Museum of Art, 26.97, Gift of Frederic H. Hatch.)

should be underscored here is that succeeding revival styles were considered both adaptive and modern. Gothic or Renaissance styles were chosen because they spoke symbolically, or even functionally, but not because people longed to be back in a past historical period. Never was the embrace of the modern world more emphatic than in the bourgeois nineteenth century, and the old notion of a century of Goths manqué must be revised. Nineteenth-century furnishings represented a direct commitment to the progressive values of the moment much as plastic furniture does today. And, in fact, the 1960s were more romantically reactionary in their enthusiasms for art nouveau and art moderne than was the Renaissance revival of the 1860s and 70s, whose characteristic style was based on what was considered the modern style of contemporary Paris, where the very concept of modernity was invented and given an urban context.

Kramer, in pushing for folk art, seemed to suggest that things that were intended as art in their own day are not, whereas less ambitious objects are. His view is yet another reflection of the modernist interest in folk art and the acceptance of folk art on the basis of formal and abstract values as correlatives of observation, but it is important to remember that folk art in America should not be confused·with a purely native or indigenous art. In crafts there are certain folk traditions that span both centuries and cultures, and in folk painting the point of reference is as much to high art as it is to life. The relationship between the gradual disappearance of folk art and the increased distribution of works of art through inexpensive color lithographs on the one hand and the rise of photography for portraiture on the other remains to be defined. Folk art is offbeat, colorful, and human, but it is not necessarily deeper philosophically than high art.

The arts of certain separatist groups, communitarians of social or religious bent, are another and independent category of folk art, with other values operative. Philosophical and religious attitudes play a part not evident in related folk manifestations, but, frankly, not enough has been done to ferret out the differences of influence (native background, motivating philosophy, and so on) and mutations produced by contact with ongoing cultures. Surely these groups played a role in the complex entity that was the America of the nineteenth century, and their absence from the exhibition represents an inconsistency of titling at least.

Kramer, however, saw other inconsistencies in the show.

(The Met seems not at any point to have made a firm decision on whether its exhibition should primarily serve the interests of art or only the interests of social history—a confusion traceable, perhaps, to the Centennial occasion.) At the highest levels of American pictorial art in this period—in the work of Stuart, Alston [*sic*], Cole, Bingham, Inness, Church, Kensett, Heade, Blakelock, Ryder, Eakins, Homer, Whistler, Cassatt, Twatchtman, and a few others—there is, I think, little question that the sheer expressive force of these artists places them beyond comparison with the productions of their folk contemporaries. But at the next level, questions abound, and it is no longer clear—at least to me—why certain atelier painters are given critical priority over certain folk painters.[10]

It is curious that Kramer insists on rigid commitment to either social history or to aesthetics, for within the context of nineteenth-century America, folk art deserves a place not only for its aesthetic interest but also for its articulation of social history. As Amy Goldin suggested in *Art News:* "In 19th-century art detail needs to be read, and 20th-century indifference to subject matter is inappropriate for this exhibition. Unfortunately, the Metropolitan has not tried to exploit contemporary narrative interests."[11]

Goldin is right, for if painting deserves a place within the context of the nineteenth-century show, it does so not as an aesthetic sampling but as a visual index of American life. That is why what Kramer called "Leutze's pictorial rubbish," *Washington Crossing the Delaware,* deserves a place in the exhibition, for seldom has a picture spoken to and for an age with such clarity. Important pictures are not always successful ones and

the tradition of the fine arts in America is shorter and has shallower roots than that of the applied arts of design. Therefore, since the exhibition was cast as a survey of the period, it had to include works by those artists who are considered important today and those whose works were valued in their own day. If the museum erred, it did so in the direction of dealing too much with inner art historical concerns—milestones of artists' careers or firsts of a certain pictorial type—so that visual or narrative qualities gave way to bookish ones.

The inconsistencies in the choice of paintings noticed by Kramer were echoed by several critics. Gabriel Laderman, writing in *Art Forum,* suggested that the exhibition was "not a total success either as spectacle or as art history." While enjoining the curator to be free of the temptations to value the past largely through the fog of current taste in art, assigning value and quality as work approaches today's taste in today's art, he found the museum's attempt to deal with the century on its own terms unsuccessful, mixing "history and nostalgia . . . with the appreciation of art." He suggested that American high art, as it deviated from European models, might be seen as primitive, and thus, "It seems strange to include eccentric work full of obvious provincialisms and errors while excluding the work of true primitives." Laderman felt that the critical choices were further complicated by the installation. "The prominence given the mixture of paintings of quality and paintings of historic or sociological interest in the first room (Fig. 13) automatically assigns quality to them all," and he concluded that the skying of works in other galleries (Fig. 12) "inevitably leads to lower estimations of their quality." While it may be stretching a point to suggest that the contemporary viewer understands the criticism that skying implied in the nineteenth century, it is true that the double hanging was not done with enough conviction to suggest a true period installation. Laderman remarked further that

If the entire show was hung in some version or other of the neo-Victorian salon, most of my arguments would be truncated, if not wholly short-circuited, but the two rooms hung pretty much as we hang paintings now [Fig. 13] contain what must be taken as the curatorial conception of the "best" of the work produced in the late Victorian era. . . . The choice of treating the art in these two rooms in the manner to which modern museum-goers are accustomed is, in the context of this

---

[10] Kramer, "Recovering the American Past."
[11] Goldin, "Coy Women, Purple Upholstery, Cosmic Landscapes," *Art News* 69, no. 3 (May 1970): 42.

Fig. 15. Gallery; mid-nineteenth-century paintings. "Three Centuries of American Painting," Apr. 9–Oct. 17, 1965. (Metropolitan Museum of Art.)

show, a most unfortunate one. It says, "Look, here is the real art. What you have seen earlier was just for the sake of nostalgia, but this is the real goods." And of course it isn't.[12]

The selection and installation of the "Taste of the Seventies" or the more recent (1965) "Three Centuries of American Painting," both assembled principally from the Metropolitan's own collection, would not only have been more consistent with the period room approach of "19th-Century America" but would also have permitted a wider range of works than the later show offered. Sadly lacking were some of the typical allegorical, sentimental, and religious pictures that would have helped to complete the setting that the period rooms began to define. Thus a work such as Henry Peters Gray's *The Wages of War,* visible over the door in the view of "Three Centuries of American

[12] Laderman, "19th Century American Art at the Met, 2. On the hanging of the show," *Art Forum* 8, no. 10 (June 1970) : 78–79. See also Jerrold Lanes, "19th Century American Art at the Met, 1. On the organization of the show," in the same volume, pp. 76–77.

Painting" (Fig. 15), which was considered so important in its own day that a subscription was raised among the Metropolitan's trustees for its acquisition—the first American painting in the museum's collection—was not included in "19th-Century America."

The "Life in America" exhibition, organized by A. Hyatt Mayor and Herman W. Williams at the Metropolitan during the New York World's Fair of 1939, could be cited as another example of a survey with an approach that might have functioned fruitfully for "19th-Century America," and incidentally it included many pictures on view in the later exhibition. "Life in America" was a true landmark exhibition, a finely honed selection of pictures that spoke with clarity and wit of the complex intermingling of factors that was nineteenth-century America. Whether the museum visitor would have been prepared to read the narrative content of such a range of pictures is a perplexing question. "Ideally," wrote Katherine Kuh of "19th-Century America" in the *Saturday Review,* "the viewer should have some previous knowledge of the period, for where our native art is concerned, tolerance results less from final standards than from an understanding of the sources, interrelationships, and difficulties that produce this art."[13] Kramer would have found this view nostalgic, and James R. Mellow, writing in *The New Leader,* regarded such possibilities as untenable.

Unfortunately, no serious student of the period is likely to buy the 19th century the Met is selling. It is one of those nice places to visit that one wouldn't want to dwell on or in for any great length of time. Visitors to the exhibition will have to bring along their own ideas as to what was significant in American art—and, indeed, in American political and social life—during the time; the Met's show is simply too limited and special in its view.

He went on to suggest that,

the important artists of the period—Eakins and Homer, Bingham and Ryder—maintain their excellence, but they are nearly buried in an avalanche of knick-knacks and gewgaws and hideous furniture. All too often, *19th Century America* represents the triumph of Kitsch and Camp.[14]

Mellow seemed not to realize that the definition of kitsch and camp resides not so much in objects as in how they are perceived. It is precisely because the museum has, in its decorative arts selection, rejected the knickknacks and gewgaws in favor of an intelligent selection of the best of each genre of object that the objects displayed cannot be labeled kitsch and camp. The viewer was asked to see objects on their own terms rather than on the basis of today's attitudes towards fun objects or period pieces. The selection of objects was serious and so was the attitude of their creators. They are not subject to the accusations of "bizarre" or "intellectually sleazy" that could be applied to the works of European contemporaries. If American productions are at times naïve and overreaching and if attempts are made to endow objects with a broader range of reference (e.g. Ott and Brewer's Baseball Vase) than the decorum of today's purist aesthetic would allow, is this not a clue to the nature of the age and one of those bits of evidence that Mellow found lacking?

[13] Kuh, "A Panorama of Nineteenth-Century America," *The Saturday Review* 53 (May 30, 1970) : 40.

[14] Mellow, "Centennial Kitsch," *The New Leader* 53, no. 13 (June 22, 1970) : 28.

Kitsch and camp are easy and loaded terms, and their use suggests an unwillingness on the part of the critic to penetrate beyond surfaces. We are in the arena of serious creation, not the field of casual by-products of a manufacturing and consumer society that could fit Mellow's description. That the nineteenth century itself understood the distinction is evidenced by a cartoon appearing in *Life* magazine for April 22, 1886 (Fig. 16). The cartoon lampoons the museum's Cesnola collection, which was criticized in the press as being not high art but common objects. If the claims were true, then the exhibition of the Cesnola collection within the museum was as inappropriate as the exhibition of Americana conjured up in the cartoon. It should also be remembered that one of the founding tenets of the Metropolitan Museum was the encouragement of good design in contemporary manufactures, thus suggesting contemporary awareness of the unsatisfactory state of design in general. A number of objects in the 1970 show were acquired by the museum in the nineteenth century directly from their makers, evidence that they were viewed as exemplars of quality in manufacture and design at the time they were made.

The critics of "19th-Century America" tended to review the selections of decorative arts and paintings separately, and although a great deal was said about the assumed premises on which the exhibition was based, very little was said about the selection of specific decorative objects. Some commentators went so far as to suggest that the juxtaposition of decorative arts and paintings was detrimental to the latter, for the general view was that "19th-Century America" was an exhibition of painting and sculpture fleshed out by the addition of decorative objects. Given the familiarity of painting and the relative unfamiliarity of furniture and other decorative arts of the century, it is easy to see why the critics found it convenient to view the exhibition in this way. Barbara Novak, who devoted the better part of her review of the catalogs to a postmortem reproach of the exhibition, assumed the point of view that there could be no aesthetic intercourse between painting, sculpture, and decorative arts (or Americana, as she classed the latter category).

The American artistic past is, in 1970, firmly established. The art needs neither yellow-brocaded couches nor patriotic rhetoric to indicate either its profound root in the American experience or its artistic integrity.

IN THE YEAR TWO THOUSAND.
WHAT DR. HAMMOND'S BALD-HEADED AMERICAN OF THE XXI. CENTURY WILL SEE AT THE METROPOLITAN MUSEUM.

FIG. 16. W. A. Rogers, *In the Year 2000,* cartoon from *Life,* Apr. 22, 1886. H. 10⁹⁄₁₆", W. 16¼". (Photo, Winterthur.)

Its subtleties and eloquence insulted by overpowering irrelevancies, could only have been brought out by the most stringent and sparing display. The exhibition drowned out this quiet voice, and, by allusion, juxtaposition, and operatic nostalgia, overemphasized what was excessive and vulgar in American art. . . . At the Metropolitan, one was pained by art as decoration and decoration as art.

Since the "decision was made on too many occasions to relegate the art to a subsidiary role," she concluded, . "We are in the peculiar position of hoping people read these documents [the catalogs] but missed the show."[15] The views of the exhibition included in this paper provide clear proof to refute Novak's belief that the paintings were "drowned out" (or "buried," as Mellow suggested).

Many people, in fact, looked without seeing, and finding themselves incapable of overcoming their preconceived notions or of summoning the requisite knowledge, especially in the area of decorative arts, went away disliking what they had viewed: "those heavy, overblown pastiches of established European styles that remain an offense to the eye and an oppression to the spirit. As history, these suffocating examples of Louis XVI Revival, Renaissance Revival, and Victorian respectability may be interesting and instructive. As art objects, they alternate between the monstrous and the ludicrous."[16] Perhaps Kramer could have made these comments seem believable if he had compared one of the pieces cited to a Shaker chair, but when actually contrasted to European prototypes, American versions appear to be models of simplicity and restrained good taste.

The illustrations given to refute Kramer's

[15] Novak, "An Uncertain Nostalgia," *The Art Gallery* 14, no. 2 (Nov. 1970) : 45–46.

[16] Kramer, "Nostalgia Helps Guide Art Choice."

claims were purposely selected (Figs. 17, 18, 19).
It would certainly have been possible to illustrate
things that come closer to his assertions, but the
fact remains that the entire century, or its manifestations in the exhibition, cannot be dismissed
without a careful examination of all the evidence.
The either/or stance assumed by most critics is entirely unrewarding as criticism or scholarship.
Amy Goldin pointed out: "these rooms have the
considerable merit of exploring the concept of
style rather than merely assuming it. The assump-
tion that stylistic purity is identical with artistic

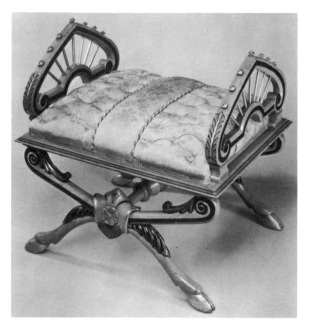

FIG. 18. Alexander Roux, Curule bench, New York, ca.
1865. Painted and gilded wood; H. 23¾", W. 23⅞",
D. 19¼". (Metropolitan Museum of Art 69.108, Ed-
gar J. Kaufmann Charitable Foundation Fund.)

FIG. 17. Leon Marcotte, Library table, New York, ca.
1872. Black cherry and amboina veneer; H. 30¾",
W. 50", D. 29". (Metropolitan Museum of Art 34.140.1,
Gift of Mrs. Robert W. deForest.)

quality is necessarily baffled by the range and
giddy energy of 19th century eclecticism."[17]

It was the forms and forces of that giddy energy
that the museum set out to investigate. What it
found was a young nation burning for culture as
established by old world precedents, but tempered
by a characteristic faith in progress as represented
by contemporary technology. In its earliest decorative forms America clung to the stylistic lead of
England, whose political control had just been
sloughed off. But these forms were bent to a political purpose, and the ornamental vocabulary
became symbolic of the new nation. When the
Renaissance borrowed from the antique, the trans-
ference of forms is called iconography; when

America does the same kind of borrowing, it is
called eclectic bad taste. Nineteenth-century bor-
rowings are seen as a slavish imitation without
comprehension of informing principles. In fact,
the use of the past changed radically over the
course of the century, and only in the later decades did it become mere academic fashionmonger-
ing. Analogous changes in the relationship of
American and European styles occurred as well.
American taste was tentative and searching, and
the excellent essay and catalog entries of the decorative arts volume point out the meanings and mo-
tives behind stylistic change.

Considering the subtle selection of objects
within and adjacent to the period rooms and the
indications of extensive thought behind the show
provided by the catalog, one wonders how Mellow
arrived at his final judgment. "It is largely a series
of period rooms—parlor studies—the Metropolitan gives us. It has dusted off the bric-a-brac and
polished up the furniture, but in the main, the
Met has left the 19th century pretty much in its
storeroom state—unexamined."[18]

To a certain extent, criticisms like this can be

---

[17] Goldin, "Coy Women, Purple Upholstery," p. 44.

[18] Mellow, "Centennial Kitsch," p. 29.

blamed on the lead established by Kramer's article, for more often than not reviewers were content to mirror his remarks without going further in their critical investigation. Thus appeared such criticisms as Alfred Werner's in *Pantheon*. "Interior designers of Victorian America often pandered to the crude tastes of an instant bourgeoisie that aped the worst features of the more vulgar, more exaggerated historicizing French and English fashions."[19]

There is really no basis for an assertion such as this, but visitors to the show, who, incidentally, were generally enthusiastic about the exhibition, had no way to check such judgments against fact. Werner probably could not prove that American designers copied only "the worst features of the more vulgar, more exaggerated," but the museum did nothing to prove otherwise. American museum visitors have few opportunities to test their perceptions of American arts against comparable European examples. Must comparisons of prototypes or sources of borrowing be reserved for discussion in scholarly articles? Is this not an area where visual evidence can be exciting and revealing? If the fifty years that American furniture has been studied seriously by museums is not sufficient to establish the value of the native school and to override notions of cultual inferiority, then it is time to eliminate American objects instead of including them out of pity. If they merit consideration, they do so within the broader context of the history of design, and American museums should not be afraid to show them in that context.

American arts are not alone in the cultural isolationism with which they are displayed. Only recently have cases of European decorative objects been reinstalled in order to suggest migrations of stylistic vocabulary and craft technique. For too long silver and ceramics have been dealt with as precious objects lacking comprehensible cultural roots. Where period rooms exist, they have suffered a similar loss of cultural associations in the transplantation process. A major value of European rooms in American museums is to establish a sense of space and scale unfamiliar to the museum visitor, but the cultural myopia of such rooms is astonishing. The situation at the Metropolitan Museum is close to scandalous. There are,

at the present time, nine eighteenth-century period rooms of French or English derivation, one eighteenth-century Venetian room, and three rooms that span the seventeenth century, English, Swiss, and Franco-Bolognese. Present plans call for the installation of a Renaissance room, another French eighteenth-century room, and an art nouveau room. The museum is also avidly collecting in the art moderne period. Specialized exhibitions of American arts rarely include related European examples, and in the decorative arts of Europe a visitor is usually subjected to the same seventeenth-eighteenth-century bias evident in the Met-

Fig. 19. J. & J. W. Meeks, Desk and bookcase, New York, 1836–1850. Rosewood and satinwood; H. 91¾″, W. 52⅜″, D. 23¼″. (Metropolitan Museum of Art 69.19, Rogers Fund.)

---

[19] Werner, "19th Century America," *Pantheon* 28, no. 4 (July–Aug. 1970): 345.

ropolitan's rooms. How then is one expected to be able to view the productions of the nineteenth century intelligently?

The employment of period rooms worked against the reading of the nineteenth-century show on any level except that of taste, bringing concern down from considerations of quality of design to questions of could I live in this room? The failure of the show was not that the works were tasteless and unworthy of a place in the museum but that they were selected and displayed at levels on which viewers could only concentrate on their value as objects of taste. The rooms were conceived as idealizations of period rooms, symbols of the best taste of their period and, consequently, too good to be true. The furnishings of the rooms were complete, or nearly so, but the images of their inhabitants were not. Period rooms become confining and repetitious in a museum where similar room types and furnishing patterns prevail. It would appear that the two most important reasons for installing period rooms are either that the room is of such quality in its own interior details, proportions, and so on, that it might be considered a work of art, or that a suite of rooms can be used within the context of social-historical considerations and be interpreted at such levels. Granted that "19th-Century America" was a temporary exhibition aiming at effect, one is still hard pressed to accept the inclusion of such complete period rooms, which veil the object in the hazy aura of a perfected taste and increase the artificiality of the museum setting. The objects in the exhibition were chosen for another purpose —a curator's selection carefully plotted to suggest such basic furniture history concerns as regional variation, use of materials, stylistic permutations, and so forth. But related examples of these concerns were often orphaned in adjoining areas. There was, in fact, an abrasive discontinuity between these controlled settings and the related display areas where the humdrum reality of the crowded museum gallery forcibly yanked the visitor back to the present. How was the visitor to read the objects placed in display areas, settled as they were around the perimeters of the galleries? Were these objects to be read with the same or greater emphasis than the objects in the rooms?

The rooms, it should be noted, were built around suites of furniture owned by the museum, and the rooms were trial runs for ones that will eventually be installed in the new American Wing. It is to be hoped that, at that time, the museum will study the pros and cons of the period room concept and its desirability in the museum, where fixed rooms freeze space and can become obstacles to the natural maturation of a collection. For nineteenth- and twentieth-century arts, they also impede a social-historical interpretation by emphasizing a domestic bias that the Metropolitan has just begun to transcend. When the concept of the period room evolved in the field of American arts with the installation of the first period rooms at the Essex Institute and the opening of the American Wing, there were few historic houses open to the public, and the available ones were not adequate restorations. Today the situation is quite different. The number of house museums has doubled and redoubled, raising questions as to the value of period rooms in the museum context not only on the basis of the tremendous space they require but also because it is now unclear as to how they are to function and how they can be interpreted to the visitor.

In the "19th-Century America" show, the vignettes, or niches, of mid-century Gothic and rococo revival furniture (Figs. 20, 21) struck a happy medium between rooms and galleries. In these vignettes the path of ornament coursing its way around a room could be studied. Shared details among various forms were apparent and readable, and even the form types themselves suggested further interpretation. There was, for instance, a preponderance of desk and bookcase forms in the Gothic area (Fig. 20), revealing that the Gothic style tended to be reserved for library or study areas—another suggestion of the symbolic rather than nostalgic interest in the past. Incidentally, the only reminder that religion even existed in the nineteenth century was in the few pieces of ecclesiastical silver displayed in the Gothic niche. Religion is another area in which paintings could have carried our knowledge of the century further, but the closest the show came to the typical religious or moralizing picture was Thomas Cole's *Voyage of Life*.

The rococo revival vignette on view in the Metropolitan during the 1930s is a handy comparison of an exhibit of period furnishings that suggested the customs and aspirations of the day (Fig. 22). In the earlier vignette, familiar furniture forms implied daily household functions, and if the set

FIG. 20. Gothic revival vignette; furniture by Alexander Roux, J. & J. W. Meeks, and John Jelliff; table and chairs in center designed by A. J. Davis for Lyndhurst. "19th-Century America." (Metropolitan Museum of Art.)

FIG. 21. Rococo revival vignette; furniture by Alexander Roux, J. Dessoir, and Brooks Cabinet Warehouse. "19th-Century America." (Metropolitan Museum of Art.)

Fig. 22. Rococo revival vignette; mid-nineteenth-century furniture. On view in the 1930s. (Metropolitan Museum of Art.)

was too grand with the Nuns and Clark piano, made for exhibition at the 1851 Crystal Palace, it was brought back to reality by the mixture of prints and paintings that surely would have occurred in even the more fashionable residences. But there were no popular prints in evidence in "19th-Century America," although the rococo niche from the present exhibition did function like its Gothic counterpart to suggest stylistic affinities. Here it was seating furniture and parlour forms that implied the importance of polite society, and the inclusion of genre subjects and the wildly flamboyant Severin Rosen still life clearly established links between the fashionable taste and painting of the period (Fig. 21). The rococo vignette provided an ideal opportunity for the inclusion of wallpaper, certainly a common element of every nineteenth-century house, but the only wallpaper in the exhibition was a William Morris reproduction in the aesthetic niche. These

niches served the function of both period room and gallery installation, setting the scene without clouding the view of the objects. Furniture was, after all, made in a workroom and viewed by the craftsman at close range. Its qualities should be apparent to the viewer at an equally close range, and if he is not prepared to look in this way, it is precisely here that a museum's educational responsibility to suggest ways of seeing to the untutored takes over. The object can then be viewed for its intrinsic museum qualities rather than as a well-placed prop.

It is interesting to note that the two rooms with perhaps the greatest documentation as specific rooms, the John Taylor Johnston (Fig. 5) and Jedediah Wilcox rooms (Fig. 6), were curiously incomplete. The rooms depicting earlier styles were fictions of architectural fragments conceptually joined together with contemporary furniture. Fiction, however, worked better than truth, for in

FIG. 23. Beechwood Lodge, the Jedediah Wilcox house, Meriden, Connecticut, built 1868–1870. View of parlor prior to removal of woodwork showing original decoration of cornice and ceiling. (Metropolitan Museum of Art.)

the later rooms judicious editing (and lack of time) left walls and ceilings devoid of the decorative paintings that were an integral part of their design. Johnston, in addition to having been the president of the museum, was an important collector of paintings, some of which were installed in the Johnston parlor, but only American pictures from his collection were shown, a selection that implied a provincialism in taste that is inconsistent with the facts. How fascinating it would have been to see American pictures hanging next to typical French salon works or the great J. M. W. Turner *Slave Ship*, which Johnston also owned. Americans were so art hungry in Johnston's time that he opened his home to the public, and news of important additions to private collections was carried in daily newspapers and illustrated in weeklies such as *Harpers*. This was also the mo-

ment when William Wilson Corcoran was building his gallery, considered an American Louvre, in Washington. Johnston, Corcoran, William T. Walters in Baltimore, are all typical of the broadening interest in the fine arts at the time of the Civil War. Was there any correlation between increasing sophistication in matters of art and in interior design?

The Renaissance revival room (Fig. 6), from the Jedediah Wilcox house in Meriden, Connecticut (Fig. 23), the most complete in terms of original architecture and furniture, was likewise chastened, in the interest of taste, by the decision to show the room in spring decor, which removed the darker figured carpet and heavy hangings and replaced them with straw mats, lace curtains, and spare furniture.

But the period room scheme broke down com-

FIG. 24. Detail of the Furniture Wareroom; suite made for Jay Gould by Herter Brothers, New York, 1882. "19th-Century America." (Metropolitan Museum of Art 69.146.1–69.146.5, Gift of Paul Martini.)

pletely at this point. The furniture wareroom installation (Fig. 24) implied certain things about the advanced state of manufactures, but the period also saw the rise of great decorating firms that could supply all the much loved and desired incunabula. This was the moment when Americans were becoming serious and intelligent collectors of European and Oriental arts and antiques, and surely this taste deserved some notice. The "Back Bay Boston" show, with which the Museum of Fine Arts inaugurated its centennial, made a halting step in this direction with a section devoted to collectors, but even here the selection of a single item from these great Boston collections hardly sufficed to set the scene. The catholicity and voraciousness of such memorable collectors and personalities as Isabella Stewart Gardner was not even hinted at in the Metropolitan's show. The vignette of the aesthetic era, which could have suggested the popularization of

the collecting mania, the desirability of clutter, and particularly the interesting developments in the collecting and manufacture of ceramics was, instead, virtually devoid of ornament (Fig. 25).

By comparison with the committed or seemingly direct course of the earlier decades of the century, the period following the Civil War, if we are to believe the selection of the Metropolitan, was ragtag and dog-eared, marred by confusion and seemingly haphazard lack of direction. The very rich, in fact, disappeared, if they were ever evident in the show. There was nothing to suggest the elaborate splendor the life of the wealthy assumed under the beaux arts blessings of Richard Morris Hunt and McKim, Mead, and White. The closest the show came to this style was the Herter suites made for Jay Gould, while, replacing the more intimate objects of use, there were an increasing number of grand ceremonial and exhibition pieces—surely an inconsistency with the

FIG. 25. Aesthetic era vignette; furniture by Herter Brothers, H. H. Richardson, Tiffany and Co., and Pottier & Stymus. "19th-Century America." (Metropolitan Museum of Art.)

domestic emphasis of the earlier part of the exhibition. "19th-Century America" presented the furniture of middle-class reformers, but not the furniture they were trying to reform. The viewer was asked to compare apples and oranges, to judge Wright, Stickley, or the Greene brothers (Fig. 26) against a horn chair (Fig. 27), cut glass bowls, or the Magnolia Vase. Of the academic styles that swept the country at the end of the century, which may be the reason America had very little real art nouveau, nothing at all was shown, and the colonial revival, which preceded and accompanied the academic style, was likewise eliminated. And what of the influence of the Metropolitan Museum on the arts of design in the last third of the century? Most museums numbered among their founding principles the desire to improve the state of design. Could not this very interesting question have been considered?

But part of the function of an exhibition is to raise questions as well as to answer them, and the "19th-Century America" show stands at the threshold of many interesting and necessary investigations. Of course, many questions are answered, and can only be answered, by the catalog, for even if the visitor has no prior information, he at least has recourse to the accompanying text. The catalog of the decorative arts section is interesting in its consideration of areas of influence, both stylistic and technological, and the role of the patron, designer, tastemaker, and craftsman. The introductory essay is a useful guide to what has previously been a bewildering panoply of styles. It is regrettable, however, that the museum saw fit to issue separate catalogs to cover the decorative arts and painting and sculpture. This separation of text surely contributed to the misreading of the premises of the exhibition. The *Classical America* catalog on which Berry Tracy worked with his then fellow curator at the Newark Museum, William Gerdts, should have served as a model for the present volume. Not only were most visitors to "19th-Century America" forced, by economy, to choose between the two volumes, but the paint-

Eighteenth-Century Cultural Process in Delaware Valley Folk Building

Henry Glassie

THE people of the past wrote little. A progressive agriculturist may have left a diary in a trunk for modern discovery; an egotistic public servant may have endured his sunset years longhanding reminiscence, but most of those who are now dead wrote formally about themselves no more than people do today. Like us, they allowed posterity to depend on the external observer for a record of their thought. Reliance on the journalist or the literate elite for our glimpses of deceased cultures skews our view of the past in a definite direction—the direction formalized in those history texts to which the intellectual reformer and the black spokesman for today's minorities object. Reading the words of the past, we can accumulate the fragments for a fair mosaic of the life of the wealthy, which they and their literate retainers bequeathed to us, and we can uncover occasional references, usually maddeningly superficial, to workaday life in the chancy journals of travelers. The comments of an Andrew Burnaby or a Pehr Kalm are invaluable, but we have been left no understanding of the culture of the majority: those who farmed or tinkered with sufficient success—the kind of people who now live in modest, solid brick houses, drive a late model sedan, and spend the day tightening bolts at the Caterpillar factory or keeping the house clean to the rhythm of "The Secret Storm"; just folks who are more excited by the World Series than they are by the latest show at Museum of Modern Art.

Today, the average person is a consumer; in the eighteenth century he was a maker. If he left no books, he did leave artifacts by the thousands. The wagon or the rifle or the shape of a field outlined by walls of rock is as direct an expression of culture as the book—all are artifacts. These artifacts, many now inflated in value as antiques, have attracted different sorts of scholars. Some, trained as historians, have selected a few things associated with specific events—a blood stained chair from Ford's Theater, say—to use as visual props for historical notions set in print. Others have treated objects as if they were art, selecting the few which measure up to modern taste and arranging these about the walls of museums in chronological schemata to illustrate the sequence of detail called "style." Selection on the basis of contemporary need has demonstrable social worth, whether it is mythological (in the case of the historian striving to justify the current situation) or aesthetic (in the case of the antiquarian working to preserve some old-fashioned charm in a drab and jerry-built present); but as scholarship it is incomplete, and incompleteness is wrong—except by accident.

A methodological limitation to print binds the scholar to studying only the handful of people who were literate. The artifact is potentially democratic; artifacts from the past are so abundant that they can be utilized to replace romantic preconceptions with scientifically derived knowledge.[1] This is not, however, inevitable. Often the historian treats only the genealogically relevant things, artifacts which fit the scheme of progress.

A modified version of this paper was presented on October 11, 1969, at a conference sponsored by the Winterthur Program in Early American Culture, entitled "The Delaware River Region in the Eighteenth Century." I would like to express my indebtedness to Craig Gilborn, who suggested the topic, and to Professor Fred Kniffen, who first showed me what the landscape could yield.

[1] Ivor Noël Hume, *Historical Archaeology* (New York: Alfred A. Knopf, 1969), p. 20.

To parody Herbert Read's statement on art history,[2] the history of artifacts is often presented as a line from progressive thing to progressive thing. The usual historical treatment of agricultural implements, for example, is not a description of the tools in use at given times and places; rather, it is a chronological list of rare tools that suggests the "evolution" of modern machinery. This constrictively linear approach to the past, as Claude Lévi-Strauss has shown in his magnificant book, *The Savage Mind*,[3] leaves most people and most artifacts out of consideration.

A similarly ethnocentric approach treats past artifacts only if they are judged appealing by contemporary standards. The prevailing opulent taste of most critics causes them to single out some things as better than others on the basis of their richness of decoration. The application of modernist aesthetic criteria to past artifacts causes a violent change; it eliminates from greatness the things that are untrue to their media.[4] Chippendale highboys and Gothic cathedrals are banished (both have characteristics appropriate to sculpture rather than to furniture and architecture), and their places in art appreciation classes are taken by milking stools and the stone cabins of the Hebrides. Taste is an important subject for study, but the modern critics' evaluations teach not of past but of present culture. Connoisseurship and the optimistic notion of progress have prevented the study of artifacts from becoming a means for making history the rigorous study of past cultures.

Some scholars—they may be historians, archaeologists, cultural geographers, anthropologists, or folklorists—have begun to appreciate the artifact as a powerful source of information. They view objects as books that, no matter how pretty the bindings, are worthless until read. A hammer and a quilt may look nice behind the museum's glass, but they are merely chance associations of hard or soft substances unless enough is known about their source and function to make accurate interpretation possible.[5] A building may enhance the landscape, but it remains a heap of old wood and stone until it is analyzed. The analysis leads away from a concern with the fabric itself toward the ideas that were the cause of the fabric's existence. Strictly speaking, the ideas in the mind of a maker can never be enumerated, but the scholar can venture near a comprehension of the mind's activities and the maker's intent through deep play with components, sources, and models of process, as John Livingston Lowes did in his study of Samuel Taylor Coleridge's two greatest poems.[6] From sticks of wood joined into a chair, from the burned clay mortared into a dwelling, we can get an idea of ideas, a feeling for the concepts that are culture, an understanding, perhaps, of the anguish and pleasure, the joy of innovation and the pain of compromise of men long dead.

The spoor of culture on the land is amazing and easily followed. The dangers in interpreting from artifact back through behavior to culture are obvious, but it is the best means we have; we will never understand the eighteenth century if we read only books. By reading artifacts, if we will read enough of them and not be trapped by a shapely cabriole leg or a scrap of molding, we can learn of past culture, the repertoire of learned concepts carried by those people who framed not only our basic law, but our environment and social psychology as well.

In using things to teach of the past, some classes of artifacts are more useful than others. This usefulness is a function of the ease with which objects can be related to their time and place, of a complexity sufficient to eliminate the probability of polygenesis, and of the existence of enough material to prevent theory from being built on chance survival. Architecture—complex objects that can be sensed inside and out and are such direct and conscious expressions of culture that for both scholar and builder they become symbol—is one of the most useful kinds of objects.

This paper deals with two matters of Delaware

[2] "The history of art is a graph traced between points which represent the appearance in history of a great artist." *Art and Alienation: The Role of the Artist in Society* (New York: Viking Press, 1969), p. 22.

[3] (Chicago: University of Chicago Press, 1969), chaps. 8, 9, especially p. 257.

[4] For an interesting statement of modernist criticism, see Clement Greenberg, "Modernist Painting," in Gregory Battcock, ed., *The New Art: A Critical Anthology* (New York: E. P. Dutton and Co., 1966), pp. 100–10.

[5] See J. Geraint Jenkins, "Folk Museums: Some Aims and Purposes," *Museums Journal* 69, no. 1 (June 1969): 17–20; William C. Sturtevant, "Does Anthropology Need Museums?" *Proceedings of the Biological Society of Washington* 82 (1969): 619–50.

[6] *The Road to Xanadu* (1927; reprint ed., New York: Vintage Books, 1959).

Valley architecture—houses and farm plans. It is based on fieldwork conducted in the eastern United States between 1961 and 1970. It is intended not as a study but as a metaphor for a study. The paper itself is an abstraction, an impression of study based on social-scientific rather than art historical philosophy. It does not include the kind of information normally presented in art historical publications but is made of the stuff familiar to readers of cultural geographic or folkloristic publications. It is offered in this context to increase understanding and communication and to illustrate an alternative to art historical considerations of vernacular architecture and is intended not to replace but to complement. The full study of a subject as large as building in the Delaware Valley should involve the art historian's emphasis on diachronic methodology, concentrating on the few fine houses and public buildings remaining and on the decorative elements of a dwelling's facade. It should also involve the social scientist's emphasis on synchronic methodology, focusing on the quantitatively dominant humble buildings, and on the economic functions of a building's internal volumes.

The attempt to account for all building is fundamental to the social scientist's approach to architecture. When the totality of building is taken into account, the mansions and gems considered worthy of preservation form such a tiny portion of the whole that they deserve little attention. Similarly, by considering all of each building, crockets, brackets, and twitches of stylish trim become unimportant when compared with matters of basic form. The architect Clovis Heimsath expressed the notion succinctly in his intriguing book on Texas architecture. "It's the form that really counts in architecture. Decoration buzzes around the form to dress it up."[7]

It is easy and voguish but incorrect to think of these basic forms as following function (folk buildings frequently have a Bauhaus clarity, which calls to mind the functional style of recent architecture). The basic forms were useful; people lived and worked in them, and they did function —to return to the anthropological sense of the word—both economically and aesthetically. But they were not designed to suit idiosyncratic need;

they were traditional components, traditionally structured into traditional organizations of space required for psychological comfort. The forms lay in the minds of their makers until some problem caused them to be drawn out. When drawn out, the forms were defined by some material, stone, log, or brick, frame filled or sided. Then, the form might have been decoratively encrusted, and it might have had other, distinct forms added onto it. Forms are types—plans for production—and buildings are examples of types or composite types. It is definitively characteristic of folk buildings, and most buildings are folk buildings, to be examples of types that persist with little change through time. The invariant aspects of a form are the aspects of deepest necessity to the people who must use the form.[8]

This paper, accordingly, will concentrate on basic folk types and will be concerned more with architecture as internally usable space than as externally viewed art. A democratic examination of Delaware Valley building leads to a series of conclusions about the cultures of the area during the eighteenth century. These will be exemplified through an examination of certain forms, but the major regional patterns are sketched here as forewarning.

Since Fred Kniffen's classic paper, "Louisiana House Types,"[9] scholars have used folk architecture to suggest spatial patterning in the United States. Fieldwork reveals that the Delaware River runs through two major American cultural regions. The Delaware Valley is divided horizontally at about the southern limits of the Pocono and Kittatinny mountains; the portion above this line belongs with New England and New York in the broad culture region of the North, the portion below fits into the Mid-Atlantic, the architectural region including southern Pennsylvania

---

[7] *Pioneer Texas Buildings: A Geometry Lesson* (Austin and London: University of Texas Press, 1968), p. 100.

[8] The adjective "folk" when applied to an object indicates that the object was produced out of ideas that were old to the producer and out of style with regard to the overtly supported mass culture. For more on the subject see Henry Glassie, "Artifacts: Folk, Popular, Imaginary and Real," in Marshall Fishwick and Ray B. Browne, eds., *Icons of Popular Culture* (Bowling Green: Bowling Green University Popular Press, 1970), pp. 103–22; and Henry Glassie, "Folk Art" in Richard M. Dorson, ed., *An Introduction to Folklore and Folklife Studies* (Chicago: University of Chicago Press, currently in press).

[9] Most recently published in Philip L. Wagner and Marvin W. Mikesell, eds., *Readings in Cultural Geography* (Chicago: University of Chicago Press, 1962), pp. 157–69.

and parts of adjacent Maryland, Delaware, and New Jersey. There is an approximate consensus on the regional boundaries among scholars from different disciplines working with different manifestations of culture. The Mid-Atlantic architectural region outlined on the accompanying map (Fig. 1) is quite similar to Midland speech areas seven and eight in Hans Kurath's *A Word Geography of the Eastern United States*.[10] The northern border is in close agreement with that on the map, "Folk Housing Areas: 1850," recently offered by Kniffen.[11] On the southern and western boundaries there is less general agreement, though the line through southern Maryland is compatible with the one drawn by Wilbur Zelinsky after studying several different cultural traits.[12] Though some of the disagreement in the various maps of cultural phenomena is the result of a difference of interpretation,[13] most of the apparent disagreement results from the distributional differences exhibited by varying aspects of culture. Alan Lomax's map of the English language folk song styles of North America[14] locates the southern boundary of the cultural region of the North far south of the line in figure 1 or the divisions made by Kurath or Kniffen. This reflects the actual state of difference in the spatial patterns of dialect and folk architecture as opposed to song and fiddle style. The dif-

ferences in the cultural maps of the East offered to date are small when contrasted with the truly striking similarities. Cultural regions are scientifically valid; they can be clearly delineated even in these days of supposed national homogeneity.

The lower Delaware Valley, an area, dominated by Philadelphia, that fits into the Mid-Atlantic region, will be the focus of this paper. The lower valley's areas of close cultural connection are found throughout the remainder of the Mid-Atlantic region. The Mid-Atlantic region has been defined by compromising the distribution of major architectural forms and techniques of construction: for example, north of the region, log construction is rare;[15] the Dutch barn found nearby in New Jersey and New York is generally absent from the region;[16] and the external west British[17] chimney, which is characteristic of areas south of the region, is restricted to a handful of examples in Chester County, Pennsylvania,[18] and in the Alleghenies. The boundaries of the regions are not arbitrary lines scratched through the border country between influential centers. Locations within a region, even when greatly separated, are culturally more alike than juxtaposed locations in different regions. Still, the culture of the Mid-Atlantic exhibits certain extraregional connections (Fig. 1), especially between central New Jersey and Long Island, between southern New Jersey and the Chesapeake Bay area, and among southeastern Pennsylvania, central Maryland, and the Valley of Virginia.[19]

Also, the region is not perfectly homogeneous; it can be divided and subdivided into subregions

[10] (1949; reprint ed., Ann Arbor: University of Michigan Press, 1967), fig. 3.

[11] "Folk Housing: Key to Diffusion," *Annals of the Association of American Geographers* 55, no. 4 (Dec. 1965): 571.

[12] "Where The South Begins: The Northern Limit of the Cis-Appalachain South in Terms of Settlement Landscape," *Social Forces* 30, no. 2 (Dec. 1951): 172–78.

[13] The greatest conflicts lie in the South, which has been less efficiently studied than the Mid-Atlantic and the North. The problem relevant to the Mid-Atlantic is whether or not the Upland South is an extension of the Mid-Atlantic or a separate region. Crucial to the solution of this problem is the source of the major Upland house types, most significantly the I house. Kniffen in "Folk Housing," p. 561, feels that the I house of the Upland South and the Midwest is a Mid-Atlantic contribution. He is followed by Peirce F. Lewis, "The Geography of Old Houses," *Earth and Mineral Sciences* 39, no. 5 (Feb. 1970): 34. On the other hand, I feel that the I house of the middle of the United States comes out of the Chesapeake Bay area and that both Kniffen and Lewis have vastly underestimated the influence and cultural significance of the coastal South. See Henry Glassie, *Pattern in the Material Folk Culture of the Eastern United States* (Philadelphia: University of Pennsylvania Press, 1969), pp. 37–39, 64–67, 75.

[14] *The Folk Songs of North America in the English Language* (Garden City, New York: Doubleday & Co., 1960), front end papers.

[15] Fred Kniffen and Henry Glassie, "Building in Wood in the Eastern United States: A Time-Place Perspective," *The Geographical Review* 56, no. 1 (Jan. 1966): 40–66, especially 60, 64, 66.

[16] For some reason John Fitchen, *The New World Dutch Barn* (Syracuse: Syracuse University Press, 1968), considers only the Dutch barns of upstate New York. A couple remain on Long Island and there are many just outside the Mid-Atlantic region in New Jersey; see Peter O. Wacker, *The Musconetcong Valley of New Jersey: A Historical Geography* (New Brunswick: Rutgers University Press, 1968), pp. 94–97.

[17] M. W. Barley, *The English Farmhouse and Cottage* (London: Routledge and Kegan Paul, 1961), pp. 98, 112, 145, 156, 221; Sir Cyril Fox, "Some South Pembrokeshire Cottages," *Antiquity* 16, no. 64 (Dec. 1942): 312.

[18] Eleanor Raymond, *Early Domestic Architecture of Pennsylvania* (New York: William Helburn, 1931), pp. 72–77.

[19] The Valley of Virginia is the area between the Blue Ridge and the Allegheny mountains in western Virginia.

FIG. 1. The Mid-Atlantic folk architectural region and major Mid-Atlantic subregions with directions of extraregional connection. (By the author.)

by plotting the distribution of traits restricted to but not found throughout the region, by establishing the local proportions of traits found everywhere in the region, and by examining the difference in association and significance of regional traits. For example, the drive-in corncrib, called "old fashioned" in *Radford's Practical Barn Plans,*[20] is found for the length and breadth of the Mid-Atlantic region, but it is more common in some areas than in others and is treated differently in the subregions. In New Jersey the drive-in corncrib is a major farm building located in a position of importance within the farmyard; it is fitted with doors and sheds and serves multiple purposes, such as implement storage (Fig. 2). In Pennsylvania it is a dependency of the barn, generally located to one side of the barn's ramp; it often lacks sheds, occasionally, the doors, and frequently serves only as a corncrib (Fig. 3). In the Midwest the drive-in corncrib is a large building with a cupola,[21] and in the southern Appalachian region

it is a small structure frequently built of logs.[22]

Paradoxically, although the Delaware River is the threshold of the Mid-Atlantic, it also amounts, roughly, to a boundary between the major Mid-Atlantic subregions, separating the almost wholly English New Jersey sphere from the syncretistic British and Germanic Pennsylvania sphere (Fig. 1). But there are major intrusions across the river, so that in western New Jersey around Phillipsburg, Pennsylvania characteristics are in evidence, and parts of Chester, Delaware, and New Castle counties are as English as the country to the east. The observable pattern is readily explainable by settlement history, but settlement history might not suggest that this river is as neat a regional border as contemporary fieldwork reveals it to be.

In viewing the Delaware Valley from the other organizational coordinate, time, it is possible to distinguish distinct building phases. By focusing on decorative detail, the architectural historian

[20] William A. Radford (New York: Radford Architectural Co., 1909), p. 274. The drive-in corncrib can also be found in Byron David Halsted, *Barn Plans and Outbuildings* (New York: Orange Judd, 1881), pp. 219–30.

[21] Kniffen, "Folk Housing," pp. 576–77.

[22] Henry Glassie, "The Old Barns of Appalachia," *Mountain Life and Work* 40, no. 2 (Summer 1965): 22–25.

FIG. 2. The Drive-in Corncrib, west of Roadstown, Cumberland County, New Jersey. (Photo, the author.)

FIG. 3. The Drive-in Corncrib, at Clear Spring, south of Dillsburg, York County, Pennsylvania; see also Fig. 25. (Photo, the author.)

can chop the past into a lengthy and complicated series of style periods.[23] Most buildings were completely unaffected or only superficially affected by the sequence of "style," so only three major phases emerge from a consideration of the totality of building. The first, lasting in the Mid-Atlantic area from the period of first settlement to about 1760, was a time of ethnic solidarity in architecture, of the retention of diverse Old World forms and technics with a resultant heterogeneity on the land. The second major time segment included an initial acceptance of new ideas and a blending of the old and new to create a New World repertoire with resultant regional homogeneity on the land. The point at which the regional culture lost its dominance in building practice (though it is nowhere entirely dead and its manifestations still rule the environment) varies from region to region. R. W. Brunskill writes that the end of English regional building can be marked by the com-

[23] A fine recent work is Marcus Whiffen, *American Architecture Since 1780: A Guide to the Styles* (Cambridge: M.I.T. Press, 1969).

FIG. 4. The Georgian House Type. With its double pile plan and rhythm of five openings per floor on the front and two per floor on the end, this house is a perfect example of the eighteenth-century Georgian form expressed in a nineteenth-century structure. Note the Gothicized Palladian window. The plan of this house type can be found in Fig. 5A; other examples of the type can be found in Figs. 10 and 21. Middleburg, Snyder County, Pennsylvania. (Photo, the author.)

ing of the railway in 1840.[24] About the same date seems to hold for the northeastern United States. In the Mid-Atlantic area, regional building practices were retained more tenaciously, and it was not until the era of the First World War that the regional culture was dissolved into the national. In the South the date was still later.[25] Temporally this paper will focus on the early part of the second building phase—the time of extensive and intensive innovation—the third quarter of the eighteenth century; for better than a century later, its legacy was the stable pattern of Delaware Valley building, and the patterns that continue to characterize the landscape today are the products of cultural clash and mesh in the mid-eighteenth century.

It should be noted that most of the illustrations for this paper picture nineteenth-century expressions of eighteenth-century ideas. Late buildings, rather than structures that actually date to the eighteenth century, were chosen to illustrate the points in this paper for two reasons, both of them

crucial to the paper's intent. In the first place, basic house forms, because of the conservatism of builders and inhabitants, persisted unchanged despite the fluctuations of taste represented by architectural detail. Secondly, the major Mid-Atlantic house types of the eighteenth century continued to be erected for better than a century after their introduction or development, so that forms of eighteenth-century origin are not now rarities on the landscape. Buildings worth study are not difficult to locate, and contemporary fieldwork can teach much about eighteenth-century cultural patterns.

The earliest forms of human shelter in the valley changed with the insertion of the Georgian house type (Figs. 4, 5A) into the awareness of builders in the middle of the eighteenth century. As a form it was a century old in England and on the Continent; as a geometric structure of geometric components, it was a Renaissance-inspired notion of classical planning. The form, primly symmetrical, was employed in America as early as 1700 and was accepted for the home of affluent gentlemen the length of the Atlantic seaboard for the last three quarters of the eighteenth century, although its impact was not great until after the publication of handbooks advocating the Georgian style in the

[24] "The Study of Vernacular Architecture," *Architecture North West* (Apr. 1966).

[25] Henry Glassie, "The Impact of the Georgian Form on American Folk Housing," in Austin and Alta Fife and Henry Glassie, eds., *Forms Upon the Frontier* (Logan: Utah State University Press, 1969), pp. 23–25.

FIG. 5. Major Transformations of the Georgian House Type: A. Full (see also Figs. 4, 10, 21); B. Two-thirds (see also Figs. 6, 9, 22); C. One-third (see also Figs. 7, 8). (By the author.)

1740s and 1750s.[26] Like the drama of an earlier period, the Georgian form is an English interpretation of an Italian interpretation of Roman practice (with an optional half-step through Dutch interpreters). The Georgian form is usually considered an English contribution to American domestic architecture, but while that notion connotes accurately the acculturative situation, English Georgian was part of an international Renaissance style. Distinctively Scottish and Germanic expressions of the style were built in Pennsylvania, and the fact that the basic Georgian form was known in seventeenth-century central Europe facilitated its acceptance by Continental settlers in the Mid-Atlantic region.[27] The definitive elements of the type rarely varied: externally, a low pitched roof (hipped on finer houses but usually gabled) and two openings per floor on the ends, five on the facade; internally, a double pile plan with two rooms on each side of a central hall containing the stair.

The new idea was not radically different from older European folk practice. Medieval building was not wholly lacking in symmetry; bilateral symmetry was, in fact, an essential feature of western European folk design. The roof of the new type was shallow, but it was still a triangle that could be framed and covered in the old manner. A central passage, though hardly a formal hall was, as M. W. Barley points out in his excellent *The English Farmhouse and Cottage,* "a characteristic feature of the medieval house."[28] The idea of a symmetrical cover for a two room depth was alien to most old British building, but it was familiar enough to those who came in great numbers from central Europe. The Georgian form was new, but not too new, and backed by the taste makers of the period, it became firmly lodged in the Mid-Atlantic architectural repertoire. From the middle of the eighteenth century to the close of the nine-

FIG. 6. Two-thirds Georgian House Type. The plan of this house is basically that of Fig. 5B. The wing off the hall gable is characteristic of country New Jersey. Northeast of Mt. Airy, Hunterdon County, New Jersey. (Photo, the author.)

teenth, the type was constructed as a stalwart farmhouse in stone, brick, log, or frame throughout the Mid-Atlantic region, achieving dominance at the region's western end in the area of Somerset County, Pennsylvania, and standing as a very familiar form along the Delaware River and throughout New Jersey.

Being an idea, existing fully in the mind before its achievement as an object, the Georgian type was not only built of a variety of materials (form and technics being separate architectural subsystems),[29] it was subject to formal modification. The most common transformation within the Georgian type consisted of a subtractive step yielding two-thirds of the complete idea, a house with two rooms on one side of the hall (Figs. 5B, 6). Houses of the kind are seen occasionally as farmhouses through southern Pennsylvania and adjacent Delaware and Maryland. It is also the predominant, traditional town house type even beyond the region, being found commonly in cities such as Washington, D.C., and Richmond, Virginia,[30] where Georgian house subtypes are unusual in the

[26] Hugh Morrison, *Early American Architecture from the First Colonial Settlements to the National Period* (New York: Oxford University Press, 1952), pp. 288–91, 317.

[27] Charles Morse Stotz, *The Early Architecture of Western Pennsylvania* (New York and Pittsburgh: William Helburn, 1936), pp. 89–91; William J. Murtagh, *Moravian Architecture and Town Planning* (Chapel Hill: University of North Carolina Press, 1967), pp. 79–82, 101–104, 124–25; C. Gillardon, "Das Safierhaus," *Schweizerisches Archiv für Volkskunde* 48, no. 4 (1952): 201–32; cf. G. Edwin Brumbaugh, *Colonial Architecture of the Pennsylvania Germans* (Lancaster: Pennsylvania German Society, 1933), pp. 7–8.

[28] P. 24.

[29] On this and many other points essential to the understanding of building, Christian Norberg-Schulz, *Intentions in Architecture* (Cambridge: M.I.T. Press, 1968) is extremely useful; for this matter see p. 102.

[30] Paul S. Dulaney, *The Architecture of Historic Richmond* (Charlottesville: University Press of Virginia, 1968), pictures many examples.

FIG. 7. An Urban Row Composed of Houses of the One-third Georgian House Type. These houses—some masonry, some wooden; some of the eighteenth century, some of the nineteenth—illustrate the variety of one-third Georgian facades. This sketch represents the 200 block of North Darlington Street in West Chester, Chester County, Pennsylvania. (By the author.)

surrounding countryside. In New Jersey the two-thirds Georgian type is extremely common on the farm and in the village. Generally, it has a kitchen wing, lower and narrower than the bulk of the basic house, built off the gable along which the hall runs. An additional rural New Jersey Georgian modification amounts to a two-thirds form in a single story expression (Fig. 22). The occurrence of this house in central New Jersey is an example of the connections between New Jersey and Long Island, where the type is also found with frequency. On Long Island and in northeastern New Jersey, the chimney was often placed internally, New England fashion; in the part of New Jersey located within the Mid-Atlantic region, chimneys were built inside the gable end as they were nearly always in Pennsylvania and Maryland.

If the Georgian form could be reduced by one-third, it could be reduced by two-thirds, and the new form, one room wide and two deep, was a common town house in the Delaware Valley, as it was in London (Fig. 5C). Like larger town houses, it was often built as half a pair in the vicinity of the Delaware (Fig. 7). In southeastern Pennsylvania, nearby Delaware, and particularly in the area of New Jersey just east of Philadelphia, it can be found, built of frame or log, brick or stone, as a farmhouse, generally with a wing off the non-

chimney gable (Fig. 8). The gable of this house, one-third of the Georgian type, is the same as that of houses that are two-thirds or all of the fundamental form, but the openings per floor on the facade are reduced from five to three to two (Fig. 5).

The transformations of the Georgian type tell a simple story. Ernest Allen Connally teaches the same lesson in his study of Cape Cod houses.[31] People, being innovative, can modify ideas and fragment forms to suit economic and environmental needs. Houses that are portions of the entire idea were doubtless built by the same masters who built the full houses, though for people who had smaller families, less cash, or a smaller piece of land. The narrow, deep proportions of the one-third and two-thirds Georgian subtypes made them suited to small lots and crowded situations. The fact that when the architectural repertoire was rummaged for town houses partial Georgian subtypes were chosen as the forms to fit the context[32] reveals a traditional, rural element in Mid-Atlantic town planning. If the builder were designing from

[31] "The Cape Cod House: An Introductory Study," *Journal of the Society of Architectural Historians* 19, no. 2 (May 1960): 47–56.

[32] Christopher Alexander, *Notes on the Synthesis of Form* (Cambridge: Harvard University Press, 1967), pp. 18–24.

Fɪɢ. 8. One-third Georgian House Type. The basic house is of the type pictured in Fig. 5C. It is located between New Hope and Wrightstown, Bucks County, Pennsylvania. (Photo, the author.)

a problem rather than out of a limited collection of folk components, he would likely have constructed a thin house, its gable to the street, like the ones found in pictures of old European towns or in the late nineteenth-century mill and mine company towns of Pennsylvania. But the planner's repertoire was rural, and even though it meant that the rafters had to span a long distance, he wanted his house in the town to be structured and positioned as it was in the country. Behind the house he had a plot for a garden and a tiny barn, so that the town consisted of rows of miniature farms, the houses, country fashion, with their long sides, or what purported to be their long sides, to the road (Fig. 9). Our innovator was a conservative man: he comforted his innovation by placing it in a traditional structure (the relationship between entrance, ridge line, and road), and he limited his innovations to simple matters of addition and subtraction—addition because the partial form could be enlarged subsequent to its building to produce the full form, and the full form could

be enlarged by an additional one-third or two-thirds (Fig. 10).

The little family of house types on the Georgian plan is a major characteristic of the Mid-Atlantic region. In neither of the adjacent coastal regions, North or South, did the Georgian set of ideas become as deeply embedded in the thinking of traditional builders. The existence of the Georgian type did more than inspire novel forms that collectively signal a new, impurely folk phase in architectural chronology. The basic form was dissected, and some of its components were fused with elements from pre-Georgian building to produce, in a flurry of eighteenth-century innovation, two new house types, both of which showed much more creative thought than occasional refinements within the Georgian form and style such as Cliveden in Germantown or Mount Pleasant in Philadelphia's Fairmount Park.[33]

[33] Irwin Richman, *Pennsylvania's Architecture* (University Park: Pennsylvania Historical Association, 1969), pp. 17–19.

Fig. 9. Mid-Atlantic Townscape. This photograph shows the characteristic orientation of traditional urban housing in the Mid-Atlantic region. To the left is a house of the two-thirds Georgian type. The next house is an example of the Pennsylvania farmhouse type, as in Fig. 13. The main street through Dover, York County, Pennsylvania. (Photo, the author.)

Fig. 10. Full Georgian House with Additions. The stone house is of the full Georgian form. It has had an additional one-third in frame added with lateral symmetry to one gable; beyond that is another frame addition. The house is situated south of Norton, Hunterdon County, New Jersey. (Photo, the author.)

FIG. 11. Continental Central Chimney House Type. Weather-boarded log house. The plan of this house is as in Fig. 12A. The small upstairs windows and bunched window spacing are typical of early houses of this kind. The one story rear ell is a washhouse—common in southern Pennsylvania as an appendage or detached dependency; see too Figs. 13, 27. Between Bermudian and York Springs, Adams County, Pennsylvania. (Photo, the author.)

In the German areas of the region, including spots in West Jersey[34] as well as the more predictable broadening arc in Pennsylvania from Northampton to York counties, an off-center chimney characterizes a common house type, built regularly up to about 1770. Rendered, generally, in stone or log, it exists in one and two story examples. Typically, it has a three room plan; an offset door opens into a long, narrow kitchen incorporating the house's deep fireplace. Behind the chimney, a broader front room serves as a parlor, a smaller back room as the chamber (Figs. 11, 12A).[35] The

size of the house cues internal modifications, such as partitioning the kitchen of a large house or eliminating the wall between bedroom and parlor in a small house.[36] The plan is like that of peasant dwellings in Switzerland and the Rhine Valley.[37] Its depth and proportions, products of the late medieval Continent, are not completely incompatible with the Georgian intent; its plan is not wholly unlike the two-thirds Georgian house subtype. This similarity surely supported acceptance of the new Georgian form, and it facilitated the merger of the old and new forms into the type most common in the heartland of the Mid-Atlantic area from Bethlehem, Pennsylvania, to Frederick, Maryland (Figs. 12B, 13). The flattish roof and ex-

[34] For an example: Peter O. Wacker and Roger T. Trindell, "The Log House in New Jersey: Origins and Diffusion," *Keystone Folklore Quarterly* 13, no. 4 (Winter 1968): 253.

[35] Donald Millar, "An Eighteenth Century German House in Pennsylvania," *The Architectural Record* 63, no. 2 (Feb. 1928): 161–68; Henry Kinzer Landis, *Early Kitchens of The Pennsylvania Germans* (Norristown: Pennsylvania German Society, 1939), pp. 15–16; Robert C. Bucher, "The Continental Log House," *Pennsylvania Folklife* 12, no. 4 (Summer 1962): 14–19; Henry Glassie, "A Continental Log House," *Pennsylvania Folklife* 18, no. 2 (Winter 1968–69): 32–39.

[36] For examples see Glassie, *Pattern in the Material Folk Culture of the Eastern United States*, pp. 50–51.

[37] Max Gschwend, *Schwyzer Bauernhauser* (Bern: Paul Haupt, 1957), pp. 20–21; Franz von Pelser-Berensberg, *Mitteilungen über Trachten, Hausrat Wohn- und Lebenweise im Rheinland* (Dusseldorf: L. Schwann, 1909), pp. 49–53; Karl Rumpf, *Deutsche Volkskunst: Hessen* (Marburg: Simons, 1951), p. 23.

Fig. 14. Pennsylvania Farmhouse Gable. The Georgian house types—full, two-thirds, and one-third—and the Pennsylvania farmhouse type (Figs. 12, 13, 23) share this Georgian gable; it is, therefore, a major visual symbol of the Mid-Atlantic region. The shutters—paneled below, louvred above—are also typical of the Mid-Atlantic landscape; see too Figs. 16, 19. This house has a four opening facade with two front doors and a four room plan. It is located north of Yorklyn, New Castle County, Delaware. (Photo, the author.)

the New World,[40] it was commonly built in all the English colonies north of the middle of the North Carolina coast during the seventeenth and early eighteenth centuries. The early form, in most instances, consisted of two rooms on the ground floor, one of which was square, called a hall, and used for most living; it was often a bit longer than the other room, the parlor.[41] In New England, logically enough, the East Anglian[42] central chimney form was most usual; in the Chesapeake Bay

area, west British external chimneys were most characteristic. In the Mid-Atlantic area, the chimneys were built flush within each gable wall.[43]

The introduction of the Georgian form into I house country engendered the same results in the Chesapeake and Mid-Atlantic areas. The I house retained its one room depth (without which an example would be classified as a different type), but its new plan approximated the front half of the Georgian house with rooms of about equal size separated by a hall (Figs. 15, 16, 17). The five opening facade became standard, so that from the front a Georgian house and a Georgian-influenced

[40] Barley, *The English Farmhouse and Cottage*, p. 178.

[41] A good English plan of the type can be found in W. Galsworthy Davie and W. Curtis Green, *Old Cottages and Farmhouses in Surrey* (London: Batsford, 1908), p. 16.

[42] For English plans: Harry Forrester, *The Timber-Framed Houses of Essex* (Chelmsford: Tindal Press, 1965), p. 15; Elizabeth Melling, *Kentish Sources: V: Some Kentish Houses* (Maidstone: Kent County Council, 1965), p. 44.

[43] For a good example, see Ned Goode, "An Album of Chester County Farmhouses," *Pennsylvania Folklife* 13, no. 1 (Fall 1962): 20.

I house are indistinguishable. The gable view, however, is quite different. The gables of early I houses were normally blank (Fig. 16), though an off-center window per floor became common on later Pennsylvania houses. Particularly throughout southern New Jersey and the Maryland Eastern Shore, there are often two windows on each floor, disguising the old I house even more completely as a Georgian house (Fig. 17).

Most extant Mid-Atlantic I houses are frame, though some in the Alleghenies, on the region's western frontier, are log. In Bucks and Chester counties particularly they are of stone. They were frequently built of brick, most notably in southern New Jersey, and in Salem and Cumberland counties where glazed headers were worked into elaborate diamond and zigzag patterns and into dates

and initials (Fig. 18)[44]—a mode of decoration that was quite common in Tudor England and occasional along the southern Atlantic coast.[45]

The I house concept, expressed like all basic

[44] Joseph S. Sickler, *The Old Houses of Salem County* (Salem: Sunbeam, 1949); Paul Love, "Patterned Brickwork in Southern New Jersey," *Proceedings of the New Jersey Historical Society* 73, no. 3 (July 1955): 182–208; Roger T. Trindell, "Building in Brick in Early America," *The Geographical Review* 58, no. 3 (1968): 484–87.

[45] Harry Batsford and Charles Fry, *The English Cottage* (London: Batsford, 1950), p. 109; "Brickwork Details," *The Domestic Architecture of England During the Tudor Period* (Boston: n.p., 1913); Lewis Coffin, Jr. and Arthur C. Holden, *Brick Architecture of the Colonial Period in Maryland and Virginia* (New York: Architectural Book Publishing Co., 1919), p. 8; Henry Chandlee Forman, *The Architecture of the Old South: The Medieval Style, 1585–1850* (Cambridge: Harvard University Press, 1948), p. 150.

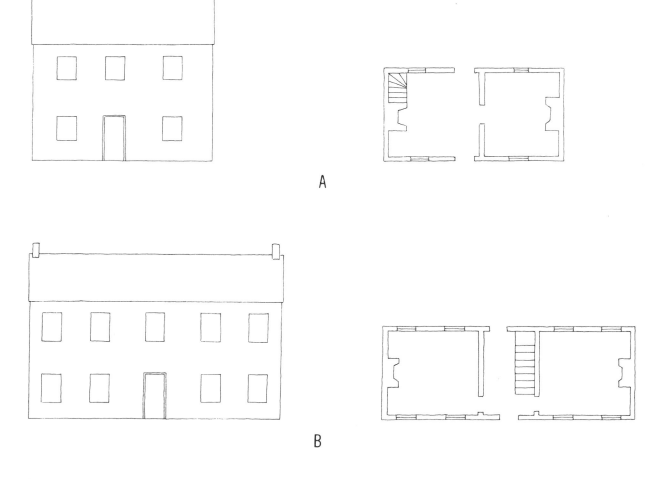

FIG. 15. Schematic Representation of the Development of the Georgian I House Type: A Early two room—"hall and parlor"—plan; B. Georgian I house plan (see also Figs. 16, 17, 24). (By the author.)

FIG. 16. Georgian I House Type. Stone house with a brick facade. Northwest of Middletown, Dauphin County, Pennsylvania. (Photo, the author.)

FIG. 17. Georgian I House Type. Greek Revival era I house. The gable fenestration is typically Georgian (see Figs. 4, 14), though the tall, narrow proportions of the old British yeoman's house remain intact. The exposed chimney back of the internal end chimney, which is characteristic of New Jersey and southeastern New York, is found occasionally throughout the southern United States; the automatic ascription of this feature to some continental—Dutch or Flemish—source is simplistic at best. South of Norton, Hunterdon County, New Jersey. (Photo, the author.)

Fig. 18. I House. The original section of this building was an early two room I house. The gable was subsequently altered—the roof flattened and a double chimney added—in accordance with Georgian taste, and a room (laid in common bond where the original house was laid up in Flemish bond) was added bringing the house into the double parlor form. The overall, zigzag pattern on the gable is less common in the fancy brickwork of southern New Jersey than dates and initials. The house stands south of Hancocks Bridge, Salem County, New Jersey. (Photo, the author.)

concepts in diverse materials, underwent expansion through various kinds of shed and ell additions to the rear (Figs. 17, 19, 20) —if not actual additions, these are still conceptual additions like suffixes on words. Also, a two story room—square in good English fashion, like the house's main rooms—was occasionally added onto one gable, producing a double parlor house (Fig. 18), a form that, owing to its popularity in England, one would expect to have been more usual in America. Like the Georgian house, the I house could be split, and houses that are two-thirds of the full form, one room and a hall, are found in Pennsylvania villages and in the countryside of southwestern New Jersey and eastern Delaware (Fig. 19).

Once introduced, the Georgian form was worked upon in many ways: it was built unaltered of a variety of materials; it was reduced and enlarged systematically to fit spatial or economic requirements; and it was broken down so that some of its

components could be combined with components from pre-Georgian architectural repertoires, both British and Germanic, to produce new house types.

Culture is an inventory of learned concepts. The cultural process consists of selecting from among the concepts, some of them new, some of them old, when a problem such as walking, courting, or building a barn has to be solved. Some concepts are fully accepted, some are modified, some are torn apart and combined with others, and some are rejected. The acceptance of the Georgian form meant not only the appearance of new things but also the disappearance of old things. Some old ideas were specifically incompatible: if the Georgian ideal of chimneys poking up at either gable were embraced, the central fireplace of the three room Continental house could not remain, despite the elaborate flues constructed to that end in at least one house. Some ideas were lost as a part of the general but rapid move during the third quarter of the eighteenth century toward a prosperous

FIG. 19. Two-thirds Georgian I House Type. The perfect Gothic trim and frontal gable and the rear appendages do not entirely obscure the basic house, which conforms to the two-thirds Georgian I house type, a hall along one gable with a room with a fireplace next to it; compare this house with Figs. 15B, 16, 17. This late nineteenth-century expression of an old concept is located east of Woodstown, Salem County, New Jersey. (Photo, the author.)

FIG. 20. New Jersey Farm. Built on the courtyard plan with the house and barn at right angles. The house is a late nineteenth-century I house; the barn is an example of the three bay, English barn type. East of Canton, Salem County, New Jersey. (Photo, the author.)

homogeneity—a move facilitated by a new and prestigious architectural concept, offered at once to all people, and to all somewhat foreign, somewhat familiar. A few manifestations of the ethnically distinct architectural ideas of the early period in Mid-Atlantic building can still be found to give the fieldworker an impression of the early heterogeneity—of the ideas that were rejected. Among the lost forms was the Swiss bank house,[46] although its multi-level concept may have survived in the semisubterranean cooking cellars of many Mid-Atlantic farmhouses. The low, stone Scotch-Irish cabin[47] was also lost as New World Ulstermen moved into larger, more fashionable dwellings. Although translated into log or frame, the little northern Irish cabin did persist with tenacity on the Appalacian frontier.[48] Apparently never of much importance, Scandinavian log construction, too, was lost during this period when an acceptable but limited folk architectural repertoire was built up in the New World out of Old World stuff.[49] By mid-century Scandinavian log construction had been completely overwhelmed by the totally different kind of log construction usual in America, which was introduced from central Europe.[50]

The houses and other folk buildings that typify the Mid-Atlantic landscape—the barns and mills, meeting houses and corncribs—can be explained as artifacts largely by reference within the architectural system. Unlike a utopian designer, the folk planner employs an old and established form, despite changes of use and environment. In arranging a complete form in a spatial relationship to other forms, the folk planner finds himself with an abundance of problems. The lay of the land, the ranges of wind, rain, and temperature, the changes in the social and economic systems—all make adherence to a type, a traditional template for correctness, more difficult in the construction of composite, noncontinuous forms, such as towns or farms, than it is in the construction of unitary, continuous forms, such as houses or bridges. Exactly the same house type might work nicely in a metropolis or a wilderness, but different settings obviously require quite different relationships between the house and other structures.

Two distinct, fundamental farm plans exist in the Delaware Valley; in their ideal forms they stay pretty obediently on opposite sides of the river, though both tend to lose the rigor of their pattern at the Delaware and especially on the Jersey bank above Philadelphia. In southern New Jersey, the

---

[46] Robert C. Bucher, "The Swiss Bank House in Pennsylvania," *Pennsylvania Folklife* 18, no. 2 (Winter 1968–69): 2–11. The Schaeffer, Spangler, and Ley houses pictured are good examples of the type; the Matz house is a good example of a German–Georgian Pennsylvania farmhouse with a banked cellar.

[47] Åke Campbell, "Irish Fields and Houses: A Study in Rural Culture," *Béaloideas* 5, no. 1 (1935): 57–74; E. Estyn Evans, "The Ulster Farmhouse," *Ulster Folklife* 1 (1955): 27–31.

[48] Henry Glassie, "The Types of the Southern Mountain Cabin," in Jan H. Brunvand, *The Study of American Folklore: An Introduction* (New York: W. W. Norton, 1968), pp. 338–70.

[49] Harold R. Shurtleff, *The Log Cabin Myth* (1939; reprint ed., Gloucester: Peter Smith, 1967), pp. 166–71.

[50] Kniffen and Glassie, "Building in Wood in the Eastern United States." It has been more difficult to kill the erroneous notion of the Swedish-Finnish origin of American log construction, traceable to Henry C. Mercer's pioneer article, than it was for Harold R. Shurtleff to do away with the idea that log construction was the earliest building mode in the English colonies. Some scholars, probably as a result of American affection for the underdog and the melting pot, seem bent on giving the little settlement of New Sweden—whose population never reached a thousand souls and which was destined for early acculturation—credit for the introduction of a host of major American cultural traits. Martin Wright, for example, traced the essentially English dog-trot house of the deep South to Scandinavia, and Thomas Tileston Waterman somehow located Swedish origins for the Germanic three room house and for the

most usual kind of English town house. The best scholars continue to write about the Scandinavian provenance of American log construction, yet the hewn, chinked, box-cornered log construction that predominates in the United States is definitely different from that of Sweden and Finland. Sigurd Erixon, the foremost authority on Scandinavian building, came to America believing that American log construction was Swedish in origin; after examining a few houses, he decided that it definitely could not be. Henry C. Mercer, "The Origin of Log Houses in the United States," *Old-Time New England* 18, no. 1 (July 1927); 18, no. 2 (Oct. 1927); and in *Collection of Papers Read Before the Bucks County Historical Society*, 5:568–83; Stevenson Whitcomb Fletcher, *Pennsylvania Architecture and County Life: 1640–1840* (Harrisburg: Pennsylvania Historical Museum Commission, 1950), pp. 42–44; Martin Wright, "Antecedents of the Double-Pen House Type," *Annals of the Association of American Geographers* 48, no. 2 (June 1958): 109–17; Thomas Tileston Waterman, *The Dwellings of Colonial America* (Chapel Hill: University of North Carolina Press, 1950), pp. 43, 125, 128–34; information on Erixon comes from an interview with Professor Stith Thompson, internationally known folktale scholar, Cooperstown, New York, May 1, 1965. Erixon is the author of, among other things, "The North-European Technique of Corner Timbering," *Folkliv* 1 (1937): 13–60, a description of Scandinavian log construction that implicitly reveals the vast difference between north European and North American construction.

FIG. 21. New Jersey Farm. This farm is built on the most common courtyard pattern with the house and barn related within a parallel structure. The house is of the full Georgian type; the barns and the open shed are of English derivation and are typical of New Jersey. South of Elmer, Salem County, New Jersey. (Photo, the author.)

ideal from which reality varies is a hollow square (Figs. 20, 21).[51] It consists of a house, an I house or some Georgian subtype, generally, facing the road with the barn, almost always a three bay, side-opening barn of one level, such as was most common in England,[52] directly behind it or set a bit to one side. In some cases the ridge lines of house and barn are set at right angles (Fig. 20) though a parallel arrangement is more common and seems to have been the ideal (Fig. 21). On one side a line of buildings, consisting mainly of a long shed open on the inside, connects the spheres of house and barn. A few other dependencies are placed opposite this line forming a courtyard, a hollow rectangle—house at the front, barn at the rear, with one boundary typically a little ragged. As one moves northward through New Jersey, this tight plan loosens up. Some farms exhibit the major structural elements, the parallel relation of house and barn, but they lack the sheds enclos-

ing the square. In others the barn and sheds form a courtyard of sorts— what would be called a "fold-yard" in England[53]—but the house is not a part of the rectangular layout. This situation is common in the North and suggests that such farms may be products more of Northern than of Mid-Atlantic thinking.

When the house is rarely an I house and the barn is usually a Yankee style basement barn,[54] the fieldworker is likely to be near the Kittatinny Mountains, and his suspicion that he is leaving the Mid-Atlantic region is confirmed. In this hilly section of western New Jersey, farms on which there is no clear statement of the square are common; there is instead the simple clustering of some outbuildings around the barn and others around the house with a psychological separation between the two areas (Fig. 22). The groups of buildings may be considered, respectively, as extensions of house or barn and the two areas as spheres of sexual control, the barn being the man's domain, the

[51] Fred Kniffen mentions the New Jersey courtyard plan in his "Neglected Chapters of Pioneer Life," *Pioneer America Society Newsletter* 2, no. 4 (July 1969 [supplement]): 1–4.

[52] George Ewart Evans, *The Farm and the Village* (London: Faber and Faber, 1969), pp. 82–83.

[53] Joscelyne Finberg, *Exploring Villages* (London: Routledge and Kegan Paul, 1958), pp. 70–71.

[54] Glassie, *Pattern in the Material Folk Culture of the Eastern United States*, pp. 135–41.

Fig. 22. New Jersey Farm. This farm is not built on the courtyard plan. There is some suggestion of the parallel relation of house and barn, except, unlike the true courtyard plan (Fig. 21), in this case the house faces the barn, and the layout is composed of separate house and barn areas. The house is a two-thirds Georgian house of one story; as with two story houses of the kind, the kitchen wing is lower than the basic dwelling (compare Fig. 6); the barn is the usual English three bay type. Between Unionville and Wertsville, Hunterdon County, New Jersey. (Photo, the author.)

house, the woman's. While it takes different forms in different subregions, this loose dual arrangement appears to be an Americanism with multiple origins, lacking sufficient precision to enable the scholar to make confident assertions about Old World provenance or New World antiquity. The hollow square, which predominates in flat southern New Jersey but breaks up in the stony hills of the upper Delaware Valley, is an English form. Probably related to similar plans in northern Europe,[55] the hollow square, including or omitting the house, dates to Saxon times in England, where it is still regularly found, and in Ireland it is restricted to the English-planted areas.[56] In America,

derivative plans are found not only in New Jersey but also on Long Island and in upstate New York.[57] The farms of New England[58] occasionally consist of a house and barn in a parallel arrangement, though the two are joined by a service wing; the similarities are suggestive of a possible genetic relationship in old England between these two tight farm plans, which are outstanding in a country characterized by loose farm planning.

The ideal in southern Pennsylvania and its areas of cultural continuity, west central New Jersey, central Maryland, and the northern Valley of Virginia, consists of lining up the house and barn gable to gable and positioning this linear structure so that the fronts of both the house and the barn face south, east, or somewhere in between (Figs.

[55] Hollow square plans are found in many parts of Northern Europe. Their appearance in northern Schleswig and Denmark is most relevant to the historic situation of England: R. Mejborg, *Nordiske Bøndergaarde* (Copenhagen: Lehman and Stages, 1892), 1:169–220; six of the farmsteads at the Danish Open-Air Museum (from Eastern Jutland, Sweden, Zealand, and Funen) are of the type, as Kai Uldall's valuable guide shows. *Frilandmuseet* (Lyngby: Danish National Museum, 1966), nos. 42, 54, 55, 63, 68, 71.

[56] M. E. Seebohm, *The Evolution of the English Farm* (Cambridge, Harvard University Press, 1927), p. 100; Finberg, *Exploring Villages*, pp. 70–71; C. Henry Warren, *English Cottages and Farm-Houses* (London: Collins, 1947),

p. 26; Sydney R. Jones, *English Village Homes and Country Buildings* (London: Batsford, 1947), pp. 72–75, 115; E. Estyn Evans, *Irish Folk Ways* (New York: Devin-Adair, 1957), p. 112.

[57] Henry Glassie, "The Wedderspoon Farm," *New York Folklore Quarterly* 23, no. 3 (Sept. 1966): 163–87.

[58] See Wilbur Zelinsky, "The New England Connecting Barn," *The Geographical Review* 48, no. 4 (Oct. 1958): 540–53.

FIG. 23. The Linear Mid-Atlantic Farm Plan. This farm consists of (from left to right) hog house, bank barn (of the Dornbusch and Heyl, *Pennsylvania German Barns,* type F-G), chicken coop, washhouse, and Pennsylvania farmhouse type. Southwest of Dillsburg, York County, Pennsylvania. (Photo, the author.)

FIG. 24. The Linear Mid-Atlantic Farm Plan. This farm consists basically of a Georgian I house and a bank barn (of Dornbusch and Heyl type H). Later nineteenth-century Georgian I houses in the Mid-Atlantic region, such as this one, tend to have three rather than five openings per floor on the front; compare this house with Figs. 16, 17. North of Frederick, Frederick County, Maryland. (Photo, the author.)

FIG. 25. The Linear Mid-Atlantic Plan, bent to correspond to the topography. The house and barn of this farm were constructed directly parallel to slopes that intersect at an angle, causing the linear plan to bow. The bank barn is of the Dornbusch and Heyl type F-G; in front of it, built into the stone wall around the barnyard, is a hog house; behind it is a drive-in corncrib. The house is an altered example of a two-thirds Georgian type. The farm is situated near Clear Spring, south of Dillsburg, York County, Pennsylvania. (Photo, the author.)

23, 24, 26A). The front of the house is obvious, but the barn's front, in traditional terms, is the side with the doors into the stables—the side on which the manure, a sign of agricultural success, is displayed in early spring—and not necessarily the side into which one would drive a wagon or truck. Many different kinds of houses and barns were plugged into the slots in this linear structure. Around the southern and western borders of the Mid-Atlantic region, in Maryland and Virginia particularly, the house slot was usually filled with an I house (Fig. 24). Through the center of the region the house was generally a Georgian or Germanic farmhouse (Fig. 23), and one often sees modern bungalows neatly inserted in the dwelling's traditional position on the farm. In hilly areas of rocks and subsistence farming, eastern Northampton, northern Chester and York, and Bedford counties, Pennsylvania, especially, the barn is often one level. Through most of the western subregion of the Mid-Atlantic area, the barn slot in the farm structure is filled with some variety of bank barn. Prefab and cement block barns, even those lacking any formal connection with the old tradition, still tend to be related traditionally to the rest of the farm's buildings.

As long as the barn was one level, the problems involved in the achievement of the ideal layout were not hard to conquer. With the development of the bank barn, the planning problem became complicated. The bank barn developed at about the same time as the pair of syncretistic Mid-Atlantic house types, and it was, like them, a product both of the fragmentation of preexisting forms and of the reordering and meshing of their elements. It seems to be an application of the multi-level, banked concept, common on barns in northwestern England and on barn and house combinations in north central Switzerland and the Black Forest, to the single level double-crib barn of Swiss ancestry.[59] The bank barn of the Mid-Atlantic is typified by a cantilevered forebay over the stabling doors at the front and a ramp leading to its upper level at the rear (Figs. 23, 24, 25, 27).[60] The prob-

[59] See Henry Glassie, "The Double-Crib Barn in South Central Pennsylvania," 4 parts, *Pioneer America* 1, no. 1 (Jan. 1969): 9–16; 1, no. 2 (July 1969): 40–45; 2, no. 1 (Jan. 1970): 47–52; 2, no. 2 (July 1970): 23–34, especially part 4.

[60] For the Pennsylvania bank barn see: Charles H. Dornbusch and John K. Heyl, *Pennsylvania German Barns* (Allentown: Pennsylvania German Folklore Society, 1958); Alfred L. Shoemaker, ed., *The Pennsylvania Barn* (Kutztown: Pennsylvania Folklife Society, 1959); Henry Glassie, "The Pennsylvania Barn in the South, Part Two," *Pennsylvania Folklife* 15, no. 6 (Summer 1966): 12–25.

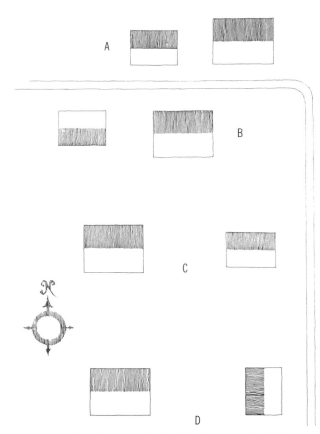

FIG. 26. Variety in the Relationship between the Linear Plan and the Road: A. House and barn face the road and the south (see also Fig. 23, 24); B. House faces the road, barn faces the south; C. House and barn face the south, ignoring the road; D. House faces the road, barn faces the south (see also Fig. 27). (By the author.)

lems involved in planning a farm that included a bank barn were not solely the linear arrangement and southerly exposure but also the location of a grade into which the barn could be built. Despite the complexity of the requirements, the ideal generally materialized on the land although topography occasionally caused compromise. In some areas houses were not traditionally backed into a bank, so that the barn was constructed slightly uphill of the house, crooking the plan. Generally, the house and the barn were positioned squarely to the rise of the land, like English bank barns,[61] which seem to have provided part of the suggestion for the Pennsylvania barn, so that a curved piece of terrain caused the buildings to be related along the

[61] James Walton, "Upland Houses: The Influence of Mountain Terrain on British Folk Building," *Antiquity* 30, no. 119 (Sept. 1956): 144.

contour, bending the plan (Fig. 25). In these ways topography served to distort the ideal.

When it became fashionable to have the house front on the road, an additional factor of confusion was introduced. If the road ran east-west and the farm were on the north side of the road, no trouble arose (Fig. 26A). If the farm were on the road's south side, a choice had to be made. Some farm planners ignored the road, situating the house with its back turned to it, leaving the house and barn in alignment facing the early sun. Others compromised by placing the front of the house and the back of the barn to the road (Fig. 26B); in this way, the aesthetic arrangement of ridge lines was retained, though the practical tradition of the dwelling's orientation was lost. A road running in an inconvenient direction, northwesterly say, presented even greater problems. Many ignored the road, letting it run through or by the farm without influencing the organization of the buildings (Fig. 26C), so that an appropriate slope for the barn and the cardinal points were the only factors considered in the accomplishment of the ideal. Others built the house on the road, even if it meant that the house faced into the coldest winds. The barn could have been placed in alignment, preserving the aesthetic tradition while violating the practical tradition; however, the barn was left so that the morning sun bathed the barnyard, and the farm's plan became L-shaped—a compromise that is frequently seen (Figs. 26D, 27). When neither hillside nor road allowed the expression of the ideal, disruption of both the practical and aesthetic—economic and artistic—traditions resulted. But the first step in planning was site selection, and such sites were usually avoided; farms lacking any suggestion of linear organization and southern orientation are rare.

The forces that affect change in the cultural process are easily ordered in an examination of the problems solved in structuring a farm's components. Given an ideal, there are aesthetic forces for its continuation (the familiarity of the linear or the rectangular plans) and aesthetic forces for its disruption (the desire to orient the house to the road). There are practical forces for its continuation (the warmth of the southerly aspect, the utility of the courtyard arrangement) and practical forces for its disruption (the need for a slope in Pennsylvania, the need for flat land in New Jersey).

The two ideal farm layouts of the Delaware

Fig. 27. The L-shaped Variant of the Linear Mid-Atlantic Plan. The house of this farm faces the road, while the barn faces southward. The house is of the Pennsylvania farmhouse type (as in Fig. 13); the barn is Dornbusch and Heyl type F-G. The locations of the hog and chicken houses at the front of the barn and the washhouse at the rear of the dwelling are characteristic of southern Pennsylvania and adjacent Maryland. This farm is north of Bermudian in York County, Pennsylvania. (Photo, the author.)

Valley act as modulations between European and American farm patterns. In both, unlike the plans found throughout most of the United States, the house and barn were considered as parts of a single, formal unit rather than as separate foci for units related only by extra-architectural systems. The separation one senses between the house and barn in the Midwest, or indeed in southwestern Pennsylvania or northwestern New Jersey, is not present in the older Delaware Valley farms. Still, in general, the Delaware Valley farm plans, as sets of spaces set aside for particular uses, were not as tight or intergrated as farm-plans in the Old World.

The origin of the linear plan may lie in buildings or ranges of buildings that housed the farmer at one end and his stock at the other. These are found in many of the parts of the Old World from which the Mid-Atlantic settlers came: in England, Wales, Ireland, Scotland, Switzerland, and the Rhine Valley.[62] Germans in nineteenth-century Wisconsin erected buildings housing both people and stock, and there are reports by a traveler and two tax assessors of similar buildings in Pennsyl-

[62] Sidney Oldall Addy, *The Evolution of the English House* (London: Swan Sonnenschien, 1898), pp. 69–74; Seebohm, *The Evolution of the English Farm*, pp. 282–328; P. Smith, "The Long-House and the Laithe-House: A Study of the House-and-Byre Homestead in Wales and the West Riding," in Idris L. Foster and L. Alcock, eds., *Culture and Environment* (London: Routledge and Kegan Paul, 1963), pp. 415–37; Christopher Stell, "Pennine Houses: An Introduction," *Folk Life* 3 (1965): 16, 20–21; Barley, *The English Farmhouse and Cottage*, pp. 110–12; Iowerth C. Peate, *The Welsh House: A Study in Folk Culture* (Liverpool: Hugh Evans, 1946), pp. 51–84; Alwyn D. Rees, *Life in a Welsh Countryside* (Cardiff: University of Wales Press, 1950), pp. 47–51; Caoimhín Ó Danachair, "The Combined Byre-and-Dwelling in Ireland," *Folk Life* 2 (1964): 58–74; I. F. Grant, *Highland Folk Ways* (London: Routledge and Kegan Paul, 1961), pp. 75, 145, 150; Hans Schwab, "Das Bauernhaus in der Schweiz," *Schweizerisches Archiv für Volkskunde* 31, no. 3–4 (1931): 177–78. A very

vania.[63] The first house built by the Moravians at Bethlehem, Pennsylvania, was a twenty-by-forty log building that housed people at one end and animals at the other.[64] But clearly the pattern was never usual. Arriving in the New World with the tradition of a combined house and barn, the farm planner seems to have exploded the old building. The building's components were individually unaltered, and they were ordered linearly, but he let daylight in between them.

The activities on the farm were spread out and separately housed; the holdings that were loosely bound into the agricultural community were similarly scattered. In Britain before and during the Roman presence, farms were independently possessed and isolated.[65] This ancient European pattern survived through the Middle Ages only in those mountainous areas of the Continent and the British Isles that were relatively undisturbed by the waves of violence called history.[66] In the most densely settled sections, where the land had many stomachs to support and was worth fighting over, the agricultural village with its clustered habitations, outfield system, and cooperative style became the norm. But the old, individualistic sense of status dependent upon the accumulation of territory and chattels was not wholly lost in the medieval, communal setting;[67] and although tight agricultural villages were planned in Spanish, French, and English America, the settlers of those villages scattered rapidly and greedily into the country-

side, claiming and working isolated holdings,[68] with exceptions only in extremely authoritarian situations such as those that existed in early New England and Mormon Utah.[69] With antecedents in the land-use patterns of the Scotch-Irish and with support from the land allotment schemes of William Penn,[70] the separate, single-family farm became the usual pattern for the Mid-Atlantic and for the United States.[71]

The availability of land is the most obvious among the factors that made up the New World environment and that functioned causally to encourage an abrupt change in planning. The Delaware Valley settler's holding was much larger than his European father's; he could spread his buildings and farms around; more significantly, he probably felt that he had to. After the fact, we can wax ecstatic about the vastness of the new country, though at the time only a few philosophers gloried in the creeks and trees. We might wish that those folk who found themselves on the banks of the Delaware two hundred and fifty years ago had related to the environment like Thoreau or a crusading member of the Sierra Club, but they were peasants. The forests were enemies, strange and evil, existing only to be cleared. The forests caused the immediate invention of nothing—men do not work that way—but they did cause the selection and elaboration of old traditions through which the trees could be utilized—or rather, exploited, for wood was wasted and what was used was ripped out of natural shape and hidden. Then as now, the ash-tough American on the move felt that the physical environment was something to devastate. America to the newcomer, as Leo Marx has pointed out, was *"both* Eden and a howling des-

important study with relevance to this topic is Richard Weiss, *Haüser und Landschaften der Schweiz* (Erlenbach, Zurich, and Stuttgart: Eugen Rentsch, 1959), especially the fourth and fifth sections; see also Adolph Spamer, *Hessische Volkskunst* (Jena: Eugen Diedrichs, 1939), pp. 20, 24–25; Heinrich Götzger and Helmut Prechter, *Das Bauernhaus in Bayern* (Munich: Callwey, 1960), pp. 81–180.

[63] Richard W. E. Perrin, "German Timber Farmhouses in Wisconsin," *Wisconsin Magazine of History* 44, no. 3 (Spring 1961): 199–202; and the same scholar's "'Fachwerkbau' Houses in Wisconsin," *Journal of the Society of Architectural Historians* 18, no. 1 (Mar. 1959): 29–33; Don Yoder, ed., "The Pennsylvania Sketchbooks of Charles Leseur," *Pennsylvania Folklife* 16, no. 2 (Winter 1966–67): 34; Shoemaker, *The Pennsylvania Barn*, p. 9.

[64] Murtagh, *Moravian Architecture and Town Planning*, p. 23.

[65] A. L. F. Rivet, *Town and Country in Roman Britain* (London: Hutchinson, 1966), pp. 39–40, 43, 108–21.

[66] Hermann Kallbrunner, "Farms and Villages: The European Pattern," *Landscape* 6, no. 3 (Spring 1957): 13–17.

[67] H. S. Bennett, *Life on the English Manor: A Study of Peasant Conditions, 1150–1400* (Cambridge: Cambridge University Press, 1962), chap. 2.

[68] John W. Reps, *Town Planning in Frontier America* (Princeton: Princeton University Press, 1969), pp. 3, 66, 68, 89, 92, 147–53, 183, 259, 386.

[69] See Sumner Chilton Powell, *Puritan Village: The Formation of a New England Town* (Garden City: Doubleday & Co., 1965); Lowry Nelson, *The Mormon Village: A Pattern and Technique of Land Settlement* (Salt Lake City: University of Utah Press, 1952).

[70] E. Estyn Evans, "The Scotch-Irish: Their Cultural Adaptation and Heritage in the American Old West," in E. R. R. Green, ed., *Essays in Scotch-Irish History* (London: Routledge and Kegan Paul, 1969), pp. 73–74, 84–85; Anthony N. B. Garvan, "Proprietary Philadelphia as Artifact," in Oscar Handlin and John Burchard, eds., *The Historian and The City* (Cambridge: M.I.T. Press, 1966), p. 187.

[71] Lowry Nelson, *American Farm Life* (Cambridge: Harvard University Press, 1954); chap. 5.

ert," a wilderness and a garden;[72] the idea of wilderness produced fear, but the idea of the garden gave him strength, and the American "environment-buster"[73] tore fearfully and optimistically through the land. The limitless spaces he faced had to be controlled to eliminate the fear and to realize the optimism. Great expanses of land had to be turned from wilderness into material culture; they had to be subdued by the surveyor's chain and mile upon mile of fencing; they had to be claimed by buildings, tall, inharmonious signs of conquest dropped across the landscape—manmade forms spread out as far and lonesome as they could be, without leaving too much space between for the wilderness to slip in.

Transition can be read in the characteristic spatial arrangements of the Delaware Valley; there is a lingering sense of the tightness of the English or German peasant with his clustered, cooperative modes, but there is also the beginning and fulfillment of the dominant style of America, loose, worried, acquisitive individualism. Dispersion—separate buildings, separate holdings—is the major material manifestation of cultural response to the New World environment, and it has been from the beginning of European settlement. Jamestown was only fifteen years old when an English visitor complained that the buildings seemed scattered about.[74] Three hundred and thirteen years later, Le Corbusier noted that the American desire for "a little garden, a little house, the assurance of freedom"[75]—the capitalistic possession of a bit of land—had resulted in the failure of the American city and the American way of life. From the Delaware Valley westward go separate holdings where the nuclear family works for itself, where ownership is an end in itself, where noncooperative capitalism flourishes. The single farmstead, symbol of individualistic endeavor, is compatibly systematic with other segments of the culture: the constricted, unaccompanied solo singing,[76] the literature demanding authority, the art and architecture stressing symmetry, the strict sex roles, the restrictive morality with its attendant modesty, guilt, and partrifocality,[77] the politics of individual power, and the hope for upward mobility within what Henry Nash Smith calls "the fee-simple empire."

Individualism suggests conformity and breeds repetition. The irony of cultural freedom in America has not been better expressed than by D. H. Lawrence:[78] masterless, the American is mastered; free, the American has conservatively chosen to restrict freedom. The land of the free is paradoxically not a land of endless variety. The critic might react differently to an eighteenth-century farmhouse and a modern rambler (and the old house is objectively assisted in its appeal by the soft edges that come with age and the subtlety that, as James Agee wrote,[79] results from the attempt to achieve stark symmetry with less than perfect hand methods), but there are no more basic eighteenth-century farmhouse types in the Delaware Valley than there are different house models in many subdivisions. The colonial American would have had no more trouble finding the whitewashed kitchen in the home of an unknown contemporary than today's suburbanite would have finding the knotty pine rec room in the split-level of a new neighbor.

Books may not tell us, but buildings do. The eighteenth-century average guy in the Delaware Valley was an individualist but a conformist—a wary adventurer. He felt anxious in his adjustment to the changing times and chose to appear modern while acting conservatively. He cared more for economics than for aesthetics. He does not sound unfamiliar.

---

[72] *The Machine in the Garden: Technology and the Pastoral Ideal in America* (New York: Oxford University Press, 1967), p. 43.

[73] The phrase is from Wallace Stegner, "The Meaning of Wilderness in American Civilization," in Roderick Nash, ed., *The American Environment* (Reading, Mass.: Addison-Wesley, 1968), p. 194.

[74] Nathaniel Butler, quoted in Wayne Andrews, *Architecture, Ambition and Americans: A Social History of American Architecture* (New York: The Free Press, 1967), pp. 1–2.

[75] Francis E. Hyslop, Jr., trans., *When the Cathedrals Were White* (1947; reprint ed., New York, Toronto, London: McGraw-Hill, 1964), p. 174.

[76] Alan Lomax, *Folk Song Style and Culture* (Washington: American Association for the Advancement of Science, 1968), pp. 99–100.

[77] Conrad M. Arensberg and Solon T. Kimball, *Culture and Community* (New York: Harcourt, Brace, and World, 1965), chaps. 11–13.

[78] *Studies in Classic American Literature* (1923; reprint ed., Garden City, New York: Doubleday & Co., 1953), chap. 1.

[79] *Let Us Now Praise Famous Men* (1941; reprint ed., New York: Ballantine 1966), pp. 131–33.

"Designed, Drawn and Lithographed by James Akin."

Akin's talents extended beyond those of engraver and caricaturist. He was also a profile portraitist, silhouettist, and watercolorist. Among the earliest of his watercolor portraits were those of Judge Timothy Pickering,[2] his good friend ("Squire") Thomas Leavitt and his wife Hannah.[3] In 1841, Akin exhibited two watercolors at the Pennsylvania Academy: *Durham Bull Collostra* and *Colossal Bull Nero.* In 1853, a watercolor, *English Lane Scene,* by James Akin was exhibited posthumously at the Pennsylvania Academy.[4]

Engraving on silver was a related skill practiced by Akin. Approximately one month after his arrival in Newburyport, Massachusetts, in 1804, the Merrimack Humane Society recorded a payment to James Akin for engraving a lifesaving medal smithed by Ebenezer Moulton.[5] This medal, with the possible exception of his daughter's monogrammed silver mentioned in Akin's will, is the only recorded example of his engraving on silver. Its present location is unknown.

Little recognition has been granted James Akin. Standard thumbnail sketches of the life of this colorful engraver are consistently brief. "Born about 1773, probably in South Carolina; died in Philadelphia, July 17, 1846, 'aged 73 years.' Akin came to Philadelphia from Charleston, S.C. and

was for a time a clerk in the State Department under Timothy Pickering (1795–1800)."[6] It is possible, however, to expand his biography in order to afford a substantially more comprehensive picture of his life and work.

Exactly when Akin arrived in Philadelphia is not certain; apparently he was born in Charleston, although he is not listed in the Charleston directories. Dr. John Shecut's *Medical and Philosophical Essays,* published in Charleston, 1819, records that: "Among her [Charleston's] sons, we would make honorable mention of Thomas Coram, James Akin, Washington Alston, . . . as holding a distinguished rank among the amateurs of portrait painting and engraving." Akin maintained family and business ties with his native state throughout his life.[7]

He does not appear in the Philadelphia city directories until 1799, but a "James Aitken, engraver, 33 So. Second" was listed in the 1794 guide. The fact that other sources locate Akin in Philadelphia prior to 1799 may indicate that the 1794 listing was a variant spelling. In June 1797, "James Akin of Charleston, South Carolina" was established at "Powell street, 4 doors from 5th st. between Spruce and Pine Streets [Philadelphia]." From this address he submitted a prospectus for three "patriotic" prints, *The Battle of Eutaw Springs, The Battle of Cowpens,* and the *Capture of Major Andre.* The proposal provides the largest single body of autobiographical information concerning Akin's training and the extent of his circle of professional acquaintances. The undertaking was ambitious as evidenced by the proposed size and price. His prospectus boasts that he had "employed a considerable part of [his] life in acquiring a knowledge of the fine arts, from the most celebrated and esteemed masters in Europe." The

[2] *Merrimack Magazine and Ladies Literary Cabinet* 1 (Nov. 2, 1805) : 47. Akin proposed to engrave a portrait of Judge Pickering "from a water coloured drawing, taken with the Judge's permission from life, at his seat near Danvers, Oct. 26, 1805, by Mr. Akin, (one of his clerks when Secretary of State) ."

[3] Theodore Bolton, *Early American Portrait Painters in Miniature* (New York: Frederic Fairchild Sherman, 1921), nos. 74, 75. Bolton described the portrait miniatures, but his reference, F. B. Sanborn, "Thomas Leavitt and His Artist Friend, James Akin," *Granite Monthly* 25 (Oct. 1898) : 225, said only that they were "portraits drawn by . . . Akin, 1808." Sanborn, Leavitt's grandson, noted that although Leavitt was a strong Republican and Akin an ardent Federalist, the two men shared a friendship that lasted even after Akin moved from New England. Sanborn recalled that through Akin's life Akin and his grandfather maintained correspondence—the engraver sending the latest examples of his work to delight the Squire. Leavitt was a prominent citizen of Hampton Falls, New Hampshire.

[4] Anna Wells Rutledge, "Cumulative Record of Exhibition Catalogues, The Pennsylvania Academy of the Fine Arts, 1807–1870, The Society of Artists, 1800–1814, The Artists' Fund Society, 1835–1845," American Philosophical Society *Memoirs* 38 (1955) : 196, 204, 320.

[5] John J. Currier, *History of Newburyport, Massachusetts, 1764–1909,* 2 vols. (Newburyport: John J. Currier), 2:139.

[6] David McNeill Stauffer, *American Engravers upon Copper and Steel,* 2 vols. (New York: Grolier Club, 1907), 1:4–5.

[7] John Shecut, *Medical and Philosophical Essays* (Charleston: A. E. Miller), p. 54. Assuming that the Akin spelling of the artist's name was original and not a shortened signature adopted after arriving in Philadelphia, the engraver can be quickly distinguished from the more numerous Aitkens and Aikens of Charleston. The extant Charleston directories are few. Those for 1782 and 1784 do not list an Akin, but that of 1790 cites "Thomas Akin, Mariner, 97 East-bay." And in 1794, "Thomas Akin, Shopkeeper, 30 Pickney" and "Ann Akin, Boarding School, 76 Church" are noted.

print of Eutaw Springs was to be taken from a painting by

the much celebrated STOTHARD, and a few very valuable pictures I have which were painted by this distinguished artist, and which may be seen in my possession, will serve as specimens of my friend's great talents, to those who are unacquainted with his works. The prints will be engraved in the *line* manner, from two original pictures, and their size will be 2 feet 1 inch by 1 foot 6 inches. The price for each will be 15 dollars; one half to be paid at the time of subscription, for which a receipt will be given. . . . In addition to the above prints, I propose engraving as a centerpiece, the *Capture of Major Andre;* from STOTHARD. . . . The price will be 8 dollars—payable as above. The size will be 1 foot 2 inches by 1 foot. . . . Subscriptions for the above prints, or either of them will be received by C. W. Peale at his museum; Thomas Dobson, and John Ormood, booksellers and Henry Bembridge, jun. South Front street, near the Drawbridge, Philadelphia; by C. Tiebout, engraver, No. 29, Golden hill street New York; by R. R. Peale at the Museum, Baltimore; and by Major Shubrick (who was aid-de-camp [*sic*] to Gen. Greene, at the Eutaw Springs), and Thomas Coram, Charleston, S.C. N.B. The painting of the EUTAW SPRINGS may be seen at Peale's Museum.

June 17[8]

Akin's boast that he had spent a considerable part of his life studying under "the most celebrated and esteemed masters in Europe," suggests that Stothard was not an American unknown but the well-known English painter, designer, and book illustrator, Thomas Stothard (1755–1834). In 1794, Stothard had begun a series of history paintings for Bowyer's Historic Gallery.[9] The pictures to which Akin referred in his prospectus were probably history paintings by Thomas Stothard.

It is interesting to note the far reaching circle of business ties listed in the prospectus but perhaps

impossible to interpret its full significance. Were these men strictly business acquaintances—or was there a more amiable connection between various members of Akin's artistic circle? Thomas Coram, portrait and landscape painter, engraver of copper-plate prints and on metals, came to Charleston, South Carolina, in 1769, from his native Bristol, England, and remained in Charleston until his death in 1811.[10] Perhaps the English-born engraver was influential in directing the younger Akin to England for more intensive study.

The Peales, whom Akin specified as ready to accept subscriptions for the proposed prints, were mentioned in reference to Akin's engravings on several occasions.[11] The mention of R. R. Peale in Baltimore indicates that Akin's work was not unknown in Baltimore. It is possible that his trade card for the Baltimore cabinetmaker, William Camp, was commissioned directly between patron and engraver—or indirectly between patron and a Baltimore member of a sympathetic coterie of artists and artisans.

Akin's connection with Cornelius Tiebout is not clear, but like the other subscription-takers whom Akin listed, Tiebout's name occurs in association with Akin's in more than one instance. Akin and Tiebout both studied abroad, perhaps at the same time, although nothing more is known of Akin's years abroad, except that he does not appear on the lists of students at the Royal Academy Schools from 1768 to 1830. In 1801, Akin and Tiebout apparently collaborated on a plate for Mathew Carey's Philadelphia edition of *The Holy Bible*. This illustration, *The Good Samaritan,* is signed "etched by James Akin / engraved by C. Tiebout."[12] A further indication that Akin belonged to a coterie of artists is the fact that

[8] *American Daily Advertiser* (Philadelphia), June 20, 1797; *City Gazette and Daily Advertiser* (Charleston), July 31, 1797. For South Carolina readers, Akin included the names of those who were pictured in the *Eutaw Springs* and the *Cowpens*.

[9] "Stothard, Thomas," *Dictionary of National Biography* (London: Oxford University Press, from 1917), 18:1320–24. Stothard's designs were often engraved by Medland and by Blake. In 1792 his illustrations for Milton's works were engraved by Bartolozzi. In 1794 he was elected an Academician, and in 1806 he received a commission to paint *Canterbury Pilgrims setting forth from the Tabard Inn*—a commission which had previously been offered to his friend William Blake. The bitter rivalry that resulted brought their friendship to an abrupt end.

[10] "Coram, Thomas," in George C. Groce and David H. Wallace, *The New-York Historical Society's Dictionary of Artists in America, 1564–1860* (New Haven: Yale University Press, 1957), p. 148.

[11] Akin and Harrison's portrait of *Thomas Jefferson* (checklist No. 66) was taken from Charles Willson Peale's oil. Mantle Fielding, *American Engravers upon Copper and Steel* . . . (Philadelphia: Wickersham Press, 1917), no. 19, states that one of Akin's etchings of fossil bones (checklist No. 2A) was taken from a wash drawing by Titian Peale.

[12] "Tiebout, Cornelius," in Groce and Wallace, *Dictionary of Artists in America,* p. 630. Tiebout (ca. 1773–1832) was born in New York and apprenticed as an engraver on silver. He travelled to London in 1793, returned to New York, where he worked until 1799, and then moved to Philadelphia. Sidney C. Hutchinson, "The Royal Academy Schools, 1768–1830," *The Volume of the Walpole Society* 38 (1960–62): 123–91.

Jeremiah Paul's *Venus and Cupid* was exhibited at the office of "James Akin, engraver, No. 22 Mulberry Street," in 1811.[13]

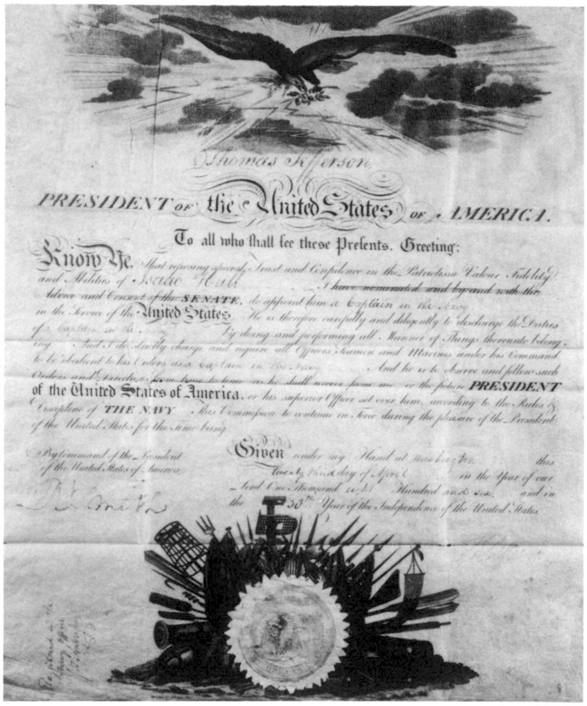

In the early years of Akin's Philadelphia residency, he consistently produced engravings of fine quality such as encyclopedia plates and book illustrations. His work with William Harrison, Jr., on the United States Naval Commission form (Fig. 1) may have been a commission granted as a favor to the engraver who was currently employed as a clerk in the office of Timothy Pickering, United States secretary of state (1795–1800).[14] Sometime in 1803, the threat of yellow fever in Philadelphia, combined with promises of profitable employment in Newburyport, Massachusetts, influenced Akin to remove his business from Philadelphia to New England. In June, 1803, Edmund M. Blunt, editor of the *American Coast Pilot,* had advertised in the *Newburyport Herald* that: "Any person who is acquainted with the different branches of copperplate Engraving may have constant employ and good wages."[15] Not receiving the desired response, Blunt turned to Philadelphia—and Akin. With the knowledge that both Edmund M. Blunt and Jacob Perkins, inventor of stereotyped steel plates, had need of his services, Akin embarked on what proved to be an economically unfortunate venture. He apparently left Philadelphia late in 1803, and was in Newburyport by January 1804.

Akin came to Newburyport with no written agreement—but with Blunt's elaborate assurances of a rewarding stay. On February 4, 1804, a bond was signed between the two men assuring Akin constant employ for five years. The vagueness of the contract and the temperaments of the two parties involved led to difficulties that were terminated in court. Akin stated that "I [had] met repeated disappointments and shiffling excuses from . . . Blunt . . . and [had] been at last

FIG. 1. James Akin, United States Naval Commission. Philadelphia, ca. 1798. Engraving and etching; H. 17", W. 14¼" (sheet). (Winterthur 57.1413.)

obliged to sue him."[16] At a settling of accounts in October 1804, Blunt concluded that Akin was in debt to him for $214.71½, a sum that Akin grudgingly agreed to pay.[17]

On October 27, 1804, Akin and Blunt met in the hardware store of Josiah Foster. Blunt confronted the engraver with accusations of stealing copperplates and paper. Akin publicly challenged Blunt to a duel, but the New Englander "refused [the South Carolinian] the satisfaction of a gentleman."[18] Instead Blunt picked up a footed skillet

---

[13] Currier, *History of Newburyport,* 2:377. Currier's citation of Akin's address as "22 Mulberry" is probably a typographical error. The city directory for 1811 lists Akin at No. 32 Mulberry.

[14] Stauffer, *American Engravers upon Copper and Steel,* 1:4–5.

[15] Quoted in Lewis C. Rubenstein, "James Akin in Newburyport," *Essex Institute Historical Collections* 102, no. 4 (Oct. 1966) : 285.

[16] Case 107, Blunt vs. Aken; Case 108, Blunt vs. Aken, The Supreme Judicial Court of the County of Essex, Massachusetts, Record Book C, p. 174, Office of the Clerk of the Courts, Salem, Massachusetts.

[17] Rubenstein, "James Akin in Newburyport," p. 292.

[18] Case 108, Blunt vs. Aken, The Supreme Judicial Court of the County of Essex, Massachusetts, Record Book C, p. 174, Office of the Clerk of the Courts, Salem, Massachusetts.

INFURIATED DESPONDENCY!

Fig. 2. James Akin, *Infuriated Despondency*. Newburyport, Mass., 1805. Engraving; H. 7⅜", W. 5¹³⁄₁₆" (plate). (Worcester Art Museum.)

from Foster's stocks and hurled it at Akin. Akin was jailed for proposing his challenge. The engraver revenged himself with a satirical print of Blunt, *Infuriated Despondency* (Fig. 2). Akin accompanied his portrait of Blunt with a verse that he entitled "A Skillet Song."

A SKILLET SONG

(Written in the *Iron Age*. Tune, "Yankee Doodle.")

In Newburyport, a famous place
  For trade and navigation,
A man was slapped upon the face
  For uttering defamation;

CHORUS

And peoples will remember long
  The story, to a tittle,
That gave rise to my Muse's song,
  About an iron kettle

You've heard, no doubt, a pratling clown.
  An ugly, sland'rous fellow,
Revile at folks thro' all the town,
  With one eternal bellow.

CHORUS, AS ABOVE

But sudden he was made,—good lack!
  To bawl a different way, sirs;
With thumps which brought him on his back,
  Crying out, "You'll raise the neighbors";
For lo! his courage now had fled,—
  He'd neither strength nor spittle;
Like Matthew Lyon, who, 'tis said,
  Spit,—when he had no kettle.

Such clamor soon the people drew,
  Who gathered in amazement;
When through the crowd the skillet flew,
  An shattered on the pavement.

One would have thought you had forgot
  The tricks of Dalton's kitchen;
And not to throw a dirty pot,
  When you for spite were itching;
Because it is a greasy thing
  Used merely to boil victual;
The very cook-girls scorn to fling
  Their dirty iron kettle.

Now this in Newburyport is made
  A finable offence sir,
To heave a skillet at the head,
  On whatso'er pretence, sir.

CHORUS

Poor, miserable hobbling wight,
  Your dirty tricks have failed, sir,
To place me in a doleful plight,—
  (Being sure I'd not be bailed, sir.)
For the grand jury soared above
  A verdict low or little
Which showed they'd neither fear nor love
  For crumble-toes nor kettle.[19]

The engravings were sold as single sheets, as broadside portraits, and as writing-book covers: "Book Covers just published and for sale by James Akin, by the single sheet or hundred, three numbers of Plate I entitled No. 1 Turkeys No. 2 Sailor's Glee No. 3 Infuriated Despondency,—calculated for Writing Book covers for children, and adapted with singular taste to amuse their juvenile fancy."[20] The otherwise unexplained plate number is probably the number that Akin planned to assign to each caricature in a forthcoming collection which he proposed to publish.

As soon as I can conveniently remove to Philadelphia, it will be put to press, and shall contain the full value of One Dollar, at which price subscribers are solicited. Many plates from entire new and original designs made expressly for the occasion shall accompany the work; and the politician, the moralist and the critic shall find a record of events as strange as they are true.

JAMES AKIN
Author of the "Prairie Dog,"
"Infuriated Despondency,"
"Bug a boo," &c. &c.[21]

It is said that Akin sent his design for *Infuriated Despondency* to England by a local sea captain, Nicholas Brown, where it was transferred to Liverpool pitchers and "chamber vessels." Blunt and his friends bought up and destroyed as many of these vessels as they could. Consequently, they are rare.

The dispute between Akin and Blunt raged for three years. The litigation became so involved that the court appointed a committee of three to rule on the case. Akin was awarded three decisions out of six, but his victory was not financially satisfying. He barely broke even.

Although his bond with Blunt had gone badly, Akin was not entirely devoid of business sense,

---

[19] Quoted in F. B. Sanborn, "Thomas Leavitt and His Artist Friend, James Akin," pp. 225–26.

[20] *Newburyport Herald,* June 25, 1805.

[21] *Newburyport Herald,* Nov. 14, 1806.

and his Newburyport years were not totally abortive. Launching out on his own in February, 1805, Akin took quarters "directly over Messrs. Thomas and Whipple's Bookstore."[22] The arrangement was beneficial to both parties. Akin illustrated various publications issued by Thomas and Whipple, and they in turn sold Akin's prints. A commission by Jacob Perkins to engrave his stereotype steel plates[23] and Akin's use of the physiognotrace for profile portraiture[24] were two more facets of his career in Newburyport. One of his cleverest works during these years was a caricature portrait of *Lord Timothy Dexter.*

In October 1807, Akin gave notice of his intention of leaving New England. His statement rings with characteristic wit as he alludes to his recent experiences:

To the Inhabitants of Newburyport:

The public are respectfully informed of my intention of removing to Philadelphia by way of New York, where, if uninterrupted health prevails, shall be *traced* and *bitten* with acid for their amusement some Phantasmagorial subjects. Those who benevolently encouraged my *Little* labors to prevent the *blunt* wearing of my *points* in *Legal* executions will please accept my sincere thanks.

I flatter myself that no distance will ever lessen the gratitude I feel and those endeavors to please which I have manifestly displayed on all occasions where I have been employed.

Claimants are requested to present their accounts for settlement, and should there be delays my friend, Mr. Jacob Perkins, will receive applications in my absence.[25]

There is no indication that Akin stayed long in New York—if at all.

In 1808, Philadelphians were notified that Akin had returned to their city and was residing: "just above the upper Ferry, over the Schuylkill, where he means to pursue his business."[26] For the next four or five years, Akin apparently chose employment of an uncontroversial nature. The major portion of his output from 1808 to 1813, as testified to by extant works, was book illustration and a few trade cards. But his spirit was not completely

stilled as evidenced by his caustic cartoon of *Dickey Folwell,* a scurrilous Philadelphia journalist.

In 1811, Akin appeared in the directory as "engraver and draftsman, 32 Mulberry." By 1813 his address had changed to 39 North 6th Street, but his profession remained that of engraver and draftsman. He then disappeared from the directories until 1819 when he was cited as "James Akin, engraver, 166 Locust above Eleventh." He remained there until 1823. His extant works indicate little output during the years 1813 to 1824.

For the next seven years Akin's listings are difficult to interpret: he apparently left the art of engraving and became first (1823–1824) the proprietor of a "rural lodge, opp. new penitentiary," and second (1829) the proprietor of an "eating-house, 17 Chestnut." This ambivalence of profession might be interpreted as hard times— or it might indicate that Akin was a man of somewhat independent means and restless temperament.

By the mid-twenties he was producing some cartoons, and, in 1830, the directories indicate that he had left the eating-house and reestablished himself as "engraver, 63 Dock [St.]." From this time until his death in 1846, his work was almost exclusively cartoons and caricatures.[27]

At the time of his death, in July 1846, Akin and his wife were living at 18 Prune Street.[28] His will

---

[22] *Newburyport Herald,* Feb. 12, 1805.

[23] *Newburyport Herald and Country Gazette,* May 14, 1799 quoted in Currier, *History of Newburyport,* 2:363.

[24] *Newburyport Herald,* Feb. 12, 1805.

[25] *Newburyport Herald,* Oct. 30, 1807.

[26] Currier, *History of Newburyport,* 2:376.

[27] In 1831, Akin was listed at 177 S. 11th Street where he remained until 1835 when he moved to 18 Prune St. In 1837 Akin was listed as a druggist "from Prune St" at the Southeast corner of Brown and Second. His caricatures, which probably sold for only a few pennies, would not have provided enough income to support a family. Perhaps as a druggist Akin was sustained by his shop while he looked to his lithographic caricatures. In 1839 "Akins, James, druggist, 51 Brown" was listed in the current city directory— and not James Akin. This is no doubt a typographical error. "Akins, James, Designer, 51 Brown" appeared in the 1840 directory, and "Akin, James, Designer, 51 Brown" was cited in the 1841 directory. By 1842 James Akin, engraver, had returned to his Prune St. (No. 18) address where he remained until his death in July 1846.

[28] The marriage of James Akin to Eliza Cox on November 30, 1797 in Christ Church, Philadelphia, is recorded in the Christ Church, Philadelphia, Marriage Records, p. 4560. Apparently the first Mrs. Akin was familiar with the art of engraving, if only superficially. A simple wood engraving signed Eliza Akin appears in [Anna Barbauld,] *Lessons for Children, Part II. From Four to Five Years Old* (Wilmington: James Wilson, 1800), which was "Adorned with Cuts Engraved by James Akin." A more sophisticated, unsigned piece, The Orphans Assylum Certificate, has traditionally

and inventory, which were probated in the Philadelphia courts, show that his colorful life had not left him penniless. The inventory and appraisal of Akin's estate, January 18, 1847, valued his household furnishings at $195.45. Akin's profession was reflected in the unusual number of pictures and prints listed among his furnishings: six pictures valued at $3.00, thirteen framed pictures valued at $1.50, three pictures valued at $3.00, seven paintings valued at $7.00, and one hundred and fifty prints valued at $6.00. Another unusual possession was a microscope valued at $15.00. In addition Akin left his wife, Ophelia, his "best friend in this world, his house and lot, No. 18 on the south side of Prune Street, and "Two hundred shares of Stock of the Bank of South Carolina, and twenty-five shares of the Planters and Mechanicks [*sic*] Bank—both of which banks are located in Charleston, South Carolina." To his executrix, Ophelia Akin, and the executors of his estate, he bequeathed responsibility for the management of "certain legacies left to [his] children by will of my late sister Eliza Akin of Charleston South Carolina." He also left a silver tumbler, a silver waiter, and silver teaspoons to his daughter Caroline Christie. The tumbler and spoons were inscribed with her initials,[29] and it is possible that Akin himself had engraved the pieces.

William Murrell in his *History of American Graphic Humor* has observed that James Akin, Elkanah Tisdale, Amos Doolittle, and "Peter Pencil" were the precursors of the American cartoonist.[30] Undoubtedly Akin made an important contribution to the art of American political cartooning. His clever delineation and astute insight establish him as one of the more talented American cartoonists and caricaturists of his day. Akin's work is candid in its criticism. As a critic of society, he was both humane and forceful. His criticisms were sound and tempered with a strong feeling for mankind.

Like the well-known James Gillray, whose work Akin so closely mirrors, Akin's greatest talent was his ability to successfully combine well-delineated

and penetrating personal caricature with popular symbols while retaining a keenly developed sense of design. The soft etching ground and later the equally pliable lithographic stone allowed the artist to compose as he etched so that his engravings have a real freedom of composition and expression. Gillray and later George Cruikshank were cartoonists who took full advantage of the etching medium for a freedom necessary to their art. Akin's work is reminiscent of the work of both Gillray and Cruikshank.[31]

In his political art Akin did not rely on any one consistent style. Many artists exhibit a progression of maturing styles, but Akin employed different styles simultaneously. He never adopted a new style to the exclusion of an old one. His work is characterized by two dissimilar approaches to design: sparsely filled frames in which he relied on clear-cut, terse, personal caricature, or extensively filled frames in which his figures pun expansively on elements of the subject that Akin is editorializing. *The Prairie Dog*, Akin's earliest known signed political work, *The Man*, and *The House That Jonathan Built* are examples of Akin's sparse, concentrated designs, while *Caucus Curs*, *The Holy Alliance*, and *My Card* rely on a number of figures and complex explanatory dialogue. In this latter type of design not only the frame but also the horizontal margin below the frame are filled with complementary verse, a technique that was employed in the eighteenth century and had indeed originated earlier, in the seventeenth century. Akin handled either of these approaches successfully. Even in his most complicated conceptions he never lost sight of the overall design, though the directness of his simply conceived caricatures may appeal to the twentieth-century eye more readily than the involved allegorical conceits of his complex and crowded designs.

In his drawing Akin also employed two styles: well-delineated, slender forms, for example, those in *Dress*, *An Unexpected Meeting of Old Friends*, and *The Prairie Dog*, and well-rounded, balloon-like forms, such as the figures in *Liberty and Right*, *A Kean Shave*, and *Philadelphia Taste Dis-*

---

been attributed to Eliza Akin's hand. Mrs. Eliza Akin's death, November 11, 1834, was recorded in [Poulson's] *American Daily Advertiser* (Philadelphia), Nov. 11, 1834.

[29] James Akin, Will no. 174 (1846), Will Book no. 18, p. 434. Philadelphia City Archives.

[30] Murrell, *A History of American Graphic Humor*, p. 79.

[31] For examples of the work of Gillray and Cruikshank see James Gillray, *Fashionable Contrasts: Caricatures by James Gillray* (London: Phaidon Press, 1966); Dorothy M. George, *English Political Caricature, 1793–1832*, 2 vols. (Oxford: Oxford University Press, 1959).

FIG. 3. James Akin, *The Prairie Dog Sickened at the Sting of the Hornet.* Newburyport, Mass., 1803–1804. Etching (watercolored); H. 11^{15}⁄$_{16}$″, W. 15^{15}⁄$_{16}$″ (sheet). (Courtesy Prints Division, Library of Congress.)

played. In each instance he was close to his English prototypes.

According to Murrell, American political cartooning was a dormant art in the period from 1817 to 1830,[32] but scattered examples of Akin's work during this period are extant, although the majority of his political works date from after 1830. In addition some of Akin's important later cartoons have rarely been illustrated and infrequently discussed.

Akin's cartoons and caricatures fall into two broad catagories: local and national politics, and patriotic themes. Akin's earliest known signed political cartoon, *The Prairie Dog Sickened at the Sting of the Hornet* (Fig. 3), portrays a patriotic, or nationalistic, theme. In 1806, Akin advertised himself as the author of the cartoon,[33] but the

subject matter, President Jefferson's embarrassment over the question of West Florida, suggests that the print was completed earlier, in 1803 or 1804.

In settling the United States' claims to West Florida under the terms of the Louisiana Purchase, Jefferson publicly called upon Congress to press Spain for her "trespasses." Secretly, he asked Congress for two million dollars to purchase West Florida and secure the United States' claim without incident. For certain financial considerations to herself, France offered to act as go-between. Akin's portrayal of Jefferson in the prairie dog print reflects his characteristic anti-Republicanism and anti-Francophilism.

At the left of the frame, a figure with the body of an emaciated dog and the head of a man (Thomas Jefferson) coughs up gold coins, which fall into a pile at his feet. A hornet with the characteristic Bonaparte hat on a Napoleon head

---

[32] *A History of American Graphic Humor*, p. 135.
[33] *Newburyport Herald*, Nov. 14, 1806.

stings the dog from behind. At right, a gentleman dances about in front of the dog. In his right hand he holds a map of West Florida, in his left a map of East Florida. Talleyrand's instructions are in his pocket.

Although he drew at least two other political cartoons in the early 1800s, Akin's talents were directed toward nonpolitical subjects until the confusion of issues and candidates in the national election of 1824 stimulated him to produce at least two cartoons satirizing the differing personalities in the presidential race. *An Unexpected Meeting of Old Friends* is one of his commentaries on the election of 1824. The figure dominating the right half of the frame, Old Kanetuck, half-horse and half-alligator, a folk figure of the boasting frontiersman, is undoubtedly a reference to the Kentucky senator Henry Clay and his attempt to gain strategic Philadelphia votes. Akin drew Old Kanetuck in skeletal form, displaying a petition adorned by a laurel wreath. At the left of the picture, a man throws up his hands and bends backward in fright. Between the two figures, political papers flutter to the ground.

Caucus Curs in Full Yell, Or a War-Whoop to Saddle on the People, A Pappoose President (Fig. 4), another pictorial statement on the 1824 election, is Akin's only known expression of sympathy for President Jackson, who was more often the target of Akin's trenchant humor. The political stance of the cartoon is anti-Clay, anti-Crawford, and anti-caucus system. It may well be the subject of Akin's letter to Ralph Eleaser Whiteside Earl, the husband of Jackson's niece, dated November 9, 1824. The letter mentions a caricature sympathetic to the General. "I enclose you a Caricature in favour of General Jackson, in opposition to the miserable herd of wretches who publish their pitiful resentments against the Man who saved them from the Grasp of British Tyranny. Accept as my testimony of my high respect this feeble Effort to put down the clamours of so base a herd." Murrell cites this letter as proof that Akin was occasionally productive during the years 1820 to 1830, but he did not uncover the print to which Akin's letter referred.[34] Although *Caucus Curs* tells its story by means of a pack—not a herd—the subject is that which Akin described,

"wretches who publish pitiful resentments against [Jackson]."

The date of the letter, November 9, 1824, also argues the case for *Caucus Curs*. The election of 1824, the subject of this cartoon, was a landmark election in that it dealt a deathblow to the caucus system, which until that time had assured the selection of national tickets by congressional caucuses excluding the direct vote of the people. The candidates in the hotly contested election were William H. Crawford, John C. Calhoun, John Quincy Adams, Henry Clay, and Andrew Jackson. Four of these, Crawford, Clay, Adams, and Jackson, claimed to be Republican candidates. Because the caucus system had fallen into disrepute, only sixty-nine members attended the caucus that selected Crawford as the Republican candidate.

Thus, William Crawford, secretary of the treasury, entered the race the strongest of the five participants. Jefferson's personal sanction supported Crawford's claim that he was the true Jeffersonian Republican in the race. The Virginia dynasty which in alliance with New York had controlled the presidency for twenty-four years, seconded Jefferson's support of Crawford. Martin Van Buren also supported Crawford and worked against strong popular pressures to insure his state's backing for the secretary of the treasury. Crawford's strong commitment to the caucus system proved to be a source of weakness in an era of growing popular democracy. His appeal was mainly to the wealthy class of the South, and his strength on other fronts depended on politicians who were beginning to fear the rising tide of popular opinion against the caucus system.

In Akin's representation of the election issues, Martin Van Buren stands in front of "Uncle Sam's Treasury Pap House" holding a bowl full of dollars. The New York politician tells a woman and an Indian, "here's a bowl full of solid pappose meat." In this instance pap and "pappose meat" are colloquialisms for official patronage dispensed by Crawford and his "Amalgamation Tool," the treasury department. Van Buren's statement, "better marry our wild Indians than foreigners good or bad," probably refers to his scheme to persuade Henry Clay to accept the vice presidential nomination, rather than permit the Swiss born Albert Gallatin to run on the Crawford ticket.

In the foreground Akin depicts the press as a pack of skulking curs barking at the military hero,

[34] Quoted in Murrell, *A History of American Graphic Humor*, p. 135.

Andrew Jackson, whose sword bears the inscription "Veni, Vidi, Vici." *The National Gazette,* Crawford's press, is branded with the words, "British Influence." The *Pittsburgh Statesman* bears the inscription, "Let the purloining of Letters be sounded through the Clarion of ill fame and be blown by Walter Lowrie." Walter Lowrie was the senator who asked Gallatin to withdraw from the campaign because of the former treasury secretary's unpopular foreign connections.[35] The

reference to the purloining of letters and the Hartford Convention, the five-headed dog, recalls Crawford's strike at Andrew Jackson through the publication of the Jackson-Monroe correspondence of 1816. The correspondence revealed that Jackson had, in 1816, urged Monroe to put a Federalist in his cabinet. Eight years later, in 1824, this recommendation was unfathomable to Jackson's would-be supporters. The incident caused such clamor that Jackson's friend and backer, John Eaton, was forced to publish the entire correspondence; Federalists as well as Republicans were dismayed. Not only had Jackson advocated a Federalist in

[35] George Dangerfield, *Era of Good Feeling* (New York: Harcourt, Brace and World, A Harbinger Book, 1964), p. 336.

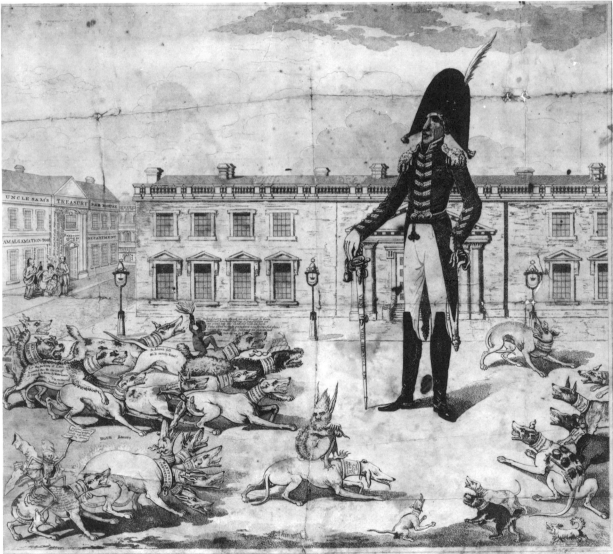

FIG. 4. James Akin, *Caucus Curs in Full Yell.* Philadelphia, 1824. Aquatint and etching; H. 17¾", W. 20" (outer border). (Courtesy Prints Division, Library of Congress.)

the Republican administration, but he had written that if the Hartford Convention had been held within his military jurisdiction, he would have hanged its leaders.[36]

Seated on the *Richmond Whig* is a Negro woman, who speaks in dialect, saying, "Name o' God! no body gwine feard now for Crawford ghose! look pondat sleepy dog . . . Can't bark no mo for Crawford." The reference is to Crawford's paralytic stroke, suffered in 1823. The *Boston Gazette,* which bears its teeth at the commanding figure of Jackson, is cleverly portrayed with a cod fish tail.

The *Raleigh Register,* whose head appears at the upper right, has been credited with establishing the "dark and fruitful precedent" of unnecessary personal abuse of public figures. On October 12, 1824, the paper criticized Jackson's duel fought in defense of his wife's good name as "A disgusting detail of squabbling and quarreling—of pistolings dirkings & brickbattings and other actions reconciliable neither to regulations nor morals." On November 5, 1824, the *Raleigh Register* had become bolder and made a "solemn appeal to the reflecting part of the community, and beg[ged] of them to think and ponder well before they place[d] their tickets in the box, how they [could] justify it to themselves and posterity to place such a woman as Mrs. Jackson! at the head of the female society of the U. States."[37]

In another of his less known cartoons dealing with national subjects, *The Holy Alliance,* drawn in 1830, Akin turned to a religious theme with strong political overtones. *The Holy Alliance* (Fig. 5) caricatures fundamentalist groups who wished to halt the delivery of mails on Sunday. Akin's portrayal of the issue shows his concern for free thought and his fear of bigotry.

In the center of the frame, a United States mail coach is halted by two groups of men dragging trees across the path. Women praying and reading Sunday school tracts are seated on benches in the lower left of the picture. A long "PETITION against the MAILS Travelling on SUNDAY" is rolled out in the center foreground. Behind a pulpit in the upper left is a clergyman wearing an exaggeratedly high mitre. In his right hand is a gallows and in

his left hand the flames of hell-fire. Akin probably found the prototype for the clerical figure in George Cruikshank's *Clerical Magistrate,* who was similarly surrounded by symbols of repression and death, a gallows, a cat'-o-nine-tails, and shackels, but Cruikshank's cleric was a Janus figure while Akin's is not.[38] In front of the cleric, a demon-figure dances before an altar or pulpit. To the right of this group is a church ridden by a clergyman who sits in the "GREAT STATE SADDLE." His standard is a banner depicting hell-fire surmounted by a skull. A domed building, the U.S. Capitol, whose entablature is lettered with the traditional American freedoms that the fundamentalists threaten, is seen in the background to the right.

In contrast to Akin's earlier sympathetic treatment of General Jackson, *Caucus Curs,* are two bitingly critical anti-Jackson productions: a broadside entitled *The Man* and a pamphlet entitled *The House That Jonathan Built. The Man* (Fig. 6), a Janus portrait of President Andrew Jackson, viewed from one perspective renders a profile bust of a man, "A brainless, sappy, lump of lead. The card turn'd—shows the Brute!!!"; the head becomes that of a "JACK ASS." The conjoined or double headed image had its birth in the Reformation token and became a popular conceit in both England and France in the late eighteenth century. The original address lithographed on the American Antiquarian Society's copy of the print, 177 South 11th, was inked out, and 18 Prune added by a contemporary hand. The city directories list Akin at 177 South 11th from 1831 to 1833, which provides the basis of the date, 1831–1833 for the first state. He was listed at 18 Prune (the inked in address) from 1835 to 1836 and from 1842 until his death in 1846.

The House That Jonathan Built or Political Primer for 1832 purports to be "A Straw Thrown Up—To See Which Way The Wind Blows." This anonymous tract, illustrated with twelve cleverly conceived and well-executed wood engravings, is dedicated to the "Little Magician." "To Martin Van Buren & the Money Changers at Albany, The First Being the LITTLE Political Magician of the United States, The Last His Worthy & Obedient Satellites, THIS WORK IS RESPECTFULLY DEDICATED, as A tribute Worthy the Master Spirits of the Kit-

[36] Marquis James, *Andrew Jackson: Portrait of A President* (New York: Grosset and Dunlap, 1961), p. 81.

[37] James, *Andrew Jackson,* p. 93.

[38] George, *English Political Caricature,* 1:182, pl. 71.

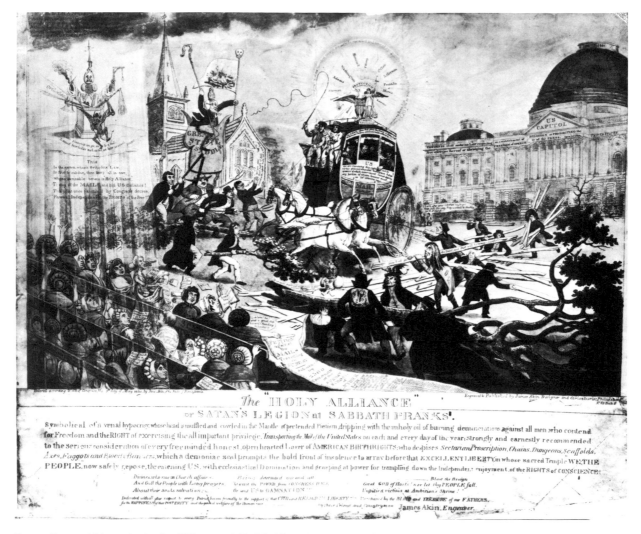

Fig. 5. James Akin, *The Holy Alliance*. Philadelphia, May 5, 1830. Aquatint; H. 13¾", W. 21¹³⁄₁₆". (Courtesy of the American Antiquarian Society.)

chen Cabinet, By the Public's Humble Servant."

The House That Jonathan Built is an adaptation of the traditional English nursery rhyme, "The House That Jack Built." The parody was not original to the anonymous author of this anti-Jackson tract. The first author to parody the rhyme was William Hone whose *The Political House That Jack Built,* published in 1819, was illustrated with woodcuts by George Cruikshank. By 1820 Hone's pamphlet had gone through fifty editions and had created a vogue for adapting the rhyme to political purposes. This craze died out in the late twenties, but there was an attempt to revive it in 1832, the date of the publication of *The House That Jonathan Built* illustrated by James Akin.

Akin had used a similar rhyme meter two years earlier in the verse accompanying *The Holy Alliance.* In fact, *The Holy Alliance* provides a further link between Akin and the English prototype because the clerical figure in *The Holy Alliance,* which Akin adopted from Cruikshank, had originally appeared as an illustration in Hone's *Political House That Jack Built.* At least three other anti-Jackson caricatures modeled on "The House That Jack Built" rhyme are known. In each case,

FIG. 6. James Akin, *The Man!* Philadelphia, 1831–1833. Lithograph; H. 10¼″, W. 4¾″. (Courtesy of the American Antiquarian Society.)

their publication dates are post-1832.[39] *The House That Jonathan Built* and its English prototype are more sophisticated productions than these single sheet broadsides; they supply their own appropriate verse composed on the original rhyme scheme and written specifically to the subject. In both the Hone pamphlet and the anonymous Akin pamphlet, the author, in true nineteenth-century fashion, quotes from works other than his own to preface each verse, and these introductory lines are placed immediately below the cuts.

The title page cut (Fig. 7), *The Pen Outweighs Them All,* for *The House That Jonathan Built* is composed of a man (Andrew Jackson) in military dress uniform standing at the right of a scales. In an attempt to weight the balance, he places his sword on the right pan, which carries three documents labelled Anti-Tariff, Nullification, and Bank Veto. But the left pan still weighs the heaviest even though it holds only a quill pen, the instrument of the United States Constitution and freedom. The frontispiece (Fig. 8) is an advertisement for a broom. The slogan "Buy a broom" is a takeoff on Jackson's 1828 campaign slogan for reform—a broom to sweep the Augean stables. The text makes obvious reference to the president's advisers, the Kitchen Cabinet, and the *Globe,* the Jacksonian newspaper.

The story begins with *The House That Jonathan Built* (Fig. 9), a domed temple of Republican rule, based on the temple of the Constitution, a recurrent English symbol. Its pillared supports consist of Congressional Power, Judiciary, and Liberty and Independence. The roof of the house, which protects the treasure stored therein, is the Constitution. What better picture could an artist render of the Whigs' counter-conception of the Democrats strong, all powerful, positive executive. The Whig negative executive was silent and unseen.

The Wealth (Fig. 10) that lay in the House is the dividends of the American Revolution: the Act of Habeas Corpus, the Declaration of Inde-

[39] George, *English Political Caricature,* 1:182; Frank Weitenkampf, *Political Caricature in the United States* (New York: New York Public Library, 1953), p. 34 lists three single-sheet prints based on the Jonathan theme: *The House that Rogues Built* (n.p., 1834), at the Boston Public Library; E. W. Clay, *This is the House that Jack Built* (New York: A. Imbert, 1834), at the New-York Historical Society; and an untitled version also at the New-York Historical Society.

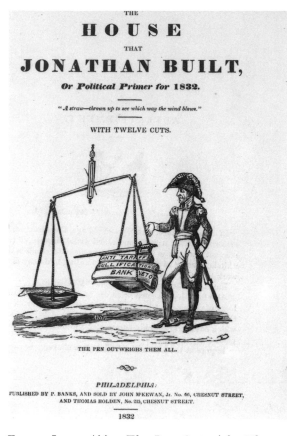

Fig. 7. James Akin, *The Pen Outweighs Them All.*
From *The House That Jonathan Built* (Philadelphia:
P. Banks, 1832). Woodcut; H. 5″, W. 7½″. (Eleuthe-
rian Mills Historical Library.)

ADVERTISEMENT.

Buy a broom!! buy a broom!! buy a broom!!

In consequence of inability and old age, the advertiser is
OBLIGED to *retire* from business, and would dispose of two
efficient slaves, who have been accustomed to scrub in the
"kitchen" and "back stairs," and are willing to do any dirty
work to which they may be put.

Inquire at the sign of the "Globe," Washington.

Also for sale, if a good price can be obtained, the Astro-
loger of the nineteenth century, or Great Magician, with all
the cups, balls, conjuring sticks, &c. &c. used by him, and
which has brought to his late master and himself immense
gain.

Inquire at the sign of the "Globe," as above.

Fig. 8. James Akin, *Advertisement*. From *The House
That Jonathan Built* (Philadelphia: P. Banks, 1832).
Woodcut; H. 4¾″, W. 3¹³⁄₁₆″. (Eleutherian Mills His-
torical Library.)

pendence, the Constitution of the United States,
and the Laws of the United States. Akin depicts
this wealth as legal documents, insurances of democratic processes, placed in and around the treasure chest.

It is the self-propogating and corrupt *Vermin*
(Fig. 11) who threaten the *Wealth* that lay in the
House that Jonathan Built. Jackson's "Spoils
System" bore them, and Jackson, the rocking
horse—the plaything of the *Vermin*—is courted
by a group of four.

The mustached figure riding the rocking horse
is undoubtedly a reference to the unsavory Eaton
affair, in which Jackson's defense of Peggy Eaton,
after her ostracism by the wife of Vice President
Calhoun, led to a major cabinet split. The group
of onlookers in the picture is composed of men
who remained loyal to Jackson in his split with
Calhoun. To the right is Peggy Eaton's husband,

Secretary of War John Eaton. Martin Van Buren
appears in the center back, and the journalistic
duo of Blair and Kendall are at the far left.
Francis P. Blair, the editor of the Jacksonian or-
gan, the *Washington Globe,* holds a globe or
sphere in his hand. Close by his side is Amos
Kendall, editorial contributor to the *Globe.* Both
men were members of the president's trusted
Kitchen Cabinet. "'Old Andy' would lie on a
couch and smoke and dictate his ideas to Kendall,
the scholar of the group, and then Editor Blair or
Kendall would write and rewrite the paragraphs
which would crackle in the *Globe* the next day."[40]
The depiction of Jackson as a rocking horse with
the crown of a king suggests the president was an

[40] Frank Luther Mott, *American Journalism: A History
1690–1960* (3rd ed.; New York: The Macmillan Co., 1950),
pp. 179–80.

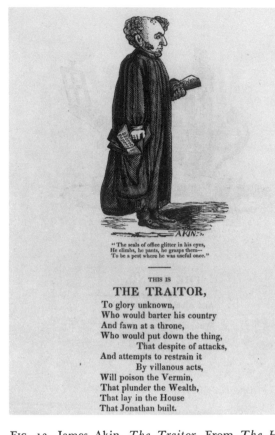

"The seals of office glitter in his eyes,
He climbs, he pants, he grasps them—
To be a pest where he was useful once."

THIS IS

THE TRAITOR,

To glory unknown,
Who would barter his country
And fawn at a throne,
Who would put down the thing,
        That despite of attacks,
And attempts to restrain it
        By villanous acts,
Will poison the Vermin,
That plunder the Wealth,
That lay in the House
That Jonathan built.

FIG. 13. James Akin, *The Traitor*. From *The House That Jonathan Built* (Philadelphia: P. Banks, 1832). Woodcut; H. 4⅛″, W. 2⅜″. (Eleutherian Mills Historical Library.)

"Ruffians are abroad—
•   •   •   •   •   •"

THESE ARE

THE VICTIMS,

Of high-handed power,
Who groan in a prison
To this very hour—
Who despise the base Traitor,
To glory unknown,
Who would put down the Thing,
        That despite of attacks,
And attempts to restrain it
        By villanous acts,
Will poison the Vermin,
That plunder the Wealth,
That lay in the House
That Jonathan built.

FIG. 14. James Akin, *The Victims*. From *The House That Jonathan Built* (Philadelphia: P. Banks, 1832). Woodcut; H. 3″, W. 4⅛″. (Eleutherian Mills Historical Library.)

hind the bar on which hangs the slogan "City privilege sell without a license." Oyster cellars did not boast a very good reputation. They were thought of as places of slothful living and dens of villainous plotting. Akin's subjects are far from villainous; they appear more suited to slothful living than to cunning intrigue.

Joseph Jackson, in his *Philadelphia Encyclopedia,* identifies the oyster cellar in Akin's lithograph as one owned by James Prossler, "a fine looking mulatto," who operated an oyster cellar at 806 Market Street (the 1890 street address) from about 1830. Prossler was among the first to introduce Philadelphians to steamed snapper. Jackson credits Akin with having made the lithograph in 1829,[43] and Akin's employment in that same year as an eating house proprietor may have provided

the inspiration for the scene. The fact that *Philadelphia Taste Displayed* was lithographed by the firm of Kennedy and Lucas also argues an early date for the print, because by the mid-1830s Akin had acquired his own lithographic equipment.

Turning to local politics, Akin's lithograph *Crib of Wolf Meat and Court Fodder* (Fig. 20) comments on the Whig Party's attempt to defeat Dr. Joel B. Sutherland, Democratic Governor George Wolf's candidate in the congressional election of 1834. Following Jackson's bank veto of 1833, the Democratic Party had split into two factions. Pennsylvania's Governor Wolf, who had been a supporter of the Bank, was forced into making an ambiguous statement on the veto that was easily interpreted as a reversal of his earlier stand. The split that ensued—although it did not seriously endanger the Democrats' chances in congressional or state elections—encouraged the Whig Party to contest incumbent Democrats. The congressional elections of 1834 were quiet with the

[43] Joseph Jackson, *Encyclopaedia of Philadelphia*, 4 vols. (Harrisburg: The National Historical Association, 1931), 2:386.

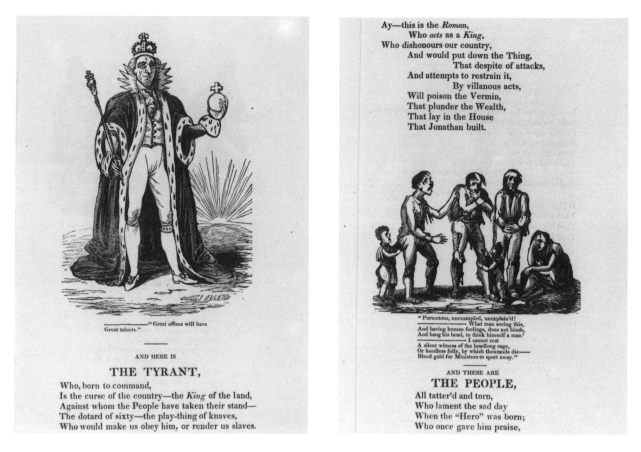

Ay—this is the *Roman*,
Who *acts* as a *King*,
Who dishonours our country,
And would put down the Thing,
That despite of attacks,
And attempts to restrain it,
By villanous acts,
Will poison the Vermin,
That plunder the Wealth,
That lay in the House
That Jonathan built.

——————"Great offices will have
Great talents."

AND HERE IS

THE TYRANT,

Who, born to command,
Is the curse of the country—the *King* of the land,
Against whom the People have taken their stand—
The dotard of sixty—the play-thing of knaves,
Who would make us obey him, or render us slaves.

" Portentous, unexampled, unexplain'd!
———————— What man seeing this,
And having human feelings, does not blush,
And hang his head, to think himself a man?
———— I cannot rest
A silent witness of the headlong rage,
Or heedless folly, by which thousands die—
Bleed gold for Ministers to sport away."

AND THESE ARE

THE PEOPLE,

All tatter'd and torn,
Who lament the sad day
When the "Hero" was born;
Who once gave him praise,

FIG. 15. James Akin, *The Tyrant*. From *The House That Jonathan Built* (Philadelphia: P. Banks, 1832). Woodcut; H. 5¼", W. 3½". (Eleutherian Mills Historical Library.)

FIG. 16. James Akin, *The People*. From *The House That Jonathan Built* (Philadelphia: P. Banks, 1832). Woodcut; H. 2⅝", W. 3¾". (Eleutherian Mills Historical Library.)

exception of the activity in Philadelphia where the Whigs made a strong showing in their unsuccessful attempt to unseat Sutherland of the First Congressional District. James Gowen, the Whig candidate, was an Irish mechanic. He brought popular support to the ticket, but the Irish issue was inevitably raised.[44]

Akin's *Crib of Wolf Meat* pictures a wolf (Governor Wolf) overseeing the electoral tug of war from his perch atop the public crib, which is stuffed with tokens of patronage. Dr. Joel, who feels the power of Jemmy (Gowen) and the Sons of Erin, holds the spoils of office in his hand. The unpleasant half-animal, half-human creatures crawling around Sutherland's feet remind the doctor of their support. The term "wolf-meat" can be

interpreted as patronage; it is an obvious and convenient pun on the governor's name.

One of the most brutal and inhumane subjects caricatured by James Akin was the anti-Catholic riots of 1844 in the City of Brotherly Love. This he did with characteristic candor and insight in the print *My Card, or a Swash Crowing from a Chicken of True Game Breed* (Fig. 21), the last of his signed, known works.

Nativism and anti-Catholicism grew in proportion to the increasing immigration during the thirties and forties. In revival-swept America the presence of the Catholic Church, the "Proprietor of Wickedness" and the agent of alien power, intensified the zealous religiosity and xenophobia of patriotic Protestants. The poor and the uneducated—the workers who had most to suffer from an influx of cheap labor—had no priority on the fear of popery. John Fanning Watson, the Philadelphia antiquarian, observed:

[44] Charles McCool Synder, *The Jacksonian Heritage: Pennsylvania Politics, 1833–1848* (Harrisburg: The Pennsylvania Historical Commission, 1958), p. 48.

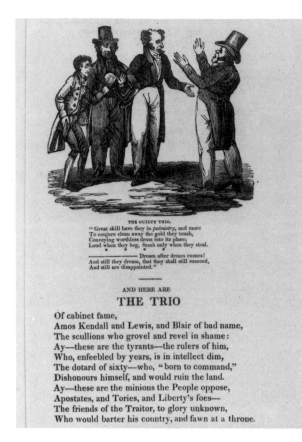

FIG. 17. James Akin, *The Trio*. From *The House That Jonathan Built* (Philadelphia: P. Banks, 1832). Woodcut; H. 3¾″, W. 3¾″. (Eleutherian Mills Historical Library.)

the Romanists are at present establishing themselves throughout our whole land. . . . This is done by erecting churches, schools, and nunneries (by aid of Foreign Funds), in all places. Many are disturbed by their presence. But the press will be too free and expansive to take undue ascendency and domination, and will urge their conductors also to divest themselves of many of their assumptions and pageantries, as fostered and indulged in foreign countries.[45]

Smouldering anti-Catholic sentiment was fanned into consuming flames by the founding of the Native American Party, whose America for the Americans theme was for some a matter of political expediency and for others the expression of ignorance and superstition. Outwardly professing an anti-alien policy, the party welcomed non-Catholic aliens.

[45] John Fanning Watson, *Annals of Philadelphia, and Pennsylvania in Olden Time,* 3 vols. (Philadelphia: Leary Stuart and Co., 1927), 3:603.

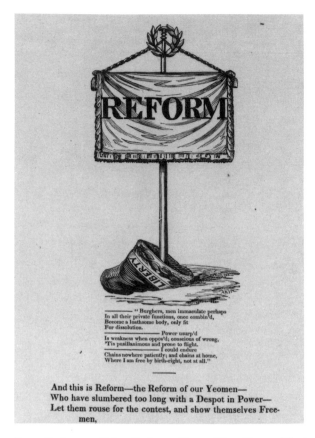

FIG. 18. James Akin, *Reform*. From *The House That Jonathan Built* (Philadelphia: P. Banks, 1832). Woodcut; H. 5⅛″, W. 2¾″. (Eleutherian Mills Historical Library.)

Philadelphia was fertile ground for the seeds of nativism. It was a city of unsynthesized nationalities and clannishness. Fire and militia companies organized on a national basis were rallying points for perennial skirmishes between different ethnic groups. Philadelphia nativists had their first meeting in 1837. They battered the public incessantly with incendiary and libelous pamphlets. When a controversy erupted over reading of the Bible in public schools, the war of words was transfigured into bloody civil disorder. In *My Card,* one of Akin's "Native Germs" shouted the significant line, "No G–d D—n Catholick Bibles/ our own will give your Soul ease."

In order to foil the papist plot to eliminate Bible reading in school, the Native Americans called a rally in the Kensington District of Philadelphia, the heart of the Irish neighborhood. The meeting took place on the evening of May 3, 1844. By the evening of May 9, Philadelphia, recoiling in horror, picked up the pieces of a riot-torn city. An exact accounting of the damage wrought by the riots is difficult to determine, but it is a "matter of record that more than forty dwelling houses were destroyed . . . , while over two hundred families were rendered homeless." The loss of life was established at forty, while some sixty persons were seriously wounded. Church property valued at over $150,000 and city property over $100,000 was destroyed. St. Michael's Church and Convent were burned to the ground as was St. Augustine's, which housed the largest Catholic library in America at the time.[46]

On July 4, 1844, five thousand Nativists turned out for the Independence Day parade in which

[46] Joseph L. Kirlin, *Catholicity in Philadelphia From the Earliest Missionaries Down to the Present Time* (Philadelphia: John Joseph McVey, 1909), pp. 304-306, 322-24.

A DOWNRIGHT GABBLER,
or a goose that deserves to be hissed —

Fig. 19. James Akin, *A Downright Gabbler*. Philadelphia, ca. 1829. Lithograph; 7¹³⁄₁₆", W. 7" (sheet) . (Worcester Art Museum.)

FIG. 20. James Akin, *Crib of Wolf Meat.* Philadelphia, 1834–1835. Lithograph; H. 11⅛″, W. 14⅞″. (Courtesy of The New-York Historical Society, New York City.)

their party's patriotic floats and banners were leading attractions. The parade was reported to be "the finest political procession that had ever been seen in the city."[47] That evening members of the Native American army, weary from the day's celebration, camped in Fisher's Woods. In the morning their rest was interrupted by a gang of about thirty whooping Irish who came to answer the Nativist accusations of the preceeding day. News of the "onslaught of murderous Irish" spread quickly. It was enlivened by the revelation that arms were hidden in the Church of St. Philip de Neri in the Southwark District,[48] the subject of Akin's cartoon.

[47] Scharf and Westcott, *History of Philadelphia,* 1:669.
[48] Kirlin, *Catholicity in Philadelphia,* p. 332.

As rumors spread and tension mounted, William Dunn, brother of the pastor of St. Philip's, and 150 volunteers stationed themselves inside the church. Crowds gathered outside demanding a search of the building. Sheriff McMichael searched the building, brought out some muskets, and surrendered them to a volunteer posse stationed in front of the church. About midnight, the City Guard took command of the church. After prodding by the crowd, the guard made another search of the building and found additional muskets. In the morning American Native sympathizers reinforced the mob, and it spilled out into the neighboring streets.

The mob was sporadically dispersed by Brigadier General Cadwalader and a mounted platoon that charged the crowd. Cadwalader petitioned

FIG. 21. James Akin, *My Card or a Swash Crowing from a Chicken of True Game Breed*. Philadelphia, 1844. Lithograph (watercolored); H. 11½", W. 18". (Historical Society of Pennsylvania.)

the mob to disband, but his request was met with hisses and dares that he open fire. Meanwhile, cannons that the mob commanded were being discharged at the rear walls of the church. Another cannon was dragged to the doors of the church. The crowd continued to issue ultimatums. They agreed to disperse only when the Hibernia Greens, an Irish militia company occupying the inside of the church, surrendered their position. Meeting this request, the Greens, escorted by two neutral militia companies, left the church and were immediately attacked by the mob. The crowd then surged into the church and attempted to put the building to the torch, but it was unsuccessful.

The troops guarding the church were faced with a more riotous mob on Sunday morning, July 6. Armed with several cannon and the mistaken assurance that the military would not fire, the crowd refused to comply with the order to clear the streets. The troops fired three volleys into the mob at Second and Queen streets and the crowd temporarily dispersed. Reorganizing under the cover of night, the native sympathizers returned to the church with additional cannon secured by long ropes and loaded with nails, chains, chisels, and broken bottles.

The governor declared a state of civil war and called for federal assistance. President Tyler dispatched Federal troops from Fort Carlisle, Fort Mifflin, and Fort McHenry. The governor sent troops from Lancaster and Harrisburg. During the night the mob lost possession of several of their cannon, and by morning peace had been restored. Within the week 5,000 troops had been brought into Philadelphia, where they remained for a month. During three days fighting fourteen people had been killed and fifty wounded.[49]

[49] Kirlin, *Catholicity in Philadelphia*, p. 339.

At the time of the execution of *My Card,* James Akin was a man in his early seventies. He pictured with keen insight the political overtones of the Philadelphia riots of 1844, which occured two years before his death. The "Whirling Sun" refers to the *Daily Sun,* edited by Lewis Levin, a leading Nativist. Within its wide-spread rays an ominous gawking bird screeches "picked Goose cackle / & street talk / for Congress ho!" Capitalizing on the Nativist ticket, editor Levin later won a seat in the U.S. Congress.

At the left of the picture, a fiery band of winged skeletons stand behind and to the left of their commander, "A Spectred DEMON, striding a pale horse!" A billowing-caped standard bearer mounted on the wheel of a caisson urges his company forward. His banner is the skull and cross bones. Behind the standard bearer, the leader, wearing a fire-radiating crown, whose head is more reptile than equine, "bandish[es] aloft a fiery Glittering sword." A bored member of the demon pack sits on the barrel of the cannon with his head in his hands awaiting action; his feet rest on a winged skull suspended at the mouth of the cannon. At right the angry mob, held at bay by two public servants, shouts and jeers. In front of the mob a gaunt, long-legged man in a coxcomb hat stretches out his arms in the direction of the assaulting cannon. A "hardware shop," an indiscriminate selection of tools, pans, furniture, and so on flies in the air above the cannon over the heads of the crowd. At the lower right, a man who has come under the plank barrier that holds back the crowd crouches and picks up a rock. A Greek Revival church, St. Philip de Neri, with the sacred monogram above the door, is seen in the background to the right of the mob. Contrary

to first impressions, the date 1840 inscribed above the door of the church does not date the scene depicted. It indicates the year in which the cornerstone of St. Philip de Neri was laid.[50]

The verse below the print reads as if intended to be the reflections of Charles Naylor whose "quick-thinking saved the day." Naylor, a lawyer and former member of congress, informed Brigadier General Cadwalader that the troops had no legal right to fire on the crowd. Naylor is seen within the frame of the picture with his arms outstretched toward the cannon. He reasons legalistically with the fiery personage of Cadwalader who has given the order to fire:

> Hail Ghastly Ministers of destruction
> Whose dread Engine purposes fell Murder
> Hold! Hold! I beeseech ye,——Don't fire
> Let mercy season justice!

In this final documented work Akin rose to the height of his powers in condemning the passions and prejudices of his fellow citizens. Opinionated he certainly was but indifferent never. Not always a great engraver in terms of technical skill, as a caricaturist he fulfilled the charge of Annibale Carracci, the father of *caricatura,* "to grasp the perfect deformity and thus reveal the very essence of a personality. The caricature, like every other work of art, is more true to life than life itself."[51]

[50] Scharf and Westcott, *History of Philadelphia,* 2:1392.
[51] George, *English Political Caricature,* 1:11.

Checklist of the Works of James Akin

The checklist entries include all the known works of James Akin. The entries are arranged chronologically within five catagories: book and magazine illustrations, bookplates and trade cards,

caricatures and cartoons, portraits, and miscellaneous works. Prints attributed to Akin are also included in the checklist, and the basis for attribution has been noted.

The entries include the title, or description, the date, medium, dimensions, and inscription for each of Akin's prints. Unless otherwise indicated the dimensions given refer to the greatest extent of the print. Inscriptions have been transcribed literally except for the omission of descriptive captions and figure numbers from technical plates and maps. Selected institutions and individuals owning copies of Akin's prints are indicated under the heading "Collections." The abbreviations used for these institutions are as follows:

AAS   American Antiquarian Society, Worcester, Massachusetts

EI   The Essex Institute, Salem, Massachusetts

EMHL   Eleutherian Mills Historical Library, Greenville, Delaware

HSP   Historical Society of Pennsylvania, Philadelphia, Pennsylvania

LC   Library of Congress, Washington, D.C.

LCP   Library Company of Philadelphia, Philadelphia, Pennsylvania

NYHS   New-York Historical Society, New York, New York

NYPL   The New York Public Library, New York, New York

PUL   Princeton University Library, Princeton, New Jersey

UD   Hugh Morris Memorial Library, University of Delaware, Newark, Delaware

WAM   Worcester Art Museum, Worcester, Massachusetts

WM   The Henry Francis du Pont Winterthur Museum, Winterthur, Delaware

In every instance the owner of the copy examined appears first under "Collections." For some works, references that reproduce or discuss specific prints are also noted.

Book and Magazine Illustrations:

1. Thomas Dobson, *Encyclopaedia; or, A Dictionary of Arts, Sciences, and Miscellaneous Literature,* 18 vols. (Philadelphia: Thomas Dobson, 1798)

A. Plate 315, vol. 12, opposite p. 380; nine genera beginning with the letter *M*
Medium: Engraving and etching
Dimensions: H. 9⅝″, W. 7½″ (sheet)
Inscription: [Lower right] 'Grav'd by James Akin of So. Carolina.
Collections: WAM (sheet); LC (sheet); WM; EMHL

B. *Navigation,* plate 338, vol. 12, opposite p. 712; geometric figures illustrating navigation
Medium: Engraving
Dimensions: H. 9⅛″, W. 7 1/16″ (plate); H. 10 7/16″, W. 8 7/16″ (sheet)
Inscription: [Top center] NAVIGATION [lower right] JAkin S. C.
Collections: WM; EMHL; LC (sheet)

C. *Navigation,* plate 343, vol. 12, opposite p. 746; three illustrations of a sextant
Medium: Engraving
Dimensions: H. 9⅛″, W. 7 1/16″ (plate); H. 10 7/16″, W. 8 7/16″ (sheet)
Inscription: [Top center] NAVIGATION. [lower right] Akin Sou Carolina
Collections: LC (sheet); WM; EMHL

D. Plate 345, vol. 12, opposite p. 792; illustrations of unrelated terms beginning with *N*
Medium: Engraving
Dimensions: H. 7½″, W. 6 9/16″ (plate); H. 10 7/16″, W. 8⅜″ (sheet)
Inscription: [Lower right] 'Grav'd by James Akin of So. Carolina
Collections: WM; EMHL

E. *Mustella,* plate 333, vol. 13, opposite p. 558; eleven species of genus *Mustella*
Medium: Etching
Dimensions: H. 10½″, W. 8½″ (sheet)
Inscription: [Top center] Mustella [below fig. 5, upper left] JAkin Aquaforti: Fecit.
Collections: WM; EMHL

F. Plate 486, vol. 18, opposite p. 40; illustrations of unrelated terms beginning with *S*
Medium: Engraving
Dimensions: H. 9⅝″, W. 6 11/16″ (sheet)
Inscription: [Lower right] 'Grav'd by James Akin
Collections: WM; EMHL

G. *Surgery,* plate 490, vol. 18, opposite p. 188; twenty pieces of surgical apparatus
   Medium: Engraving
   Dimensions: H. 9½″, W. 6¹³⁄₁₆″ (plate) ; H. 10½″, W. 8⁹⁄₁₆″ (sheet)
   Inscription: [Top center] SURGERY. [lower right] 'Grav'd by James Akin.
   Collections: WM; EMHL

H. *Surgery,* plate 492, vol. 18, opposite p. 188; fifteen pieces of surgical apparatus
   Medium: Engraving
   Dimensions: H. 9½″, W. 6¹³⁄₁₆″ (plate) ; H. 10½″, W. 8⅝″ (sheet)
   Inscription: [Top center] SURGERY. [lower right] 'Grav'd by James Akin.
   Collections: WM; EMHL

2. American Philosophical Society, *Transactions of the American Philosophical Society* 4 (Philadelphia: Thomas Dobson, 1799)

A. Plate 1, opposite p. 528; fossil bones
   Medium: Etching
   Dimensions: H. 9⁷⁄₁₆″, W. 15½″ (plate)
   Inscription: [None; attributed to Akin on the basis of the signed, companion plate of fossil bones appearing on the same page]
   Collections: LC; WM
   References: Mantle Fielding, *American Engravers upon Copper and Steel . . . A Supplement to . . . Stauffer's American Engravers* (Philadelphia: Wickersham Press, 1917), no. 19

B. Plate 2, opposite p. 528; fossil bones
   Medium: Etching
   Dimensions: H. 9⅝″, W. 15½″ (plate)
   Inscription: [Bottom] Engraved by James Akin from Chalk Drawings made (the size of the Bones) by Doctr. W. S. Jacobs: —
   Collections: LC; WM

3. [Anna Barbauld], *Lessons for Children, Part II. From Four to Five Years Old* (Wilmington, Delaware: James Wilson, 1800; and 2nd ed., 1803)

A. Title page; black stone with white lettering, 1800 and 1803 editions
   Medium: Wood engraving

Dimensions: H. 1⅞″, W. 1¾″
Inscription: [On stone] Adorned with / Cuts / Engraved by James Akin.
Collections: PUL, Sinclair Hamilton Collection (1800 ed.) ; AAS (1803 ed.)

B. Front cover; upper cut of crucifixion and lower cut of Bewick-like bird profile, 1800 ed.
   Medium: Wood engraving
   Dimensions: H. 1¼″, W. 1¾″ (upper rectangle) ; H. 1¼″, W. 1¾″ (lower rectangle)
   Inscription: [None; attributed to Akin on the basis of the title page inscription]
   Collections: PUL, Sinclair Hamilton Collection

C. Rear cover; upper cut of sunset at sea, identical to checklist No. 3L, and lower cut of Bewick-like bird profile, 1800 ed.
   Medium: Wood engraving
   Dimensions: H. 1¼″, W. 1⅞″ (upper rectangle) ; H. 1¼″, W. 1⅞″ (lower rectangle)
   Inscription: [Bottom of oval] [JA]
   Collections: PUL, Sinclair Hamilton Collection

D. Front cover; two fable illustrations: the dog and the ox and an unidentified fable, 1803 ed.
   Medium: Wood engraving
   Dimensions: H. 1¹³⁄₁₆″, W. 2⁵⁄₁₆″ (upper oval) ; H. 1¹³⁄₁₆″, W. 2⁵⁄₁₆″ (lower oval)
   Inscription: [None; attributed to Akin on the basis of the title page inscription]
   Collections: AAS

E. Rear cover; two fable illustrations: the old woman and her maids and the kid, the goat, and the wolf, 1803 ed.
   Medium: Wood engraving
   Dimensions: H. 1¹³⁄₁₆″, W. 2⁵⁄₁₆″ (upper oval) ; H. 1¹³⁄₁₆″, W. 2⁵⁄₁₆″ (lower oval)
   Inscription: [None; attributed to Akin on the basis of the title page inscription]
   Collections: AAS

F. Church modelled on St. Paul's London; 1800 and 1803 editions
   Medium: Wood engraving
   Dimensions: H. 1¼″, W. 1⅞″
   Inscription: [None; attributed to Akin

on the basis of the title page inscription]
Collections: PUL, Sinclair Hamilton
Collection; AAS

G. Cow grazing under a tree; 1800 and 1803
editions
Medium: Wood engraving
Dimensions: H. 1¼″, W. 1⅞″
Inscription: [None; attributed to Akin
on the basis of the title page inscription]
Collections: PUL, Sinclair Hamilton
Collection; AAS

H. Donkey; 1800 and 1803 editions
Medium: Wood engraving
Dimensions: H. 1¼″, W. 1¾″
Inscription: [None; attributed to Akin
on the basis of the title page inscription]
Collections: PUL, Sinclair Hamilton
Collection; AAS

I. Lamb; 1800 and 1803 editions
Medium: Wood engraving
Dimensions: H. 1¼″, W. 1¾″
Inscription: [None; attributed to Akin
on the basis of the title page inscription]
Collections: PUL, Sinclair Hamilton
Collection; AAS

J. Lion; 1800 and 1803 editions
Medium: Wood engraving
Dimensions: H. 1¼″, W. 1¹³⁄₁₆″
Inscription: [None; attributed to Akin
on the basis of the title page inscription]
Collections: PUL, Sinclair Hamilton
Collection; AAS

K. Printer's flower in the form of a ship; 1800
and 1803 editions
Medium: Wood engraving
Dimensions: H. ⅞″, W. ¾″
Inscription: [None; attributed to Akin
on the basis of the title page inscription]
Collections: PUL, Sinclair Hamilton
Collection; AAS

L. Sun setting at sea; identical to upper cut
of checklist No. 3C, 1800 and 1803 editions
Medium: Wood engraving
Dimensions: 1¼″, W. 1⅞″
Inscription: [None; attributed to Akin
on the basis of the title page inscription]
Collections: PUL, Sinclair Hamilton
Collection; AAS

4. *The Good Samaritan;* The Holy Bible (Philadelphia: M. Carey, 1801)
Medium: Engraving and etching
Dimensions: H. 5½″, W. 4⁵⁄₁₆″ (extent of
frame)
Inscription: [Lower left] Etched by James
Akin [lower right] Engraved by C. Tiebout
[centered below frame] THE GOOD SAMARI-
TAN / *Then Jesus said unto him. Go and do
thou likewise* [lower right] *St. Luke Ch. 10
v 37.*
Collections: NYPL

5. Henry Wilson Lockette, *An Inaugural Dis-
sertation on the Warm Bath Machine* (Phil-
adelphia: For the Author by Carr and Smith,
1801); the warm bath machine
Medium: Engraving
Dimensions: H. 4½″, W. 4⅛″
Inscription: [Lower right] J. Akin *sc.*
Collections: AAS

6. John Drayton, *A View of South Carolina As
Respects Her Natural and Civil Concerns*
(Charleston: W. P. Young, 1802)
A. Opposite p. 40; fossil bones.
Medium: Engraving and etching
Dimensions: H. 9⁹⁄₁₆″, W. 6¹¹⁄₁₆″ (sheet)
Inscription: [Lower right] J. Akin sc.
Collections: AAS; LC; WM

B. *Inside View of a Water Rice Machine,* op-
posite p. 122
Medium: Engraving
Dimensions: H. 9¾″, W. 12¾″ (sheet)
Inscription: [Above frame] An Inside
View of a Water Rice Machine as Used
in South Carolina [below frame on left]
H. B. Latrobe Esqr. Del. [below frame
on right] 'Grav'd for Drayton's Histy of
So. Carolina by J. Akin Philada. [cen-
tered below frame] Explanations of the
Machine
Collections: AAS; LC; WM

C. *Sketch of the Santee Canal,* opposite p. 156
Medium: Engraving
Dimensions: H. 12¹¹⁄₁₆″ (sheet), W.
6⅛″ (plate)
Inscription: [Top]   RIVER / RIVER /
SWAMP / SANTEE [left center] Sketch / of
the / SANTEE CANAL [lower right] J. Akin
sc.
Collections: AAS; LC; WM

'Graved by James Akin Philad.

The STATE HOUSE at COLUMBIA.

Taken from Rives's Tavern May 1794.

FIG. 22. James Akin, *The State House at Columbia.* From John Drayton, *A View of South Carolina As Respects Her Natural and Civil Concerns* (Charleston: W. P. Young, 1802). Engraving; H. 4⁵⁄₁₆″, W. 5¾″. (Photo, Winterthur.)

D. *The State House at Columbia,* opposite p. 210 (Fig. 22)
Medium: Engraving
Dimensions: H. 4⅚₆″, W. 5¾″
Inscription: [Centered below frame] 'Graved by James Akin Philad. / THE STATE HOUSE AT COLUMBIA. Taken from R[ive]s's Tavern May 1794
Collections: AAS; LC; WM

7. David Ramsay, *The History of South Carolina, from Its First Settlement in 1670, to the Year 1808,* 2 vols. (Charleston: David Longworth, 1809)

A. Frontispiece of vol. 1; Map of South Carolina, dated 1802 based on the inscription
Medium: Engraving (watercolored)
Dimensions: H. 16¾″, W. 19½″ (plate)
Inscription: [State seal, lower left below seal] T. Coram del. Charleston / J. Akin sc. Philada. [below frame] Engraved for Drayton's History of S.C.
Collections: WM

B. *Plan of Charleston,* frontispiece of vol. 2
Medium: Engraving
Dimensions: H. 9¹³⁄₁₆″, W. 12¼″
Inscription: [Upper left] A PLAN / OF / CHARLES / TOWN / from a survey of Edwd. Crisp / in 1704 / Engraved by / James Akin.
Collections: AAS

8. *Economical Laboratory of James Woodhouse;* James Parkinson, *The Chemical Pocket-Book of Memoranda Chemica* (Philadelphia: James Humphreys, 1802)
Medium: Engraving
Dimensions: H. 3½″, W. 6″
Inscription: [Centered below frame] Engraved for J. Humphreys [lower left] Akin del. [lower right] Tanner sc. [center] Economical Laboratory of James Woodhouse. M.D. / Professor of Chemistry of the University of Pennsylvania &c.
Collections: AAS
References: Samuel Parkes, *Chymical Catechism* (Philadelphia: James Humphreys, 1807), includes a restrike of the plate

9. *False Alarms;* from *False Alarms; or, The Mischievous Doctrine of Ghosts and Apparitions, of Spectres and Hobgoblins, Exploded* (Philadelphia: Benjamin Johnson & Jacob Johnson, 1802); boy running from church yard
Medium: Etching and engraving
Dimensions: H. 3¹⁵⁄₁₆″, W. 3″ (plate)
Inscription: [Lower right] J. Akin del. & sculp. [centered below] False Alarms
Collections: PUL, Sinclair Hamilton Collection
References: Sinclair Hamilton, *Early American Book Illustrators and Wood Engravers* (Princeton: Princeton University Library, 1958), no. 203

10. *The Juvenile Magazine or Miscellaneous Repository of Useful Information,* 4 vols. (Philadelphia: Benjamin Johnson, 1802–1803)
A. Vol. 1, p. 181; illustrations of primates, 1802
Medium: Etching and engraving
Dimensions: H. 4¾″, W. 3¼″ (sheet)
Inscription: [Below figure upper left] Long Armed Ape. [below figure upper right] Outrang Outrang. [below figure lower left] Pigmy Ape. [below figure lower right] Barbary Ape. / J. Akin sc.
Collections: LC

B. *Orphan boy,* vol. 2, p. 194; woman and girl conversing with young boy, 1802
Medium: Etching
Dimensions: H. 4¹⁵⁄₁₆″, W. 2⅞″ (plate)
Inscription: [Above frame] Orphan Boy. [lower right] JA [below frame] Published by B. Johnson No. 31 Market Street.
Collections: LC

C. Vol. 3, p. 107; sloth, great ant eater, and armadillo, 1803
Medium: Engraving and etching
Dimensions: H. 5¾″ (sheet), W. 2⅞″ (plate)
Inscription: [Figures top to bottom] Sloth / Great Ant Eater / Armadillo [lower right] J. Akin sc.
Collections: LC

11. *The Spectator* 5, no. 379 (Philadelphia: Robert Carr for Samuel P. Bradford & John Conrad, 1803); knight in armor and man with a spade in stone-walled room
    Medium: Engraving
    Dimensions: H. 5¹³⁄₁₆″, W. 3½″
    Inscription: [Lower right] J. Akin Sc.
    Collections: AAS

12. *Swiss Hospitality;* William Mavor, *An Historical Account of the Most Celebrated Voyages,* 10 vols. (Philadelphia: Samuel Bradford, 1803)
    Medium: Engraving and etching
    Dimensions: H. 5⁹⁄₁₆″, W. 3⁷⁄₁₆″ (sheet)
    Inscription: [Centered below picture within frame] Engraved by James Akin / Swiss Hospitality
    Collections: LC (sheet); NYPL (sheet); WAM (sheet)
    References: Fielding, *American Engravers upon Copper and Steel,* no. 16

13. *A Trifle for a Good Girl* (Philadelphia: B. Johnson, 1803)
    A. Arthur and Jowler; two boys playing
       Medium: Etching
       Dimensions: H. 3⁷⁄₁₆″, W. 5⁷⁄₁₆″ (sheet)
       Inscription: [Bottom center] J. Akin
       Collections: AAS

    B. The Little Fruit Seller; woman seated beside table piled with fruit
       Medium: Etching
       Dimensions: H. 5⁷⁄₁₆″, W. 3⁷⁄₁₆″ (page size includes checklist No. 13C)
       Inscription: [Text above cut] Little Fruit Seller [attributed to Akin on the basis of stylistic similarity to signed plate on the same page]
       Collections: AAS

    C. Unlucky Rogues; three boys
       Medium: Etching
       Dimensions: H. 5⁷⁄₁₆″, W. 3⁷⁄₁₆″ (page size includes checklist No. 13B)
       Inscription: [Text above cut] These unlucky rogues [below hat filled with stones] J. Akin
       Collections: AAS

    D. Naughty Boys in Danger; two illustrations, stag charging boy and horse dragging rider
       Medium: Etching
       Dimensions: H. 5⁷⁄₁₆″, W. 3⁷⁄₁₆″ (sheet)
       Inscription: [Top of page] Naughty Boys [below first cut] J. Akin Sc. [text in center of page] in Danger. [below bottom cut] J. Akin
       Collections: AAS

    E. The Rats; boy with cat opening rat trap
       Medium: Etching
       Dimensions: H. 5⁷⁄₁₆″, W. 3⁷⁄₁₆″ (sheet)
       Inscription: [Below the boy] J. Akin
       Collections: AAS
       References: Thomas Bewick, *A General History of Quadrupeds* (London: B. Quaritch, 1885), p. 230

14. Michael Walsh, *A New System of Mercantile Arithmetic Adapted to the Commerce of the United States* (3rd ed.; Portland: n.p., 1803), title page cut; seated man and flowers
    Medium: Wood engraving (relief block)
    Dimensions: H. 1⅞″, W. 3⁵⁄₁₆″
    Inscription: [On sheet at right hand of seated figure] Akin / sc
    Collections: AAS

15. *Power of Solitude;* Joseph Story, *The Power of Solitude* (Salem: Barnhart Macanulty, 1804), frontispiece; bearded man with a book seated in front of a cave
    Medium: Engraving
    Dimensions: H. 6¼″, W. 3⁹⁄₁₆″ (sheet)
    Inscription: [Above cut] POWER OF SOLITUDE. [centered below cut] Engrav'd by J. Akin. Newburyport. [lower left] Drawn by—[lower right]—Corné, SALEM [below frame] And muse, with truth in Wisdoms sacred cell. / Published by MACANULTY, SALEM.
    Collections: LC; EI
    References: Lewis C. Rubenstein, "James Akin in Newburyport," *Essex Institute Historical Collections* 102, no. 4 (Oct. 1966): 294; Harriet S. Tapley, *Salem Imprints, 1768–1825* (Salem, Mass.: The Essex Institute, 1927), p. 190

16. Abraham Rees, *The Cyclopaedia; or, Universal Dictionary of Arts, Sciences, and Literature*, 46 vols. (1st Am. ed.; Philadelphia: Samuel F. Bradford, and Murray, Firman, and Co., 1805–1825)

    A. *Quadrupeds,* vol. 46; illustrations of goats
        Medium: Etching
        Dimensions: H. 10¾″, W. 8¼″ (sheet)
        Inscription: [Top center] QUADRUPEDS. / MAMMALIA GENUS CAPRA. GOAT. [lower right] J. Akin sc.
        Collections: LC (sheet); NYPL (sheet); WAM (sheet); WM; EMHL
        References: Fielding, *American Engravers upon Copper and Steel,* no. 20

    B. *Botany,* vol. 46; illustrations of life cycle of plants
        Medium: Engraving
        Dimensions: H. 10¾″, W. 8¼″ (sheet)
        Inscription: [Top center] BOTANY. [lower right] 'Grav'd by JAkin.
        Collections: WM; EMHL

17. *Howard's Large and Small Round Text Copies with the New Rules for Learners* (Newburyport: Thomas & Whipple, 1805), title page; examples of different lettering styles
    Medium: Engraving
    Dimensions: H. 3″, W. 7¹⁵⁄₁₆″
    Inscription: Howard's / Large and Small / Round Text Copies / With the New Rules for Learners / James Akin Engraver— — Newburyport [bottom of page] Entered according to Act of Congress by Thomas & Whipple, Booksellers, Newburyport, [1805].
    Collections: AAS; EI
    References: Rubenstein, "James Akin in Newburyport," p. 292

18. *Perry's Spelling Book; or, The Only Sure Guide to the English Tongue* (Newburyport: Angier March, 1805)
    A. Fable of the farmer and the snake
        Medium: Wood engraving (relief block)
        Dimensions: H. 1⅞″, W. 2⁷⁄₁₆″ (rectangle)
        Inscription: [Possibly Akin or similar signature on hearth at right; attributed to Akin on the basis of similarity of style and format to signed plates in the book]
        Collections: AAS

    B. Fable of the hound, despised by his master
        Medium: Wood engraving (relief block)
        Dimensions: H. 1⁷⁄₁₆″, W. 2⁷⁄₁₆″ (rectangle)
        Inscription: [None; attributed to Akin on the basis of similarity of style and format to signed plates in the book]
        Collections: AAS

    C. Fable of the kid, the goat, and the wolf
        Medium: Wood engraving (relief block)
        Dimensions: H. 1⅞″, W. 2⁷⁄₁₆″ (rectangle)
        Inscription: [Below wolf's left forefoot] Akin
        Collections: AAS

    D. Fable of the wolves and the sheep
        Medium: Wood engraving (relief block)
        Dimensions: H. 1⅞″, W. 2⁷⁄₁₆″ (rectangle)
        Inscription: [Lower left of oval] Akin
        Collections: AAS

    E. Fable of the two thieves and the butcher
        Medium: Wood engraving (relief block)
        Dimensions: H. 1⅞″, W. 2⁷⁄₁₆″ (rectangle)
        Inscription: [Bottom center] Akin
        Collections: AAS

    F. Fable of the shepherd's boy and the farmers
        Medium: Wood engraving (relief block)
        Dimensions: H. 1⅞″, W. 2⁷⁄₁₆″ (rectangle)
        Inscription: [Between extended forelegs of fleeing fox] Akin
        Collections: AAS

    G. Fable of the dog and the ox
        Medium: Wood engraving (relief block)
        Dimensions: H. 1⅞″, W. 2⁷⁄₁₆″ (rectangle)
        Inscription: [Below ox's forelegs] Akin
        Collections: AAS

    H. Fable of the dove and the bee
        Medium: Wood engraving (relief block)

FIG. 23. James Akin, *Jupiter.* From William Sheldon, *History of the Heathen Gods and Heroes of Antiquity* (Worcester: Isiah Thomas, Jr., 1810). Wood engraving; H. 4¼″, W. 2⅜″. (Princeton University Library, Sinclair Hamilton Collection: Photo, Wilford P. Cole.)

C. Jupiter reclining on bed of clouds (Fig. 23)

    Medium: Wood engraving (relief block)

    Dimensions: H. 4¼″, W. 2⅜″

    Inscription: [Centered within border of frame at bottom] J. AKIN. SCULP.

    Collections: PUL, Sinclair Hamilton Collection; EI

    References: Boston Museum of Fine Arts, *Catalogue of an Exhibition of Early Engraving,* no. 7; Hamilton, *Early American Book Illustrators,* no. 205; Rubenstein, "James Akin in Newburyport," p. 294

D. Mercury wearing a winged helmet

    Medium: Wood engraving (relief block)

    Dimensions: H. 4¼″, W. 2⅜″

    Inscription: [Within frame below clouds] J. AKIN SC.

    Collections: PUL, Sinclair Hamilton Collection; EI

    References: Boston Museum of Fine Arts, *Catalogue of an Exhibition of Early Engraving,* no. 7; Hamilton, *Early American Book Illustrators,* no. 205; Rubenstein, "James Akin in Newburyport," p. 294

E. Momus, a dwarf figure with a jester's costume, dances in a clearing

    Medium: Wood engraving

    Dimensions: H. 4³⁄₁₆″, W. 2¼″

    Inscription: [Centered within border of frame at bottom] J. AKIN. SCULP.

    Collections: PUL, Sinclair Hamilton Collection; EI

    References: Boston Museum of Fine Arts, *Catalogue of an Exhibition of Early Engraving,* no. 7; Hamilton, *Early American Book Illustrators,* no. 205; Rubenstein, "James Akin in Newburyport," p. 294

F. Pan carries a crooked staff and his pipes

    Medium: Wood engraving (relief block)

    Dimensions: H. 4³⁄₁₆″, W. 2⅜″

    Inscription: [Within frame lower left] Akin

    Collections: PUL, Sinclair Hamilton Collection; EI

    References: Boston Museum of Fine Arts, *Catalogue of an Exhibition of Early Engraving,* no. 7; Hamilton, *Early American Book Illustrators,* no. 205; Rubenstein, "James Akin in Newburyport," p. 294

G. Saturn on a throne in Roman military dress

    Medium: Wood engraving (relief block)

    Dimensions: H. 4³⁄₁₆″, W. 2⅜″

    Inscription: [In circle at Saturn's feet] J. Akin

Collections: PUL, Sinclair Hamilton Collection; EI

References: Boston Museum of Fine Arts, *Catalogue of an Exhibition of Early Engraving,* no. 7; Hamilton, *Early American Book Illustrators,* no. 205; Rubenstein, "James Akin in Newburyport," p. 294

H. Satyrs depicted in varying poses
Medium: Wood engraving (relief block)
Dimensions: H. 4¼", W. 2⅜"
Inscription: [Centered within frame at bottom] Engr. by J. Akin.
Collections: PUL, Sinclair Hamilton Collection; EI
References: Boston Museum of Fine Arts, *Catalogue of an Exhibition of Early Engraving,* no. 7; Hamilton, *Early American Book Illustrators,* no. 205; Rubenstein, "James Akin in Newburyport," p. 294

25. *Inside of a Hut & Dress of the Laplanders;* John Pinkerton, *A General Collection of the Best and Most Interesting Voyages and Travels, in All Parts of the World . . . ,* vol. 1 (Philadelphia: Kimber and Conrad, 1810)
Medium: Engraving and etching
Dimensions: H. 6½", W. 9⅝"
Inscription: [Below oval fireside scene] 'Grav'd by James Akin [across bottom] Inside a Hut & Dress of the Laplanders
Collections: LC (sheet); NYPL (sheet)
References: Stauffer, *American Engravers upon Copper and Steel,* no. 27

26. *The Freemason's Magazine,* vol. 1 (Philadelphia, 1811); "Demons of The Night" or The Sisters of Fate, group of obscure figures among storm clouds
Medium: Engraving
Dimensions: H. 6½", W. 3¼" (plate); H. 3½", W. 2⁵⁄₁₆" (rectangular frame)
Inscription: [Lower right] J. Akin Sc. [below frame] The sisters sail in dusky state, / And, / wrapt in clouds, in tempests tost, / Weave the airy web of fate.
Collections: NYPL; HSP
References: Fielding, *American Engravers upon Copper and Steel,* no. 13

27. *Facts Connected with the Life of James Carey Whose Eccentrick Habits Caused a Post Mortem Examination, by Gentlemen of the Faculty; To Determine Whether He Was Hermaphroditic: With Lithographed Drawings, Made at Their Request. by James Akin* (Philadelphia, 1839)

A. James Carey; hunched figure on driver's seat of an omnibus
Medium: Lithograph
Dimensions: H. 7¹⁵⁄₁₆", W. 5⅜" (sheet)
Inscription: [Top center] JAMES CAREY. [bottom] Lithographed by James Akin / Philadelphia.
Collections: LCP

B-D. Post mortem examination of James Carey, three diagramed dissections of the post-mortem
Medium: Lithograph
Dimensions: (27B) H. 7½", W. 5⅜" (sheet)
(27C) H. 7¹⁵⁄₁₆", W. 5⅛" (sheet)
(27D) H. 7¹⁵⁄₁₆", W. 5⅛" (sheet)
Inscription: (27B) [Bottom of page] Lithograph by J. Akin from / James Carey. / post mortem examination.
(27C) [none]
(27D) [bottom of page] From the Preparation of the University / of Pennsylvania.
Collections: LCP

Bookplates and Trade Cards:

28. Leslie & Price Trade Card; Neptune conversing with Father Time, 1793–1798
Medium: Engraving and etching
Dimensions: Unknown
Inscription: [Below work bench] LESLIE & PRICE / [C]lock & Watch Makers / No. 79 / Market Street / PHILADELPHIA. [clock face at right] Leslie & Price / Philada. [illegible inscription on clock face at left] [on drawers of case at left] Pendons / Ballances / Verges / Wheels / Glasses / Springs / Pinions /

Chains / Hands / Dia[ls] / A General Assortm[ent] / of Tools & / Materials. [below frame] Grav'd by J. Akin from a sketch by J. Thruston.
Collections: HSP, Dreer Collection
References: Mary E. Means, "Early American Trade Cards" (M. A. Thesis, University of Delaware, 1958), p. 65

29. Joseph Barry Trade Card; illustrations of varied furniture types, ca. 1797–1798
Medium: Engraving
Dimensions: Unknown
Inscription: [Below tables] Pier-/Tables. [top center] A Lady's Dressing Commode. [center] Joseph B. Barry. / CABINET MAKER & UPHOLSTERER. / FROM LONDON / No. 148 South Third Street / PHILADELPHIA. [above sideboard] A Side Board with knife Cases. [above chairs] Drawing-/Room Chairs. [below] Orders for the West Indies, or elsewhere Executed in the neatest manner and Attended to with the Strictest punctuality &c / Drawn & 'Grav'd by J. Akin.
Collections: Unknown
References: William M. Hornor, Jr., *Blue Book of Philadelphia Furniture: William Penn to George Washington* (Philadelphia: by the author, 1935), pp. 234–35, pl. 432; Means, "Early American Trade Cards," pp. 63–64; Advertisement of the Old Print Shop, *Antiques* 34, no. 1 (July 1938): 36

30. John Baptiste Dumoutet Trade Card; allegorical figures framing a portrait of Washington, ca. 1800
Medium: Engraving (on silk)
Dimensions: H. 5½″, W. 4¾″
Inscription: [Above oval portrait] George Washington [on monument] J. B. Dumoutet, jun. / Goldsmith, Jeweller, Hair Worker &c. / Corner of Chestnut & Second Street Philadelphia / Devices, Enamelling, / and all branches connected with the above / Departments, done on the lowest terms / and sold either Wholesale or Retail. [lower right] Drawn & Engraved by James Akin.
Collections: NYHS, Bella C. Landauer Collection
References: Means, "Early American Trade Cards," p. 67; *Early American Trade*

Cards from the Collection of Bella C. Landauer, with Critical Notes by Adele Jenny (New York: William Edwin Rutledge, 1927), pl. 10; Ruth S. Granniss, "Mrs. Landauer's Early American Trade Cards," *New York Herald Tribune*, Jan. 10, 1928

31A. Bookplate of Hector Coffin; variant of the Coffin arms, ca. 1805
Medium: Engraving
Dimensions: Unknown
Inscription: [Below chevron] J. Akin del. / F. Kearny Sc. [banner below chevron] EXSTANT / RECTE FACTIS / PROEMIA [below banner] Hector Coffin.
Collections: UD, Brewer Collection, no. 2623
References: Charles D. Allen, *American Book-Plates* (New York: The Macmillan Co., 1894), no. 174

31B. Bookplate of Hector Coffin; variant of the Coffin arms, date unknown
Medium: Engraving
Dimensions: H. 3⅞″, W. 3⁵⁄₁₆″ (sheet)
Inscription: [Banner below shield] POST TENEBRIS / SPERAMUS LUMEN / DE LUMINE [below banner] J. Akin Sculp. / Hector Coffin
Collections: UD, Brewer Collection, nos. 2621, 2623; AAS; Metropolitan Museum of Art, New York, New York
References: Allen, *American Book-Plates*, nos. 173, 174

32. Angier March Trade Card; shop interior with wares displayed, ca. 1805
Medium: Engraving
Dimensions: H. 4″, W. 5⅞″ (sheet)
Inscription: [Above central arch] LAW / DIVINITY / PHYSIC [central arch] BOOKS STATIONARY CHARTS &c. [below central arch] Angier March / Market 13 Square / NEWBURYPORT. / keeps constantly for sale / on the lowest terms, a / large & general assortment / of the above articles. / Wholesale or Retail. / Orders faithfully executed. [on left arch] Account & Record Books of all descriptions [on arcade below arch] Miscellanies / School Books / Classics / Novels. [jug on floor at left] Ink [on right arch] Patent Medicines, Fancy Articles, &c. [on

arcade below right arch] Travels / Voyages / Biography / Mathematics. [previously published attribution to Akin]
Collections: AAS
References: Stauffer, *American Engravers upon Copper and Steel,* no. 29; Means, "Early American Trade Cards," p. 66; Rubenstein, "James Akin in Newburyport," p. 292

33. J. Baldwin Trade Card; Neptune conversing with Father Time, second state of checklist No. 28, 1804–1807
Medium: Engraving and etching
Dimensions: H. 4″, W. 5″
Inscription: [Above frame] Willards Patent Clocks: an elegant assortment of Looking Glasses &c. &c. &c. [below work bench] J. BALDWIN Silver Plate & Jewelry: / Sign of the Watch / SALEM / Hair-work neatly executed [to right of scythe] rs [clock face at right] Leslie & Price / Philada. [illegible inscription on clock face at left] [on drawers of case at left] Pendons / Ballances / Verges / Wheels / Glasses / Springs / Pinions / Chains / Hands / Dia[ls] / A General Assortm[ent] / of Tools & Materials. [below frame] Grav'd by J. Akin from a sketch by J. Thruston
Collections: AAS
References: Means, "Early American Trade Cards," p. 66; Fielding, *American Engravers upon Copper and Steel,* no. 17; Rubenstein, "James Akin in Newburyport," p. 292

34. Bookplate of Ichabod Tucker; Tucker crest, 1807
Medium: Engraving
Dimensions: H. 4⅛″, W. 2¹³⁄₁₆″ (plate)
Inscription: [Below chevron] Ichabod Tucker [attributed to Akin on the basis of Akin's own description of the bookplate]
Collections: EI
References: Rubenstein, "James Akin in Newburyport," pp. 294–95; James Akin to Ichabod Tucker, Jan. 17, 1807, EI

35. Benjamin Ferris Trade Card; Neptune conversing with Father Time, third state of checklist No. 28, 1807–1813

Medium: Engraving and etching (watercolored)
Dimensions: H. 3¹³⁄₁₆″, W. 5″ (border); H. 4⁷⁄₁₆″, W. 5⁹⁄₁₆″ (sheet)
Inscription: [Below work bench] BENJN. FERRIS / Clock & Watch Maker / No. [17] / [North 2nd] Street / PHILADELPHIA [clock face at left] Ferris / Patent [clock face at right] Benj. Ferris / Philada. [on drawers of case at left] Pendons / Ballances / Verges / Wheels / Glasses / Springs / Pinions / Chains / Hands / Dia[ls] / A General Assortm[ent] of Tools & / Materials. [below frame] Grav'd by J. Akin from a sketch by J. Thruston.
Collections: Friends Historical Library, Swarthmore College, Swarthmore, Pennsylvania

36. William Camp Trade Card; illustrations of varieties of furniture, 1802–1810
Medium: Engraving
Dimensions: Unknown
Inscription: [Across top at left] A Pier Table. [center] A Lady's Cabinet & Dressing Commode. [right] A Lady's Work Table. [center] William Camp. / Cabinet-Maker and Upholsterer. / No. 25, / Water Street / Baltimore. / Orders / for the West Indies, or / any part of / the Continent. / neatly executed & / attented to with Punctuality. / James Akin / del & sculp. [above chair at left] Drawing. / Room Chair. [above chair at right] Drawing / Room Chair. [below sideboard] A Side Board with Vase Knife Cases.
Collections: Baltimore Museum of Art, Baltimore, Maryland
References: Baltimore Museum of Art, *Baltimore Furniture: The Work of Baltimore and Annapolis Cabinetmakers from 1760 to 1810* (Baltimore: Baltimore Museum of Art, 1953), p. 193

37. Jacob Coburn Trade Card; depiction of hotel buildings, ca. 1807
Medium: Engraving
Dimensions: H. 8¾″, W. 7½″ (size of plate)
Inscription: [Across top of frame] NEWBURYPORT / SUN HOTEL. [below frame] Taken

on the Spot & Engraved by James Akin / Jacob Coburn, / with deference informs his friends and the Public that / he has opened a Spacious Hotel in State Street / NEWBURY-PORT, / the former mansion of the late Honble. Nathl. Tracy Esqr. / and where Mr. James Prince last resided. / Having at considerable pains and expense put the above in a / situation suited to accommodate Gentlemen, he assures them / with confidence that they will find every convenience, / and an unremitting attention to ensure the favours of the / TRAVELLER. / Good Horses and carriages to be had at all hours.
Collections: Historical Society of Old Newburyport, Newburyport, Massachusetts
References: Rubenstein, "James Akin in Newburyport," fig. 2

38. Charles Canby Watch Paper; female figure with flower garland, ca. 1810
Medium: Engraving
Dimensions: Unknown
Inscription: [Within circular frame at top] Chains. Seals. [within circular frame at bottom] Keys. Glasses &c. [within cartouche at right of winged figure] Chas. Canby / Clock & Watch maker / 4 Doors below Post Office / 77 Market Street / Wilmington, DELa. / J. Akin sc.
Collections: Harrold Gillingham
References: Harrold E. Gillingham, "Watch Papers," *Antiques* 28, no. 2 (Aug. 1935): 66–67

39. Bookplate of Peter A. Browne; books, laurel wreath, and all seeing eye, ca. 1820
Medium: Engraving and etching
Dimensions: H. 3¾₁₆″, W. 4⅞″ (sheet)
Inscription: [On book standing on edge of table] Peter A. Browne [on table] FIAT JUSTITIA [below picture frame] Engraved by James Akin
Collections: UD, Brewer Collection; AAS; BMFA; WAM; Metropolitan Museum of Art, New York, New York (2 states)
References: Allen, *American Book-Plates*, no. 113; Boston Museum of Fine Arts, *Catalogue of an Exhibition of Early Engraving*, no. 8

40. Bookplate of Joseph Lewis; books, inkstand, and quills, ca. 1820
Medium: Engraving
Dimensions: Unknown
Inscription: Joseph S. Lewis / 'Graved by J. Akin
Collections: BMFA
References: Inscription from Boston Museum of Fine Arts, *Catalogue of an Exhibition of Early Engraving*, no. 10; American Art Association, *Illustrated Catalogue of the Remarkable Collection of American and Foreign Book Plates Formed by the Late Dr. Henry C. Eno* (New York: American Art Association, 1916), no. N-168

Caricatures and Cartoons:

41. *The Prairie Dog Sickened at the Sting of the Hornet;* an emaciated dog with the head of Thomas Jefferson, stung by a hornet with the head of Napoleon, coughs up gold coins, 1803–1804
Medium: Etching (watercolored)
Dimensions: H. 11¹⁵⁄₁₆″, W. 15¹⁵⁄₁₆″ (sheet)
Inscription: [Above pile of coins at center] Two Millions! [below feet of dog with human head] J. Akin fect. [petition in left hand of man at right] West Florida [petition in right hand] East Florida [balloon speech of gentleman] A gull for the / People [document in his pocket] Instructions / CH: Mau: Talleygrand [across bottom] The PRAIRIE DOG Sickened at the sting of the HORNET— / of a Diplomatic Puppet exhibiting his Deceptions!
Collections: LC

42. *Bug a boo;* ca. 1805
Medium: Unknown
Dimensions: Unknown
Inscription: [Unknown; attributed to Akin on the basis of his published advertisement]
Collections: Unknown
References: In an advertisement for a forthcoming collection of illustrations, Akin signed himself, "JAMES AKIN / Author of the 'Prairie Dog,' / 'Infuriated Despondency,' / 'Bug a boo,' &c. &c," *Newburyport Herald,* Nov. 14, 1806

43. *The Mandate;* a Spanish subject bows to a skelton Napoleon, ca. 1804
    Medium: Etching
    Dimensions: H. 8¾″, W. 7½″ (plate)
    Inscription: [Lower left] [Le?] Grande Armie [de la] Skillet-ton [Napoleon speaking—figure at left] Hah! rais you voice Whiskerrandos / tell dem Jean Americain / for giv you MOR MILLION / tell dem I viel have eit [between two men] Confield Defence! [Spanish agent—figure at right speaking] Imperiale Mastaire / eit shall bee donne. [upper right] the MANDATE [lower right] Grave par un bon Loyal / sujet de su Majesta [attributed to Akin because the reverse of the etched plate bears Akin's signed design for Jacob Coburn's trade card]
    Collections: Historical Society of Old Newburyport, Newburyport, Massachusetts (the engraved plate)
    References: Rubenstein, "James Akin in Newburyport," p. 291

44A. *Infuriated Despondency;* caricature of Edmund M. Blunt wielding a skillet, 1805
    Medium: Engraving
    Dimensions: H. 7⅜″, W. 5¹³⁄₁₆″ (plate)
    Inscription: [Upper left] PLATE 1 [centered below] INFURIATED DESPONDENCY: / DESIGNED, ENGRAVED & PUBLISHED BY JAMES AKIN, NEWBURYPORT; WHERE WRITING-BOOK COVERS MAY BE HAD. / ENTERED ACCORDING TO LAW, JUNE 1ST. 1805.
    Collections: AAS; EI (Crowinshield-Bentley House) ; WAM
    References: John J. Currier, *History of Newburyport, Massachusetts,* 2 vols. (Newburyport: John J. Currier, 1906–1909), 2:372–74; William Murrell, *A History of American Graphic Humor: 1747–1865* (New York: Whitney Museum of Art, 1933), p. 52; Rubenstein, "James Akin in Newburyport," pp. 290–91; F. B. Sanborn, "Thomas Leavitt and his Artist Friend, James Akin," *Granite Monthly* 25, no. 10 (Oct. 1898): 226–27

44B. *Infuriated Despondency;* design identical to engraving of *Infuriated Despondency,* checklist No. 44A, but executed on earthenware pitcher, ca. 1805.
    Medium: Transfer-printed earthenware

Dimensions: Unknown
Inscription: [Above Blunt's head] A DROLL SCENE IN / NEWBURYPORT
Collections: Anna Knapp of Newburyport (1898) ; Society for the Preservation of New England Antiquities, Boston, Massachusetts
References: Currier, *History of Newburyport,* 2:372–74; Nina F. Little, "The Cartoons of James Akin upon Liverpool Ware," *Old-Time New England* 28, no. 3 (Jan. 1938): 103–106; Murrell, *A History of American Graphic Humor,* p. 52; Rubenstein, "James Akin in Newburyport," pp. 290–91; Sanborn, "Thomas Leavitt and his Artist Friend, James Akin," pp. 226–27

45. *Lord Timothy Dexter;* caricature of a Newburyport eccentric walking with his dog, 1805
    Medium: Engraving and etching
    Dimensions: H. 4¹³⁄₁₆″, W. 4″
    Inscription: [Upper left] "I am the first in the East, / the first in the West / and the greatest Philosopher, / in the Western World! /. Affirmed by me, / Timothy Dexter," [lower left] Engraved from the Life [lower right] by James Akin Newburyport. [center] The most Noble / Lord Timothy Dexter. / What a piece of work is Man! / how noble in reason! how infinite in faculties! in form & moving, how express & admirable! / Entered according to act of Congress June 1st. 1805 by James Akin Newbury / AND SOLD BY THOMAS & WHIPPLE.
    Collections: AAS; John J. Evans, Jr.; HSP (Photographic reproduction that does not include the dog) ; WAM
    References: Currier, *History of Newburyport,* 2:423; Murrell, *A History of American Graphic Humor,* no. 46; *Newburyport Herald,* Jan. 31, 1806; Rubenstein, "James Akin in Newburyport," p. 291; Stauffer, *American Engravers upon Copper and Steel,* no. 13

46. *Timothy Dexter's Dog;* short-legged dog, 1806
    Medium: Relief block (woodcut or type metal)
    Dimensions: Unknown
    Inscription: [Text of page set in type] Strange, Wonderful and Philosophic. / THE MOST NOBLE Lord TIMOTHY DEXTER, / *First in the East!* / This day / published, / and

FIG. 24. James Akin, *Dress, the Most Distinguishing Mark of a Military Genius.* From *Advice to the Officers of the Army, To the Officers of Ordinance, and to the Secretary at War* (1st Am. ed.; Philadelphia: Matthew McConnel, 1813). Etching; H. 5⁷⁄₁₆″, W. 3½″ (sheet). (Courtesy of the American Antiquarian Society: Photo, Wilford P. Cole.)

for sale at the / Bookstore of / THOMAS AND / WHIPPLE, Sign / Johnson's Head, / Market Square, / A full length Portrait of this Ec-/centric Character, with his *Dog,* engraver from / Life, by *James Akin.* / Jan. 31.
Collections: Unknown
References: *Newburyport Herald,* Jan. 31, 1806

47. *Dickey Folwell;* caricature of Richard Folwell, a Philadelphia journalist, ca. 1808
    Medium: Etching (watercolored)
    Dimensions: H. 8″, W. 6⅛″
    Inscription: [Upper left] THE / "SPIRIT of the PRESS." / "Nothing Extenuate nor set down / aught in Malice" / Sic Sum ut Vides. [lower left] J. Akin sc. [centered] "Dicky Folwell"
    Collections: HSP
    References: Murrell, *A History of American Graphic Humor,* p. 54, no. 47; Stauffer, *American Engravers upon Copper and Steel,* no. 14

48. *Dress, the Most Distinguishing Mark of a Military Genius;* frontispiece, *Advice to the Officers of the Army, to the Officers of Ordinance, and to the Secretary at War: With the Addition of Some Hints to the Drummer and Private Soldier . . .* (1st Am. ed.; Philadelphia: Matthew McConnel, 1813); caricature of a military dandy (Fig. 24)
    Medium: Etching
    Dimensions: H. 5⁷⁄₁₆″, W. 3½″ (sheet)
    Inscription: [Below officer] Designed & Engraved by James Akin Philada. / DRESS, / the most distinguishing mark of a military Genius.
    Collections: AAS
    References: Stauffer, *American Engravers upon Copper and Steel,* no. 25; Murrell, *A History of American Graphic Humor,* p. 52

49. *An Unexpected Meeting of Old Friends;* half-horse, half-alligator figure confronting local politician, ca. 1824
    Medium: Aquatint and etching
    Dimensions: H. 9⁵⁄₁₆″, W. 12¹³⁄₁₆″
    Inscription: [Upper left] Avaunt! / and quit my Sight [below Kanetuck—lower right] Old Kanetuck, / Half Horse-Half Alligator [Kanetuck's petition] Kentucky / Returns / Philada / Ward / Mee/tings [papers falling to ground between Kanetuck and politician] Custom / House Blanks / Wrested / from / the / Widow / and / Helpless / Orphan / Government / Favours / [?] [illegible inscription on tombstone lower right] [lower right] J. Akin [center below] AN UNEXPECTED MEETING OF OLD FRIENDS

Collections: AAS; Harvard University, Cambridge, Massachusetts
References: Fielding, *American Engravers upon Copper and Steel*, no. 12; Murrell, *A History of American Graphic Humor*, p. 141; Weitenkampf, *Political Caricature in the United States in Separately Published Cartoons: An Annotated List* (New York: New York Public Library, 1953), p. 23

50. *Caucus Curs in Full Yell, or a War-Whoop to Saddle on the People, a Pappoose President;* dogs representing newspapers snap at Andrew Jackson, 1824
Medium: Aquatint and etching
Dimensions: H. 17¾″, W. 20″ (outer border)
Inscription: [Title on frame] CAUCUS CURS in full YELL, or a WAR-WHOOP to saddle on the PEOPLE, a PAPPOOSE PRESIDENT. [below frame] What would you have, you Curs that like not peace, nor war? / Who deserves Greatness, deserves your hate: and your affections are a sick man's appetite. / With every minuet you do change a mind; and call him noble, that was now your hate, / Him vile, that was your Garland! Shakespeare's Coriolanus.

[Inscriptions within frame are recorded in a counterclockwise direction starting in upper left] [building at left] UNCLE SAM'S TREASURY PAP HOUSE / ALMAGAMATION-TOOL / Pappoose / meat by / W. H. C. / DEPARTMENT [Indian speaking] Rum for de baby [woman holding baby] Oh! Stuff your mouth / you brat! Treasury pap is better than rum. [man holding bowl bearing inscription] Dollars / Here's a Bowl full of solid pappoose meat / that's a good Girl better marry our wild Indians than Foreigners good or bad / Report to Congress
[inscriptions on collars and dogs in the pack at left] Salem Gazette / National Gazette / British Influence / Pittsburgh Statesmen / Let the purloining of Letters / be sounded through the Clarion of ill fame & be blown by Walter Lowrie / Philadelphia Gazette / Boston Gazette / Cape Cod / Washington / City / Gazette / National Advocate / Tunis / Richmond Whig / In Adam's fall / We'll surely bawl!

[riding on the Richmond Whig is an Indian] mas Andra I carry dis eah jew dog blongst to Tunis, / barkloud, someboday tief way ee Paper & show um / one ghose, wite like CLAY, dat mak um feard. Name o' God! no body gwine feard now for Crawfud ghose! / Look pon dat sleepy dog; jumbea [?] da ride um, can't / bark no mo for Crawfud [between two groups of dogs at left] Blue lights [torch in woman's hand] old [Fienney] [dog's collar—lower left] Democratic Press [skeleton astride Democratic Press] Immortal memory / Revd James Quigley / basely sacrificed / conscience Avaunt' [in skeleton's coat pocket] letter [hind quarter of skeleton's dog] SHAMOKIN [on dog's tail] Pike berry brig [forequarters] Good sprite, / In Mercy / lash me / with a / dry corn / STALK; / I'm so jaded by / stable swooning / smoke house steams / & Hog Cellar Sweats! !

[five headed dog] Hartford Convention / Cabot / Lyman / Otis / Griswald / Waldo [tail of five headed dog] Port of Attraction [dog in center ridden by demon figure] Still / it cried / *sleep, sleep* on / Sentinel [dog pack at right] Butler Sentinel / National Intelligencer / Amalgamation Implements W. H. C. / scalp / scalp / scalp / Trenton True American / Nashville Whig / Raleigh Register / Traiterous / Statesman / thee knows [on General's sword] Veni, Vidi, Vici
Collections: LC
References: Murrell, *A History of American Graphic Humor*, p. 135; Stauffer, *American Engravers upon Copper and Steel*, no. 16

51. *A Downright Gabbler;* caricature of Fanny Wright in the guise of a goose, ca. 1829
Medium: Lithograph
Dimensions: H. 7¹³⁄₁₆″, W. 7″ (sheet)
Inscription: [Lower right] Published by J. Akin Philada. [centered] A DOWNRIGHT GABBLER, / or a goose that deserves to be hissed.
Collections: WAM

52. *Philadelphia Taste Displayed, or, Bon-Ton Below Stairs;* scene in an oyster house, 1829–1830

    Medium: Lithograph (watercolored)
    Dimensions: H. 21½″, W. 34″ (sheet)
    Inscription: [Cross top of clock] Music has charms [scroll hanging from bar] City / Privilege / sell / without / License   [below border within frame] PHILADELPHIA TASTE DISPLAYED, OR, BON-TON BELOW STAIRS.— [lower left] Drawn on Stone by James Akin [lower right] Kennedy & Lucas, Lithographic Printers
    Collections: HSP
    References: Joseph Jackson, *Encyclopedia of Philadelphia*, 4 vols. (Harrisburg: The National Historical Association, 1931), 2:386–87; T. Harry Peters, *America on Stone* (New York: Doubleday, Doran and Co., 1931), p. 74; Nicholas B. Wainwright, *Philadelphia in the Romantic Age of Lithography* (Philadelphia: Historical Society of Pennsylvania, 1958), no. 290; George C. Groce and David H. Wallace, *The New York Historical Society's Dictionary of Artists in America, 1564–1860* (New Haven: Yale University Press, 1957), p. 365

53. *The Holy Alliance;* a United States mail coach halted by groups who oppose Sunday mail delivery, May 5, 1830

    Medium: Aquatint
    Dimensions: H. 13¾″, W. 21¹³⁄₁₆″
    Inscription: [Below frame—lower left] Entered according to Act of Congress, the 5th day of May 1830, by James Akin of the State of Pennsylvania [lower right] Engrav'd & Published by James Akin Designer and Caricaturist Philadelphia / No 63 Dock St.

    [centered below frame] The "HOLY ALLI-ANCE" / or SATAN'S LEGION at SABBATH PRANKS. / symbolical of a venal hypocrisy, whose head is muffled and cowled in the Mantle of pretended Pietism dripping with the unholy oil of burning denunciations against all men who contend / for privilege, *Transporting the Mail of the United States* on each and every day of the year; Strongly and earnestly recommended / to the serious consideration of every free minded, honest, open hearted Lover of AMERICAN BIRTH-

RIGHTS, who despises *Sectarian Proscription, Chains, Dungeons, Scaffolds, Axes, Faggots, and Bloody Banners,* which a demoniac zeal prompts the bold front of insolence to array before that EXCELLENT LIBERTY in whose sacred Temple "WE THE / PEOPLE," / now safely repose, threatening US. with ecclesiastical Domination and grasping at power for trampling down the Independent enjoyment of the RIGHTS of CONSCIENCE! / Divines, who [rule] in Church affairs. / And Gull the People with long prayers, / About their souls salvations! / Being Determin'd one and all / To wrest the Great GOD of Hosts! nor let thy PEOPLE Fall. Unpitied victims at Ambition's Shrine! / Dedicated with due respect, to every Patriot bosom friendly to the support of that CIVIL and RELIGIOUS LIBERTY [?] Purchased by the BLOOD and TREASURE of FATHERS, / for the HAPPINESS of their POSTERITY and the general welfare of the Human race. by their Friend and Countryman / JAMES AKIN, Engraver.

[within frame—above pulpit] "A STRANGE DREAM!!! / Away with your philosophy and vain deceit! You who advo-/cate the rights of conscience and the transportation of the / MAIL on sunday, shall be delivered over to your father the Devil, / who will torment you with everlasting burnings in HELL'S hottest / furnace of FIRE & BRIMESTONE." [from scepter on pulpit] Orthodox [below pulpit] "An little pleasure it can git, e'en to a Deil; / To scaud poor bodies such as we, an hear us squeel / BURNS"

[verse] This / Is the system, whose Orthodox Law, / Is first to subdue, then keep all in awe, / Whose damnable tenets is "HOLY ALLIANCE," / To stop all the MAILS, and bid US. defiance, / This point once sanction'd by Congress decree, / Farewell Independence, The RIGHTS of the Free!!! [benches at left] SUNDAY SCHOOL / In Ten years the Power will be in the hands of Sunday Schools / [?] UNION [books and tracts held by congregation] Visits of / Mercy / Tract Depository, / Tracts / Tracts / Tracts / Tracts / Tracts / Who / putteth / forth / innocent / pam-/phlets / Ascendency in / Christian politics / or ye become / Infidels. [back of woman praying] I wonder after all this fuss / what

chance a body will stand / to get a hus-band. / Every Church / shall be a Disci-plined / Army! / PLAN for / establishing a / NATIONAL Religion. [woman on bench says] Look here! See! what a great step / towards Sunday schools!!!

[long petition] PETITION / against / the MAILS / Travelling / on SUNDAY / subscribed by 2500 / Children of the / Sunday / School / of N. York. / That a Law / be made to / Stop all prea-/chers of the / Gospel / and / the MAIL / from travell-/ing on SUN-DAY / and that both houses / of / CONGRESS / Pass a vote / that col. R. M. / Johnson is in-sane! [along side of petition] As regards the Children the memorial [t s] it has not been thought necessary to enquire see report of [Comm] of examination in N. York [in Bishop's hand] on either hand marched a multitudeness Army. / Crossier & mitre in grand array. / Here ye of Long ears! / Ex-clude all men / who are not orthodox / by Sunday school union systems!! [behind bishop] Their infidel friends will suspend you in their / parlours, taverns / and / fac-tories. [bishop's mitre] Canon Law. [demon figure] JOHN CALVIN / verses Servetus / who was burned / to the stake! / see his Letter / Life of Leo Xth / 3d. VOL. [log in hand of figure in front of church] I say Doctor how will this / Beech tree do to kindle Griffin / Blast of Brimstone / 10 times / hotter than / Hell / You'll all go to the Devil. [saddle on church] GREAT STATE SADDLE [figure in front of church] Stop I say "lest you enter / that path of Hell / paved with [infants] skulls not a span long!" [ray encircling eagle atop mail coach] ["In the] free Land the thoughts of the humblest citizen are not to be man-nacled and fettered nor punished whether orthodox or not" Col. Johnson / on [print-ing] the report. [names surrounding "Lib-erty"] Marion / Barry / Sherman / Adams / Washington / Hancock / P. Henry / St. Clair / Jefferson / Franklin / Morris / Laurens / Protection / Liberty / Independence [sides of stage] Tis Liberty alone that given the flower of fleeting life / its [?] and perfume and we are weeds without it. / US / We are exercising this right not in / virtue of Gov-ernmental indulgence but as RIGHTS of which

Government cannot deprive / any portion of citizens, however small, / see Colo. Johnson's report / Mail [?] [inscription within coach is illegible] [on wheel of coach] [?] by acts of Benevolence. / See Colo. Johnsons . . . Look after your Liberties my Boys! / that just the way, they wanted to shackle / us in Ireland!!! [domed building] US / CAPITOL / Congress shall make no Law respecting an establishment of Religion or Prohibiting the / Free exercise thereof or abridging the FREEDOM of SPEECH or the PRESS. *Constitu-tion* / UNITED STATES. / All be damn'd in everlasting HELL'S FLAMES Forever. / You'll all go to the Devil . . . , and that will be some Comfort! [lower right] "There are some souls that must be saved and some that must be [?] / Ere 50 years millenium will come / Then stage and steamboat ye shall cease / and that's one Great and Glorious consolation. [remaining inscription in lower right corner illegible]

Collections: AAS

References: Fielding, *American Engravers upon Copper and Steel,* no. 11

54. *The House That Jonathan Built or Political Primer for 1832* (Philadelphia: P. Banks, 1832)

A. *The Pen Outweighs Them All,* title page cut; Andrew Jackson and a scale with doc-uments and pen

    Medium: Woodcut

    Dimensions: H. 5", W. 7½"

    Inscription: [Rolled documents on right side of scale] ANTI TARIFF / NULLI-FICATION / BANK VETO [below scale] Akin [centered below] THE PEN OUTWEIGHS THEM ALL.

    Collections: PUL, Sinclair Hamilton Collection; EMHL

    References: Stephan Lorant, *The Pres-idency, a Pictorial History of Presiden-tial Elections from Washington to Tru-man* (New York: The Macmillan Co., 1954), pp. 124–26

B. *Advertisement,* frontispiece; two men, one with a broom

    Medium: Woodcut

    Dimensions: H. 1", W. ½"

Inscription: [Above cut] ADVERTISE-MENT [below cut] *Buy a broom!! buy a broom!! buy a broom!!* [attributed to Akin on the basis of stylistic similarity to signed illustrations in the book]

Collections: PUL, Sinclair Hamilton Collection; EMHL

References: Lorant, *The Presidency, a Pictorial History of Presidential Elections*, pp. 124–26

C. *The House That Jonathan Built;* temple supported by symbolic columns

Medium: Woodcut

Dimensions: H. 4¾″, W. 3¹³⁄₁₆″

Inscription: [Across entablature of temple] CONSTITUTION [three pillars, left to right] CONGRESSIONAL POWER / JUDI-CIARY / LIBERTY & INDEPENDENCE [lower right] Akin sc. [inscription below cut] "A distant age asks where the fabric stood."

Collections: PUL, Sinclair Hamilton Collection; EMHL

References: Lorant, *The Presidency, a Pictorial History of Presidential Elections*, pp. 124–26

D. *The Wealth;* American rights depicted as wealth

Medium: Woodcut

Dimensions: H. 3½″, W. 4″

Inscription: [Documents in chest] HA-BEAS CORPUS / DECLARATION OF / INDE-PENDENCE! / CONSTITUTION / OF THE / UNITED STATES [volume beside chest] LAWS / OF THE / UNITED STATES [inscription below chest]—"Not to understand a treasure's worth, / Till time has stolen away the slighted good, / Is cause of half the poverty we feel, / And makes the world the wilderness it is." [attributed to Akin on the basis of stylistic similarity to signed illustrations in the book]

Collections: PUL, Sinclair Hamilton Collection; EMHL

References: Lorant, *The Presidency, a Pictorial History of Presidential Elections*, pp. 124–26

E. *The Vermin;* caricature of Andrew Jackson as a horse wearing a crown

Medium: Woodcut

Dimensions: H. 3¼″, W. 4″

Inscription: [Center ground] Akin [inscription below cut] "—A race obscene. / Spawn'd in the muddy beds of Nile, came forth / Polluting Egypt; gardens, fields, and plains, / Were cover'd with the pest; / The Croaking nuisance lurk'd in every nook' / No places, nor even chambers, scap'd; / And the land stank— so numerous was the fry."

Collections: PUL, Sinclair Hamilton Collection; EMHL

References: Lorant, *The Presidency, a Pictorial History of Presidential Elections*, pp. 124–26

F. *The Thing;* a printing press

Medium: Woodcut

Dimensions: H. 3¼″, W. 4½″

Inscription: [On bed of press] KNOWL-EDGE / IS POWER [left of base of press] Akin [text below cut] "Once enslaved, farewell!" / Do I forbode impossible events, / And tremble at vain dreams? Heav'n grant I may!"

Collections: PUL, Sinclair Hamilton Collection; EMHL

References: Lorant, *The Presidency, a Pictorial History of Presidential Elections*, pp. 124–26

G. *The Traitor;* caricature of Martin Van Buren as a magician

Medium: Woodcut

Dimensions: H. 4⅛″, W. 2⅜″

Inscription: [Left hand] Magician [right pocket] Secret papers [lower right] Akin [sc] [text below cut] "The seals of office glitter in his eyes, / He climbs, he pants, he grasps them— / To be a pest where he was useful once."

Collections: PUL, Sinclair Hamilton Collection; EMHL

References: Lorant, *The Presidency, a Pictorial History of Presidential Elections*, pp. 124–26

H. *The Victims;* Andrew Jackson depicted as a king

Medium: Woodcut

Dimensions: H. 3″, W. 4⅛″

Inscription: [Below king Andrew's rifle] My Will [below king's feet] Akin [above man standing immediately right of king] Indian Embassy [below two men standing shackled at right] Missionary [inscription below] "Ruffians are abroad—

Collections: PUL, Sinclair Hamilton Collection; EMHL

References: Lorant, *The Presidency, a Pictorial History of Presidential Elections,* pp. 124–26

I. *The Tyrant;* Andrew Jackson depicted as a king

Medium: Woodcut

Dimensions: H. 5¼", W. 3½"

Inscription: [Bottom of left breeches leg] H O N [lower right] J. Akin [inscription below cut]——"Great officers will have / Great talents."

Collections: PUL, Sinclair Hamilton Collection; EMHL

References: Lorant, *The Presidency, a Pictorial History of Presidential Elections,* pp. 124–26

J. *The People;* group of ragged, suffering people

Medium: Woodcut

Dimensions: H. 2⅝", W. 3¾"

Inscription: [Below cut] "Portentous, unexplain'd! / ——What man seeing this, / And having human feelings does not blush, / And hang his head, to think himself a man? / ——I cannot rest, / A silent witness of the headlong rage, / Or heedless folly, by which thousands die— / Bleed gold for ministers to sport away." [attributed to Akin on the basis of stylistic similarity to signed illustrations in the book]

Collections: PUL, Sinclair Hamilton Collection; EMHL

References: Lorant, *The Presidency, a Pictorial History of Presidential Elections,* pp. 124–26

K. *The Trio;* Kendall, Lewis, and Blair conversing

Medium: Woodcut

Dimensions: H. 3¾", W. 3¾"

Inscription: [Below cut] THE GUILTY TRIO. / "Great skill have they in *Palmistry,* and more / To conjure clean away

the gold they touch, Conveying worthless dross into its place; / Loud when they beg, dumb only when they steal. / ——Dream after dream comes! / And still they dream, that they shall still succeed, / And still are disappointed." [between feet of man on right] A

Collections: EMHL

References: Lorant, *The Presidency, a Pictorial History of Presidential Elections,* pp. 124–26

L. *Reform;* banner and liberty cap

Medium: Woodcut

Dimensions: H. 5⅛", W. 2¾"

Inscription: [Banner reads] REFORM [on cap] LIBERTY [lower right of cut] Akin [below cut] "Burghers, men immaculate perhaps / In all their private functions, once combin'd, / Become a loathsome body, only fit / For dissolution. / ——Power usurp'd / Is weakness when oppos'd; conscious of wrong, / [Tis] pusillanimous and prone to light. / ——I could endure / Chains nowhere patiently; and chains at home, / Where I am free by birth-right, not at all."

Collections: EMHL

References: Lorant, *The Presidency, a Pictorial History of Presidential Elections,* pp. 124–26

55. *The Man;* Janus portrait of Andrew Jackson as a man or a mule, first state, 1831–1833.

Medium: Lithograph

Dimensions: H. 10¼", W. 4¾"

Inscription: [Below profile of man] THE MAN! / What have we here? A human head! / "The tree known by its fruit"! / A brainless, sappy, lump of lead; / The card turn'd —shows the Brute!!! / Sold by J. Akin Lithographer [177 South 11th] Street Phila. [below profile of ass] THE JACK ASS. / A stupid Jack he now appears! An awkward dolt—a Beast! / "By the Eternal," Uncle Sam fears, / On Liberty he'll feats!!! / Sold by J. Akin Lithographer [177 South 11th] Street.

Collections: AAS

56. *The Union Pie, No. 1;* large pie and eggs representing states with nullification monster and angel, 1832–1833

> Medium: Lithograph
> Dimensions: H. 9″, W. 11¼″ (frame); H. 10″, W. 11⅝″ (including text)
> Inscription: [Across top of frame] NULLIFICATION OF A PEEP AT SOUTH CAROLINA IN 1832–3 [title below frame] THE UNION PIE NoI / Being the first one, and Introduction to the Collection of *Ten Pictures* illustrating the rise, progress & [issue] of the whole Subject of Nullification by an Artist & Politician from South Carolina: price 25cents each— New York. [pie filled with eggs bearing initials of States—within frame at left] Flo. / Ga / N.C. / La / ARK. / K [?] TENN. / MISS. / Va / ALA. / M [?] / [?] / IND. / OHIO / Pa / Md / DEL. / N.J. / CON. / R.I. / MAINE / N.H. / VERMONT / N. York / MASS. [egg at top of pie cracking open] S. Carolina [tree growing out of egg] Fair Palmetto [man waving banner] NUL. [winged angel-like figure, "Gabriel," says] Out power here is Union of / Th ree! Seek shelter Nully / in thy Palmetto tree!!! [winged monster, "Nully," asks] Gabriel! What / are you about? With Proclamations from Heaven to kick a gen-/ tleman out!! I saluted you friendly, but / you bad me begone!! But mark me you'll / have more of this business anon! / It encouraged I show in variety's dress. For mark me! There's more / of this matter in press. [two speeches below Nully's speech are illegible] [on sail of boat abreast of Union Pie] Bunker Hill / [of] / Cape Cod [John Bull stands on a rock labelled] England [John Bull says] The Belgian pie / Greek pie I've devoured And now / for the *American*. my stomach's em-/powered! In '76 & '13 tho' thwarted in my pride. If I cannot eat all now. I'll see it divide!! / ha! ha!! [previously published attribution to Akin, although the New York address on the inscription raises doubts about the attribution]
> Collections: NYHS; AAS
> References: Murrell, *A History of American Graphic Humor*, p. 136; Weitenkampf, *Political Caricature in the United States*, p. 32

57. *A Frontispiece For A Journal;* caricature of Fanny Kemble as both a begger and a lady, 1835

> Medium: Lithograph
> Dimensions: H. 10¾″, W. 6″ (sheet)
> Inscription: [Across top] A FRONTISPIECE FOR A JOURNAL [petition in beggar's right hand] Pity kind / YANKEES. / friends to Humanity, / Give me a / rich husband / and I will / be gone. [play-bill for the Beggars Petition in beggar's left hand] Beggars / Petition / Pity the longings of / a poor young maid / hem! [play-bill in Lady Fanny's left hand] Beggars Opera / A Bold stroke / for a husband. [Lady Fanny speaks] "Mercy God! What's here? / A poor bread-hunter!!!" / Journal Vol. II, p. 16. [below figures of Beggar Kemble and Lady Fanny Butler] James Akin Draughtsman & Lithographer No. 18 Prune Street Philadelphia [text of broadside—below] "Born to good luck" by "Scene-shiftin" in "Fortune's Frolicks," / or the English beggar Girl's elevation to a Butler's lady!!! [Verse]

> Fan Pulldedock, a Beggar low!
> From England came to join the show
> She long secur'd in British "Fa-me." ∅
> A brag about her Family "Na-me," ∅
> Which "Jon'than" heard shell'd out his mite
> To give poor "Puddledock" a bite,
> But she preferr'd to Pit or boxes
> A "Call-boy's" Butler—Orthodoxies
> And now a wife she damns all stages,
> Returning Jonathan "Pain and A-ches," ∅
> By publishing loose tittle tattle,
> Of stage flirts vulgar coars lewd prattle;
> All what she saw, heard, lov'd or hated,
> Two Volumes filld of gossip prated;
> Hence the Proverb trite and known well
> A Beggar hors'd soon rides to _____.

*Family Appelation Journal Vol. I., p. 16. ∅ Vide John P. Kemble's vile pedantic pronunciation / for which he was very properly hissed!!! [below verse] Entered according to act of Congress in the year 1835, by James Akin, in the Clerk's Office of the District Court / of the Eastern District of Pennsylvania.—
> Collections: NYPL
> References: Stauffer, *American Engravers upon Copper and Steel*, no. 29; Murrell, *A History of American Graphic Humor*, pp. 138–39

58. *Crib of Wolf Meat;* caricature of patronage
politicians, 1834–1835
Medium: Lithograph
Dimensions: H. 11⅛″, W. 14⅞″
Inscription: [Men left to right] Hurrah for
a Son of Erin, / Pull all together! / rattle
the Shuttle my Boys! / That's your sort—
This Gown pattern, Joel my honey! /
Warped around you will save the Treasury /
filling-Whig con-cords too strong for Joel's
Meshes of low Intrigue. / Pull away Jemmy-
Give a long pull, / and leave the Corrup-
tionists nothing but what Paddy shot at;
then send the / Doctor home to take his own
Physick [man at right] Silence ye greedy
Cormorants!!! / Cease all this Turbulence,
or We shall lose the whole CRIB, & all the
Fat. You then becom paupers or starve. [roof
of crib] PUBLIC CRIB [on pediment of Public
Crib] [Ica]Dien [Kerge] / Before we proceed
as regards these Licences, / I hold it fit that
we know how the applicants Vote. / aye /
courteous Brothers of King's Bench!

   [contents of Public Crib] drops / For dizzy
heads / wolf belly Guts / Strengtheners of
Weak Stomach / Public Work / Bravers for /
Quulmish Folk / County Bridges / APS /
Candy / Waffle bread / Plumbs / Auditor-
ships / King fritters Protho notoryships /
Muffins / Joels / Joels Court Compouns /
Office / Ginger Bread / Hot from Court /
The kings sugar plmubs / Joels composing
powders &c / Infatution Drops / for Gripy
Folks / Jumbles / Nervous Cordial / Court-
belly Guts / AP's / Lozenges for Weak / Con-
sciences / Court Cake / Comfits / Anodynes /
Judgeships / Wolfe Meat / n dollar Wine /
Shares of Rail Road Stock / licences / Stock /
Southward Rail Road / Wolf Meat / tit
bits / office [papers in hand of man at right]

   [papers in Joel's (?) hand] Joels Jumbles /
Gull cake / Joels jumbles / Licences / fa-
our'd Tavern Licences / Licence / AP for
King fat office / clerkships. [animal figures
from left to right] I'll secure you votes Dr. /
bubbling from the mud of Society!!! / Dont
forget the Tipstaves Dr. / Oh Dr. Dr. / Dont
forget poor old / Moll Foster / I bully the
Wh__s / mace / I smell as a faetidu teufel's
[?] Let me get in / Ill gull em! / oak crutches
aid Informers to / ford over dirty Puddles /

Whole hog / curried or not curried / A gut-
ter commissioner! / why he's fitter for scav-
enger / a mere reptile in office / give it to me
Dr. / I've the Stomach / Commissioner
Southwark [lower right] Lithographed. 18
Prune St. JAkin.
Collections: NYHS

59. *A Hickory Apology;* confrontation between
Andrew Jackson and French king, 1834–1836
Medium: Lithograph
Dimensions: H. 9⅞″, W. 14¾″
Inscription: [Title line below frame] Set-
tling the French question on our responsi-
bility or / a Hickory apology, to assure
Monsier Bag and Tail. / that *'Uncle Sam,*
isn't quite sich a tarnal mean crittur as to
give up 25,000.000 of Francs; for fear of a
French dab in the Chops *!!! Ah ha / ! ! !*
[within frame—lower left] Designed,
Drawn and Lithographed by James Akin, /
No. 18 Prune Street. [below frogs at left]
Les corps de Legisla[i]eurs [dialogue of frogs
—ballons numbered left to right] [1] Vive
le Roi! / Vive la bagatelle! / Bourgre l'Amer-
icaine Generale! c'est unebete! [2] Vive le
Valaze! General / Zhackson. God damne. [3]
Largent, l'argent, gardons / l'argent. [4] Ar-
retex l'argent. [5] Une pologie se demand' /
raisonabla, si cele Generale / is now make
one growl / avec ses ames— [6] une explica-
tion est indespensable / il est un Homme a
cariatre. [frog between king's legs] "Blood
on [own] / now he sou [?]

   [French king's dialogue] Eh bien slit mon
sher ami, / Je m'etatis bien doute, que vou
etes / au fait make on 'pologie wis de wif
Hickorie vil make / satisfy tout les Nations
so well / le dam Fean Bool! [Jackson's dia-
logue] Genl. Valaze wants an apology does
he? / By the eternal, he shall have a taste /
of old Virginia Rep—Raps, in shape of a /
tough hickory whip; to make you belch
compliance as / our old Bainbridge, Hull &
Decatur, made your crusty neighbor Johnny
Bull.' [Neptune's dialogue] Fowl him Andy!
Give him a belly-/breaker my boy! Old Iron-
sides and a / Hull—even the Pennsylvania
will do, to make / Johnny Crapauds squeam-
ish stomach, / belch up 25,000,000 of Francs!
His next / door neighbour knows d__d
well, / what a punch in the Guts means!!!

64. *United States and England;* two dogs quarreling over a bone labeled Oregon, ca. 1846
   Medium: Unknown
   Dimensions: Unknown
   Inscription: [Unknown; previously published attribution to Akin]
   Collections: Unknown
   References: Sanborn, "Thomas Leavitt and His Artist Friend, James Akin," p. 226; Stauffer, *American Engravers upon Copper and Steel,* no. 28

Portraits:

65. *General Pinckney;* half-length portrait of Charles Cotesworth Pinckney, 1799
   Medium: Stipple engraving
   Dimensions: H. 8%₁₆″, W. 7¼″ (frame)
   Inscription: [Below oval frame] From an Original Picture by James Earle in the Possession of Major Thos. Pinckney / General Pinckney / late Envoy Extraordinary to the French Republic. [print trimmed at this point; imprint data missing; previously published attribution to Akin]
   Collections: NYPL
   References: Stauffer, *American Engravers upon Copper and Steel,* 2:6, no. 20; Childs Gallery, *An Exhibition and Sale of American Historical Prints* (Boston: 1971), no. 10

66. *Thomas Jefferson;* three-quarter length portrait, Jan. 10, 1800
   Medium: Stipple engraving
   Dimensions: H. 5⅜″, W. 4¼″
   Inscription: [Left of oval frame] Painted by C. W. Peale 1791 [right of oval frame] Engraved by Akin & Harrison Junr. [below frame] Thomas Jefferson Esqr. / Vice President of the United States & President of the American Philosophical Society. / Philada. Pub. by A. & H. Junr. Jany. 10, 1800.
   Collections: Atwater Kent Museum, Philadelphia, Pennsylvania
   References: Stauffer, *American Engravers upon Copper and Steel,* no. 17; Alfred L. Bush, *The Life Portraits of Thomas Jefferson* (Charlottesville: The Thomas Jefferson Memorial Foundation, 1962), p. 32; *Aurora* (Philadelphia), Jan. 11, 1800

67. *George Washington;* 1800
   Medium: Engraving
   Dimensions: Unknown
   Inscription: *G. Washington. / Born 11th Feby O.S. 1732 / Comr Contl Army 1755 / Prest Fed: Convention 1787. / Prest United States 1789. / Declined Election 1796. / Comr Fedl Army 1798. / America lamenting her Loss at the Tomb of* [General Washington] *Intended as a Tribute of respect paid to departed Merit & Vertue, in / the remembrance of the illustrious Hero & most Amiable man who Died Decr 14, 1799. / Design'd Engraved and Published by Akin & Harrison Junr Philada Jany 20th 1800. Hart, 147*
   Collections: Unknown
   References: Inscription quoted from Stauffer, *American Engravers upon Copper and Steel,* 2:7; Childs Gallery, *American Historical Prints,* no. 23

68. *Benjamin Rush;* 1800
   Medium: Engraving
   Dimensions: H. 7%₁₆″, W. 6%₁₆″
   Inscription: *Painted by J. Paul Junr—Engraved by J. Akin / Dr Benjamin Rush / To the Gentlemen of the Faculty & Medical Students throughout the / United States, this Plate Engraved with the Drs Permission & at the request / of his Pupils from the Original Picture in the Proprietor's Possession is / Inscribed by their Obedt Humble Servt / James Akin / Published March 20th 1800 & Sold by J. Akin, Engraver, Johnson's Court Nth 8th St Philadelphia.*
   Collections: Unknown
   References: Dimensions and inscription quoted from Stauffer, *American Engravers upon Copper and Steel,* 2:6

69. *Patrick Lyon;* portrait with background of prison walls, ca. 1800
   Medium: Engraving
   Dimensions: H. 5⅝″, W. 4½″ (cut and inscription block)
   Inscription: [Lower right] 'Grav'd by J. Akin [centered below cut] PATRICK LYON, / who suffered Three months severe imprisonment on merely a vague suspicion for the

internal Robbery of the Bank / of Pennsylvania.
Collections: NYPL
References: Stauffer, *American Engravers upon Copper and Steel*, no. 19

70. *Timothy Pickering;* Oct. 1805
Medium: Watercolor
Dimensions: Unknown
Inscription: [Unknown; attributed to Akin on the basis of his letter mentioning the finished portrait and his proposal to engrave a print from the portrait]
Collections: Unknown
References: James Akin to Timothy Pickering, Oct. 31, 1805, Massachusetts Historical Society, Boston; *Merrimack Magazine and Ladies Literary Cabinet* 1 (Nov. 2, 1805) : 47

71. *Thomas Leavitt;* profile bust, 1808
Medium: Watercolor
Dimensions: Unknown
Inscription: [Unknown; previously published attribution to Akin]
Collections: Unknown
References: Theodore Bolton, *Early American Portrait Painters in Miniature* (New York: Frederic Fairchild Sherman, 1921), no. 74; Rubenstein, "James Akin in Newburyport," p. 297; Sanborn, "Thomas Leavitt and His Artist Friend, James Akin," p. 225

72. *Hannah (Melcher) Leavitt;* 1808
Medium: Watercolor
Dimensions: Unknown
Inscription: [Unknown; previously published attribution to Akin]
Collections: Unknown
References: Bolton, *Early American Portrait Painters in Miniature*, no. 75; Rubenstein, "James Akin in Newburyport," p. 203; Sanborn, "Thomas Leavitt and His Artist Friend, James Akin," p. 225

Miscellaneous:

73. United States Naval Commission; commission of Isaac Hull as a captain, decorated with American eagle and Navy seal, ca. 1798
Medium: Engraving and etching
Dimensions: H. 17", W. 14¼" (sheet)
Inscription: [Text of commission omitted] [below emblem of arms] Written by S. Lewis Senr. / Designed & Engraved Akin & Harrison Junr.
Collections: WM; Atwater Kent Museum, Philadelphia, Pennsylvania
References: Stauffer, *American Engravers upon Copper and Steel*, no. 24

74. Merrimack Humane Society Medal; 1804
Medium: Engraving on silver
Dimensions: Unknown
Inscription: [Unknown; previously published attribution to Akin]
Collections: Unknown
References: Currier, *History of Newburyport*, 2:139; Rubenstein, "James Akin in Newburyport," p. 289

75. *A Perpetual Almanack;* ornately decorated calendar chart, Jan. 1, 1805
Medium: Engraving
Dimensions: H. 13¼", W. 18¾"
Inscription: [Within swirled banners left and right of title] U. States / America / Engraved by / J. Akin, NBuryport. [arched across top of chart] A PERPETUAL ALMANACK, / by which may be found in a few seconds of time, the DAY of the WEEK in any YEAR to come. [within columned arch to left] Explanation. / Look at the top for the CENTURY / then to the Right or the Left / for the Odd Year [&] in a line / with that odd year directly / under the CENTURY is the / Dominical Letter for the years. [within columned arch at right] Explanation. / Under the given Dominical Letter / find the DAY of the WEEK / and in a line with it / in the Calendar you have / the date of the / MONTH. [below chart] [Patented &] Published by Act of Congress by G. Goold January 1st 1805.
Collections: WAM; AAS; EI
References: *Newburyport Herald*, Dec. 11, 1804; Rubenstein, "James Akin in Newburyport," p. 292; Childs Gallery, *American Historical Prints*, no. 45

76. *Turkeys;* print intended for a copy-book cover depicting two turkeys and a peacock or peahen, June 1, 1805

Medium: Etching and engraving
Dimensions: H. 5⁵⁄₁₆″, W. 7⅜″ (plate)
Inscription: [Across top] TURKEYS. PUB-
LISHED ACCORDING TO LAW BY JAMES AKIN,
ENGRAVER. [across bottom] JUNE 1, 1805 AND
SOLD WHOLESALE OR RETAIL BY THOMAS AND
WHIPPLE, BOOKSELLERS & STATIONERS, NEW-
BURYPORT.
Collections: AAS
References: Rubenstein, "James Akin in
Newburyport," p. 290; *Newburyport Her-
ald,* June 25, 1805

77. *Sailors Glee;* print intended for a copy-book
cover depicting sailors drinking and dancing,
June 1, 1805
Medium: Engraving
Dimensions: H. 5⅜″, W. 4⅝″ (sheet)
Inscription: [Below frame] SAILORS GLEE. /
"Singing Laughing. / Dancing Quaffing, /
Both Cheerily, / And Merrily, / And all for
the Sake of his girl on Shore" / ENTERED AC-
CORDING TO LAW JUNE 1st 1805, & PUBLISHED
BY JAMES AKIN ENGRAVER, / SOLD BY HIM &
THOMAS & WHIPPLE, BOOKSELLERS & STATION-
ERS, NEWBURYPORT.
Collections: WM; AAS
References: Rubenstein, "James Akin in
Newburyport," p. 290; *Newburyport Her-
ald,* June 25, 1805

78. Profile Cut; three-quarter front silhouette
bust used as an advertisement for profile likenesses, 1805
Medium: Relief block (woodcut or type
metal)
Dimensions: Unknown
Inscription: [To right of cut] PROFILE
LIKENESSES. / THE Subscriber ex-/pects to
be ready on Thursday / next to *paint & cut*
profile Like-/nesses. He will attend from
2 / o'clock till 9 in the evening at his house
in Temple-Street, near Mr. / Mihon's Meet-
ing-house. Price / for Paint 2 to 4 dollars—
for / cutting 6 cents each. J. Akin. / An assortment of frames just received and for
sale at Thomas & Whipple's. [attributed
to Akin because the cut was used to illustrate his advertisement]
Collections: Unknown

References: *Newburyport Herald,* Feb.
19, 1805

79. Massachusetts Currency; printed by Jacob
Perkins's patented stereotype plate process for
discouraging counterfeiting, ca. 1805
Medium: Engraving (stereotype plate)
Dimensions: Unknown
Inscription: [Face of bill] COMMONWEALTH
OF MASACHUSETTS / V / V / 5 PATENT / K /
FIVE / V / V / FIVE / FIVE / FIVE / FIVE / FIVE
DOLLARS / [inscribed over innumerable Five
Dollars] The President, Directors, & Com-
pany of the [blank for name of bank to be
inserted] promise to pay [blank for name
to be inserted] or bearer on demand / FIVE
DOLLARS / [blank] 18 [blank] Cashr.—Presd.
/ Patent stereotype steel plate / FIVE / FIVE /
FIVE / FIVE / V / V / 5 / FIVE / K / FIVE / 5 / V /
V [attributed to Akin on the basis of Akin's
earlier endorsement of Perkins's process
and Perkins's published announcement that
Akin had engraved his plates]
Collections: AAS
References: *Newburyport Herald and
Country Gazette,* May 14, 1799, quoted in
Currier, *History of Newburyport,* 2:363–67;
Newburyport Herald, Mar. 8, 1805

80. *Plan of Hampton,* New Hampshire; 1806
Medium: Engraving
Dimensions: Unknown
Inscription: [In circular frame lower
right] Plan of Hampton / Containing 3129
Acres / 1825 being salt Marsh / from actual
survey by / Thomas Leavitt Esqr. / 1806 /
Engraved by James Akin.
Collections: Unknown
References: Joseph Dow, *History of the
Town of Hampton, New Hampshire,* 2 vols.
(Salem, Mass.: Salem Publishing and Print-
ing Co., 1893) 1: facing 285; Rubenstein,
"James Akin in Newburyport," p. 295; San-
born, "Thomas Leavitt and his Artist
Friend, James Akin," p. 229–30

81. Record Pitcher; coopers arms and view of the
ship *Merremack* on Nicholas Brown and Lucy
Lamprey Brown's pitcher, ca. 1806–1808
Medium: Transfer-printed Liverpool-type
pitcher

Dimensions: Unknown
Inscription: [Unknown; previously published attribution to Akin]
Collections: Unknown
References: Sanborn, "Thomas Leavitt and his Artist Friend, James Akin," p. 227

82. Cow Pitcher; John Bull and Napoleon pulling a cow by the horns and tail, while Jefferson milks the cow, ca. 1808
    Medium: Transfer-printed Liverpool-type pitcher
    Dimensions: Unknown
    Inscription: [None; previously published attribution to Akin]
    Collections: Society for the Preservation of New England Antiquities, Boston, Massachusetts; Philadelphia Museum of Art, Philadelphia, Pennsylvania
    References: Williard E. Keyes, "The Cow & The Sleeping Lion," *Antiques* 39, no. 1 (Jan. 1941): 26–30; Little, "The Cartoons of James Akin upon Liverpool Ware," pp. 103–106; Murrell, *A History of American Graphic Humor*, p. 52; *Newburyport Herald*, Nov. 11, 1806; Stauffer, *American Engravers upon Copper and Steel*, no. 18

83. Essex County Seals; 1807
    Medium: Engraved seals
    Dimensions: Unknown
    Inscription: [Unknown; previously published attribution to Akin]
    Collections: Unknown
    References: Rubenstein, "James Akin in Newburyport," pp. 294–95; James Akin to Ichabod Tucker, Jan. 17, 1807, EI

84. Tucker Seal; Jan. 1807
    Medium: Engraved seal
    Dimensions: Unknown
    Inscription: T [previously published attribution to Akin]
    Collections: Unknown
    References: Rubenstein, "James Akin in Newburyport," pp. 294–95; James Akin to Ichabod Tucker, Jan. 17, 1807, EI

85. *Implements of Torture;* depiction of iron gag, 1835

Medium: Lithograph
Dimensions: H. 8¾", W. 5⅞"
Inscription: [Above iron gag] IMPLEMENTS OF TORTURE / and their dangerous Effects, Illustrated / By James Akin, No. 18 Prune Street Philadelphia / Taken from Mcelwee's detailed Statements [within iron gag] THE IRON GAG / of its natural size Locked upon Mathias Maccumsey, / a convict of Lancaster County sentenced to the Cells for / Manslaughter; who Died with it in his mouth, in the Eastern STATE PENITENTIARY, of / PENNSYLVANIA / June 1833 [on lock on lower left of iron gag] 8 [below iron gag] "IN OPEN DEFIANCE of all the known maxims of Law, and / Contrary to Legislative enactments, a convict was compelled / to endure the appalling tortures of this infernal contrivance, formerly speaking to a fellow prisoner. In a Land too, where / Tyranny, and Oppression, is held in utter abhorence, and Liberty, Equality, and a just enjoyment of rights are the constant / boasting of the people!!! The Spanish inquisitions, can not / exhibit a more fearful and barbarous mode, beyond all / human endurance! it ought to be forever abolished !!!" / Entered according to Act of Congress, in the year 1835, by James Akin in the Clerk's office at the / District Court, of the Eastern District of Pennsylvania.
Collections: HSP; LC

86. *Durham Bull Collostra;* ca. 1841
    Medium: Watercolor
    Dimensions: Unknown
    Inscription: [Unknown; attributed to Akin on the basis of published exhibition]
    Collections: Unknown
    References: Anna Wells Rutledge, "Cumulative Record of Exhibition Catalogues, The Pennsylvania Academy of the Fine Arts, 1807–1970, The Society of Artists, 1800–1814, The Artists Fund Society, 1835–1845," *American Philosophical Society Memoirs* 38 (1955): 196

87. *Colossal Bull Nero;* ca. 1841
    Medium: Watercolor
    Dimensions: Unknown
    Inscription: [Unknown; attributed to

Akin on the basis of published exhibition]
Collections: Unknown
References: Rutledge, "Cumulative Record of Exhibition Catalogues," p. 204

88. *English Lane Scene;* ca. 1840s
     Medium: Watercolor

Dimensions: Unknown
Inscription: [Unknown;   attributed   to
Akin on the basis of published posthumous
exhibition]
Collections: S. B. Fales in 1853
References: Rutledge, "Cumulative Record of Exhibition Catalogues," p. 320

The Shaker Mission
to the Shawnee Indians

Edward Deming Andrews

TWELVE years after "Mad Anthony" Wayne, in August 1795, concluded a treaty with the Indians of the Northwest at Greenville, and four years before Governor William Henry Harrison, in 1811, defeated the forces of Tecumseh at Tippecanoe, the religious society of Shakers dispatched a mission to one tribe of these Indians, the restless Shawnee, in southern Ohio. The hoped-for conversion of the "savages" to the Shaker faith was their primary purpose. Though the Believers in Christ's Second Appearing had little knowledge of ethnology and Indian culture, they had heard rumours of a religious "commotion" among the Shawnee and talk that the spirit of the recent Kentucky Revival had been "given to the Heathen."[1] In accord with the Shaker custom of propagating "the one true gospel" wherever there were "awakenings," it was decided to try to bring the Shawnee into the fold. Rumours of Indian warfare against the white settlers, instigated, it was said, by the British,[2] were also rife, and the investigation of these rumours may have been a secondary motive

for the arduous undertaking. The peace-loving Shakers had heard that the Prophet, Tecumseh's brother, whose influence among his people was in the ascendency, was in the region. To meet and talk with him was their immediate objective.[3]

The three brethren chosen to carry the gospel to the Shawnee were Benjamin S. Youngs, David Darrow, and Richard McNemar. Youngs, or "little Benjamin" as he was affectionately called, was a man of profound convictions and was one of three missionaries sent out from the central Shaker society at New Lebanon, New York, early in 1805 to open the testimony of Christ's Second Appearing in the wake of the Kentucky Revival. Darrow followed him soon afterwards, and for twenty years was the leading minister at Turtle Creek, the central society in Ohio.[4] McNemar, "a commanding influence" in the Revival, was one of the first western converts to the faith of Mother Ann Lee, the foundress of the United Society. When these men, in fulfilment of a prophesy and a vision, set out from Turtle Creek on March 17, 1807, the sect had been established

---

[1] The religious excitement known as the Kentucky Revival was first manifested along the western frontier around 1800 and continued during the early years of the nineteenth century. Eventually denominational rivalries and doctrinal quarrels resulted in the formation of new sects. For the Shaker involvement see Edward Deming Andrews, *The People Called Shakers* (1953; reprint ed., New York: Dover Publications, Inc., 1963), pp. 72–74.

[2] British influence was strong in the area occupied by the Indians before the Treaty of Ghent ended the War of 1812 and established American claims in the Northwest with finality. In the period between the end of the Revolutionary War and the end of the War of 1812, the English encouraged the Algonquian Indians to resist the Americans. The Shawnee were an Algonquian tribe. Clark Wissler, *Indians of the United States* (Garden City, New York: Doubleday, Doran & Co.), pp. 77–79.

[3] Tecumseh, a Shawnee chief, attempted to form a confederation of tribes and to establish the Ohio River as the permanent boundary between the American and Indian nations. Tecumseh's political appeal was supported by the religious vision of his brother, the Prophet, who preached that the Great Spirit had ordered the Indians to assemble in the valley of the Ohio. Wissler, *Indians of the United States*, pp. 79–82; Glenn Tucker, *Tecumseh: Vision of Glory* (Indianapolis: Bobbs-Merrill Co., 1956).

[4] Turtle Creek was the site of the first Shaker settlement in the West. In 1812 it was renamed Union Village. Andrews, *People Called Shakers*, p. 79. By 1831 the settlement was known as "*Union or Shakertown*, a remarkably neat settlement, inhabited by Shakers, . . . 4 miles west of Lebanon." John Kilbourn, *The Ohio Gazeteer; or Topographical Dictionary* (10th ed.; Columbus: John Kilbourn, 1831), p. 285.

in the valley of the Great Miami River for about two years. It is to the credit of the Shaker order, and a measure of its convictions, that so early in the organization of the church in the West, when the believers were living under rude frontier conditions, they should thus have diverted their time and energy to such an enterprise.

The following narrative indicates that in spite of the gulf separating the beliefs, customs, and language of the Shawnee and those of the Shakers, unusual rapport was established between the two parties. One cannot but admire the way the missionaries, by tact, courtesy, and use of the simplest language, managed to communicate the Christian Shaker faith to the Shawnee prophet and chiefs. Intuitively they sensed that by referring to God as the "good spirit," or "great spirit," the gulf between two civilizations might be crossed. The words "good," "evil," "wicked," "foolishness," "hatred," "falsehood," "salvation from wickedness," were concepts they were sure could be readily understood. Faced with a tribe that had been mistreated by the whites and was suspicious of them, they took care to dissociate themselves from those ministers who had branded Indian beliefs as "foolishness" and "nonsense."

The journal provides interesting insights into the morals of the Shawnee, especially in their condemnation of drunkenness, of wife-abuse, of murder, and particularly of witchcraft. The Indians were admittedly superstitious, but to the missionaries their good qualities and intentions outweighed their ignorance. A curious belief, repeatedly asserted by George Bluejacket, the interpreter, was that wickedness and the capacity to do evil, as well as the advent of the rite of confession (probably learned from the Roman Catholics), began at the age of seven years.

The most probable author of the narrative was Youngs.[5] He proved himself to be a meticulous observer. Aside from the doctrinal exchanges between the two parties, Young's descriptions of the country, Indian encampments and customs, and

encounters with various strangers clothe the narrative with a lively interest. His account of the Shawnee meeting house is so detailed that its appearance can be readily visualized.

It is significant that one passage in the journal, where the missionaries told the interpreter that they "believed in no books of man's invention," was crossed out. Also, in another place, they stated that books "written by wicked men only corrupted the mind." The deletion and the use of the adjective "wicked" are doubtless explained by the fact that McNemar was publishing his account of the Kentucky Revival this same year, 1807, and that Youngs, on his part, was already engaged in writing *The Testimony of Christ's Second Appearing,* the standard work on Shaker theology, sometimes called "the Shaker bible," which was published at Lebanon, Ohio, the following year.

Though the missionaries left the great fort and the Indians "fully satisfied in finding such a real work of God among a noble & resolute people"; nevertheless the mission must be accounted unfruitful, at least as far as conversions to Shakerism and the spirit of the Kentucky Revival are concerned. No Indians joined the society.

As for the Prophet, it is not clear whether, as has been said, "some scraps of his system" came from the Shakers or whether he really sought the good of his people.

In a letter from Thomas Jefferson to John Adams, the Prophet was characterized as follows:

The Wabash Prophet is more rogue than fool. . . . He rose to notice while I was in the administration. . . . His declared object was the reformation of his red brethren, and their return to their pristine manner of living. He pretended to be in constant communication with the Great Spirit; that he was instructed by Him to make known to the Indians that they were created by Him distinct from the whites, of different natures, for different purposes, and placed under different circumstances, adapted to their nature and destines; that they must return from all the ways of the whites to the habits and opinions of their forefathers; they must not eat the flesh of hogs, of bullocks, of sheep, etc., the deer and the buffalo having been created for their food; they must not make bread of wheat, but of Indian corn; they must not wear linen for woollen, but must dress like their fathers, in the skins and furs of animals; they must not drink ardent spirits; and I do not remember whether he extended his inhibitions to the gun and gunpowder, in favor of the bow and arrow.

---

[5] Although the journal of the mission to the Shawnee Indians, which is now in the Edward Deming Andrews Memorial Shaker collection in the Winterthur Museum Libraries, is not signed, the script closely resembles Benjamin Youngs's known handwriting. However, John P. MacLean, who published verbatim excerpts from the narrative in his *Shakers of Ohio: Fugitive Papers Concerning the Shakers of Ohio* (Columbus: F. J. Heer Printing Co., 1907), credits authorship of the account to Richard McNemar.

Jefferson concluded that the Prophet was

a visionary, enveloped in their entiquities, and vainly endeavoring to lead back his brethren to the fancied beauitudes of their golden age. I thought there was little danger of his making many proselytes from the habits and comforts they had learned from the whites, to the hardships and privations of savagism, and so great harm if he did. But his followers increased until the British thought him worth corrupting, and found him corruptible.[6]

Opposition to the Prophet's leadership developed among neighboring chiefs, and at one time he carried out a veritable inquisition against his enemies, denouncing them as witches and cruelly condemning them to death.[7] This opposition created a confused situation in the relations between the Indians and the Shakers at their colony in Busro near Vincennes in the Indian Territory. In 1811, according to letters written from that outpost by Elder Issachar Bates, "a number of Indians of the prophets party came in to get their tools repaired these were Shawnees Kickapoos Wyandots Potowattomes." Governor Harrison issued orders against any "smith work" declaring that the hoes and other tools were for war, though the Indians indignantly denied the charge saying

"we do not go to war." In July, under the leadership of Tecumseh and his brother, Indians from different tribes were summoned by Harrison to a council at Vincennes but unrest and fear of an outbreak of hostilities continued. The Busro Shakers, as a result of the theft of four horses, became more suspicious of the Indians. Elder Bates, who still trusted the Prophet, "condemned the theft as a trick carried on by the 'wicked Potowatomies' who followed the Prophet's Party and stole in order that it might be blamed on the Prophet." At the battle of Tippecanoe, in November, 1811, "the Gov proceeded and burnt the prophets town and all that was in it among which was 5000 bushels of corn."[8]

The narrative of the Shakers' journey to meet the Indians has been transcribed verbatim. The few misspellings have been retained. "Priara" means prairie. Youngs spells women "weomen." There are variant spellings of "Ske lah way." The prophet's Indian name, according to the narrator, was "Lallawasheka," not "Lawlewasikaw" as in other accounts.[9] Youngs's capitalization and punctuation have also been retained except where minor changes were necessary to clarify meaning. For a largely self-taught man his writing is clear and accurate, and always earnest. That his was an essentially scholarly mind is abundantly proven by his later book, *The Testimony of Christ's Second Appearing.*

[6] Quoted in Edward Eggleston and Lillie E. Seelye, *Tecumseh and the Shawnee Prophet* (New York: Dodd, Mead & Co., 1878).

[7] In 1810, a Wyandot chief known as Leatherlips was executed by his own people for practicing witchcraft after six warriors sent by Tecumseh visited the tribe. Ohio State Journal Company, *The Ohio Railroad Guide* (Columbus: Ohio State Journal Co., 1854), p. 55.

[8] Quoted in Mary Lou Conlin, "The Lost Land of Busro," *Shaker Quarterly* 3, no. 2 (Summer 1963): 50–52.

[9] The name meant loud voice. At one point in the Prophet's career, he adopted a new name, Tenskwatawa, meaning the open door.

A Journey to the Indians

Miami near Lebanon, Ohio, 3d. month 1807.

Both before & since the gathering of the Church of God at New Lebanon & other places since the year 1780, Many visions, Indian tongues, prophecies, revelations & signs were given to the people of God respecting the Gentile nations or *Indians* in the Western parts of America, from time to time predicting their coming into the Gospel— Also since the commencement of the gospel in this Western country there had been much feeling & fervent prayr among the believers in behalf of our red brethren, & many pointed signs had been given from time to time of the spirit of God being at work among them, but no express information had reached us neither where they lived, nor of what nation they were, nor what the work was among them, except some vague reports, which stated first that a number of Indian tribes had come over their boundary & were going to make war with the whites & then again that it was not for war they had come but . . it was on a religious account & that they had prophets among them who told of great things at hand & c.[10] Sometimes we heard one thing & sometimes another, but we fully believed the spirit of God was at work among them.

About the beginning of the third month we began to feel a great concern for them which continually increased on our minds with great weight. At length their situation & need of help became so urgent & impressive that we could feel no longer justified with out going to see them & seek out the truth of the matter—accordingly on the 17th day of the month El. David Darrow, Benjamin S. You[ngs] & Richard M[c]N. set out like Abram of old not knowing whether we went, but gathering assuredly from our feelings that the people lay somewhere to the North & that it was our Duty to find them, intending in the first place to follow the best direction we could find by making distant enquiries in order to keep our business concealed from the advantage of enemies [Fig. 1].

The first day we rode N. 22 miles to the believers at Beulah on Beaver creek[11]—the next day

[10] The boundary, or American line, referred to here and elsewhere in the journal was the boundary between settled and Indian land established by the treaty signed at Greenville fort in 1795. The Indian lands lay on the western side of the boundary. Tucker, *Tecumseh*, p. 149.

[11] In 1818 the Shaker settlement at Beulah was renamed Watervliet. Andrews, *People Called Shakers*, p. 84.

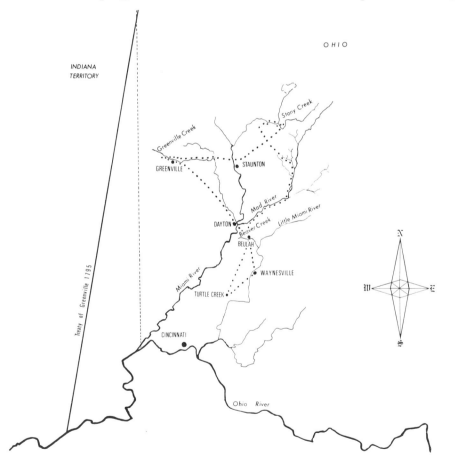

Fig. 1. Route of the Shaker Missionaries, 1807. (Map drawn by Rob Howard: Photo, Winterthur.)

still N. 5 miles to Mad-river—thence up the river N.E. by E. 16 miles to *Pickaway* once an old Indian town, having passed by many miles of large Prararo's, or wild meadows, between us & the river; very antient & extensive to the eye—Also we passed over large upland plains on which were extensive entrenchments & all the evident marks that the country was once inhabited by a great & warlike people whose name like Amolek [Amolet's] is now out of rememberance & blotted out from under heaven—in the midst of these plains were artificial mounts or hills, called Mounds cast up by hands—one of these was about 180 yards in circumference & 35 feet high, said to contain the bones of those who are supposed to be slain in their wars—These Mounds are covered with trees as large as any in the woods around them, & shew it impossible to form any calculation when, or by whom this country was once inhabited—all these mounds & the prospects around them are great marks of antiquity & are very striking to the eye.[12]

From *Pickaway* we crossed *Mad-river* just below the forks & went up the North fork. N.E. 8 miles to one Kysers mill in a low rich & very level country although the waters were clear & very rapid from whence came the name *Mad-river*— here we tarried all night & received some untelligiable information about the Indians who were whether they were 30 or 40 miles to the NW. or N. or NE. they could not tell, but said that they frequently came to this mill.

The next day being still severe cold weather we left *Kysers* & went N.E. 6 miles up the river to the mouth of Nettle creek, & thence up the creek to the head N.W. by W. 14 miles.—& about noon having no satisfactory inteligence we left the frontier settlements & entered the trackless wilderness, & continued N.W. by W. 14 miles & encamped in the woods, with no other accomodation but a little hut erected against ye side of an old log with sticks & barks—but as we had no fire & the night was very cold & freezing we were under the necesity of traveling back & forth during great part of the night so that by sun rise we had a plain & beaten path.—

The fourth day of our journey after sunrise we took our course N.E. lest we should leave those Indians to the right hand of us whom we understood lived on the waters of the Great Miami called Stony Creek—In about 3 miles we came to a river which we afterward found to be the Great Miami & soon discovered a canoe lying upon the opposite side but could not ford the river till we went up about 3 miles on the South side for it ran here from East to West, & having crossed we tied our horses, & two of us went down the river thinking it probable that some trace might lead from the canoe which we had seen [to] some inhabitants; but we found the canoe had only floated down ye river & lodged in a thicket from whence we concluded that the inhabitants were higher up the river, accordingly after returning to our horses we continued up the river on the N. side & in about 6 miles came to an old Indian Sugar camp—& soon after came to 3 fresh horse tracks on an Indian trace from the N. & had just crossed the river towards the S.—We recrossed the river above the mouth of Stony Creek & followed those tracks & within a mile at a camp of Indians we overtook 3 french traders who had just come from the *Mingo* town 7 miles off, & from the *Stawa* town 15 miles off both lying to the North[13] —these traders could talk English—from whom we received information that the Indian town or village was close by, but that the chief with most of the Indians were at their sugar camps—We soon went to the village which contains Nine log & bark houses, & perhaps abt. 80 or 100 inhabitants—We soon discovered the spirit of the people to be totally in the dark; & did not tarry among them but a few minutes—from thence we were conducted by two of those traders to another small village 2 miles off; their chief they told us, whose English name was *Capt. John,* was out at his sugar camp about a mile further[14]—We went to see him in company with the above mentioned traders—a number of Indians were at the camp

---

[12] Indian mounds were a common feature in many parts of Ohio. They were presumed to be grave structures. Kilbourne, *Ohio Gazeteer,* pp. 40, 42; Ohio State Journal Company, *Ohio Railroad Guide,* p. 30.

[13] Mingo and Stawa, or Tawa, like Pickaway were apparently Indian settlements. It is no longer possible to reconstruct their precise locations because the Indian names were applied to other geographic features. For example: The area in southwest Ohio near the Ohio River was known as Mingo bottom, Pickaway was a county in western Ohio, and by the 1850s Tawawa springs near Xenia had become a fashionable resort. Kilbourne, *Ohio Gazeteer,* pp. 212, 239; Ohio State Journal Company, *Ohio Railroad Guide,* p. 40.

[14] The Shawnees made maple sugar for sale to white settlers. Tucker, *Tecumseh,* p. 97.

but we had no feeling to open any thing to them —the chief was gone a hunting & we waited several hours before we could see him, & when he came we could feel nothing in him or any of the people that felt like the spirit of God but their conversation was light & carnal—this chief was naturally an able & likely man & could talk tolerable good English—from some distant enquiries we made, they told us of a Shawnee tribe that lay abt. 70 miles to the S. of W. in a line through the woods near *Greenvill fort,* among whom, they said was one LALLAWASHEKA that was called a prophet who had prayed mightily among the people & told many strange things, but they represented him as a very bad character, that he had deceived the people & enriched himself with their property, but said they "The people have found him out, & will not believe him now, nor let him speak any more"—he says [he] can talk with God Almighty, but he can talk with the devil better." —This however did not discourage us from continuing our search it was rather an evidence that God was among them—It was now late in the evening when we set off—We returned 3 miles back to the first village & were about an hundred miles from home the way we came—these Indians were a mixture of Shawneese & Mingo's, & some intermarried with the French.

About sun set we left the village & went about a mile into the woods & having got a flint & some punk, we had some m . . . p . . . gent but it would not catch, from the Indians we kindled a fire & erected a small hut by the side of a log & there lodged all night very comfortably, considering the severity of the weather.

The fifth day of our journey we set out about sun rise. In the course of ye forenoon we were much surprised at 3 different times with—[illegible] singular of vast multitudes of pigeons & blackbirds flocking together & no difference between them except ye colour & melodious singing of ye latter; otherwise ye actions of both were perfectly alike, most of that day we traveled through the woods for the distance of about 30 miles S.W. by S. from the Indian town on Stony ck. to Jarretts Mills on the Great Miami, which here runs from N to S. bearing W its general course 3 miles above Stamton & 23 miles above *Dayton,* at ye mouth of *Mad River* where we lodged at night.

The 6th Day of our journey we left Jarretts &

having crossed the Great Miami—we took a West course 12 miles to a Settlement note if there is but one family it is called a settlement in ye country on the Greenville fork of the Great Miami by some improperly called *Still Water* but by the Indians *Kithwathala.* at this Settlement we bought some corn for our horses & some cornbread & bacon for ourselves to take with us—here we crossed that river abt. 25 miles above the mouth which is at Dayton & found a blind trace in a Western direction leading to the *great fort;* this we followed 12 miles keeping up ye river on ye S. Side & lodged that night on an old Indian camping ground 8 miles from the *fort.*

The seventh day of our journey, the second of the week & 23d of the month we came to the *fort* —The aspect of the country appeared awfully sublime, many hundreds of Acres around the garrison was entirely stript of timber & afforded a very extensive & level prospect, the remains of the old stockades discovered still the extent of the fort which we supposed contained not less than 50 to 60 Acres of land, covered with thick grass & it being the place where the peace was established between the Indians, & Americans rendered it still more solemn—Near the fort we found two french traders from *Detroit* who told us of an Indian town about two miles off up a fork of the Creek near the head of a great *Priara*—We found a plain road leading South up the W. side of the *Priara* & after traveling a mile we came on a point of *oak wood land* which overlooked the *Priara* towards the E. & the *fort* towards the N. where the *Wiandot* nation had held their religious campmeetings last summer[15]—We were sensibly struck with ye resemblance this place bore to places of encampment during the late revival, In Kentucky & Ohio, etc.

Two rows of hew'd logs were extended E. & West in the form of Seats about 150 feet in length & perhaps 12 or 14 feet apart affording a larg walk which from appearance had been beat as smooth as a house floor, around on ye outside of this *walk* were the bodies of small trees as if intended for seats for Spectators, & Many tents—one principle tent stood on the South side of the walk facing it about the middle & was floored with puncheons & open at ye sides something resembling the old

---

[15] The Wyandots, an Iroquois tribe, were Tecumseh's allies. Tucker, *Tecumseh,* pp. 129–30.

stands for preaching—On this ground we felt exceeding solemn, but hastened on toward the town—on our left hand was a fence made of poles & forks about a mile in length enclosing certain spots of ground along on the border of the Priara & generally a hut on each spot of ground where corn was raised last summer.

When we came in sight of the town or village the first object that attracted our view was their meeting house an immense building, & about 57 smoking cottages stood around on every side—We rose up & saluted some Indians but could get no answer in English—at length one of them signed to a tent where we must go, naming *George,* & as we advanced one came out & with a motion of his hand beckoned to us to come thither—here we found one who could talk English whose name by interpretation was PETER CORNSTALK—We asked him how they felt towards us, if their feelings were friendly? He answered, O Yes, we are brothers—*Ques.* Where are your chiefs, we wish to have conversation with them? *Ans.* They are about 4 miles off making sugar—Ques. What are their names? A. One is LALLA-WASHEKA & his brother TEKUMSAW. *Q.* Can any of them talk English? A. No, but there is a good Interpreter there that can talk English better than I, he has been to School & can read, his name in English is GEORGE BLUEJACKET—We enquired how we should find the way to them? He pointed to one who he said would pilot us.—We then set out with our pilot, but had not gone far 'till a runner came after us & called us back—we were told that one of the chiefs had come in from the camps, & would presently return & show us the way.—

In the meantime we asked PETER several questions—

Q. What is that great house for? A. To worship the great spirit.—Q. In what way do you worship? A. Mostly in speaking.—Q. Have you any public speakers? A. Yes, several. Q. Who is your chief speaker? A. Our prophet LALLAWASHEKA, he can converse with the good spirit, & tells us the way to be good.—Q. Do all of you that are here believe in him? A. Yes we believe in him, he can dream to God! All the village seemed to be moved & look'd serious, & some appeared very solemn in tears & could scarce take their eyes off us—While we were waiting for the chief to get ready, whose name was TEKUMSAW, before mentioned, several set off before us to the *camps,* one

in perticular who we were told was a king whose name was WASEEKEEKAPOW, a Deleware chief.

As soon as TEKUMSAW was ready he got on his horse & went on before us taking with him some public papers for our information, etc. On the way we met three men who appeared very solemn & under the fear of God, loving & kind spirited—with these the Chief talked for some time & then went on again when we came to the *camps*—we found a large number there—& the chiefs & prophet & Interpreter were holding a council in a Close *tent* & together with our pilot continued in the *tent* for about an hour—after which the Interpreter came out & presented us several papers—from the Governor of *Ohio,* from the Governor of *Detroit* & from other public men, to show the spirit of friendship that existed between them & the *whites*—

We enquired for the prophet & desired conversation with him. GEORGE answered that he was very sick & could not talk—we repeated our desires of seeing him but were again answered in the negative; He is too sick to talk, he has been sick a long time, he has a bad pain in his head, he cannot sit up—to these he added his preaching is different from the *white* people, the ministers of the white people don't believe what he says. They call it foolishness what he believes & we don't like to tell them much about it because they don't understand what it means—We answered, we are not of those kind of ministers, we are a people that are separated from them by the work of the *great spirit,* they count us foolish too & speak against us—He asked if we believed that a person could have the Knowledge of the *good spirit* & know what was good by an inward feeling without going to school & learning letters? we told him we believed they might & that was the best kind of knowledge that we felt in the heart—he told us that their prophet had that knowledge & had been encreasing in it for two years & had great understanding & was still seeing more and more wonderful things which he taught the people—but added, I cannot tell you the wonderful strange things which he speaks so you can understand me. I cannot Interpret to you what he says—We told him that we believed it was the work of the *good spirit,* & that we knew the work of the good spirit was foolishness to many ministers of the white people, & that we wished them to understand that we were not of them, & that they hated us & spoke evil of us because they did not understand the work of [the] *good spirit* which was among us—& these things we wished to be communicated to the prophet—& desired to be informed of what they believed & of the work of the Spirit among them more perticularly, adding that we were free & willing to answer them any questions, & inform them what the *good spirit* had taught us.—

Again they entered the prophets *tent* & had a long talk for near or quite an hour. At this time things appeared dark & every communication shut up, but we could by no means feel free to leave them so, & determined if possible to let them know what we were, before we should leave them—for we could see no way of entrance unless we committed ourselves to them first.

After a long time GEORGE came out & sat with us round the fire, & soon after the prophet also made his appearance smoking in a large pipe [Fig. 2]—he came forward & sat down among the rest. he evidently appeared under great sufferings & in deep labour & distress of mind, & not under any real bodily disorder—He was divested of all his tinkling ornaments but a round tire on his breast, that—fastened his garment, his dress plain & decent, his countenance grave & solemn—his person of a common size, rather slender, & of no great appearance—all was silent for some time—He began to speak, & with his eyes closed continued his speech about half an hour in a very eloquent & emphatical manner; he sensibly spake by the power of God—his solemn voice, grave countenance, with every motion of his hand & gesture of his body, were expressive of a deep sence & solemn feeling of eternal things—about five & twenty men were in & about the tent paying attention—five of whom George told us were *Deleware* chiefs who had come to hear the prophet—at every remarkable pause or sentence, a solemn assent sounded through ye tent in the word *"Sequy"* which signified their approbation of the things that were spoken.—

After he had done speaking GEORGE, told us that he spake wonderful things which he could not communicate in *English,* they were strange things. "I am not able to Interpret them, what is told to the *ministers* of the *white* people they called *foolishness,* & say it is *nonsense,* & want us to quit such foolish ways but the prophet says he never will quit this way so long as he lives.—["]

We now saw the way in some measure open to free our minds as we had felt & concluded; & accordingly we told George the Interpreter that we had a feeling to communicate to them something of what we believed & what the good spirit had done for us—& then they might be just as free in their communications to us as they felt proper, & they gave us liberty.—

We asked them if they believed that all the world, all mankind were lost from the good spirit by wicked ways? We were answered, We do believe that all are gone away from the *good spirit.* —We asked if they believed that the *good spirit* once made himself known to the world, by a man that was called *Christ,* to make men good? George answered, Yes, we do believe it.—We then told them, first, that this man who was called *Christ* was the Son of God, of the *good spirit,* & that many believed on him, & followed him & were made *good,* but after a long time them *good* people were all gone & were no more, & another kind of people rose up in their place & pretended to know the *good spirit* & *Christ* his Son, but they have deceived mankind a great while & will preach to people to be *good* but will not put away their own wicked ways, they will quarrel & fight among one another & they will go to war & shed blood, & they will be unjust & cruel to other people & wherever the good spirit works they will hate it & call it foolishness & nonsense, & speak against it; we do not believe in such ministers, the good spirit never sent them—they are not *good people*—but the Great spirit has promised by his holy prophets long ago that he would have a good people to serve him on the earth in the last days—We then told them how the *great spirit* had begun to fulfill his promises, by raising up witnesses to tell people how to be *good*—& how these witnesses were moved by the good spirit to come all the way from England over the great water to *Nisqueunia* in the state of *New York,* & how the *great spirit* told them to settle in a swamp there & how they could settle nowhere else only where the *great spirit* told them.[16] & how they told people to be *good* & put away all wicked ways—& how a great many believed them & became a *good people* all united in *one*—We also told them of the *Great Spirit* that had been in

[16] Niskeyuna, later Watervliet, New York, was the first Shaker settlement in America.

FIG. 2. George Catlin, *The Open Door, known as the Prophet.* 1830s. Oil on canvas; H. 29″, W. 24″. (National Collection of Fine Arts, Smithsonian Institution.)

Kentucky & between the Miami's, in Ohio of the camp meetings, convictions for sin, & fervent prayrs to the *great spirit* that he would open some way of deliverance, & of the visions & prophecies among the people that the *great spirit* would have a good people soon. & of the Witnesses that had been sent from the *state of New York* & traveled about a thousand miles on foot, & were led by the *great spirit* to the house of one of the chief prophets who lived in the Miami country & could go no further, but there opened to the people what they must do to be saved & that many believed what they said, & were obedient & put away all their sins & wicked ways & had set out to be a *good people*—but that the *white people* all round hated them because they would not be wicked any longer, & called the work of the good spirit which was among them *foolishness* & *delusion*—& told them of some things that were reported of them that we believed were false, & that we knew that all those who served the *good spirit* would be hated & much evil spoken of by all the rest of the world—& that the true work of the *good spirit* always was *foolishness* to the ministers & people that would be wicked, & that they could not understand it.—We also told them that the *Great Spirit* had promised by his Son & by his holy prophets long ago that he would have a good people to serve him, & that the Gentile nations or *red people,* should be his people, & that all his people out of all nations, that would be good & put away their wicked ways, & should be united in *one,* & the *good spirit* should dwell among them, & we believed yt the time was come for that work, and that the *great spirit* had begun it. & that they were the beginning & foundation of that great work, for the good of the nations of the *red people,* & that we knew it was the work of the *great & good spirit,* & we were come to encourage them & to help them—& we desired them to be free in communicating to us what they believed & what the work of the spirit was among them, & how it began & that we were willing to inform them, & answer them any question they felt to ask.

These are the outlines & about ye Substance & manner of our communications before them all— They listened with great attention, & when we had closed, after some silence George began to Interpret & to communicate to the prophet & people what we had said, & spake in a solemn & feeling manner for about the same length of time

that we did, to which the prophet gave several vocal assents while the Interpreter was speaking— & after he had got through the prophet returned to his tent & took his bed. &—the Interpreter then began in communicating to us some of the prophets speech & other matters in relation to the work among them—the substance of which is as follows.—

That he (the prophet) had formerly been a very wicked man until about two years ago, there happened to be great sickness among ye people at Stawa Town, at that time he lived on *White river,* & being a doctor was sent for to attend the sick at Tawa, while he was there he fell under deep conviction for sin, & was in great distress & prayed to the *good spirit* to shew him how he must be saved, & while under this distress & exercise of mind he had a vision or revelation made known to him from the good spirit, as follows.

He saw, & behold he was traveling along a road & came to where it fork'd—the right hand he was told led to heaven & the left to hell—the forks of the road where they parted was explained to him as the place or time of conviction—those who took the right hand road left off all evil & wicked ways & became *good,* but those who took the left hand *way* were all *bad wicked* people who would not *be good* after they had an offer by light & conviction—these moved along slowly untill they had passed the fork of the road & then they went very swift—On this left hand road he saw three houses —from the first & second were path ways that led across into the right hand road, which was discovered as shewing a posibility of being finally saved after rejecting the first light for some time —but he discovered no way that led from the third & last,—this he called *eternity*—Those who went to this last house were such as were obstinate & would not leave off their wickedness—& the perticular crimes that led to that place were *Witchcraft,* or the art of hurting & tor[tur]ing one another with a certain kind of poison—drinking spirituous liquors—beating & abusing their fellows wives,—& murder—he saw vast multitudes of every colour going this left hand road, & many would not forsake it but were runing swiftly to the last house—he saw vast crouds in each of those habitations under awful torments, & heard them roaring like the falls of a river—he saw the punishment assigned to each transgressor according to his wickedness, & mentioned perticularly that of the *drunkard*. One stood before him with a cup full of a certain liquid that resembled melted lead & gave it to him to drink, & when he had drank it his bowels were seized with an awful burning—when he would refuse to drink any more his attendant would urge him, saying, come drink, sure you used to love liquor—now you must drink it.—

He saw nothing at that time that was on the right hand road, nor went any further than the fork, but was told by the *great spirit* to go back & tell the people what he had seen & warn them of their danger.

In another vision afterwards he was taken along the right hand road & conducted into a beutiful habitation which was full of blossoms, & flowers, & fruit of the most delicious smell & every thing that was delightful & pleasant—but after his first revelation he began to speak to the people in great distress for their situation, & would weep & tremble while he was addressing them.

Some believed & were greatly alarmed; & began to turn from their wicked ways, which spread the alarm & caused others to come & hear; & from this it spread into differant tribes & encreased to other nations of the *red people*.—

He testified perticularly against *witchcraft* & the use of their *poison*, & had a perticular gift of discernment to know & point out those who practis'd it, even if they were strangers among a great multitude, & could tell those who had the *poison*, where they kept it hid if it was at the distance of a thousand miles—This *witchcraft* (continued the Interpreter) is a very wicked thing—they can go a thousand miles in less than an hour & back again & poison any body they hate & make them lame & torment them in many wicked & cruel ways—they can go into houses with their *poison* if the doors are locked ever so tight & the people cannot get awake till they are gone—this *witchcraft* has prevailed greatly & been very common among our people & some of the white people have learned it & practise it, & it is a very wicked thing & all such go to *eternity* of torment & misery who will not throw away their *poison* & *witchcraft*.

On this subject arose great opposition, many of the chiefs used *witchcraft* & had the *poison* & would not throw it away—he was then told by the *great spirit* to separate from these wicked Chiefs & their people & come over & settle within the American line—accordingly all that believed

& were obedient to what he taught them set out from *White-River* toward the *great fort* where the peace was made; & came about 10 miles over the line to the spot where the *great spirit* told him he must settle & make preparation to receive all of the different nations that would become good— He said he knew the white people claimed the land & many wanted to have them drove off—but he was not concerned, they might come & settle there by thousands if they had a mind to drive them, but they would not go until the *great spirit* bid them, & that the land all belonged to the *great spirit* & he would convince them in two years & they would see a day of *Judgment* at that time—He said if they staid among the wicked nations, that they could not be good, & all their good impressions of the *great spirit* would die away, & there was no other place where they could follow the right way but there—he said that many white people thought they were going to make war but they were very foolish to imagine that they would hurt them—they felt great pity & love to all mankind & wanted them all to be *good*—he said that thousands were coming there next summer from ye nations to hear the prophet—but many were afraid to come, & some would not come, because they would not throw away their *poison*—but none could come & keep their wickedness conceal'd. all began to do wicked at seven years old, & he could tell all the sins & bad things every one has done from that time.—

These are the outlines of what they communicated to us by way of history—but that weighty & spiritual concern, & that solemn sence, love & simplicity that we felt in the assembly cannot be put into words.—

When our communications were about through a young man came along with a large wooden bowl in which he had a boiled wild turkey—of this he handed to every one of them a piece, of which we had a share—this was divided between near or quite 30 men who were at & about the tent with us. & how many men weomen & children more we could not tell—the men were generally by themselves—the weomen were diligently employed about their fires & tent affairs, but we saw but few of them—uncorrupted manners, & unaffected modesty & simplicity was evident among them—that was not to be found among the whites.—

Some time after the turkey was divided, the

broth of it was brought in a tin kettle containing about 6 or 8 quarts with one spoon—of this broth each man eat in his turn—this was all they had perhaps during the whole day without a morsel of bread, by this we discovered that they were scant for provisions—but what they had, they eat with peace & contentment.

It was now near night, & being greatly satisfied with the opening we had had, we concluded to return back to the town with the Interpreter & some others.—We asked them how they made out for provisions? they told us they had none, that the great multitudes who had been there last summer to attend their meetings had consumed all their provisions—We asked if they had any money wherewith to buy? they said they had not any—We then concluded to give them from our traveling expences for their present relief, & handed them Ten dollars to buy corn, which the Interpreter gave to the prophet. We now took a friendly leave of them & got on our horses & as we sat waiting abt. a minute One of their public speakers, a cousin to the prophet named SKE LAW WAY stood up in an open passage about the middle of the encampment & spoke for about fifteen minutes in a very powerful manner—surely it was not the preaching of *Antichrist*—but it was completely out of his sight & comprehended all his ministers!

Several were standing around him, & those who sat in their tents were all attention, & gave a very solemn & vocal assent at every pause—the daylight was just departing, & the full moon just appearing above the horizon; our feelings were like Jacobs when he cried out, "how terrible is this place, surely God is in this place & the world know it not["]—The shrill voice of the eloquent *Shawny* might have been distinctly heard at the distance of a mile or more; & when he closed his discourse a low shout of approbation reiterated from *tent* to *tent,* till it went through the whole—he immediately turned from the camp & with the Interpreter & a number of others went to the town & we followed after—when we got to the town the Interpreter GEORGE provided for us a *tent*—in the middle of which we had a fire made with wood provided by the weomen, for this was their common custom for the weomen to do all their work & the men to spend their time chiefly in hunting.

We saw many heathenish & superst[it]ious prac-

tices among them such as shaving part of their heads, painting their heads & faces with diverse colours—wearing feathers on the top of their heads—wearing tinkling ornaments of silver on their heads & garments, earrings & nose jewels & many other costly ornaments & idle practices of superstition—but notwithstanding, such was truly the work of the spirit of God among them that these things were no obstruction to our feeling it.—At night we lay by the side of our fire on some puncheons or split pieces of timber, & did not suffer much although it was very cold.

Early the next morning we were sent for into the tent of GEORGE BLUEJACKET the Elder, who was the principal chief, & father to our Interpreter & was the first that went into the great fort & made the treaty the Indians & Americans[17]—several other persons of note were present—They enquired several things concerning our people—

Q. Do you drink any whiskey? A. Nay, not at all we never taste it.—this appeared to give them great joy to find any among the *whites* so far reformed from wicked ways—

They told us of several missionaries that had been sent to preach to them, & perticularly one *Hugh's* a presbyterian minister who they said would drink whisky after he had done preaching, & would allow his people to drink it in harvest, & at house raisings & log rollings etc. & they did not believe that such were truly religious people, or that any man was truly religious who would drink whisky, & they believed those kind of ministers would almost all drink it. We enquired many things concerning the vices which their prophet spake against, & how far they had light to discover the evil nature of sin—We were told, that he had great light concerning man in his first creation & how he fell into evil, & what the *great spirit* had made known to many generations—We asked, what are the perticular evils that he speaks against? Ans. We all begin to do evil at 7 years old & he can tell all that we do from that time—

Q. Does he say anything against fornication, you know what that is, viz. young men & weomen being together in the carnal works of the flesh?

Ans. O yes, from seven years old he can tell it all.

[17] George Bluejacket had been the Indian commander at the Battle of Fallen Timbers. Wissler, *Indians of the United States,* pp. 78–79.

Ques. What do those do who have been wicked when they believe the prophet?

Ans. They confess all that they have done.

Ques. Who do they confess to?

Ans. to the prophet & four Chiefs in council.

Ques. Do they confess all the bad things they have done & lay open their whole life?

Ans. Yes, from 7 years old, they confess all, & cry & tremble when they do it.

Ques. How did they learn this, the Roman Catholicks practice the confessing of sins?

Ans. A great many *Wiandots* have belonged to the Roman Catholicks at *Detroit,* but they have left them & now believe in our prophet—the Roman Catholics would confess their sins but would still go on & be wicked, but our people forsake their evil ways when they have confess'd.

Ques. Do the white people ever bring Whisky among you to sell?

Ans. Not any, we will not have it, we would knock the head out of their vessels & let it run, if they would bring it here.—

Ques. Is there anything more that your prophet speaks against?

Ans. This *witchcraft* & *poisoning* is the greatest —they learn it from some old men & keep it hid, & learn it again to others—it is a very wicked thing, & them that will not throw it away go to *eternity* of torment & misery, & all such as beat & abuse their wives & drive them away because they dont have childrens.—

They asked us concerning books, whether we believed they were of any use?—We told them we believed in the Bible, that the true prophets had spoken what was written in that book; but other books yt were written by wicked men only corrupted the mind, & our people did not read them.—

They enquired the distance to where we lived & promised that some of them would come & see us in a few weeks

Soon after this conversation we had a bason & a spoon brought us with some wild Turky & broth, & some cakes in it of wheat flour—prepared by our Interpreter, & we had a comfortable breakfast.—

But it was scarcely light when one of the public speakers mounted a log near the south-East corner of the village, & began the morning service with a loud voice in thanksgiving to the great spirit—he continued his discourse for near an

hour—the people were all in their tents, some at the distance of 10, 20, & 30 rods yet they could all distinctly hear & gave a solemn & audable assent which sounded from *tent* to *tent* at every pause— During the scene we stood in his view at the end of the meeting house & the ground being a little rising we had a fair prospect of the whole village & the vast open plain or *Priara* to the South & East & for the distance of 3 miles which looks over the great fort towards the North.—It felt as if we were among the tribes of the children of Israel on their march through the wilderness to Canaan— their uneffected zeal for the increase of the work, & ardent desires for the salvation of their unbelieving Kindred—their willingness to undergo hunger, fatique, & hard labour to make preparation to receive & accomodate all that would come to hear the truth—the high expectations they had of thousands flocking down among them in the summer to hear the prophet, & the great burden & concern they felt that they might believe & obey the truth—these considerations were truly affecting not so much from their words or from what could be seen, as from the spirit which we felt among them—While SKE LAH WAY, hailed the opening day with loud aspirations of gratitude to the *great spirit* & encouraged the obedient followers of divine light to persevere, It seemed, if ever the saying of the prophet Habbakkub was fulfilled it was on that ground, "I saw the tents of Cushan in affliction, & the curtains of the land of Midian did tremble." Ten thousand people might have distinctly understood him & his voice might have been heard over the plains for the distance of at least two miles.

The afflictions & mortification that this people were under for the truth's sake appeared to be designed to prepare for supplanting the kingdom of darkness among those wild & barbarous nations at the appearance of which there was evidently great fear & trembling among the tribes.—

After these things we wrote a letter to the prophet & delivered it to the Interpreter which was as follows.—

To LAL LA WA SHE KAH the Shawneese prophet & brothers—By GEORGE BLUE JACKET Interpreter. At the plains of the great-fort by the River *Kitwathaka*

Brother, We have heard strange things of you & your people—Some red men & some white men say bad things of you, but it is because they do not understand the work of the spirit which is among you, we understand it, & have come to see you because we know it is the work of the good spirit.—

Brother, we are free to let you know what srange things the *good spirit* has done for us, & we desire that you also would be free—We believe the *bad spirit* that once made us wicked & that made you wicked will now be done away, & the *great good spirit* will have a great & good people to serve him that will all be united in *one*—& them that will not put away their wicked ways the *great spirit* will destroy them from the earth, & that the *good people* will have it for the *great spirit* has promised it to them long ago.—

Brother, we believe that the same *good spirit* is working in you & in us, which has told us how to put away all wicked ways & be a *good people* & we have come to encourage you & help you.—

Brother, Be assured that we love that *good spirit* which is working among you & that we are your nearest & best friends, & we hope that we shall have a right understanding of each other— We are glad to see you so careful about receiving ministers of the *white people*—many of them are wicked & do not know the work of the *good spirit,* & will speak against it in us & in you—The true work of the *good spirit* which saves us from wicked ways is very *foolish* to the ministers of this world, & to all wicked people—We are not of them.

We will not believe any bad thing people say of you, & we hope you will not believe any thing they say against us.

Brother, we feel very free that some of your Chiefs should come & see what the *good spirit* is doing among us—it may be a help to you; & we hope the *good spirit* will tell you what to do, & will shew you the right way & bless you, for all power is in the hands of that *great & good spirit.*

Near the Great fort	David Darrow
24th 3d month	Benjamin S. Youngs
1807	Richard McNemar

After we had written this letter & delivered it to *George* our Interpreter, we asked the privelege of going into their meeting house which was readily granted, but they said they did not commonly allow white people to go in because they would mock.—We went in & view'd it & could not have felt more solemn in viewing throughout the

temple of Solomon with all its magnificence & glory. It was 150 feet in length from East to West & 34 in bredth—this immense building was raised upon three rows of large hew'd posts set in the ground—the middle row contained ten posts elevevated to a proper height to form the roof— large hew'd beams extending from post to post, supporting the rafters which were also hew'd & neatly covered with lath & clapboards, & the whole stockaded round with split & hew'd plank set in the ground & extending upwards to the foot of the rafters—even the weight poles on the roof were neatly hew'd & everything look'd new & white—there were four doors to the house—one at the middle of each end—& one at the middle of each side—& on each side of the house within were hew'd logs for seats from end to end—there was no floor laid to the house, but the ground was beaten hard & level as the floor of an house & everything very neat & clean & in good order—in the N.E. & S.W. corners were two piles of wood split & neatly piled up, & in the middle of the house between the posts of the middle row were two trammels, which appeared designed for cooking. The whole order & appearance of things, but perticularly the spirit we felt there brought on our minds a very striking & solemn sence of what God was doing in the earth & the world knew it not—& although both ministers & people would come & see & hear yet they can neither discern nor comprehend it—but we are all of them by these poor *Shawneese* both discerned & comprehended.

We enquired if they offered any kind of sacrafice to the *great spirit?* they answered in the negative, & said the provisions that were cook'd in the meeting house were for *union* & *feasts* of *love,* in which they all eat together as one family.

We now felt at liberty to depart—& beyond our expectations were fully satisfied in finding such a real work of God among a noble likely & resolute people. At about 10 o'clock we set out to return in a cold snow & rain storm which lasted abt. 3 hours.

On our return homeward several things struck our minds with a pleasing reflection—that our journey had been directed by a wise providence, in going first to the Stony creek Indians for had we gone directly to the *Shawneese* at the great fort we could not have received the least communication from them by word or letter, tho' they were nearly 200 in number of adult persons—PETER

CORNSTALK the only one that could talk English was gone from home trading among the whites, & had but just returned perhaps within 48 hours of the time we got there—& what was still more extraordinary—GEORGE BLUEJACKET the best Interpreter & who could read English had also but just come 200 miles from *Detroit* & was immediately going to return. It appeared as though he had been sent on purpose. George is 26 years old a likely sensible man—has a wife & two children & carries on farming at *Detroit* where he got his learning—He was a long time Interpreter with the presbyterian missionaries among the Indian tribes, he treated us with great kindness—there are numbers at *Detroit* who believe in the prophet.—And likewise when we came to the Stony Creek Indians Interpreters were there provided by providence, in the very hour that we wanted them—for among them all not one could speak English except the Chief called Capt John —before mentioned who was gone a hunting, & did not return till near night—so that in the natural course of things we must have returned without one sentence of verbal communication or inteligence, had not things been directed just as they were. And by going first to these Stony Creek Indians we not only discovered their state but also that of other tribes & their spirit of opposition & evil repute against the work of God among the *Shawneese*—Also our traveling through the woods & laying out at nights proved a peculiar blessing to *us* & thereby we found ourselves much better prepared to be among the *Shawneese* than if we had went directly there. Another circumstance appeared Singular, as we intented to keep our way & business conceal'd from the wicked had we come one hour sooner our way if not our business would certainly have been discovered by five wicked men who were coming towards us from the great fort & had taken a path that led out of our trace to their left hand perhaps not 15 minutes before we came along so yt we passed on undiscovered by any. Note these men had went from the frontier Settlements & staid some time among ye Indians in order to find out whether they were preparing for war or not—This we found out on our return homeward. It seemed all agreed they were for peace. But besides these reflections one was more weighty & striking than all the rest, & that was a reflection on the late preparitory & wonderful work of God which had been in *Ken-*

tucky & *Ohio*. In all places where the great & powerful camp meetings were held—2 & 3 & 4 & 5 & 6 years ago, we now see their great *stand*s for preaching & their solemn places of worship which were once awful with the presence of God—lay desolate—places resembling the habitation of owls & satyres—a solemn & striking fact, evident throughout the land wherever those great campmeetings have been.

But here we turn our eyes towards the wilderness & we see it begin to bud & blossom as the rose & the solotary places beginning to be glad—Here we see the work of God preparing the heathen nations to be his people that were not his people— Here we see the poor Indians zealously engaged in confessing & forsaking all their sins & wicked ways —a thing which none of the *Antichristians* with all their high professions ever yet did!—& here we see them erecting places for the worship of the *Great spirit* that smile with his presence—& the very air filled with his fear & a solemn sence of eternal things—& this light shines in darkness & the darkness comprehends it not.

A question may here arise, How came that great work of God which was manifest in the revival to be lost? & how is it now among the Indians? To which it is observed that the great work which God wrought in Kentucky & Ohio etc during the late revival, is not lost—but in many living witnesses has already accomplished that whereunto it was sent, & in the end brought Salvation to those who had sincerely prayed for it— from their hearts—But when the gospel came to this land two years ago this spring, the greater part of the *revivalers* rejected it & from thenceforth they began to loose their life & power—& from that very spring the power & operation of the holy spirit was taken from them by degrees as they rejected the gospel & was given to the Heathen, that they should bring forth the fruits of it, & In them was expressly fulfilled yt which was spoken by the holy Spirit—saying "It was necessary that the word of God should first have been spoken to you, but seeing ye put it from you & judge yourselves unworthy of everlasting life, lo, we turn to the Gentiles," & both in them & in those who receive the gospel God will most surely accomplish the full purpose of all his work whereunto he sends it, & in its accomplishment will yet make the nations tremble & all faces turn pale. for so hath the Lord commanded *us* saying, ["]I have set thee a light [to] ye Gentiles yt thou shouldest be for salvation unto ye ends of the earth."

After we had left the great fort & came to the camping ground where we had staid the night before last, we found a fire just kindled with the wood which we had gathered & left there—we found not the least appearance or probability that any person had lately been there—after warming & refreshing ourselves we rode on & lodged that night at a settlement abt. 22 miles N.W. by N from *Dayton*—The next day we rode to *Dayton* & from thence 5 miles S.E. by E. to the believers at *Beulah* where the next evening we held meeting at JOHN PATTERSONS.

The next day being 6.27.3[18] we returned home in very pleasant weather, by the way of Waynesville, on the Little Miami a settlement of a kind of *Quakers*—we came home about sun set having been a rout of about 260 miles in eleven days— besides our labours & traveling a great part of the time through the woods without any track or mark but the Sun—& find the distance from Turtle Creek near Lebanon to the *Shawneese* Indians at the *great fort* called *Greenville* fort to be about 70 miles the nearest way—to the North West by North.

[18] March 27, the sixth day of the week.

The Pewter of William Will: A Checklist

Suzanne Hamilton

WILLIAM WILL (1742–1798) has long been recognized as the outstanding pewterer of eighteenth-century America. Ledlie I. Laughlin in his authoritative *Pewter in America* found in Will's products "a distinction and an originality not found thus far in the pewter of any other American maker."[1] Fine workmanship, ambitious designs, and an impressive variety of forms contribute to the high esteem in which this craftsman is held.

Born in Nieuwied, a city on the Rhine near Koblenz, in 1742, William Will was the fourth son of a pewterer. The family came to America in 1752 and settled in New York City where his brother Henry achieved eminence in the father's trade. Exactly how William came to settle in Philadelphia is uncertain. Possibly he came with his brother Philip who advertised as a pewterer in Philadelphia in 1763.[2] The following year William Will was married, and it is the record of his marriage that has come to be used as the starting date for his career.[3]

In addition to his career as one of the most productive pewterers in eighteenth-century America, Will served the community as overseer of the

poor, sheriff of the city and county of Philadelphia, and representative to the General Assembly. During the Revolutionary War he was entrusted with responsibility for property confiscated from those who refused to support the American cause. He formed his own company of militia and held commands in the Continental Army up to regimental level. Throughout his active life he invested in real estate, including eight properties in the city and the adjoining Liberties as well as a 400-acre plot in Huntingdon County.[4] In 1789 he declared himself bankrupt and over the next two years much of his property was sold at sheriff's sales to pay his debts. Despite these difficulties he retained the respect of the community as indicated by the following notice of his death published in a local newspaper, February 14, 1798.

On Saturday morning departed this life after a lingering indisposition which he bore with christian fortitude, Colonel William Will, in the 56th year of his age; a native of the city of Nieuwidt in Germany; and on Monday his remains were interred in the burial ground of the German reformed congregation attended by the members of the German incorporated society, and a very large number of respectable citizens.[5]

Laughlin estimated the surviving number of pieces made by Will at about three dozen, and he considered pewter by this maker to be extremely rare. Thanks to the untiring efforts of collectors and dealers over the past thirty years, the number

[1] Ledlie I. Laughlin, *Pewter in America: Its Makers and Their Marks* (Barre, Mass.: Barre Publishers, 1969), 2:54. First published in two volumes (Boston: Houghton Mifflin Co., 1940), the 1969 edition is bound as one volume but the pagination of the 1940 edition is preserved.

[2] *Staatsbote* (Philadelphia), Sept. 19, 1763. For more biographical information on William Will see Laughlin, *Pewter in America*, 2:51–55; for the Wills of New York, 2:12–17.

[3] Records of the First (German) Reformed Church of Philadelphia, III, 2098, Collections of the Genealogical Society of Pennsylvania, the Historical Society of Pennsylvania, Philadelphia, Pa.

[4] Suzanne Hamilton, "William Will, Pewterer: His Life and His Work, 1742–1798" (M.A. diss., University of Delaware, 1967), p. 21. Additional details on Will's land holdings as well as many details of his life not included in Laughlin's biographical sketch are included in this work.

[5] *Poulson's American Daily Advertiser* (Philadelphia), Feb. 14, 1798.

is now approaching two hundred. Of the 197 pieces listed in the checklist, 128 are marked with one or more of Will's touches. The remaining pieces are attributed on the basis of association with marked pieces, or because their contours suggest that they came from the same molds as pieces bearing Will's marks.

An example of attribution by association is the Aaronsburg communion service which consists of flagon, ewer, chalice, and baptismal bowl. Only the bowl is marked, but it is assumed that the other pieces were ordered from Will at the same time. All pieces are of equally fine quality and most authorities agree they came from the same shop. The Aaronsburg service is still owned by the church to which it was given by a Jewish donor in a burst of ecumenical fervor 180 years ago. Since its discovery by Paul Auman in the late forties, it has become a touchstone for many attributions to Will.[6]

The other method of attribution, based on similarity of profiles, is possible because of the peculiar technology of the craft. Unlike the silversmith who created hollowware by hammering a disc of silver, and who was at least theoretically free to make any shape he wished, the pewterer was limited by his molds. The better molds were made of brass and were expensive. There was every incentive for the pewterer to limit the number of shapes he could cast; the test of his ingenuity lay in discovering multiple uses for each shape. Thus the domed lid of a tankard also served as the base of a chalice, and on close examination it appears that both came from the same mold.[7] The interchangeability of parts was the pewterer's stock in trade. Clever sleuthing by modern collectors has revealed the extent of the practice and has aided enormously in identifying makers of unmarked pewter.

Will employed an astonishing variety of marks. Six marks contain his name or initials, while four others are identified as his because they at times appear in combination with the name marks. It is customary in writing about American pewter to specify maker's marks according to the ap-

propriate figure number for that mark in Laughlin's *Pewter in America*.[8] The following list gives the marks illustrated in this article with their Laughlin numbers.

Fig. 1	Wᵐ WILL / PHILADEL/PHIA	Laughlin 534
Fig. 2	Lamb and dove in oval	Laughlin 535
	Crowned x	—
Fig. 3	Wᵐ WILL / PHILADELPHIA in scrolls	Laughlin 537
Fig. 4	Crowned x	—
	Wᵐ WILL	Laughlin 539
	Scales	Laughlin 538
Fig. 5	Eagle in oval	Laughlin 540
Fig. 6	ww in two concentric circles	Laughlin 541
Fig. 7	Wᵐ WILL / PHILA=/DELPHIA	Laughlin 542
Fig. 8	Four pseudo-hallmarks	Laughlin 536

Laughlin identifies variants of some marks, such as the ww mark without the two concentric circles, but the variants appear to be poor impressions of the same mark and are not counted in the total. The so-called crowned x is actually an x with five dots above it. While this is a conventional way to describe this mark, it should not be confused with similar marks used by other makers where the representation of a crown appears over the letter. The crowned x and scales may have been used by Will to suggest the quality marks used traditionally by English pewterers. More curious are the four small touches consisting of a lion rampant, initials IC (or possibly TC), a rosette, and a fleur-de-lys. These marks which always appear together in the order mentioned are referred to in the checklist as four pseudo-hallmarks.

Dating of individual pieces in the checklist is based on one of four methods. Will's working dates, 1764–1798, are given where there is no reliable evidence for a narrower range. Those pieces exhibiting characteristics of the neo-classical style are arbitrarily dated 1785–1798. Thus, coffeepots and other forms with urn shaped bodies and all pieces with beaded decoration are assigned to this

---

[6] Paul M. Auman, "New Finds in Old Pewter by William Will: The Aaronsburg Communion Service," *Antiques* 57, no. 4 (Apr. 1950) : 274–75.

[7] Charles V. Swain, "Interchangeable Parts in Early American Pewter," *Antiques* 83, no. 2 (Feb. 1963) : 212–13, fig. 3.

[8] Plates LXV and LXVI, figures 534–42a.

FIG. 1. William Will, Mark: wᵐ WILL / PHILADEL/PHIA (Laughlin 534) on hot water plate. Pewter. (Winterthur 58.658.)

FIG. 2. Will, Marks: Lamb and dove in oval (Laughlin 535) and crowned x on hot water plate. Pewter. (Winterthur 58.658.)

FIG. 3. Will, Mark: wᵐ WILL / PHILADELPHIA in scrolls (Laughlin 537) on plate. Pewter. (Winterthur 53.26.)

FIG. 4. Will, Marks: Crowned x, wᵐ WILL (Laughlin 539), and scales (Laughlin 538) on hot water plate. Pewter. (Winterthur 54.97.2.)

FIG. 5. Will, Mark: Eagle in oval (Laughlin 540) on plate. Pewter. (Winterthur 53.26.)

FIG. 6. Will, Mark: ww in two concentric circles (Laughlin 541) on bedpan. Pewter. (Winterthur 61.103.)

FIG. 7. Will, Mark: wᵐ WILL / PHILA-/DELPHIA (Laughlin 542) on teapot. Pewter. (Winterthur 58.656.)

FIG. 8. Will, Pseudo-hallmarks (Laughlin 536) on plate. Pewter. (Winterthur 58.659.)

date range. The eagle mark suggests a still narrower date range, not only because it is an eagle in combination with stars, but because it has in the inscription the word "FEDERAL." Pieces with this mark are presumed to have been made between the time of the Constitutional Convention (1787) and Will's death (1798). Lastly, the Aaronsburg communion service cannot have been made before 1789 because the church did not exist before that date.[9]

Creation of the checklist was possible mainly through the cooperation of collectors and museum curators who furnished the information. Inevitably, however, information acquired from such a variety of sources varied in its degree of completeness; this explains why some pieces are better described than others. Verification of recent ownership was sought wherever possible. Unfortu-

nately, a few pieces published in earlier years cannot be located. Such pieces are included in the checklist only if there is little likelihood of duplication.

Bibliographical references in the checklist cite the source of information concerning the specific piece mentioned. These citations include letters from owners or museum curators, articles, books, and catalogues. Complete facts of publication accompany references to articles and catalogues; the facts of publication are not repeated in references to Laughlin, Kerfoot, and Myers.[10] Since the author had direct access to the pewter in the Winterthur Museum and to the registration files of that institution, no citation appears in the checklist.

[9] Auman, "New Finds in Old Pewter," p. 275.

[10] Laughlin, *Pewter in America;* J. B. Kerfoot, *American Pewter* (Boston and New York: Houghton Mifflin Co., 1942) ; Louis G. Myers, *Some Notes on American Pewterers* (Garden City, N.Y.: The Country Life Press, 1926) .

Checklist

1. Basin
   Circular form with flat bottom and flared sides; pint capacity. Diam. 6⅜″
   Mark: Initials ww (Laughlin 541a)
   Date: 1764–1798
   Owner: The Henry Francis du Pont Winterthur Museum (58.651) ; ex coll. Mr. and Mrs. Richard S. Quigley

2. Basin
   Circular form with flared sides and molded rim; incised circle on bowl. Diam. 6⁵⁄₁₆″
   Mark: Lamb and dove in oval (Laughlin 535)
   Date: 1764–1798
   Owner: The Brooklyn Museum (45.10–192), Museum Purchase, John W. Poole Collection
   Bibliography: Robert Hendrick to author, Feb. 15, 1967

3. Basin
   Diam. 6⁵⁄₁₆″
   Mark: wᵐ WILL / PHILADELPHIA in scrolls (Laughlin 537)
   Date: 1764–1798

   Owner: Yale University Art Gallery, Mabel Brady Garvan Collection (1931.207)
   Bibliography: Graham Hood, *American Pewter: Garvan and Other Collections at Yale* (New Haven: Yale University Art Gallery, 1965) , no. 191

4. Basin
   Diam. 6″
   Mark: Initials ww (Laughlin 541a)
   Date: 1764–1798
   Owner: Mr. and Mrs. George A. Jenckes
   Bibliography: Mrs. George A. Jenckes to author, Nov. 9, 1966

5. Baptismal bowl
   Circular bowl with straight sides and flattened rim; pedestal base. Diam. 8¾″, H. 4⅛″
   Mark: Lamb and dove in oval and wᵐ WILL / PHILADEL=/PHIA (Laughlin 534, 535a)
   Date: 1764–1798
   Owner: Hershey Museum
   Bibliography: John J. Evans, Jr., "Some Pewter by William Will," *Antiques* 61, no. 2 (Feb. 1952) : 178–79; John F. Ruckman to author, July 25, 1964

6. Baptismal bowl (Fig. 9)

Circular bowl with a narrow, flat rim; incised circle inside bowl; inscription engraved in roman capitals: DAS GESCHENKE / ZU DENEN / DEUTSCHEN GEMEINDEN / IN ARENSBURG / VON ARON LEVY [the gift of Aaron Levy to the German congregations in Aaronsburg]. Diam. 10¹⁵⁄₁₆″

Mark: Eagle in oval struck twice and wᵐ WILL / PHILADELPHIA in scrolls (Laughlin 540 and 537). Part of Aaronsburg communion service which consists of flagon, ewer, chalice, and baptismal bowl. The bowl is the only marked piece in the service.

Date: 1789–1798

Owner: Salem Lutheran Church, Aaronsburg, Pennsylvania

Bibliography: Paul M. Auman, "New Finds in Old Pewter by William Will: The Aaronsburg Communion Service," *Antiques* 57, no. 4 (Apr. 1950): 274–75

7. Bedpan

Circular pan with flat bottom and rolled sides with circular opening in center; straight handle screwed into side; initials WLS engraved on side. Diam. 11⅜″, H. 4¼″

Mark: Initials WW in two concentric circles (Laughlin 541)

Date: 1764–1798

Owner: The Henry Francis du Pont Winterthur Museum (61.103)

8. Chalices (2)

Plain cup supported by lightly turned baluster stem on stepped base. H. 8⅛″

Mark: None. Part of Oxford communion service which consists of two chalices, two English plates and a flagon (No. 49) bearing Will's mark. The chalices are almost identical to No. 10.

Date: 1764–1798

Owner: Presbyterian Historical Society; ex

FIG. 9. Will, Aaronsburg communion service. Philadelphia, Pa., 1789–1798. Pewter; H. (ewer) 10¾″, H. (chalice) 7¹⁵⁄₁₆″, H. (flagon) 13¹¹⁄₁₆″, Diam. (baptismal bowl) 10¹⁵⁄₁₆″. (Salem Lutheran Church, Aaronsburg, Pa.: Photo, Lane Studio.)

coll. Presbyterian Church, Oxford, Pennsylvania

Bibliography: Ledlie I. Laughlin, "The Pewter Communion Services of the Presbyterian Historical Society," *Journal of Presbyterian History* 44, no. 2 (June 1966): 83–88, fig. 2

9. Chalices (2)

Plain cup supported by lightly turned baluster stem on stepped base. H. 8″

Mark: None. The chalices were found with a flagon (No. 50) bearing Will's mark; they are almost identical to No. 10.

Date: 1764–1798

Owner: Unknown; ex coll. Mrs. James H. Krom

Bibliography: Ledlie I. Laughlin, *Pewter in America,* I, plate XXXVI, fig. 240; II, p. 54

10. Chalice

Plain cup supported by lightly turned baluster stem on stepped base. H. 8″

Mark: None. Base of chalice identical to cover of tankard (No. 152) bearing Will's mark; overall it is nearly identical to chalices 8 and 9.

Date: 1764–1798

Owner: Charles V. Swain; ex coll. John F. Ruckman

Bibliography: Charles V. Swain, "Interchangeable Parts in Early American Pewter," *Antiques* 83, no. 2 (Feb. 1963): 221–213, fig. 3; Charles V. Swain to author, Nov. 25, 1966.

11. Chalice (Fig. 9)

Cup supported by baluster stem with large knop and stepped base; inscription engraved in roman capitals on side of cup: DAS GESCHENKE / ZU DENEN / DEUTSCHEN GEMEINDEN / IN ARENSBURG / VON ARON LEVY [the gift of Aaron Levy to the German Congregations in Aaronsburg]. H. 7¹⁵⁄₁₆″

Mark: None. Part of Aaronsburg communion service which consists of flagon, ewer, chalice and baptismal bowl. Only the bowl is marked, but Laughlin has related components of the other pieces to documented examples of Will's work.

Date: 1789–1798

Owner: Salem Lutheran Church, Aaronsburg, Pennsylvania

FIG. 10. Will, Chalice. Philadelphia, Pa., 1764–98. Pewter; H. 7⅞″. (Winterthur 58.24.)

Bibliography: Paul M. Auman, "New Finds in Old Pewter by William Will: The Aaronsburg Communion Service," *Antiques* 57, no. 4 (Apr. 1950): 274–75

12. Chalice (Fig. 10)

Cup supported by large baluster stem with large knop and stepped base; engraved inscription on side of cup in fraktur: ZUR EHRE GOTTES / GESTIFFTET VON / CATHARINA ELISABETHA / MORRIN [In honor of God the gift of Catherine Elisabeth Morrin] within a flaming heart. H. 7⅞″

Mark: None. Similar to chalice in Aaronsburg communion service (No. 11)

Date: 1764–1798
Owner: The Henry Francis du Pont Winterthur Museum (58.24), purchased with
funds given by Joseph France; ex coll. St.
Peter's Lutheran Church, Freeburg, Pennsylvania

13. Chalice
Plain cup supported by baluster stem with
large knop and stepped base. H. 7¹³⁄₁₆″
Mark: None. Similar to chalice in Aaronsburg
communion service (No. 11)
Date: 1764–1798
Owner: Robert Mallory III
Bibliography: Robert Mallory III, "An Amer-
ican Pewter Collection," *Antiques* 72, no. 1
(July 1957): 40–41; John F. Ruckman to
author, July 25, 1964

14. Chalice
Plain cup supported by baluster stem with
large knop and stepped base; beading
around knop and base. H. 7¹⁵⁄₁₆″
Mark: None. Similar to chalice in Aaronsburg
communion service (No. 11)
Date: 1785–1798
Owner: Robert Mallory III
Bibliography: Robert Mallory III, "An Amer-
ican Pewter Collection," *Antiques* 72, no. 1
(July 1957): 40–41; John F. Ruckman to
author, July 25, 1964

15. Chalice
Plain cup supported by baluster stem with
large knop and stepped base with beading.
H. 7¾″, Diam. (top) 3½″, (base) 4 ⁷⁄₁₆″
Mark: None. Similar to chalice in Aaronsburg
communion service (No. 11)
Date: 1785–1798
Owner: Charles V. Swain; ex coll. John F.
Ruckman
Bibliography: Charles V. Swain, "Interchange-
able Parts in Early American Pewter," *An-
tiques* 83, no. 2 (Feb. 1963): 212–13, fig. 2;
Charles V. Swain to author, Nov. 25, 1966

16. Chalice
Plain cup supported by baluster stem with
large knop and stepped base. H. 7⅞″, Diam.
(top) 3½″, Diam. (base) 3⅝″
Mark: None. Similar to chalice in Aaronsburg
communion service (No. 11)
Date: 1764–1798

Owner: Charles V. Swain; ex coll. John F.
Ruckman
Bibliography: Charles V. Swain, "Interchange-
able Parts in Early American Pewter," *An-
tiques* 83, no. 2 (Feb. 1963): 212–13, fig. 1;
Charles V. Swain to author, Nov. 25, 1966

17. Coffeepot
Urn shaped body raised on circular pedestal;
high incurved neck; hinged, high-domed lid
with finial; S-curved spout opposite C-
curved wooden handle; beading around
pedestal, body and lid. H. 15¾″
Mark: Initials ww in two concentric circles
(Laughlin 541)
Date: 1785–1798
Owner: James B. Laughlin; ex coll. Ledlie I.
Laughlin
Bibliography: Ledlie I. Laughlin, *Pewter in
America,* I, plate XXVII; II, p. 54; Ledlie I.
Laughlin to author, July 1, 1970

18. Coffeepot
Urn shaped body raised on circular pedestal;
high incurved neck; hinged, high-domed lid
with finial; S-shaped spout opposite wooden
handle; beading. H. 15¾″
Mark: Probably marked but base is corroded.
Nearly identical to No. 17
Date: 1785–1798
Owner: Robert M. Laughlin; ex coll. Ledlie I.
Laughlin
Bibliography: Ledlie I. Laughlin to author,
July 1, 1970

19. Coffeepot
Urn shaped body raised on circular pedestal;
high incurved neck; hinged, high-domed lid
with finial; S-curved spout opposite C-
curved wooden handle; beading around
pedestal, body, and lid. H. 15⁹⁄₁₆″
Mark: Initials ww (Laughlin 541a)
Date: 1785–1798
Owner: The Henry Francis du Pont Winterthur Museum (55.624); ex coll. Mr. and
Mrs. Richard S. Quigley

20. Coffeepot (Fig. 11)
Urn shaped body raised on circular pedestal
supported by square base; high incurved
neck; hinged, high-domed lid with finial;
S-curved spout with cast ornament opposite
double scroll wooden handle; beading

FIG. 11. Will, Coffeepot. Philadelphia, Pa., 1785–98. Pewter; H. 15⅞″. (Winterthur 54.33.)

around pedestal, body, and lid. H. 15⅞″
Mark: Wᵐ WILL / PHILA=/DELPHIA and LONDON
  (Laughlin 542)
Date: 1785–1798
Owner: The Henry Francis du Pont Winter-
  thur Museum (54.33)

21. Coffeepot
[unknown shape] H. 15¾″
Mark: Initials ww in two concentric circles
  (Laughlin 541)
Date 1785–1798
Owner: Robert Mallory III
Bibliography: John F. Ruckman to author,
  July 25, 1964

22. Creamer
Pear-shaped body on three feet; double scroll
  handle; flaring lip. H. 3¹¹⁄₁₆″
Mark: Crowned x
Date: 1764–1798
Owner: Charles V. Swain
Bibliography: Charles V. Swain to author,
  Nov. 25, 1966

23. Creamer
Pear-shaped body on three feet; double scroll
  handle; flaring lip. H. 3¹¹⁄₁₆″
Mark: Crowned x
Date: 1764–1798
Owner: Charles V. Swain; ex coll. John F.
  Ruckman
Bibliography: Charles V. Swain to author,
  Nov. 25, 1966

24. Creamer
Pear-shaped body on three feet
Mark: Crowned x
Date: 1764–1798
Owner: Mrs. George A. Jenckes
Bibliography: Mrs. George A. Jenckes to au-
  thor, Nov. 9, 1966

25. Creamer (Fig. 12)
Pear-shaped body on three horse-hoof feet; sin-
  gle scroll handle. H. 4¼″
Mark: Crowned x
Date: 1764–1798
Owner: The Henry Francis du Pont Winter-
  thur Museum (58.654)

26. Creamer (Fig. 12)
Pear-shaped body on three feet; double scroll
  handle. H. 3¹³⁄₁₆″
Mark: Crowned x
Date: 1764–1798
Owner: The Henry Francis du Pont Winter-
  thur Museum (55.48.26), gift of Charles K.
  Davis; ex coll. Philip Platt

27. Creamer
Pedestal base; double scroll handle; beading
  on base. H. 4½″
Mark: None. Attribution based on similarity
  of lower body and base profile to salts No.
  104
Date: 1785–1798
Owner: John H. McMurray
Bibliography: Charles V. Swain, "Interchange-
  able Parts in Early American Pewter," *An-
  tiques* 83, no. 2 (Feb. 1963): 212–13, fig. 1;
  John H. McMurray to author, Dec. 6, 1966

28. Creamer (Fig. 13)
Pedestal base; double scroll handle. H. (to
  lowest point on rim) 4″
Mark: None. Nearly identical to No. 27
Date: 1785–1798
Owner: John J. Evans, Jr.

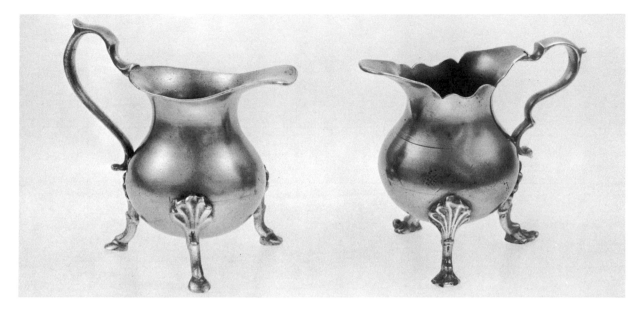

FIG. 12. Will, Creamers. Philadelphia, Pa., 1764–98. Pewter; H. (left) 4¼″, (right) 3³⁄₁₆″. (Winterthur 58.654, 55.48.26.)

FIG. 13. Will, Creamer. Philadelphia, Pa., 1785–98. Pewter; H. 4″. (Collection of John J. Evans, Jr.: Photo, Winterthur.)

29. Creamer
    Pedestal base; double scroll handle. H. (to top of handle) 4⅛″
    Mark: None. Attribution based on similarity to No. 27
    Date: 1764–1798
    Owner: Mrs. Peter Woodbury
    Bibliography: *Pewter in America 1650–1900* (Manchester, New Hampshire: The Currier Gallery of Art, 1968), no. 2

30. Creamer
    Pedestal base; double scroll handle; beading. H. 5⁷⁄₁₆″
    Mark: None. Attribution based on similarity to No. 27
    Date: 1785–1798
    Owner: Charles V. Swain; ex coll. John F. Ruckman
    Bibliography: Charles V. Swain to author, Nov. 25, 1966

31. Creamer
    Pedestal base; scroll handle; beading. H. 4¼″
    Mark: None. Attribution based on similarity to No. 27
    Date: 1785–1798
    Owner: Lola S. Reed
    Bibliography: Lola S. Reed to author, Dec. 6, 1966

32. Creamer
    Pedestal base; scroll handle; beading. H. 4⁷⁄₁₆″
    Mark: None. Attribution based on similarity to No. 27
    Date: 1785–1798
    Owner: Lola S. Reed
    Bibliography: Lola S. Reed to author, Dec. 6, 1966

33. Creamer
    Pedestal base; double scroll handle. H. 4½″
    Mark: None. Attribution based on similarity to No. 27
    Date: 1764–1798
    Owner: The Detroit Institute of Arts
    Bibliography: Graham Hood to author, June 3, 1970

34. Church cups (2)
    Two-handled cup with midband and stepped pedestal base; beading around base, midband and rim; heavy cast double C-scroll handles with acanthus leaf decoration. H. 5⅜″
    Mark: None. Tradition of having been purchased with patens (No. 74) bearing Will's mark
    Date: 1785–1798
    Owner: Presbyterian Historical Society; ex coll. Presbyterian Church, Lost Creek, Pennsylvania
    Bibliography: Ledlie I. Laughlin, "The Pewter Communion Services of the Presbyterian Historical Society," *Journal of Presbyterian History* 44, no. 2 (June 1966) : 83–88, fig. 1; Ledlie I. Laughlin to author, Nov. 23, 1966

35. Dish (Fig. 14)
    Circular form; narrow rim with beaded edge. Diam. 10⅝″
    Mark: Eagle in oval struck twice and wᵐ WILL / PHILADELPHIA in scrolls (Laughlin 540 and 537)
    Date: 1787–1798
    Owner: The Henry Francis du Pont Winterthur Museum (53.43)

36. Dish
    Circular form. Diam. 12″
    Mark: wᵐ WILL / PHILADELPHIA in scrolls (Laughlin 537)
    Date: 1764–1798
    Owner: Mrs. George A. Jenckes
    Bibliography: Mrs. George A. Jenckes to author, Nov. 9, 1966

37. Dish
    Circular form; molded edge; incised circle inside booge. Diam. 12⅛″
    Mark: Eagle in oval struck twice and wᵐ WILL / PHILADELPHIA in scrolls (Laughlin 540, 537)
    Date: 1787–1798
    Owner: The Metropolitan Museum of Art (43.162.42), Gift of Joseph France
    Bibliography: Mary Glaze to author, Nov. 15, 1966

38. Dish
    Circular form; hammered booge. Diam. 12¼″
    Mark: Eagle in oval struck twice and wᵐ WILL / PHILADELPHIA in scrolls (Laughlin 540, 537)
    Date: 1787–1798
    Owner: John H. McMurray
    Bibliography: John H. McMurray to author, Dec. 6, 1966

39. Dish
    Circular form; rim with rolled edge. Diam. 13″
    Mark: Crowned x and four pseudo-hallmarks, lamb and dove in oval struck twice (Laughlin 535, 536)
    Date: 1764–1798
    Owner: J. Lawrence Cummings (1937)

FIG. 14. Will, Dish. Philadelphia, Pa., 1787–98. Pewter; Diam. 10⅝″. (Winterthur 53.43.)

Bibliography: "The Editor's Attic: Another William Will Pewter Mark," *Antiques* 32, no. 5 (Nov. 1937) : 229

40. Dish

Circular form. Diam. 16¼″

Mark: Lamb and dove in oval, wᵐ WILL / PHILADEL/PHIA and four pseudo-hallmarks (Laughlin 535, 534, 536)

Date: 1764–1798

Owner: The Brooklyn Museum (45.48), Museum Purchase, Dick S. Ramsay Fund

Bibliography: Robert Hendrick to author, Feb. 15, 1967

41. Dish

Circular form; rim with rolled edge; circle incised on rim and inside booge; initials E B (?) engraved on underside. Diam. 16½″

Mark: Lamb and dove in oval struck twice, wᵐ WILL / PHILADEL/PHIA, and four pseudo-hallmarks (Laughlin 535, 534, 536)

Date: 1764–1798

Owner: The Henry Francis du Pont Winterthur Museum (58.642); ex coll. Philip G. Platt; Maurice Brix

Bibliography: Ledlie I. Laughlin, *Pewter in America,* II, Plate LXV (534, 535, 536) and p. 55

42. Ewer (Fig. 9)

Spherical body mounted between high pedestal (on circular base) and elongated neck with extended pouring lip; double scroll handle with cast acanthus leaf; beaded decoration; inscription engraved in roman capitals on body: DAS GESCHENKE / ZU DENEN / DEUTSCHEN GEMEINDEN / IN ARENSBURG / VON ARON LEVY [the gift of Aaron Levy to the German Congregations in Aaronsburg]. H. 10¾″

Mark: None. Part of Aaronsburg communion service which consists of flagon, ewer, chalice, and baptismal bowl. Only the bowl is marked, but Laughlin has related components of the other pieces to documented examples of Will's work.

Date: 1789–1798

Owner: Salem Lutheran Church, Aaronsburg, Pennsylvania

Bibliography: Paul M. Auman, "New Finds in Old Pewter by William Will: The Aaronsburg Communion Service," *Antiques* 57, no. 4 (Apr. 1950) : 274–75

43. Ewer

Pitcher-shaped body on circular stepped base; unturned pouring lip opposite single scroll handle with acanthus leaf decoration; incised lines around widest portion of body. H. 9⅞″

Mark: Crowned x and wᵐ WILL (Laughlin 539)

Sugar bowls 9 through 16 are attributed to Will on the basis of this piece. It appears the same mold was used for the lower body of the ewer as for the sugar bowls.

Date: 1764–1798

Owner: The Hershey Museum, Hershey, Pennsylvania

Bibliography: John J. Evans, Jr., "Some Pewter by William Will," *Antiques* 61, no. 2 (Feb. 1952) : 178–79

44. Flagon

Spherical body mounted between high pedestal (on circular base) and elongated neck; hinged domed lid with pierced thumbpiece; covered beak spout opposite double scroll handle H. 11¼″

Mark: None. Body same as ewer, spout same as flagon in Aaronsburg communion service

Date: 1764–1798

Owner: The Art Institute of Chicago (38.844) William Goodman Collection; ex coll. Congregational Church, Farmington, Trumbull County, Ohio

Bibliography: David A. Hanks to author, May 21, 1970

45. Flagon (Fig. 9)

Urn shaped body mounted between high pedestal (on circular base) and high incurved neck with beak spout; high-domed hinged lid with thumbpiece; single scroll handle; beaded decoration; inscription engraved on body under spout in roman capitals: DAS GESCHENKE / ZU DENEN / DEUTSCHEN GEMEINDEN / IN ARENSBURG / VON ARON LEVY [the gift of Aaron Levy to the German congregations in Aaronsburg]. H. 13¹¹⁄₁₆″

Mark: None. Part of Aaronsburg communion service which consists of flagon, ewer, chalice, and baptismal bowl. Only the bowl is marked, but Laughlin has related components of the other pieces to documented examples of Will's work.

Date: 1789–1798

Owner: Salem Lutheran Church, Aaronsburg, Pennsylvania

Bibliography: Paul M. Auman, "New Finds in Old Pewter by William Will: The Aaronsburg Communion Service," *Antiques* 57, no. 4 (Apr. 1950): 274–75

46. Flagon

Urn shaped body mounted between high pedestal (on circular base) and high incurved neck with beak spout; high-domed hinged lid with thumbpiece; single scroll handle; beaded decoration. H. 13½"

Mark: None. Almost identical to flagon in the Aaronsburg communion service (No. 45)

Date: 1785–1798

Owner: John J. Evans, Jr.

47. Flagon

Urn shaped body mounted between high pedestal (on square base) and high incurved neck with beak spout; high-domed hinged lid with thumbpiece; single scroll handle; beaded decoration; inscription engraved on side in fraktur: ZUR EHRE GOTTES GESTIFFTET / VON UNDREAS MORR=/IN DIE EVANGELISCH =/LUTHERISCHE=ZION / KIRCHE, IN PENNS= TOWNSHIP / NORTHUMBERLAND COUNTY / DEN 29TEN JULY ANNO DOM. / 1795 [In honor of God a gift from Andreas Morrin to the Evangelical Zion-Lutheran Church in Penns Township, Northumberland County, the 29th of July, Anno Domini 1795]. H. 13¾"

Mark: None. Almost identical to flagon in the Aaronsburg communion service (No. 45)

Date: 1785–1798

Owner: Charles V. Swain; ex coll. John F. Ruckman

Bibliography: John F. Ruckman to author, Jan. 18, 1965; Charles V. Swain to author, Nov. 25, 1966

48. Flagon (Fig. 15)

Urn shaped body mounted between high pedestal (on square base) and high incurved neck with beak spout; high-domed hinged lid with thumbpiece; single scroll handle; beaded decoration. H. 13¹⁵⁄₁₆"

Mark: None. Almost identical to flagon in the Aaronsburg communion service (No. 45)

Date: 1785–1798

Owner: The Henry Francis du Pont Winterthur Museum (58.649)

FIG. 15. Will, Flagon. Philadelphia, Pa., 1785–98. Pewter; H. 13¹⁵⁄₁₆". (Winterthur 58.649.)

49. Flagon

Tall tapered cylindrical body with midband and molded base; stepped and domed lid with finial and thumbpiece; double scroll handle opposite beak spout. H. 10½"

Mark: Crowned x, scales struck twice, w^m WILL (Laughlin 538, 539)

Date: 1764–1798

Owner: Presbyterian Historical Society; ex coll. Presbyterian Church, Oxford, Pennsylvania

Bibliography: Ledlie I. Laughlin, "The Pewter Communion Services of the Presbyterian Historical Society," *Journal of Presbyterian History* 44, no. 2 (June 1966): 83–88, fig. 2; Ledlie I. Laughlin to author, Nov. 23, 1966

50. Flagon

Tall tapered cylindrical body with midband and molded base; stepped and domed lid with broken finial and thumbpiece; double-scroll handle opposite beak spout. H. 9½″

Mark: Crowned x, scales struck twice, w^m WILL (Laughlin 538, 539)

Date: 1764–1798

Owner: Unknown; ex coll. Mrs. James H. Krom

Bibliography: Ledlie I. Laughlin, *Pewter in America*, I, plate XXXI, fig. 218; II, plate LXVI, figs. 538, 539 and p. 54

51. Hot water plate

Circular plate with hollow interior; hinged cover in rim; two bail handles.

Mark: Crowned x, scales struck twice and w^m WILL (Laughlin 538, 539)

Date: 1764–1798

Owner: Robert Mallory III

Bibliography: Robert Mallory III, "An American Pewter Collection," *Antiques* 72, no. 1 (July 1956) : 40–43

52. Hot water plate (Fig. 16)

Circular plate with hollow interior; hinged cover in rim; two bail handles. H. 1¾″, Diam. 9¼″

Mark: Crowned x, lamb and dove in oval struck twice, and w^m WILL / PHILADEL/PHIA (Laughlin 534, 535)

Date: 1764–1798

Owner: The Henry Francis du Pont Winterthur Museum (58.658)

FIG. 17. Will, Inkstand. Philadelphia, Pa., 1764–98. Pewter; H. 1¹⁵⁄₁₆″, Diam. (base) 3⅜″. (Winterthur 52.19.)

53. Hot water plate

Circular plate with hollow interior; hinged cover missing from rim; two bail handles. H. 1⅜″, Diam. 9¼″

Mark: Crowned x, scales struck twice, and w^m WILL (Laughlin 538, 539)

Date: 1764–1798

Owner: The Henry Francis du Pont Winterthur Museum (54.97.2)

54. Inkstand (Fig. 17)

Cylindrical form tapering slightly toward top; two pairs of incised lines around body; top has large hole in center containing glass inkwell and three equidistant smaller holes for quills. H. 1⅞″, Diam. 3¼″

Mark: Initials ww in two concentric circles (Laughlin 541)

Date: 1764–1798

Owner: The Henry Francis du Pont Winterthur Museum (52.19)

55. Ladle (Fig. 18)

Hemispherical bowl with beaded rim; long curved handle with hole in end. L. 15″

Mark: w^m WILL / PHILA=/DELPHIA (Laughlin 542)

Date: 1785–1798

Owner: The Henry Francis du Pont Winterthur Museum (58.664) ; ex coll. Mrs. Henry H. Benkard

Bibliography: Ledlie I. Laughlin, *Pewter in America*, I, plate XXVI, fig. 182

FIG. 16. Will, Hot Water Plate. Philadelphia, Pa., 1764–98. Pewter; Diam. 9¼″. (Winterthur 58.658.)

FIG. 18. Will, Ladle. Philadelphia, Pa., 1785–98. Pewter; L. 15". (Winterthur 58.664.)

56. Ladle
Hemispherical bowl with beaded rim; long
curved handle. L. 15"
Mark: w^m WILL / PHILA=/DELPHIA (Laughlin
542)
Date: 1785–1798
Owner: John J. Evans, Jr.
Bibliography: J. J. Evans, Jr., "A Flat-Top
Tankard," *Antiques* 57, no. 4 (Apr. 1950):
276–77, fig. 1

57. Ladle
Hemispherical bowl and long curved handle.
L. 10"
Mark: w^m WILL (Laughlin 539) badly worn
Date: 1764–1798
Owner: Joseph H. Kler. On permanent loan
to Smithsonian Institution
Bibliography: Joseph H. Kler to author, Nov.
7, 1966; Anne Golovin to author, Mar. 12,
1971

58. Mug
Tapered cylindrical body with handle; pint
capacity. H. 4⅜"
Mark: w^m WILL / PHILA=/DELPHIA (Laughlin
542)
Date: 1764–1798
Owner: Joseph H. Kler. On loan to New
Jersey State Museum (L61.1.10)
Bibliography: Joseph H. Kler to author, Nov.
7, 1966; James R. Mitchell to author, Mar.
11, 1971

59. Mug
Tapered cylindrical body with heavy molded
base and single scroll handle; pint capacity.
H. 4⁵⁄₁₆"
Mark: Initials ww in two concentric circles
(Laughlin 541)
Date: 1764–1798
Owner: The Henry Francis du Pont Winter-
thur Museum (58.661); ex coll. Mr. and
Mrs. Richard S. Quigley; P. G. Platt
Bibliography: The Anderson Galleries, Inc.,
New York, N.Y., Sale No. 2246, Mar. 15,
1928, No. 109 (illust.)

60. Mug
Tapered cylindrical body with molded rim
and base; scroll handle; flat thumbpiece.
H. 4½"
Mark: Scales struck twice (Laughlin 538)
Date: 1764–1798
Owner: The Metropolitan Museum of Art
(41.34.1), Gift of Mrs. J. Insley Blair
Bibliography: Mary Glaze to author, Nov.
15, 1966

61. Mug
Tapered cylindrical body with scroll handle.
H. 5⁷⁄₁₆"
Mark: w^m WILL (Laughlin 539)
Date: 1764–1798

Owner: The Philadelphia Museum of Art
(15–222)

Bibliography: Beatrice B. Wolfe to author,
Nov. 3, 1966

62. Mug (Fig. 19)
Tapered cylindrical body with single scroll
handle; quart capacity; initials H B scratched
on base. H. 5¹³⁄₁₆″
Mark: wᵐ WILL / PHILA=/DELPHIA (Laughlin
542)
Date: 1764–1798
Owner: The Henry Francis du Pont Winterthur Museum (58.662)

FIG. 19. Will, Mug. Philadelphia, Pa., 1764–98. Pewter;
H. 5¹³⁄₁₆″. (Winterthur 58.662.)

63. Mug
Tapered cylindrical body with midband; sin-
gle scroll handle; quart capacity. H. 6¹⁄₁₆″
Mark: Initials ww in two concentric circles
(Laughlin 541)
Date: 1764–1798
Owner: The Henry Francis du Pont Winter-
thur Museum (58.652)

64. Mug
Tapered cylindrical body with double scroll
handle; quart capacity. H. 5¹⁵⁄₁₆″

Mark: wᵐ WILL (Laughlin 539)
Date: 1764–1798
Owner: Museum of Fine Arts, Boston, Massa-
chusetts; ex coll. Mrs. S. S. Fitzgerald;
Dwight Blaney
Bibliography: H. H. Schnabel to author, Mar.
7, 1967

65. Mug
Tapered cylindrical body with handle; quart
capacity. H. 5⅝″
Mark: wᵐ WILL (Laughlin 539)
Date: 1764–1798
Owner: Thomas D. Williams; ex coll. Charles
K. Davis
Bibliography: Mrs. L. W. Stevenson to author,
Mar. 12, 1971

66. Mug
Tapered cylindrical body with handle; pint
capacity. H. 4½″
Mark: Scales struck twice and wᵐ WILL
(Laughlin 538, 539)
Date: 1764–1798
Owner: Wilmer Moore
Bibliography: Wilmer Moore to author, June
22, 1967

67. Mug (Fig. 20)
Bulbous body on stepped pedestal base; mid-
band and double scroll handle with acan-
thus leaf decoration; quart capacity. H.
6⁷⁄₁₆″
Mark: Initials ww in two concentric circles
(Laughlin 541)
Date: 1764–1798
Owner: The Henry Francis du Pont Winter-
thur Museum (53.27)

68. Mug
Bulbous body on stepped pedestal base; han-
dle; quart capacity. H. 6⅛″
Mark: Initials ww in two concentric circles
(Laughlin 541)
Date: 1764–1798
Owner: The Brooklyn Museum (46.191), Mu-
seum Purchase
Bibliography: Robert Hendrick to author,
Feb. 15, 1967

69. Mug
Bulbous body on stepped pedestal base; han-
dle; quart capacity. H. 6¼″
Mark: Initials ww in two concentric circles

FIG. 20. Will, Mug. Philadelphia, Pa., 1764–98. Pewter; H. 6⁷⁄₁₆″. (Winterthur 53.27.)

(Laughlin 541)
Date: 1764–1798
Owner: John J. Evans, Jr.
Bibliography: J. J. Evans, Jr., "A Flat-Top Tankard," *Antiques* 57, no. 4 (Apr. 1950): 276–77

70. Mug
Bulbous body on stepped pedestal base; midband and double scroll handle with acanthus leaf decoration; quart capacity. H. 6½″
Mark: Initials ww in two concentric circles (Laughlin 541)
Date: 1764–1798
Owner: Ledlie I. Laughlin
Bibliography: P. G. Platt, "American Pewter as a Collectible," *Antiques* 18, no. 5 (Nov. 1930): 399–403, fig. 2; Ledlie I. Laughlin, *Pewter in America,* I, plate XX, fig. 127; Ledlie I. Laughlin to author, Nov. 23, 1966

71. Mug
Bulbous body on stepped pedestal base; single scroll handle; quart capacity. H. 6⁵⁄₁₆″
Mark: Initials ww (Laughlin 541a)
Date: 1764–1798
Owner: The Henry Francis du Pont Winterthur Museum (58.663)

72. Mug
Quart capacity.
Mark: Lamb and dove in oval (Laughlin 535a)
Date: 1764–1798
Owner: Unknown; ex coll. Mrs. James H. Krom
Bibliography: Ledlie I. Laughlin, *Pewter in America,* II, plate LXVI, fig. 535a

73. Mug
Pint capacity.
Mark: wᵐ WILL / PHILADELPHIA in scrolls (Laughlin 537)
Date: 1764–1798
Owner: Mrs. George A. Jenckes
Bibliography: Mrs. George A. Jenckes to author, Nov. 9, 1966

74. Patens (2)
Circular body with shallow, slightly concave top incised with two concentric circles; beaded upper and lower rims. Diam. 6″
Mark: Crowned x and wᵐ WILL / PHILADELPHIA in scrolls (Laughlin 537). Only marked pieces in communion service consisting of one tankard, two church cups, and two patens. A unique form of paten
Date: 1764–1798
Owner: Presbyterian Historical Society; ex coll. Presbyterian Church, Lost Creek, Pennsylvania
Bibliography: Ledlie I. Laughlin, "The Pewter Communion Services of the Presbyterian Historical Society," *Journal of Presbyterian History* 44, no. 2 (June 1966): 83–88, fig. 1

75. Plate
Circular plate with broad smooth rim; incised circle inside booge. Diam 5⅝″
Mark: Crowned x and wᵐ WILL (Laughlin 539)
Date: 1764–1798
Owner: The Henry Francis du Pont Winterthur Museum (58.650); ex coll. Mr. and Mrs. Richard S. Quigley
Bibliography: Ledlie I. Laughlin, *Pewter in America,* I, plate X, fig. 51, and p. 29

76. Plate
Diam. 6⅛″
Mark: Initials ww (Laughlin 541a)
Date: 1764–1798
Owner: Robert Burkhardt

Bibliography: Robert Burkhardt to author, Nov. 5, 1966

77. Plate
Diam. 6¾6″
Mark: wᵐ WILL / PHILADELPHIA in scrolls (Laughlin 537)
Date: 1764–1798
Owner: Yale University Art Gallery, Mabel Brady Garvan Collection (1930.758)
Bibliography: Graham Hood, *American Pewter: Garvan and Other Collections at Yale* (New Haven: Yale University Art Gallery, 1965), no. 192

78. Plate
Diam. 6¼″
Mark: Scales struck twice (Laughlin 538)
Date: 1764–1798
Owner: Mrs. George A. Jenckes
Bibliography: Mrs. George A. Jenckes to author, Nov. 9, 1966

79. Plate
Circular plate with reeded rim and incised circle. Diam. 6¼″
Mark: Initials ww (Laughlin 541a)
Date: 1764–1798
Owner: The Henry Francis du Pont Winterthur Museum (52.10)

80. Plate
Circular plate with reeded rim and incised circle inside booge
Diam. 6¼″
Mark: wᵐ WILL / PHILADELPHIA in scrolls (Laughlin 537)
Date: 1764–1798
Owner: The Henry Francis du Pont Winterthur Museum (58.655)

81. Plate
Circular plate with single reed on narrow rim; incised circle inside booge. Diam. 6¼″
Mark: Initials ww in two concentric circles (Laughlin 541)
Date: 1764–1798
Owner: Museum of Fine Arts, Boston, Massachusetts
Bibliography: H. H. Schnabel to author, Mar. 7, 1967

82. Plate
Diam. 6¼″

Mark: Initials ww in two concentric circles (Laughlin 541)
Date: 1764–1798
Owner: Gordon E. Perrin; ex coll. Charles K. Davis.
Bibliography: "Pewter Collection of C. K. Davis at Highwood, Fairfield, Connecticut, Exhibited at meeting of the Pewter Collectors' Club of America, June 9, 1945," stenciled typescript in pamphlet file, Winterthur Libraries; Mrs. L. W. Stevenson to author, Mar. 12, 1971

83. Plate
Circular plate with single reed on rim. Diam. 7⅞″
Mark: wᵐ WILL / PHILADELPHIA in scrolls and eagle in oval struck twice (Laughlin 537, 540)
Date: 1787–1798
Owner: Ledlie I. Laughlin
Bibliography: Ledlie I. Laughlin to author, Nov. 23, 1966

84. Plate
Diam. 7¹⁵⁄₁₆″
Mark: wᵐ WILL / PHILADELPHIA in scrolls (Laughlin 537)
Date: 1764–1798
Owner: Mrs. George A. Jenckes
Bibliography: Mrs. George A. Jenckes to author, Nov. 9, 1966

85. Plate
Circular plate with hammered booge. Diam. 8″
Mark: Eagle in oval struck twice and wᵐ WILL / PHILADELPHIA in scrolls (Laughlin 540, 537)
Date: 1787–1798
Owner: John H. Carter
Bibliography: John H. Carter, "Important Inventory," *Bulletin, Pewter Collectors' Club of America* 4, no. 4 (Sept. 1960) : 53–57; John H. Carter to author, Nov. 22, 1966

86. Plate
Diam. 8″
Mark: Lamb and dove struck twice and four pseudo-hallmarks (Laughlin 535, 536)
Date: 1764–1798
Owner: D. R. Schimmel
Bibliography: D. R. Schimmel to author, Feb. 13, 1971

87. Plate
Diam. 8¼″
Mark: Lamb and dove struck twice and four
pseudo-hallmarks (Laughlin 535, 536)
Date: 1764–1798
Owner: Mr. and Mrs. C. P. Hinshaw
Bibliography: C. P. Hinshaw to author, Feb.
12, 1971

88. Plate
Diam. 8⅜″
Mark: Eagle in oval struck twice and wᵐ WILL
/ PHILADELPHIA in scrolls (Laughlin 540 and
537)
Date: 1787–1798
Owner: Wilmer Moore
Bibliography: Wilmer Moore to author, June
22, 1967

89. Plate
Diam. 8⅜″
Mark: Lamb and dove in oval, wᵐ WILL /
PHILADEL/PHIA and four pseudo-hallmarks
(Laughlin 534, 535, 536)
Date: 1764–1798
Owner: Samuel Statland
Bibliography: Samuel Statland to author, Jan.
12, 1971

90. Plate
Diam. 8⅜″
Mark: Eagle in oval struck twice and wᵐ WILL
/ PHILADELPHIA in scrolls (Laughlin 540,
537)
Date: 1787–1798
Owner: Mr. and Mrs. C. P. Hinshaw; ex coll.
P. W. Mobberly
Bibliography: C. P. Hinshaw to author, Feb.
12, 1971

91. Plate
Circular plate with single reed on rim; ham-
mered booge
Diam. 8⁷⁄₁₆″
Mark: Eagle in oval struck twice and wᵐ WILL
/ PHILADELPHIA in scrolls (Laughlin 540,
537)
Date: 1787–1798
Owner: Museum of Fine Arts, Boston, Massa-
chusetts; ex coll. Mrs. Stephen S. Fitzgerald
Bibliography: H. H. Schnabel to author, Mar.
7, 1967

92. Plate
Circular plate with single reed on rim; incised
circle inside hammered booge. Diam. 8⁷⁄₁₆″
Mark: Eagle in oval struck twice and wᵐ WILL
/ PHILADELPHIA in scrolls (Laughlin 540,
537a)
Date: 1787–1798
Owner: Joseph H. Kler. On permanent loan to
Smithsonian Institution
Bibliography: Anne Golovin to author, March
12, 1971

93. Plate
Circular plate with single reed on rim, incised
circle inside booge. Diam. 8⁷⁄₁₆″
Mark: wᵐ WILL / PHILADELPHIA in scrolls and
eagle in oval struck twice (Laughlin 537,
540)
Date: 1787–1798
Owner: The Henry Francis du Pont Winterthur Museum (53.26)

94. Plate
Circular plate with hammered booge. Diam.
8⁷⁄₁₆″
Mark: Eagle in oval struck twice and wᵐ WILL
/ PHILADELPHIA in scrolls (Laughlin 540,
537)
Date: 1787–1798
Owner: Clare Ingham; ex coll. Charles K.
Davis
Bibliography: "Pewter Collection of C. K.
Davis at Highwood, Fairfield, Connecticut,
Exhibited at Meeting of The Pewter Col-
lectors' Club of America, June 9, 1945,"
stenciled typescript in pamphlet file, Win-
terthur Libraries; Mrs. L. W. Stevenson to
author, Mar. 12, 1971

95. Plate
Circular plate with hammered booge. Diam.
8½″
Mark: Eagle in oval struck twice and wᵐ WILL
/ PHILADELPHIA in scrolls (Laughlin 540,
537)
Date: 1787–1798
Owner: Mr. and Mrs. Frank Beaven
Bibliography: Mrs. Frank Beaven to author,
Jan. 23, 1971

96. Plate
Circular plate with hammered booge. Diam.
8½″

Mark: Eagle in oval and w^m WILL / PHILA-DELPHIA in scrolls (Laughlin 540, 537)
Date: 1787–1798
Owner: Florene Maine
Bibliography: Florene Maine to author, Feb. 8, 1971

97. Plate
Circular plate with smooth rim; incised circle inside booge. Diam. 9⅜″
Mark: Lamb and dove in oval struck twice and four pseudo-hallmarks (Laughlin 535, 536)
Date: 1764–1798
Owner: The Philadelphia Museum of Art (66–18–1)
Bibliography: Miss Beatrice B. Wolfe to author, Nov. 3, 1966

98. Plate
Circular plate with smooth rim. Diam. 9⅜″
Mark: w^m WILL / PHILADELPHIA in scrolls and eagle in oval struck twice (Laughlin 537, 540)
Date: 1787–1798
Owner: Ledlie I. Laughlin
Bibliography: Ledlie I. Laughlin to author, Nov. 23, 1966

99. Plate
Circular plate with smooth rim and incised inside booge; initials M W scratched on underside. Diam. 9⅜″
Mark: w^m WILL / PHILADELPHIA in scrolls and eagle in oval struck twice (Laughlin 537, 540)
Date: 1787–1798
Owner: The Henry Francis du Pont Winterthur Museum (58.660)

100. Plate
Circular plate with smooth rim. Diam. 9⅜″
Mark: Eagle in oval struck twice and w^m WILL / PHILADELPHIA in scrolls (Laughlin 540 and 537)
Date: 1787–1798
Owner: Samuel Statland
Bibliography: Samuel Statland to author, Jan. 23, 1971

101. Plate
Circular plate with smooth rim. Diam. 9⁷⁄₁₆″
Mark: Lamb and dove in oval, w^m WILL /

PHILADEL/PHIA, and four pseudo-hallmarks (Laughlin 534, 535, 536)
Date: 1764–1798
Owner: Mrs. George A. Jenckes
Bibliography: Mrs. George A. Jenckes to author, Nov. 9, 1966

102. Plate
Circular plate with smooth rim. Diam. 9⁷⁄₁₆″
Mark: Eagle in oval struck twice and w^m WILL / PHILADELPHIA in scrolls (Laughlin 540 and 537)
Date: 1787–1798
Owner: Samuel Statland
Bibliography: Samuel Statland to author, Jan. 23, 1971

103. Plate
Circular plate with smooth rim. Diam. 9½″
Mark: Lamb and dove in oval struck twice, w^m WILL / PHILADEL/PHIA, and four pseudo-hallmarks (Laughlin 534, 535, 536)
Date: 1764–1798
Owner: The Henry Francis du Pont Winterthur Museum (58.659)

104. Salts (3) (Fig. 21)
Circular bowl with sides double incurved toward stepped pedestal base; beading on edge of bowl. H. 2⅜″, Diam. (base) 2¼″, Diam. (top) 2⁹⁄₁₆″, Diam. (stem) ⅝″
Mark: None. Attribution based on similarity of body profile to base of chalice in Aaronsburg communion service
Date: 1785–1798
Owner: Charles V. Swain; one ex coll. John F. Ruckman
Bibliography: Charles V. Swain, "Interchangeable Parts in Early American Pewter," *Antiques* 83, no. 2 (Feb. 1963) : 212–13, fig. 1; Charles V. Swain, "Unmarked Pewter Comparisons," *Bulletin, Pewter Collectors' Club of America* 5, no. 5 (June 1966) : 98–100, fig. 2a; Charles V. Swain to author, Nov. 25, 1966

105. Salts (3) (Fig. 21)
Circular bowl with sides double incurved toward stepped pedestal base; beading on edge of bowl and base. H. 2⅜″, Diam. (base) 2⅜″, Diam. (top) 2⁹⁄₁₆″, Diam. (stem) ¾″

FIG. 21. Will, Salts. Philadelphia, Pa., 1785–98. Pewter; H. (both) 2⅜″, Diam. (stem) ⅝″ (left) ¾″ (right). (Collection of Charles V. Swain.)

Mark: None. Similar to No. 104 but with a thicker bowl and stem

Date: 1785–1798

Owner: Charles V. Swain

Bibliography: Charles V. Swain, "Unmarked Pewter Comparisons," *Bulletin, Pewter Collectors' Club of America* 5, no. 5 (June 1966) : 98–100, fig. 2b; Charles V. Swain to author, Nov. 25, 1966

106. Salt

Circular bowl with sides double incurved toward stepped pedestal base; beading on edge of bowl and base. H. 2½″, Diam. 2⁹⁄₁₆″

Mark: None. Attribution based on similarity to No. 104

Date: 1785–1798

Owner: Wilmer Moore

Bibliography: Wilmer Moore to author, June 22, 1967

107. Salt

Circular bowl with sides double incurved toward stepped pedestal base; beading on edge of bowl and base. H. 2⅜″, Diam. (base) 2⅜″, Diam. (top) 2½″

Mark: None. Attribution based on similarity to No. 104

Date: 1785–1798

Owner: Yale University Art Gallery, Mabel Brady Garvan Collection (1964.55.1) , Gift of Mr. and Mrs. Charles F. Montgomery

Bibliography: Graham Hood, *American Pewter: Garvan and Other Collections at Yale* (New Haven: Yale University Art Gallery, 1965) , no. 190; Ledlie I. Laughlin, *Pewter in America*, I, plate XXX, fig. 210

108. Salt

Circular bowl with sides double incurved toward stepped pedestal base; beading on edge of bowl and base. H. 2¼″, Diam. (top) 2⁷⁄₁₆″, Diam. (base) 2⁷⁄₁₆″

Mark: None. Attribution based on similarity to No. 104

Date: 1785–1798

Owner: Lola S. Reed

Bibliography: Lola S. Reed to author, Dec. 6, 1966

109. Salt

Circular bowl with sides double incurved toward stepped pedestal base; beading on edge of bowl and base. H. 2³⁄₁₆″, Diam. (base) 2⅜″

Mark: None. Attribution based on similarity to No. 104

Date: 1785–1798

Owner: The Brooklyn Museum (27.605),
Gift of Mrs. Samuel Doughty
Bibliography: Robert Hendrick to author,
Apr. 15, 1965

110. Salts (2)
Circular bowl with sides double incurved to-
ward stepped pedestal base; beading on
edge of base. H. 2⅜″
Mark: None. Attribution based on similarity
to No. 104
Date: 1785–1798
Owner: George A. Jenckes
Bibliography: George A. Jenckes to author,
Apr. 15, 1965

111. Salt
Circular bowl with sides double incurved to-
ward stepped pedestal base; beading on
edge of base. H. 2⅜″
Mark: None. Attribution based on similarity
to No. 104
Date: 1785–1798
Owner: Ledlie I. Laughlin
Bibliography: Ledlie I. Laughlin to author,
Nov. 23, 1966

112. Salt
Circular bowl with sides double incurved to-
ward stepped pedestal base; beading on
edge of base. H. 2⅜″, Diam. (base) 2⅜″,
Diam. (top) 2½″
Mark: None. Attribution based on similarity
to No. 104
Date: 1785–1798
Owner: Ray McCloskey
Bibliography: Ray McCloskey to author, Jan.
5, 1967

113. Salt
Circular bowl with sides double incurved to-
ward stepped pedestal base; beading on
edge of bowl and base. H. 2⁷⁄₁₆″, Diam. 1⅞″
Mark: None. Attribution based on similarity
to No. 104
Date: 1785–1798
Owner: Mr. and Mrs. David W. Gordon
Bibliography: David W. Gordon to author,
Dec. 5, 1966

114. Salt
Circular bowl with sides double incurved to-
ward stepped pedestal base; no beading.
H. 2⅜″, Diam. 1⁹⁄₁₆″

Mark: None. Attribution based on similarity
to No. 104
Date: 1764–1798
Owner: Mr. and Mrs. David W. Gordon
Bibliography: Charles V. Swain, "Interchangeable Parts in Early American Pewter," *Antiques* 83, no. 2 (Feb. 1963): 212–
213, fig. 1; David W. Gordon to author,
Dec. 5, 1966

115. Salts (2)
Circular bowl with sides double incurved to-
ward stepped pedestal base
Mark: None. Attribution based on similarity
to No. 104
Date: 1764–1798
Owner: Robert Mallory III
Bibliography: Thomas D. Williams to au-
thor, Nov. 30, 1966

116. Salt
Circular bowl with sides double incurved to-
ward stepped pedestal base; beading on
edge of bowl. H. 2⅜″, Diam. 2⅝″
Mark: None. Attribution based on similarity
to No. 104
Date: 1785–1798
Owner: George W. Scott, Jr.
Bibliography: George W. Scott, Jr., to au-
thor, Nov. 18, 1966

117. Salt
Circular bowl with sides double incurved toward stepped pedestal base; beading on
edge of bowl and base. H. 2⅜″, Diam.
(base) 2⅜″, Diam. (top) 2½″
Mark: None. Attribution based on similarity
to No. 104
Date: 1785–1798
Owner: Harold B. Willis, Jr.
Bibliography: Thomas D. Williams to author, Feb. 8, 1967

118. Salt
Circular bowl with sides double incurved toward stepped pedestal base; beading on
edge of bowl and base. H. 2⅜″, Diam.
(base) 2⅜″, Diam. (top) 2½″
Mark: None. Attribution based on similarity
to No. 104
Date: 1785–1798
Owner: Merril Beede
Bibliography: Thomas D. Williams to author, Feb. 8, 1967

119. Salts (2)

Circular bowl with sides double incurved toward stepped pedestal base. H. 2⅜″, Diam. (base) 2⅜″, Diam. (top) 2½″

Mark: None. Attribution based on similarity to No. 104

Date: 1785–1798

Owner: Thomas D. Williams

Bibliography: Thomas D. Williams to author, Feb. 8, 1967

120. Salt

Circular bowl with sides double incurved toward stepped pedestal base. H. 2⅜″, Diam. (base) 2⅜″, Diam. (top) 2½″

Mark: None. Attribution based on similarity to No. 104

Date: 1764–1798

Owner: Thomas D. Williams

Bibliography: Thomas D. Williams to author, Feb. 8, 1967

121. Salt

Circular bowl with sides double incurved toward stepped pedestal base; beading on edge of bowl and base. H. 2¼″, Diam. (base) 2⁷⁄₁₆″, Diam. (top) 2⅝″

Mark: None. Attribution based on similarity to No. 104

Date: 1785–1798

Owner: Charles F. Montgomery

Bibliography: Charles F. Montgomery to author, Nov. 5, 1967

122. Sugar bowl

Circular body with sides double incurved toward base; stepped lid with finial. H. (without lid) 2¹⁵⁄₁₆″, Diam. (top) 4¼″, Diam. (base) 2¹³⁄₁₆″

Mark: None. Attribution based on similarity of body profile to lower part of ewer in Hershey Museum (No. 44)

Date: 1764–1798

Owner: Charles V. Swain

Bibliography: Charles V. Swain, "Varying Forms from One Mold," *Bulletin, Pewter Collectors' Club of America* 4, no. 9 (Mar. 1963): 147; Charles V. Swain to author, Nov. 25, 1966

123. Sugar bowl

Circular body with sides double incurved toward base; stepped lid with finial. H.
(without lid) 3″, Diam. (top) 4⅜″, Diam. (base) 2¹⁵⁄₁₆″

Mark: None. Almost identical to No. 122

Date: 1764–1798

Owner: Charles V. Swain; ex coll. John F. Ruckman

Bibliography: Charles V. Swain to author, Nov. 25, 1966

124. Sugar bowl

Circular body with sides double incurved toward base; stepped lid; beading. H. (with lid) 4¾″, Diam. (top) 4⅝″

Mark: None. Almost identical to No. 122

Date: 1785–1798

Owner: Wilmer Moore

Bibliography: Wilmer Moore to author, June 22, 1967

125. Sugar bowl (Fig. 22)

Circular body with sides double incurved toward base; stepped lid with finial. H. (with lid) 4¾″, Diam. (top) 4⅜″, Diam. (base) 2¹⁵⁄₁₆″

Mark: None. Almost identical to No. 122

Date: 1764–1798

Owner: Charles V. Swain; ex coll. John F. Ruckman; Samuel D. Riddle

Bibliography: Charles V. Swain to author, Nov. 25, 1966

FIG. 22. Will, Sugar Bowl. Philadelphia, Pa., 1764–98. Pewter; H. 4¾″. (Collection of Charles V. Swain.)

126. Sugar bowl
    Circular body with sides double incurved toward base; no lid. H. 2¹⁵⁄₁₆″, Diam. (top) 4¼″, Diam. (base) 2¹³⁄₁₆″
    Mark: None. Almost identical to No. 122
    Date: 1764–1798
    Owner: Charles V. Swain
    Bibliography: Charles V. Swain to author, Nov. 25, 1966

127. Sugar bowl
    Circular body with sides double incurved toward base; stepped lid with finial; double incised lines on rim, lid, and base of finial. H. (with lid) 4⅝″
    Mark: None. Almost identical to No. 122
    Date: 1764–1798
    Owner: The Metropolitan Museum of Art (47.111), Museum Purchase, Rogers Fund
    Bibliography: Joseph Downs, "Recent Additions to the American Wing," *The Metropolitan Museum of Art Bulletin,* n.s. 7, no. 3 (Nov. 1948): 79–85, illust. p. 84; Mary Glaze to author, Nov. 15, 1966

128. Sugar bowl
    Circular body with sides double incurved toward base; stepped lid with finial; beading on lid, body, and base. Diam. (top) 4¾″
    Mark: None. Almost identical to No. 122
    Date: 1764–1798
    Owner: The Detroit Institute of Arts
    Bibliography: Graham Hood to author, June 3, 1970

129. Sugar bowl
    Circular body with sides double incurved toward base; stepped lid with finial. Diam. (top) 4⁷⁄₁₆″
    Mark: None. Almost identical to No. 122
    Date: 1764–1798
    Owner: Lola S. Reed
    Bibliography: Lola S. Reed to author, Dec. 6, 1966

130. Sugar bowl
    Circular body with sides double incurved toward base; stepped lid with finial; beading. H. (with lid) 4⅝″, Diam. (top) 5″
    Mark: None. Almost identical to No. 122
    Date: 1785–1798
    Owner: George W. Scott, Jr.
    Bibliography: George W. Scott, Jr., to author, Nov. 18, 1966

131. Sugar bowl
    Circular body with straight sides; midband and stepped base; beading; stepped lid with finial. H. (without lid) 3⅜″, Diam. (top) 4⅜″, Diam. (base) 3⁹⁄₁₆″
    Mark: None. Lid identical in profile to base of chalice in Aaronsburg communion service
    Date: 1785–1798
    Owner: Charles V. Swain; ex coll. John F. Ruckman
    Bibliography: Charles V. Swain, "Interchangeable Parts in Early American Pewter," *Antiques* 83, no. 2 (Feb. 1963): 212–13, fig. 2; Charles V. Swain to author, Nov. 25, 1966

132. Sugar bowl (Fig. 23)
    Circular body with straight sides; midband and beading; stepped base engraved with initials FT on underside; stepped lid with finial. H. (with lid) 6″, Diam. (top) 4¾″
    Mark: None. Almost identical to No. 131
    Date: 1785–1798
    Owner: John J. Evans, Jr.

Fɪɢ. 23. Will, Sugar Bowl. Philadelphia, Pa., 1785–98. Pewter; H. 6″. (Collection of John J. Evans, Jr.: Photo, Winterthur.)

Bibliography: J. J. Evans, Jr., "A Flat-Top
   Tankard," *Antiques* 57, no. 4 (Apr. 1950):
   276–77, fig. 1

133. Sugar bowl
   Circular body with straight sides; midband
      and beading; stepped base; no lid. H. 3¼″,
      Diam. (top) 4¼″, Diam. (base) 3½″
   Mark: None. Almost identical to No. 131
   Date: 1785–1798
   Owner: Charles V. Swain; ex coll. John F.
      Ruckman
   Bibliography: Charles V. Swain to author,
      Nov. 25, 1966

134. Tablespoons (4) (Fig. 24)
   Long oval bowl with shell and floral motif on
      back; rounded handle top; initials H + S
      scratched in crude sawtooth lines on back
      of handle. L. 8½″
   Mark: wᵐ WILL / PHILA=/DELPHIA (Laughlin
      542)
   Date: 1764–1798
   Owner: The Henry Francis du Pont Winter-
      thur Museum (58.665–.668)
   Bibliography: J. B. Kerfoot, *American Pew-
      ter,* fig. 73

135. Tablespoons (2) (Fig. 24)
   Long oval bowl with shell and floral motif
      on back; rounded handle top; initials H +
      S scratched in crude sawtooth lines on back
      of handle. L. 8½″
   Mark: None. Identical to No. 134
   Date: 1764–1798
   Owner: The Henry Francis du Pont Winter-
      thur Museum (58.669, 58.670)

136. Tankard
   Tapered cylindrical body; molded base and
      midband; hinged double-domed lid with
      pierced thumbpiece; single scroll handle.
      H. (to brim) 5⅞″
   Mark: Crowned x and wᵐ WILL (Laughlin
      539)
   Date: 1764–1798
   Owner: The Currier Gallery of Art
   Bibliography: *Pewter in America, 1650–
      1900: An Exhibition* (Manchester, N.H.:
      The Currier Gallery of Art, 1968), no. 1
      (frontispiece)

FIG. 24. Will, Tablespoons. Philadelphia, Pa., 1764–98.
Pewter; L. 8⅜″. (Winterthur 58.665–670.)

137. Tankard
Tapered cylindrical body; molded base and midband; hinged double-domed lid with pierced thumbpiece; quart capacity. H. 7⅛″
Mark: Initials ww in two concentric circles (Laughlin 541)
Date: 1764–1798
Owner: Ledlie I. Laughlin
Bibliography: Ledlie I. Laughlin, *Pewter in America*, I, plate XVII, fig. 98; Ledlie I. Laughlin to author, Nov. 23, 1966

138. Tankard
Tapered cylindrical body; molded base and midband; hinged double-domed lid with thumbpiece; single scroll handle; quart capacity. H. 7½″
Mark: Initials ww (Laughlin 541a)
Date: 1764–1798
Owner: The William Penn Memorial Museum
Bibliography: Eric de Jonge to author, Mar. 10, 1971

139. Tankard
Tapered cylindrical body; molded base; hinged flat-top lid with scroll thumbpiece; engraved on lid: a six-pointed rosette within a five-petalled flower; engraved on body opposite handle: a sunburst containing the initials DK in script and the date 1815; 2¾ pint capacity. H. 7¼″
Mark: wᵐ WILL (Laughlin 539)
Date: 1764–1798
Owner: John J. Evans, Jr.
Bibliography: J. J. Evans, Jr., "A Flat-Top Tankard," *Antiques* 57, no. 4 (Apr. 1950): 276–77, fig. 3

140. Tankard
Tapered cylindrical body; molded base; triple banded around lower body; hinged double-domed lid with single scroll handle. H. 7¹³⁄₁₆″
Mark: Initials ww in two concentric circles (Laughlin 541)
Date: 1764–1798
Owner: The Henry Francis du Pont Winterthur Museum (53.34); ex coll. Charles Hutchins

141. Tankard
Tapered cylindrical body; molded base and midband; hinged double-domed lid; two concentric circles incised on lid; single scroll handle. H. 7½″
Mark: Crowned x and wᵐ WILL (Laughlin 539)
Date: 1764–1798
Owner: Thomas D. Williams
Bibliography: Thomas D. Williams to author, Feb. 12, 1971

142. Tankard (Fig. 25)
Tapered cylindrical body; molded base and midband; hinged double-domed lid; heart-shaped cutout in thumbpiece; single scroll handle; quart capacity. H. 7⅝″
Mark: Crowned x and wᵐ WILL (Laughlin 539)
Date: 1764–1798
Owner: The Henry Francis du Pont Winterthur Museum (55.48.30), gift of Charles K. Davis; ex coll. Edward E. Minor
Bibliography: Edward E. Minor, "American Pewter Tankards," *Antiques* 34, no. 3 (Sept. 1938): 137–39, fig. 8 (c); J. B. Kerfoot, *American Pewter*, fig. 72

FIG. 25. Will, Tankard. Philadelphia, Pa., 1764–98. Pewter; H. 7⅝″. (Winterthur 55.48.30.)

143. Tankard
     Tapered cylindrical body; molded base and
     midband; hinged double-domed lid with
     pierced thumbpiece; single scroll handle.
     H. 7½"
     Mark: Crowned x, scales struck twice, and
     wᵐ WILL (Laughlin 538, 539)
     Date: 1764–1798
     Owner: The Brooklyn Museum (47.182),
     Museum Purchase, Dick S. Ramsay Fund
     Bibliography: Robert Hendrick to author,
     Feb. 15, 1967

144. Tankard
     Tapered cylindrical body; molded base and
     midband; hinged double-domed lid with
     thumbpiece; single scroll handle; quart
     capacity; engraved on body opposite han-
     dle: cartouche containing initials G E B in
     script. H. 7¹¹⁄₁₆"
     Mark: Initials ww in two concentric circles
     (Laughlin 541)
     Date: 1764–1798
     Owner: Yale University Art Gallery, Mabel
     Brady Garvan Collection (1931.163)
     Bibliography: Graham Hood, *American
     Pewter: Garvan and Other Collections at
     Yale* (New Haven: Yale University Art
     Gallery, 1965), no. 189; J. B. Kerfoot,
     American Pewter, fig. 72; Louis G. Myers,
     Some Notes on American Pewterers, plate
     facing p. 72.

145. Tankard
     Tapered cylindrical body; molded base and
     midband; hinged double-domed lid with
     thumbpiece; single scroll handle; quart
     capacity. H. 7¹¹⁄₁₆"
     Mark: Crowned x and wᵐ WILL (Laughlin
     539)
     Date: 1764–1798
     Owner: Yale University Art Gallery, Mabel
     Brady Garvan Collection (1930.806)
     Bibliography: Graham Hood, *American
     Pewter: Garvan and Other Collections at
     Yale* (New Haven: Yale University Art
     Gallery, 1965), no. 188

146. Tankard
     Tapered cylindrical body; molded base and
     midband; scroll handle; hinged domed lid.
     H. 7⅝"

Mark: wᵐ WILL / PHILADEL=/PHIA (Laughlin
534a)
Date: 1764–1798
Owner: The Philadelphia Museum of Art
(02–511)
Bibliography: Beatrice B. Wolfe to author,
Nov., 1966

147. Tankard
     Tapered cylindrical body; molded base;
     banded; scroll handle with pierced thumb-
     piece; hinged domed lid with two con-
     centric circles; quart capacity. H. 7⅜"
     Mark: wᵐ WILL / PHILADEL=/PHIA (Laughlin
     534a)
     Date: 1764–1798
     Owner: Wilmer Moore
     Bibliography: Mrs. Wilmer Moore to author,
     Mar. 21, 1971

148. Tankard (Fig. 26)
     Bulbous body on stepped pedestal base;
     hinged double-domed lid incised with con-
     centric circles; thumbpiece; single scroll
     handle. H. 7¹⁵⁄₁₆"

FIG. 26. Will, Tankard. Philadelphia, Pa., 1764–98.
Pewter; H. 7¹⁵⁄₁₆". (Winterthur 55.48.29.)

Mark: Initials ww (Laughlin 541a)
Date: 1764–1798
Owner: The Henry Francis du Pont Winter-
thur Museum (55.48.29), gift of Charles
K. Davis; ex coll. Herbert Lawton

149. Tankard
Bulbous body on stepped pedestal base;
hinged double-domed lid and thumbpiece;
beaded edges on foot, body, lip and lid;
single-scroll handle; quart capacity. H.
8¼″
Mark: None. Tradition of having been purchased with patens (No. 74) bearing
Will's mark
Date: 1785–1798
Owner: Presbyterian Historical Society; ex
coll. Presbyterian Church, Lost Creek,
Pennsylvania
Bibliography: Ledlie I. Laughlin, "The Pewter Communion Services of the Presbyterian Historical Scoiety," *Journal of Presbyterian History*, 44, no. 2 (June 1966):
83–88, fig. 1; Ledlie I. Laughlin to author,
Nov. 23, 1966

150. Tankard
Bulbous body on stepped pedestal base; mid-
band, hinged double-domed lid with
pierced thumbpiece; single scroll handle.
H. 8″
Mark: Crowned x and initials ww (Laughlin
541a)
Date: 1764–1798
Owner: The Henry Francis du Pont Winter-
thur Museum (58.653); ex coll. Edward
E. Minor
Bibliography: Edward E. Minor, "American
Pewter Tankards," *Antiques* 34, no. 3
(Sept. 1938): 137–39, fig. 7

151. Tankard
Bulbous body on stepped pedestal base;
hinged double-domed lid with two incised
concentric circles and thumbpiece; in-
verted shield and dot on single scroll han-
dle. H. 6½″
Mark: Initials ww in two concentric circles
(Laughlin 541)
Date: 1764–1798
Owner: John J. Evans, Jr.
Bibliography: J. J. Evans, Jr., "A Flat-Top
Tankard," *Antiques* 57, no. 4 (Apr. 1950):
276–77, fig. 1

152. Tankard
Bulbous body on stepped pedestal base,
hinged double-domed lid with thumb-
piece; single scroll handle. H. 7½″
Mark: Initials ww (Laughlin 541a)
Date: 1764–1798
Owner: John H. McMurray
Bibliography: John H. McMurray to author,
Dec. 6, 1966

153. Tankard
Bulbous body on stepped pedestal base;
hinged double-domed lid with two incised
concentric circles and thumbpiece; midband; single scroll handle. H. 7½″
Mark: Crowned x and initials ww in two
concentric circles (Laughlin 541)
Date: 1764–1798
Owner: Charles V. Swain; ex coll. John F.
Ruckman
Bibliography: Charles V. Swain, "Interchangeable Parts in Early American Pewter," *Antiques* 83, no. 2 (Feb. 1963):
212–13, fig. 3; Charles V. Swain to author,
Nov. 25, 1966

154. Tankard
Bulbous body on stepped pedestal base;
hinged double-domed lid with incised con-
centric circles and thumbpiece; midband;
single scroll handle. H. 7½″
Mark: wᵐ WILL (Laughlin 539)
Date: 1764–1798
Owner: Unknown; ex coll. Edward E. Minor
Bibliography: Ledlie I. Laughlin, *Pewter in
America*, I, plate XVII, fig. 100

155. Tankard
Bulbous body on stepped pedestal base;
hinged double-domed lid; heart-shaped
cutout in thumbpiece; quart capacity. H.
7¾″
Mark: Erased. Thumbpiece and other details
are the same as on marked Will tankards.
Date: 1764–1798
Owner: The Brooklyn Museum (45.10–195),
Museum Purchase, John W. Poole Collec-
tion
Bibliography: Robert Hendrick to author,
Feb. 15, 1967

156. Tankard
Bulbous body on stepped pedestal base;
hinged double-domed lid. H. 7¾″

Mark: Lamb and dove in oval (Laughlin 535)

Date: 1764–1798

Owner: Mr. and Mrs. Hill Sandidge; ex coll. Charles K. Davis; Albert Good

Bibliography: "Pewter Collection of C. K. Davis at Highwood, Fairfield, Connecticut, Exhibited at Meeting of the Pewter Collectors' Club of America, June 9, 1945," stenciled typescript in pamphlet file, Winterthur Libraries; Mrs. L. W. Stevenson to author, Mar. 12, 1971

157. Tankard

Bulbous body on stepped pedestal base; quart capacity

Mark: Initials ww (Laughlin 541a)

Date: 1764–1798

Owner: Mrs. George A. Jenckes

Bibliography: Mrs. George A. Jenckes to author, Nov. 9, 1966

158. Tankard

Bulbous body on stepped pedestal base; hinged lid and thumbpiece. H. 8″

Mark: ww in two concentric circles (Laughlin 541)

Date: 1764–1798

Owner: Joseph H. Kler. On permanent loan to Smithsonian Institution

Bibliography: Joseph H. Kler to author, Nov. 7, 1966

159. Tankard

Bulbous body on stepped pedestal base; hinged double-domed lid and thumbpiece; single scroll handle; quart capacity. H. 7⅞″

Mark: Crowned x and w^m WILL (Laughlin 539)

Date: 1764–1798

Owner: Yale University Art Gallery, Mabel Brady Garvan Collection (1930.720); ex coll. Louis G. Myers

Bibliography: Graham Hood, *American Pewter: Garvan and Other Collections at Yale* (New Haven: Yale University Art Gallery, 1965), no. 187; Louis G. Myers, *Some Notes on American Pewterers*, plate facing p. 73

160. Tankard

Bulbous body on stepped pedestal base; hinged double-domed lid with punch marks around rim; pierced thumbpiece. H. 8⅛″

Mark: Initials ww (Laughlin 541a)

Date: 1764–1798

Owner: The Metropolitan Museum of Art (39.185.7), Gift of Mrs. J. Insley Blair

Bibliography: Mary Glaze to author, Nov. 15, 1966

161. Teapot

Pear-shaped body without feet; high-domed hinged lid with finial; S-shaped wooden handle opposite spout. H. 6½″

Mark: Initials ww in two concentric circles (Laughlin 541)

Date: 1764–1798

Owner: Joseph H. Kler. On loan to New Jersey State Museum (L68.1.2)

Bibliography: James R. Mitchell, *American Pewter from the Collections of Mrs. Robert D. Graff, Dr. Joseph H. Kler, Mrs. John H. McMurray* (Trenton: The New Jersey State Museum, 1968), no. 11; Dr. Joseph H. Kler to author, Feb. 21, 1971

162. Teapot

Pear-shaped body without feet; high-domed hinged lid with finial; S-shaped pear-wood handle opposite spout. H. 6¼″

Mark: w^m WILL (Laughlin 539)

Date: 1764–1798

Owner: The Brooklyn Museum (45.10–184), Museum Purchase, John W. Poole Collection

Bibliography: Ledlie I. Laughlin, *Pewter in America*, I, plate XXVIII, fig. 189; Robert Hendrick to author, Feb. 15, 1967

163. Teapot

Pear-shaped body without feet; high-domed hinged lid with finial. H. 7⅛″

Mark: w^m WILL and eagle in oval struck twice (Laughlin 539, 540)

Date: 1787–1798

Owner: Charles V. Swain; ex coll. John F. Ruckman

Bibliography: Charles V. Swain to author, Nov. 25, 1966

164. Teapot
      Pear-shaped body without feet; high-domed
        hinged lid; beading. H. 8″
      Mark: Scales struck twice (Laughlin 538)
      Date: 1764–1798
      Owner: The Bayou Bend Collection, Mu-
        seum of Fine Arts, Houston, Texas; ex
        coll. Henry Francis du Pont; Charles K.
        Davis

165. Teapot
      Pear-shaped body without feet; high-domed
        hinged lid. H. 6½″
      Mark: Crowned x and w^m WILL (Laughlin
        539)
      Date: 1764–1798
      Owner: George W. Scott, Jr.
      Bibliography: George W. Scott, Jr., to au-
        thor, Nov. 18, 1966

166. Teapot
      Pear-shaped body without feet; high-domed
        hinged lid with finial; S-shaped handle
        (lower tip broken off) opposite spout. H.
        6½″
      Mark: Crowned x and w^m WILL (Laughlin
        539)
      Date: 1764–1798
      Owner: John J. Evans, Jr.
      Bibliography: J. J. Evans, Jr., "A Flat-Top
        Tankard," *Antiques* 57, no. 4 (Apr. 1950):
        276–77

167. Teapot (Fig. 27)
      Pear-shaped body without feet; high-domed
        hinged lid with finial; beading on lid;
        S-shaped handle opposite spout. H. 7¼″
      Mark: w^m WILL / PHILA=/DELPHIA (Laughlin
        542)
      Date: 1785–1798
      Owner: The Henry Francis du Pont Winter-
        thur Museum (58.657)

168. Teapot
      Pear-shaped body without feet; high-domed
        hinged lid with finial; S-shaped handle op-
        posite spout. H. 6¼″
      Mark: Crowned x and w^m WILL (Laughlin
        539)
      Date: 1764–1798
      Owner: The Henry Francis du Pont Winter-
        thur Museum (61.1680)

FIG. 27. Will, Teapot. Philadelphia, Pa., 1785–98. Pewter; H. 7¼″. (Winterthur 58.657.)

169. Teapot
      Pear-shaped body without feet, high-domed
        hinged lid with wooden finial; S-shaped
        handle opposite spout. H. 7″
      Mark: None. Almost identical to No. 161
      Date: 1764–1798
      Owner: Reginald French
      Bibliography: Reginald French to author,
        Dec. 1, 1966

170. Teapot (Fig. 28)
      Pear-shaped body on three claw-and-ball feet;
        high-domed hinged lid with finial. H. 8¼″
      Mark: Crowned x and w^m WILL (Laughlin
        539)
      Date: 1764–1798
      Owner: The Metropolitan Museum of Art
        (49.2), Gift of Mrs. J. Insley Blair.
      Bibliography: Lydia B. Powell, "The Amer-
        ican Wing," *The Metropolitan Museum of
        Art Bulletin*, n.s. 12, no. 7 (Mar. 1954):
        194–216, illust. p. 214; Mary Glaze to au-
        thor, Nov. 15, 1966

171. Teapot
      Pear-shaped body on three feet (broken off);
        hinged high-domed lid with finial: H. 6½″
      Mark: Crowned x and w^m WILL (Laughlin
        539)
      Date: 1764–1798
      Owner: The Philadelphia Museum of Art
        (29-49-1); ex coll. Mrs. M. L. Blumenthal

Fig. 28. Will, Teapot. Philadelphia, Pa., 1764–98. Pewter; H. 8¼". (The Metropolitan Museum of Art, Gift of Mrs. J. Insley Blair, 1949.)

Bibliography: Beatrice B. Wolfe to author, Nov. 3, 1966

172. Teapot
Pear-shaped body on three claw-and-ball feet; high-domed hinged lid with finial; S-shaped handle opposite spout. H. 8"
Mark: wᵐ WILL (Laughlin 539)
Date: 1764–1798
Owner: The Brooklyn Museum (45.10–194), Museum Purchase, John W. Poole Collection
Bibliography: John M. Graham, II, *American Pewter* (Brooklyn, N.Y.: The Brooklyn Museum, 1949), no. 59 in fig. 18; Robert Hendrick to author, Feb. 15, 1967.

173. Teapot
Pear-shaped body on three feet; high-domed hinged lid with finial; S-shaped handle opposite spout. H. 7"
Mark: Crowned x and wᵐ WILL (Laughlin 539)
Date: 1764–1798
Owner: The Hershey Museum, Hershey, Pennsylvania
Bibliography: John J. Evans, Jr., "Some Pewter by William Will," *Antiques* 61, no. 2 (Feb. 1952): 178–79; John F. Ruckman to author, July 25, 1964

174. Teapot
Pear-shaped body on three claw-and-ball feet; high-domed hinged lid with finial; S-shaped handle opposite spout. H. 7"
Mark: wᵐ WILL (Laughlin 539)
Date: 1764–1798
Owner: Robert Mallory III; ex coll. Irving H. Berg
Bibliography: Ledlie I. Laughlin, *Pewter in America*, I, plate XXVIII, fig. 190; Dr. Robert Mallory III, "An American Pewter Collection," *Antiques* 72, no. 1 (July 1957): 40–43; John F. Ruckman to author, July 25, 1964

175. Teapot
Drum-shaped body with straight spout and C-shaped wooden handle; hinged lid with finial; beading around base, top of body, lid, and finial. H. 5"
Mark: wᵐ WILL / PHILA=/DELPHIA (Laughlin 542)
Date: 1785–1798
Owner: Joseph France
Bibliography: Charles F. Montgomery, "Important Early American Pewter," *Antiques* 36, no. 3 (Sept. 1939): 118–121, fig. 10a; Joseph France to author, May 13, 1967

176. Teapot (Fig. 29)
Drum-shaped body with straight spout and C-shaped wooden handle; flat hinged lid with finial; beading around top of body, rim of lid and finial. H. 6³⁄₁₆"
Mark: wᵐ WILL / PHILA=/DELPHIA (Laughlin 542)
Date: 1785–1798
Owner: The Henry Francis du Pont Winterthur Museum (58.656); ex coll. Mr. and Mrs. Richard S. Quigley
Bibliography: P. G. Platt, "American Pewter as a Collectible," *Antiques* 18, no. 5 (Nov. 1930): 399–403, fig. 1; Ledlie I. Laughlin, *Pewter in America*, I, plate XXIX, fig. 195

177. Teapot
Drum-shaped body with straight spout and C-shaped wooden handle; flat hinged lid with finial. H. 6⅛"
Mark: Crowned x and wᵐ WILL / PHILADELPHIA in scrolls (Laughlin 537)
Date: 1785–1798

Owner: The Metropolitan Museum of Art
(40.184.4), Gift of Mrs. J. Insley Blair

Bibliography: Joseph Downs, "American
Pewter," *The Metropolitan Museum of
Art Bulletin*, n.s. 36, no. 10 (Oct. 1941):
206–07, fig. 2; Mary Glaze to author, Nov.
15, 1966

178. Teapot

Drum-shaped body with straight spout and
C-shaped pearwood handle; flat hinged lid
with finial; beading. H. 6¹³⁄₁₆″

Mark: wᵐ WILL / PHILA=/DELPHIA (Laughlin
542)

Date: 1785–1798

Owner: The Brooklyn Museum (45.10–189),
Museum Purchase, John W. Poole Collection

Bibliography: Robert Hendrick to author,
Feb. 21, 1967

179. Teapot

Drum-shaped body with straight spout and
C-shaped handle

Mark: wᵐ WILL / PHILA=/DELPHIA (Laughlin
542)

Date: 1785–1798

Owner: Mrs. George A. Jenckes

Bibliography: Mrs. George A. Jenckes, Nov.
9, 1966

180. Teapot

Drum-shaped body with straight spout and
C-shaped wooden handle; flat hinged lid
with finial; beading around base, top of
body, rim of lid and finial. H. 5⅞″

Mark: wᵐ WILL / PHILADELPHIA in scrolls
(Laughlin 537)

Date: 1785–1798

Owner: Robert Mallory III

Bibliography: Dr. Robert Mallory III, "An

FIG. 29. Will, Teapot. Philadelphia, Pa., 1785–98. Pewter; H. 6³⁄₁₆″. (Winterthur 58.656.)

American Pewter Collection," *Antiques* 72, no. 1 (July 1957): 41–43; John F. Ruckman to author, July 25, 1964

181. Teapot
Drum-shaped body with straight spout and C-shaped handle. H. 6¼″
Mark: wᵐ WILL / PHILA=/DELPHIA (Laughlin 542)
Date: 1785–1798
Owner: Robert Stuart
Bibliography: Robert Stuart to author, Feb. 15, 1967

182. Warming Pan
Circular body with flat bottom and rolled sides with circular opening in center; circular hinged cover engraved with floral motifs and pierced with eleven circular holes; turned wood handle. Note: The body is same form as bedpan (No. 7); the lid is an 8-inch plate. Diam. 12″, L. 45″
Mark: wᵐ WILL / PHILADELPHIA in scrolls (Laughlin 537)
Date: 1764–1798
Owner: The Philadelphia Museum of Art (59–71–1); ex coll. J. Stogdell Stokes
Bibliography: J. B. Kerfoot, *American Pewter*, figs. 25, 26, 80

Colonial Philadelphia and Its Backcountry

John F. Walzer

THE commercial success of an entrepôt has depended on many factors in modern western history: the excellence of its harbor; its location relative to the shifting center of Atlantic trade and to extended interior trade routes; the enterprise of its merchants; its selection as a national or provincial capital; and, in at least one important case, the establishment of scheduled shipping.[1] In addition, the success of an entrepôt depended on the productiveness of the surrounding countryside and the degree to which its merchants monopolized the existing trade. Such was the case with colonial Philadelphia.[2] Perhaps no other factor was more important in the rapid rise of Philadelphia to a position of commercial preeminence in the eighteenth century. Conversely, the failure to maintain good connections with the growing backcountry was a decisive factor in the relative decline of the one-time capital mart of America.

By 1760, the merchants of Philadelphia had succeeded in controlling the trade of a rather large and populous surrounding area. Even the uninhabited pine barrens of southern New Jersey contributed to Philadelphia's trade as they yielded thousands of board feet of planks and beams as well as lighter building material referred to collectively as scantling. Approximately twenty-one counties were commercial tributaries to Philadelphia in the 1760s; these included seven or eight counties in southern, western, and northern New Jersey, eight counties in southeastern Pennsylvania, the three counties in Delaware, and the equivalent of at least two or three counties on Maryland's eastern shore (Fig. 1). Not all the people in this inland area were wholly dependent on the merchants of Philadelphia to handle their surpluses. The farmers and millers of central New Jersey often sent their produce to New York for export, and a growing number of people living west of the Susquehanna in Pennsylvania and Maryland were beginning to look to Baltimore for their muscovado sugar, Jamaica rum, and other foreign imports. On the other hand, there were many settlers living outside this twenty-one county area who sometimes favored Philadelphia merchants with their business.

A trading area is often least clearly defined where, for the purpose of graphic description, the historian wishes it were most distinct. Blurred boundaries should cast no doubts on the real existence of trading areas, but they do provide a caution against finding minute significance in the boundary lines established. If the Philadelphia trading area is arbitrarily defined by drawing its boundaries along the line where farmers and country storekeepers probably divided their business equally between Philadelphia and New York or between Philadelphia and some means of im-

[1] Robert G. Albion, *The Rise of New York Port, 1815–1860* (New York: C. Scribner's & Sons, 1939), stresses the importance of the establishment of packet lines in the rise of New York. See also Robert G. Albion, "New York and Its Disappointed Rivals, 1815–1860," *Journal of Economic and Business History* 3, no. 4 (1930/1931): 602–29. For an examination of the factors responsible for the relative success of rival commercial entrepôts, see Curtis P. Nettles, "The Economic Relations of Boston, Philadelphia, and New York, 1680–1715," *Journal of Economic and Business History* 3, no. 2 (1930/1931): 185–215.

[2] The location of Philadelphia (approximately 100 miles inland) was an advantage in colonial times, when inland transportation costs represented a more significant proportion of F.O.B. prices than in a later era. Its merchants derived business from a wide area of productive countryside and were that much closer to what the colonists sometimes called the "back country."

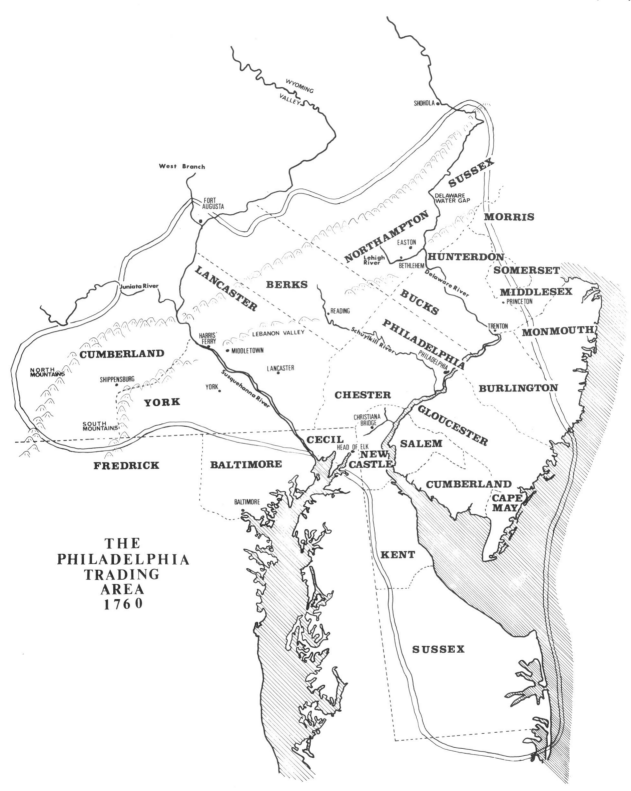

Fɪɢ. 1. The Philadelphia Trading Area, 1760. (Drawn by Rob Howard: Photo, Winterthur.)

port or export via the Chesapeake Bay, the result is an area roughly triangular in shape and extending over twenty thousand square miles, or half the size of England. Approximately three hundred and seventy-five thousand persons lived within the bounds of the area thus defined, where they could be supplied with imported gewgaws and transport their agricultural surpluses to market as a means of payment without undue cost.[3]

The merchants of Philadelphia enjoyed an almost complete monopoly of the trade in this large area. Few of the lesser ports along the Delaware and on the coast traded directly with foreign places or sister colonial ports. Only Wilmington, Delaware, was able to establish a maritime trade of significant proportions; and since the Philadelphia merchants continued to finance, direct, and control this trade until at least the end of the century, it did not represent a loss of business for the major entrepôt.[4]

The most densely populated and most productive portion of the Philadelphia trading area, and the largest consumer of West Indian and European goods unloaded at Front Street wharves, was the countryside within twenty miles of the city, which included the Schuylkill River valley and the Lancaster plain. But this was not the area most likely to grow rapidly or to change its relationship with Philadelphia, affecting the rise or decline of the commercial entrepôt relative to rival entrepôts. Instead, the potentiality for growth and change lay in the more remote parts of the trading area, especially where an alternate maritime connection was feasible.

Such an alternate connection with the rest of the Atlantic world was theoretically available to the farmers and millers of Delaware and southern New Jersey. Philadelphia lay upstream from them and was a considerable distance further inland than their own wharves and harbors. In practice the trade of Delaware Bay was seldom carried on directly with foreign places or even with interloping New England merchants, as was the common practice on the Chesapeake.[5] Trade went directly to Philadelphia because of low transportation costs and frequent opportunities to ship goods north. During ten months of the year, numerous small working sailboats, called shallops, plied the waters of the Delaware Bay and carried the grain and flour of Delaware and the fence rails, cheese, and meat of southern New Jersey to Front Street "at a trifling expense."[6] Manned by two men and a boy, these shallops transported a cargo of up to thirty-five tons, which enabled them to operate very cheaply. Since they drew no more than four or five feet of water, they wound their way up and down the long, meandering streams of New Castle, Kent, and Sussex counties, relying on tidal rather than sailing power.[7] These streams helped to extend the Philadelphia trading area well into the interior of Delaware; over one-half of the colony's farmers were located within a half-day's journey from a good shallop landing or a grist mill on tidewater.[8] Others might have had to put up for the night in order to get their crop to market, but if they turned east, there was little question that their produce would ultimately go to Philadelphia.[9] Little temptation existed to seek an alternate market at New York.

Outside the capes, the situation was somewhat

---

[3] These figures are derived from calculations based on a counting-the-square method of measuring area and on population figures from Evarts B. Greene and Virginia Harrington, *American Population Before the Federal Census of 1790* (New York: Columbia University Press, 1932), pp. 112, 117, 119, 120–21, 131; Stella Sutherland, *Population Distribution in Colonial America* (New York: Columbia University Press, 1936), pp. 98–99, 124–33, 135, 174.

[4] Peter C. Welsh, "Merchants, Millers, and Ocean Ships: The Components of an Early American Industrial Town," *Delaware History* 7, no. 4 (Sept. 1957): 321.

[5] A listing of yearly exports of produce from the several inlets on the western shore of the Delaware confirms this point. Harold Hancock, "Thomas Robinson: Delaware's Most Prominent Loyalist," *Delaware History* 4, no. 1 (Mar. 1950): 26.

[6] *Pennsylvania Gazette,* June 8, 1762.

[7] Exact information on burdens, crew, and draft is difficult to obtain. See documentary evidence and calculations based thereon, John F. Walzer, "Transportation in the Philadelphia Trading Area, 1740–1775" (Ph.D. diss., University of Wisconsin, 1967), pp. 70–74.

[8] This is estimated using eight miles as a half-day's journey, pin-pointing the known shallop landings or first known interruptions of navigation, and using the fold-out, dot maps of population distribution in Sutherland, *Population Distribution,* inside back cover.

[9] Farmers living in western Delaware, especially in Kent and Sussex, must have occasionally turned west and taken their wheat to mills on the eastern shore. Some of the resultant flour, but not all of it certainly, was shipped north to Head of Elk and ultimately to Philadelphia. There is not much evidence to determine where farmers divided their business equally between Philadelphia and some means of export on the Chesapeake, but it probably was not too far from both the provincial line and the watershed line. The Philadelphia trading area boundary has purposely been drawn conservatively in this region.

different. The surpluses of the Indian River area in southern Sussex County, Delaware, and southern Gloucester County, New Jersey, could be loaded aboard larger vessels, which were capable of taking advantage of a better price for red cedar at a New York port. But more often the boards and scantling, posts and rails, and miscellaneous truck of southern Sussex and Cape May were transported overland to the bay side and sent by shallop to Philadelphia,[10] or shallop masters risked several hours exposure to Atlantic violence and scooted through the capes. Thomas Rodney instructed his shallop master to take the risk in order to collect a cargo of pine boards along Indian River in 1775.[11] Aaron Leaming, one of the most active entrepreneurs in Cape May County in the 1740s, made no reference, in over ten years of intermittent diary records, to dealings with New York merchants, and in 1750 he discontinued his subscription to a New York newspaper.[12]

Sparsely populated south central New Jersey was another Philadelphia preserve. Rafters, joists, collar beams, and lighter building materials, dependent on water transportation because of their low value per unit weight, most often went to Philadelphia for export rather than to the coast, where they might be sent to New York.[13] The iron of the barrens was not so entirely dependent on water carriage. An advertisement for the sale of Etna Furnace, in north central Burlington County, makes it clear that the easiest transportation was to Philadelphia via a creek landing four miles distant. But "land carriage to New York market," meaning the distance to a landing on the Mullica River, was also mentioned.[14]

North of the pine barrens, on Crosswicks Creek in western Monmouth County, the attraction of the New York market was more clearly felt. In 1746, a miller, Samuel Rogers, claimed that flour could be transported to either the New York or Philadelphia market for "equally the same charge."[15] Richard Waln, whose mill was above Rogers's on the Crosswicks, dealt exclusively with Philadelphia exporters and even received wheat from down river when he could not obtain enough in southern Hunterdon and western Monmouth counties. Waln's principal business correspondents in Philadelphia were his kinsmen, and this, no doubt, offset any advantage to be gained from dealing with New York merchants.[16] The merchants of Philadelphia had dealings with storekeepers and others in places like Freehold in eastern Monmouth, but New York was definitely more convenient to the northeastern townships, where nine-tenths of the inhabitants of Monmouth County resided.[17]

The same can be said for almost all the inhabitants of Middlesex and Somerset counties in New Jersey, while northern Hunterdon County was mainly oriented toward Philadelphia. Princeton, near the common border of these three counties, clearly appears to have been on the divide between the New York and Philadelphia inland trading areas. An advertisement for the sale of a store there in 1769 neatly illustrates this fact, if it does not prove it. The store was vaunted for, "its vicinity to Philadelphia and New York, consequently will not require a large capital, as goods can so conveniently be had from either

---

[10] Aaron Leaming always had his workers haul the posts and rails they cut on the Atlantic beaches to the Bay side; see Aaron Leaming Diary, 1750–1777, Historical Society of Pennsylvania, Philadelphia (hereafter HSP).

[11] Thomas Rodney to Capt. John Simmons, Aug. 16, 1775, Thomas Rodney Letterbook, Historical Society of Delaware, Wilmington (hereafter HSD).

[12] Leaming Diary, Aug. 17, 1750, HSP.

[13] An advertisement in the *Pennsylvania Journal* (Philadelphia), Oct. 11, 1770, spoke of rafts of twenty-five hundred board feet floated daily down Ancocas (Rancocas) Creek. A petition from the inhabitants of Hattonfield and Chester Townships, Gloucester County, New Jersey, asserted that great quantities of boards and scantling were rafted and flatted down Cooper's Creek almost every week and that European and West Indian goods reached the inhabitants of Great Egg Harbor through their hands; see Petition to the General Assembly, n.d., Papers Relating to Bridges, Roads, Ferries, and Dams, New Jersey State Library, Trenton. Property for sale at Little Egg Harbor was offered in the Pennsylvania papers; see, for example, *Pennsylvania Chronicle* (Philadelphia), Jan. 23, 1769; *Pennsylvania Packet* (Philadelphia), Jan. 2, 1779. The Philadelphia merchant Stephen Collins did business with a Great Egg Harbor man; Robert Smith to Collins, June 15, 1769; July 21, 1770, Stephen Collins Papers, 9:11200 and 10:11460, Library of Congress (hereafter LC).

[14] *Pennsylvania Journal*, Oct. 11, 1770.

[15] *New York Weekly Post-Boy*, Mar. 19, 1745.

[16] Richard Waln Letterbook, 1766–1799, Waln Collection, HSP.

[17] Philadelphia merchant John Mitchell maintained a store in Allentown in the western corner of Monmouth County, on a branch of the Crosswicks. John Reynolds to John Mitchell, Jan. 17, 24, Mar. 14, Apr. 28, 1772 (sequestered), John Mitchell Papers, 1758–1781, Division of Public Records, Harrisburg, Pa. (hereafter DPR).

place, the land carriage to navigation from the former being only about twelve miles, from the latter eighteen miles, besides the conveniency of the stage wagons from both places, which meet in this town twice a week."[18]

Kingston and Stony Hill, likewise near the Hunterdon-Somerset-Middlesex border were, like Princeton, often advertised as being equally convenient to the Philadelphia and New York markets. Various New Jersey advertisements, which had to be placed in either a New York or Philadelphia paper since New Jersey had no newspaper of its own, help establish a surprisingly distinct "trading-shed" line in this region. The people of Hunterdon County almost invariably learned about plantations for sale, runaway horses, servants or slaves, and disclaimers for debts incurred by departed wives in the Philadelphia papers; Middlesex and Somerset county farmers with errant wives or horses resorted to the pages of the *New York Mercury* or *Post Boy*.[19] Most Morris County people did likewise; however property in Roxbury and Chester townships, in western Morris County, usually went up for sale in the *Pennsylvania Gazette* rather than in the New York papers.[20]

Sussex County, in northern New Jersey, was less borderline in its orientation.[21] All but the northern portion sent most of its trade down the river. On the other side of the Delaware, the Pennsylvania counties of Bucks and Northampton were

also well within the Philadelphia trading area. Like their Jersey neighbors, the Pennsylvanians living on or near the upper Delaware often made use of it to move wheat, flour, and iron to Philadelphia for export.[22] Overland conveyance of these goods to the provincial capital or to New York was not out of the question, but for those who lived close to the Delaware—or its major tributary, the Lehigh—water transportation was definitely much cheaper.[23]

On the eve of the Revolution, the settlement of this northern part of the Philadelphia trading area was very sparse beyond Blue or North Mountain. There were, however, several exceptions. Settlers had long since pushed through the Delaware water gap and up along the river on both sides. The people around Minisink, four or five miles north of the mountain, were raising enough wheat to keep several mills in operation, and the flour produced there had an excellent reputation in Philadelphia.[24] Settlers also pushed past the first continuous ridge in the Appalachians, along the West Branch of the Delaware, as the Lehigh River was then called, but the trade of this transmontane population was not so large as that on the upper reaches of the main branch of the river. One enterprising storekeeper on the upper West Branch cast an eye yet farther northward in hopes

---

[18] *Pennsylvania Chronicle*, Mar. 6, 1769.

[19] A property in Princeton, near the Hunterdon-Somerset border, was advertised in the *Pennsylvania Gazette*, Feb. 18, 1762, but in no New York paper. Another Princeton property was offered in the *New York Mercury*, Nov. 29, 1762. That same year in Amwell Township, Hunterdon County, a man offered 20/-in the *Pennsylvania Gazette*, Sept. 9, 1762, for the return of his stolen mare. A southern Hunterdon man informed the public that he and his wife were back on good terms in the *Pennsylvania Journal*, Nov. 25, 1762. Advertisements for property in Middlesex, Somerset, and Monmouth counties were placed exclusively in the *New York Mercury*, Feb. 15, Mar. 29, Apr. 19, June 14, 28, July 5, Aug. 1, Sept. 27, Dec. 27, 1762. In Plukamen Township, Somerset County, a runaway apprentice was advertised for in the *Pennsylvania Gazette*, July 1, 1762, but runaway servants and slaves were expected to head west.

[20] *New York Mercury*, June 28, 1762. The property was in East Jersey. *Pennsylvania Gazette*, Oct. 1, 1762, carried an advertisement for a property in Roxbury Township, Morris County, which was in West Jersey and at the head of the Musconetcong River, a tributary of the Delaware.

[21] Three Sussex advertisements appeared only in Pennsylvania papers. *Pennsylvania Journal*, Dec. 17, 1762; another appeared in the *Pennsylvania Journal*, Feb. 25, 1762.

[22] Samuel Powell, Jr. received three hundred barrels of flour by flatboat from [Samuel?] Depui, of Minisink, above Blue Mountain; Powell to G. Manigault, Jan. 13, 1746/47, Samuel Powell Letterbooks, HSP. The Durham Account Books show that Samuel Depui picked up iron in early 1746, and Thomas Woolson was credited with carriage of iron to Philadelphia at the water carriage rate in April 1746, Ledger A, 1744–1749, Durham Iron Works Account Books, HSP. An Easton storekeeper bargained with a miller at Trenton to supply him yearly with a large amount of wheat and later suffered a partial loss in a flatboat accident when delivering same down the river. Petition of Myer Hart, Sept. 18, 1772, to House of Representatives, Pa., Northampton County Papers, HSP.

[23] The cost of overland carriage that prevailed in all parts of the Philadelphia trading area was surprisingly uniform and stable, approximately a shilling per ton-mile (Pa. shilling per 2,240 lbs). See Walzer, "Transportation," p. 308, and especially footnote 8. The cost of carriage down the Delaware was approximately five pence per ton-mile, which allowed for the roundabout course of the river. See Walzer, "Transportation," pp. 124–25, based on Durham Account Book entries and rates quoted by Richard Smith, *Diary*, May–June 1769, in Francis W. Halsey, ed., *A Tour of Four Great Rivers, the Hudson, Mohawk, Susquehanna, and Delaware, in 1769* (Port Washington, New York: Ira J. Friedman, Inc., 1964), p. 80.

[24] Richard Waln to Daniel Arthur, June 4, 1768, Richard Waln Letterbook, 1766–1799, Waln Collection, HSP.

of establishing a trade with the people who were moving into the Wyoming Valley. His enterprise was admirable, but his affirmation in 1776 that "it is really a lively place here" was overenthusiastic.[25]

At the end of the colonial period, the people of Northampton were penetrating the Appalachian Mountains in still another location at Wind Gap, where Robert Levers, an agent for Richard Peters, established himself in the 1760s. Levers's two primary concerns were the Indian trade and supplying the garrison at nearby Fort Hamilton, but by the 1770s he had begun to supply a resident population. In October 1772, he ordered "a ream of good fool's cap and some ink powder, as the country schools now begin to open."[26] Both Levers and John Edmonds of Gnadenhuten (the enthusiastic storekeeper on the Lehigh) dealt through Bethlehem with Philadelphia merchants.

Further west, the limits of the Philadelphia trading area corresponded approximately with North Mountain except where the principal streams, such as the Susquehanna, broke through the ridges. Before the Revolution, the upper Susquehanna was the most rapidly expanding part of the Philadelphia trading area.

The Susquehanna River, as it cuts its way across the eastern seaboard from Harrisburg to the Chesapeake Bay, shows up as a broad swath of blue on a map of Pennsylvania. But this blue swath is very deceptive, at least for the colonial historian, because it was not an important inland waterway. Instead, it was, in the words of R. E. Myers, "The River to be Crossed Rather than to be Followed."[27] Not until well after Pennsylvania

had become an independent commonwealth did flatboats ply the lower Susquehanna.[28] The reason for this is fairly simple; the very breadth of the blue swath suggests the difficulty. Five miles south of the site where John Harris established his ferry across the river in 1753, the bedrock of the Susquehanna is much harder than that to the north or east. This ancient crystalline bedrock forces the river to broaden and flatten out to such a degree that nineteenth-century steamboat captains caustically described it as "miles wide and inches deep." In the late eighteenth and early nineteenth centuries, the farmers of the upper Susquehanna eventually risked their harvests on the shoals of the lower river, but during colonial times it was simply not "easier for the Pennsylvania farmer to float his produce down the Susquehanna to Chesapeake Bay than to draw it overland to Philadelphia."[29] The practice was, rather, to transship goods coming down the Susquehanna at either Harris's Ferry or Middletown to wagons, which carried them across southeastern Pennsylvania to Philadelphia.[30] Middletown was the natural break-in-bulk point, yet Harris's Ferry was the more important of the two places, owing in part to the commercial enterprise of John Harris. During the 1750s and 1760s, Harris gradually established himself as the principal intermediary in commercial matters between the inhabitants of the Juniata and upper Susquehanna River valleys and Philadelphia. Harris,

[25] John Edmonds to William Edmonds, Jan. 5, 1776; Aug. 21, 1775, Northampton County Papers, HSP.

[26] Robert Levers to Thomas Asherton, Oct. 17, 1772, Northampton County Papers, HSP. By 1775, there was a road from Wind Gap north to Wyoming. See application of Henry Sheep, Chestnut Hill Township, Northampton County, Sept. 20, 1775, for a tavern license on that "Great Road," Northampton County Papers, HSP. Richard Peters was a close associate of Proprietor Richard Penn.

[27] Richard E. Myers, "The River to be Crossed Rather than to be Followed," Lancaster County Historical Society *Papers* 57 (1953): 133–34. A surprising number of historians make this mistake. George M. Schumacher, "The Northern Farmer and His Market" (Ph.D. diss., University of California, 1948), p. 65, assumes that the lower Susquehanna was passable, or at least gives his reader that impression. Stella Sutherland says that the river served as a "highway," *Population Distribution*, p. 158. Charles H. Lincoln, *The Revolutionary Movement in Pennsylvania, 1760–1776*, Publica-

tions of the University of Pennsylvania Series in History, no. 1 (Philadelphia: University of Pennsylvania Press, 1901), p. 59, makes the same mistake, which is by no means incidental to his main concern. James W. Livingood, *The Philadelphia-Baltimore Trade Rivalry, 1780–1860* (Harrisburg, Pa.: Pennsylvania Historical and Museum Commission, 1947), p. 3, correctly states that the Susquehanna was unnavigable for fifty miles above its mouth.

[28] W. F. Warner, "Arks and Rafts on the Susquehanna," Lancaster County Historical Society *Proceedings* 34 (1930): 46–47. Despite the early nineteenth-century activity, the lower Susquehanna never really became a channel of transportation and is not one today. As Myers observes in his "River to be Crossed," p. 134, "no modern highway follows this part of the river." The Pennsylvania Railroad follows it for a short distance between Harrisburg and Philadelphia.

[29] Lincoln, *Revolutionary Movement*, p. 59.

[30] Some of the goods transferred to freight wagons at Middletown (or across the river) were carried through York County to Baltimore, as Lincoln correctly states, *Revolutionary Movement*, p. 63. What percentage went south is unknown. I believe the overwhelming bulk of trade flowed east from Middletown and Harris's Ferry as indicated by the location of both these places on the eastern bank.

of course, was a Pennsylvanian with all his business connections in Philadelphia.[31] Expansion into the upper Susquehanna area had come from the Lebanon valley and the Lancaster plain, not the lower Susquehanna and Maryland.[32] Thus, the original commercial orientation was firmly fixed in an easterly direction.

As early as 1741 settlers pushed into Shareman's Valley, just north of the first ridge. For the following two decades these people fought a running battle with the proprietary government, which sought to exclude them from what was legally Indian territory. In 1750, the Reverend Richard Peters, together with Conrad Weiser and George Croghan, led an expedition up the Juniata where they evicted a large number of families and burned their cabins. By the 1760s, the Pennsylvania authorities recognized the impossibility of preventing settlement beyond North Mountain.[33] The number of farmers there was large enough to produce a significant quantity of wheat and flour, rye and oats, and especially boards, rails, and shingles, which were sent down the Susquehanna in exchange for a great variety of West Indian and European manufactured goods. In 1770, for example, James Gollohor of Juniata ordered ninety-one gallons of rum and fifty-five pounds of sugar from John Harris.[34] And in the same year Harris supplied James Patterson of the same place with a Negro girl for £80, half of which Patterson paid in boards floated down the river.[35]

Harris was also very much interested in the trade of the Cumberland Valley, most of which flowed eastward.[36] The Shippens of Lancaster likewise helped draw Cumberland trade east. In 1751, the inhabitants of the western part of the valley warned that if the county seat were placed in the eastern end of the county their trade might go instead to Maryland, but the choice of Carlisle over Shippensburg had no such effect.[37]

Shippensburg boosters claimed that the trade of the settlements springing up beyond them in the ridge and valley west of Cumberland was in danger of being lost by Philadelphia. But at least one man, Thomas Swaine of Black Log Valley, dealt primarily with William Pollard, a Philadelphia merchant. Pollard was, in fact, Swaine's brother-in-law, and together the men were attempting to bypass the pioneer stage in agricultural development and to establish a commercially profitable farm on the frontier, while taking advantage of profitable land investments. Pollard advised Swaine to acquire cattle as cheaply as possible from his neighbors, but if that was impractical, he would send some from Philadelphia. He did send an indentured servant and instructed Swaine to brew, rather than buy, the beer he gave to the servants for their daily allowance. In addition, Pollard sent a fine stallion to Swaine, with advance instructions not to let any scrubby scoundrels get to the mares first.[38]

---

[31] The groundwork was laid for Harris by his father, the first English trader in this region, who monopolized the Indian trade there for some time. See William H. Egle, *History of the Counties of Dauphin and Lebanon* (Philadelphia: Everts & Peck, 1883), pp. 186–88. The elder John Harris died in 1749. In 1753, John Harris, Jr., whose extant ledger, at the HSP, tells us much about inland trade and transportation, acquired the ferry that bore his name.

[32] Wayland F. Dunaway, "Pennsylvania as an Early Distributing Center of Population," *Pennsylvania Magazine of History and Biography* 55, no. 2 (1931): 135.

[33] Uriah J. Jones, *History of the Early Settlement of the Juniata Valley* (Philadelphia: H. B. Ashmead, 1856), pp. 37, 43–44.

[34] Account of James Gollohor of the Juniata Valley, John Harris Ledger, p. 178, John Harris Collection, HSP.

[35] Memorandum of Aug. 27, 1769, concerning transaction with "Capt. Paterson," and account of James Paterson, entry for Jan. 16, 1773, Harris Ledger, pp. 160, 118, John Harris Collection, HSP. Another Juniata man, Marcus Hulling, supplied Harris with boards and shingles by the thousand; see account of Hulling, entries for July 5, Dec. 25, 1766;

[36] See Harris Ledger, John Harris Collection, HSP. He had dealings with people along the Conodoguinet Creek and in Carlisle, the county seat.

[37] "A Petition from the Commissioners and Assessors of Cumberland County, in the behalf, and at the desire of the far greater part of the inhabitants of the said county," June 16, 1751, *Votes and Proceedings of the House of Representatives of the Province of Pennsylvania 1682–1776*, reprinted in *Pennsylvania Archives*, 8th ser., 8 vols. (Harrisburg: Pennsylvania State Bureau of Publications, 1931–1935), 4:190 (hereafter cited as *Votes*). Placement of the county seat in the eastern end of the county encouraged settlers who had legal business or political duties to trade there and led to their establishing connections east instead of south of their dwelling places.

[38] See especially Pollard to Swaine, Mar. 4, Apr. 15, 1773; Mar. 4, Apr. 15, 30, July 4, 1774; Pollard to William Ripley, Apr. 29, 1774, where he refers to "Tho. Swaine and Co.'s farm in Black Log Valley," William Pollard Letterbook, 1772–1774, HSP.

Apr. 21, 1775, Harris Ledger, p. 124, John Harris Collection, HSP. There was considerable trade between Harris and the soldiers at Fort Augusta, at the confluence of the north and south branches of the Susquehanna. James Burd also participated in the trade with Augusta, James Burd Account Book, 1747–1748, American Philosophical Society, Philadelphia, Pa. Neither Burd nor Harris traded with the Connecticut people moving into the Wyoming Valley or upper North Branch.

Swaine's and Pollard's dealings reemphasize the importance of a man's personal acquaintances and business connections in influencing the orientation of his trade. Eventually the pressure of relatively high overland transportation costs and the existence of a rival tidewater entrepôt much closer at hand effected a contraction of the Philadelphia trading area, but only after the merchants of Philadelphia and the politicians of Pennsylvania had failed to buttress their original advantages.

In York County, the rise of Baltimore Town was more definitely felt than north of the mountains. In the 1750s, there were a significant number of petitions to the York County Court from southern townships for roads to "the temporary line," Joppa, and Patapsco, indicating that York County produce was often carried to the Chesapeake for shipment to market.[39] By 1770, petitions were forthcoming from northern townships as well, asking for new roads to Maryland and, in particular, to Baltimore.[40] It would be a mistake to conclude that all trade in York County was suddenly siphoned off to Baltimore. York County shopkeepers and merchants retained their Philadelphia and Lancaster connections and continued to buy imported articles from them.[41] Moreover, much of the wheat carried southward to tidewater ultimately came to Philadelphia. In the 1750s and 1760s, millers and merchants along the northwestern shore of the Chesapeake, including those resident in Baltimore proper, sent both wheat and flour to Head of Elk for transshipment to Christiana Bridge, the Brandywine mills, and Philadelphia.[42]

Throughout the colonial period, the trade of the upper Chesapeake in Maryland was decentralized. Individual merchants and planters dealt directly with British and New England merchants, bypassing wholesale merchants resident in some central entrepôt; but some of the trade of northern Maryland was centered in the hands of Philadelphia merchants, who supplied their Maryland correspondents with cloth, sugar, glass, rum, and various other imported goods, shipping them via the Christiana Creek and Head of Elk. The Philadelphia suppliers had to compete, of course, with the direct trade. "This day received thine per Sistey Post, informing of the remainder of the goods being shipt for Christeen," a Deer Creek retailer wrote Philadelphia merchant Stephen Collins in 1761. "Shall get [them] down as soon as possible, the others am selling though but slowly as a great many cargoes arrived about the same time from London."[43] Despite the competition, Philadelphia wholesalers were able to capture a portion of the market for imported goods even after Baltimore became established as a major entrepôt in this area.[44]

Merchants in Baltimore proper were sometimes supplied with imported goods from Philadelphia. In 1776, Tobias Rudulph, merchant and miller at Head of Elk, informed his son who was a merchant in Philadelphia that "The Last Hogsheads of sugar you sent me . . . was Very Good. I sent some to sell to Baltimore Town per Isaac Grist. The People there said they Got as Good By Way of Galbraith [a merchant at Christiana Bridge] at Thirteen Pence."[45] Trade was brisk enough be-

---

[39] See numerous petitions in York County Quarter Sessions Docket, 10 vols., 1759–1775, York County Court House, York, Pa.; for example, 3:13, 34; 4:13, 14, 30. The "temporary line" between Pennsylvania and Maryland was replaced by a permanent boundary, surveyed by Charles Mason and Jeremiah Dixon, in 1767.

[40] York County Quarter Sessions Docket, 10:13, 16, 34, 35, 65, 87–88, York County Court House, York, Pa.

[41] See the business records of Thomas and Hance Hamilton of York County, Hance Hamilton Papers, HSP. Philadelphia merchant John Mitchell had dealings in York County; Robert White to Mitchell, Apr. 14, 1772, John Mitchell Papers, DPR; George Irwin to Mitchell, July 28, 1775, York County Papers, Miscellaneous Manuscripts, HSP. The advantages that Philadelphia merchants could still offer over Baltimore were lower prices for imports, better prices for exports, better credit terms, a wider selection of imported goods, and greater dispatch in the transaction of business.

[42] Tobias Rudulph to Levi Hollingsworth and Zebulon Rudulph (Philadelphia merchants), Hollingsworth Collection, 1748–1887, Correspondence, HSP; especially Rudulph to Hollingsworth and Zebulon Rudulph, May 20, 1776.

[43] Samuel Harris to Stephen Collins, July 19, 1761, Stephen Collins Papers, 1:9709, LC. Deer Creek was in western Baltimore County and after 1772 in Harford County. See also William Cox, of Deer Creek, to Stephen Collins, Oct. 20, 1763, Stephen Collins Papers, 3:10058, LC, asking for an item to be sent via Christiana Bridge, Delaware. Harris told Collins, in 1761, to ignore his order for a loaf sugar if it was not already filled, because a large quantity of sugar was expected daily from Boston. Harris to Collins, May 25, 1761, Stephen Collins Papers, 1:96002, LC.

[44] Alexander Williamson of Frederick Town (on the Eastern Shore) dealt with Philadelphia merchant John Mitchell, and in 1772 he asked to be informed when Mitchell's spring goods came in, "as I shall come up and buy £7- or £800 worth." Williamson to Mitchell, Feb. 15, 1772, John Mitchell Papers, HSP. The difficulty is in not knowing how much of the trade in the area the merchant of Philadelphia usually handled. The delineation of the Philadelphia trading area, as it has been arbitrarily defined, is extremely difficult and uncertain in this region.

[45] Tobias Rudulph to Hollingsworth and Zebulon Rudulph, Aug. 26, 1776, Hollingsworth Collection, Correspondence, HSP. See also Rudulph to Hollingsworth,

tween Baltimore and Head of Elk in 1766 to induce Rudolph to enter into a scheme to run a stage boat between the two places on a regular twice-weekly schedule.[46] At first, Baltimore was a cross between an independent maritime entrepôt and a Philadelphia commercial subcenter. Philadelphia merchants themselves were instrumental in promoting trade there. As with Wilmington, the Philadelphia men were first attracted by the possibility of profiting from the establishment of merchant mills.[47]

Eastern Shore, Maryland, like Baltimore County, was at least partially within the sphere of the merchants of colonial Philadelphia, although it had direct maritime connections with the rest of the North Atlantic world, and although, by the eve of the Revolution, the merchants of Baltimore had begun to monopolize its trade. Property sold in Kent and Queen Annes counties was sometimes advertised in the Pennsylvania papers, and Pennsylvania and New Jersey readers learned about Cecil County slaves and horses in notices aimed primarily at Maryland readers.[48] Philadelphia merchants maintained a commercial correspondence with Eastern Shore men, sometimes collecting money for them.[49] Occasionally, it worked in reverse,[50] and, of course, there was a direct, two-way trade between the two places, consisting primarily of such things as "a box of candles, a bbl of sugar, 2 lb of tea, and 6 lbs of chocolate," which Joseph Williams at Head of Bohemia in Cecil County ordered from Hollingsworth and Rudolph, merchants in Philadelphia.[51] In return, the Marylanders sent such cargoes as "4 hhds

tobacco No 1 to 4 marked C.T., belonging to Charles Tilldon, Kent County . . . No 1 good, no 2 the same, No 3 half good, half trash, and No 4 all trash."[52] Besides tobacco and wheat, some Marylanders sent flour, both superfine and common as well as "midlens" and bread. These bulky commodities reached Philadelphia via Head of Elk and Christeen despite transshipment costs.[53] Occasionally, merchants sent the same goods to or from Philadelphia by sea. A great deal of Maryland and Virginia wheat reached mills in Delaware and Pennsylvania in this manner.

Probably the most heavily traveled road in North America before the Revolution was the one used to avoid this coasting voyage—the ten-mile distance from Head of Elk in Cecil County, Maryland, to Christiana Bridge in New Castle County, Delaware. Other overland connections between the Delaware River and Chesapeake Bay existed, but none was used so much as the Christiana Bridge road.[54] The bridge was enough of a commercial center in its own right to present certain advantages, such as frequent boats to Philadelphia and a number of resident merchants to oversee business. Indeed, the correspondence of Levi Hollingsworth and his partner Zebulon Rudolph with James Partridge, a merchant at "Christeen Bridge," who was also a partner with Hollingsworth and Rudolph in the ownership and operation of a shallop between Philadelphia and "Xteen," makes it clear that if any place in the Philadelphia trading area deserved the label of "lively place," it was Christiana Bridge.[55] The

May 20, 1766; Mark Alexander to Hollingsworth, Sept. 10, 1767; David Brown to Hollingsworth, Sept. 14, 1773, Hollingsworth Collection, Correspondence, HSP.

[46] James Partridge to Hollingsworth, Mar. 21, 1766; Partridge to Rudolph, June 30, 1766, Hollingsworth Collection, Correspondence, HSP.

[47] Charles B. Kuhlmann, *The Development of the Flour-Milling Industry in the United States* (New York: Houghton Mifflin, 1929), pp. 28–29.

[48] *Pennsylvania Chronicle*, Mar. 6, 1769. A property on the Choptank River was advertised as only fifteen miles from a landing on the Delaware, *Pennsylvania Chronicle*, Mar. 13, 1769.

[49] Stephen Collins to William Richardson, "at Gilpin's Point, Choptank River, Dorset County, Maryland," Aug. 17, 1773, Stephen Collins Papers, Memorandum and Letterbook, LC.

[50] James Hollyday to Collins, Sept. 3, 1768, Stephen Collins Papers, 8:11049, LC.

[51] Joseph Williams to Hollingsworth and Zebulon Rudolph, Oct. 1, 1767, Hollingsworth Collection, Correspondence, HSP.

[52] Tobias Rudulph to Hollingsworth and Zebulon Rudulph, Oct. 10, 1767, Hollingsworth Collection, Correspondence, HSP.

[53] Joseph Williams, miller at Head of Bohemia, Cecil County, Maryland, carried on an extensive business with the Philadelphia flour exporters, Hollingsworth and Rudulph. Williams to Hollingsworth and Rudulph, Aug. 12, 28, Nov. 3, 1767, Hollingsworth Collection, Correspondence, HSP. Thomas and Rudolph Bird to Hollingsworth and Rudulph, Sept. 21, 1770, Hollingsworth Collection, Correspondence, HSP. Apparently the Birds also sent bread and flour from Head of Bohemia. Richard Bouldin, another Cecil County miller, sent midlens (a middle grade flour) and stuff (a low grade flour) so that he could buy up wheat; Bouldin to Hollingsworth, Dec. 4, 1773, Hollingsworth Collection, Correspondence, HSP.

[54] Oliver M. Dickerson, *The Navigation Acts and the American Revolution* (Philadelphia: University of Pennsylvania Press, 1951), pp. 252–54.

[55] James Partridge to Hollingsworth and Rudulph, Mar. 21, Apr. 16, May 5, 25, June 30, July 25, Sept. 17, Dec. 12, 15, 1766, Hollingsworth Collection, Correspondence, HSP. In 1768, George Adams, a shallop master, departed from Christiana Bridge for Philadelphia on Mar. 2, 5, 18, 30;

maturation of Baltimore as an independent maritime entrepôt helped bring a quick end to the commercial flourishing of the bridge. And if Penn's capital on the Delaware did not suffer quite so evidently, it was at least adversely affected and hurried toward defeat in the race with New York for commercial preeminence on the seaboard and control of the major share of trade from the trans-Appalachian West, once that trade began to flourish.

Philadelphia merchants understood, or at least sensed, that the size and productivity of the Philadelphia trading area, its continued growth, and their monopolization of the trade of surrounding areas were related to the growth and commercial success of Philadelphia vis-à-vis its sister colonial ports.[56] They realized, too, the significance of the rise of a new seaboard rival. Yet, they did not understand these things with the drama that hindsight allows the historian or with the desperation their counterparts exhibited in the 1820s. Nor was their geographic orientation the same as ours or their horizons so distant. For American historians, the words westward and expansion almost seem to pair themselves automatically. Confronted by a map of the continent and knowing the eventual importance of the inland trade of trans-Appalachia, we can see what actions the Philadelphia merchants should have taken. But with only the seaboard and their ledger books in mind, the practical merchants of Philadelphia invested what little money they thought they could spare for internal improvements, not in improving links with the most rapidly expanding part of the Philadelphia trading area, but in the improvement of navigation on the Delaware. Concurrently, such leading merchants as Able James and Henry Drinker speculated privately in lands on the northern frontier near Shohola. In 1769, they spent a large sum of money supporting men who were to clear away the beaver dams in the area, in order to make the streams navigable and the

swampland inhabitable.[57] Ironically, beaver and other wildlife outnumbered the people in the area until almost the present.

The danger represented by Baltimore was noted in the early 1760s. By 1766, the alarm was sounded. There was, thenceforth, a constant agitation for the improvement of transportation links between Philadelphia and the west, so that the trade of York, Cumberland, Lancaster, and Chester counties would not be carried off to Baltimore.[58] This agitation was the product, primarily, of the inhabitants of Lancaster County and those articulate persons living west of the Susquehanna. The inhabitants of Bucks and Philadelphia counties suspected the westerners were motivated chiefly by a desire to have their roads improved at provincial expense. The settlers in Berks and Northampton counties were generally ready to support the Lancaster, York, and Cumberland people; Chester County, lying between Philadelphia and the west, was divided.[59] The merchants of Philadelphia may have been sympathetic to the agitators, but not so sympathetic that they applied great pressure on the legislature. The same complaint had been heard before.[60] In

---

Apr. 16; May 4, 17, 27; June 3, 9, 26; July 1, 24; Aug. 2, 10, 20, 27; Sept. 3, 11, 18, 24; Oct. 7, 22, 29; Nov. 9, 18; Dec. 4; see list of freights, Hollingsworth Collection, Invoices and Receipts, HSP.

[56] The first (size, productivity, growth, and monopoly of the inland area) did not cause the second (growth and commercial success of Philadelphia). The two were what might be called "causually reciprocal."

[57] See the long account by an unknown person of his efforts to clear a stream at Shohola, fifty to sixty miles (by water) above Blue Mountain, Northampton County Papers, 1682–1887, HSP. For James's and Drinker's involvement, see Robert Levers to Richard Peters, Dec. 29, 1769, Northampton County Papers, HSP.

[58] Petition from diverse freeholders and other inhabitants of the County of Lancaster to the House of Representatives of Pa., Dec. 20, 1774, *Votes of the House of Representatives, from Wednesday, December 29, 1773 [to December 24, 1774]* (Philadelphia: Henry Miller, 1774), p. 69 (hereafter cited as *Votes, 1773–74*); two petitions from diverse inhabitants of the Borough and County of Lancaster to the House of Representatives of Pa., Jan. 13, 1772, *Votes and Proceedings of the House of Representatives . . . the Fourteenth of October, Anno Domini 1771, And Continued by Adjournments* (Philadelphia: Henry Miller), p. 318 (hereafter cited as *Votes, 1771–72*).

[59] "A considerable number" of Chester County people petitioned for a straightening of the Lancaster-Philadelphia road, Jan. 9, 1767, *Votes*, 7:5950, and yet, the Chester County representatives opposed a strengthening of the 1772 road reform law supplement.

[60] The boosters of Shippensburg threatened the loss of their trade to Maryland in 1751, "Petition from the Commissioners and Assessors of Cumberland County," June 16, 1751, *Votes* 4:190, and the backers of Easton for county seat of Northampton warned that if their site was not chosen a great deal of trade of the upper Delaware Valley would be siphoned off to New York, Petition from the inhabitants of upper Bucks, Mar. 11, 1751, *Votes*, 4:187–88. This was probably an empty threat. Research into the extant sources, especially the Northampton County Papers, suggests that

addition, the petitions coming from Lancaster and beyond grossly exaggerated the inroads already made by the merchants of Baltimore in the Philadelphia trading area.[61]

The merchants knew that the danger, although not immediate, was nonetheless real and that remedies were available. First, they knew that transportation between Philadelphia and the upper Susquehanna could, and should, be improved and conversely, that improvement of the lower Susquehanna should be discouraged. Also, there was a demand for lowering the ferry rates across the Susquehanna and the Schuylkill, since western farmers living near, as well as far, had to pay to cross the latter before they could conduct their business in Philadelphia.[62] The improvement of transportation between Philadelphia and the Susquehanna took many forms. There was a scheme to link the upper reaches of the Schuylkill with the Susquehanna. Penn had envisioned such a link, and the Schuylkill had already been somewhat improved for local purposes;[63] however, such a scheme was still in its visionary stages in 1770. A more practical proposal was the modernization of the system by which roads were maintained in colonial Pennsylvania.[64] Finally, and most spe-

cifically, the King's Highway between Lancaster and Philadelphia, the chief artery of commerce in the province other than the Delaware, could be straightened and made more passable. This was the project most of the alarmists called for in the early 1770s.[65]

The negative act of forbidding the development of the lower Susquehanna, which cost nothing, was the easiest way of meeting the Baltimore threat and was attended to in 1771. Ferry rates were less easy to adjust. By 1770, rates across both the Susquehanna and Schuylkill were yielding high profits for those granted the right to collect them, at the price of measurably raising the cost of transportation from west to east. The charge for crossing the two rivers raised freight costs from York and Cumberland counties by 7 or 8 percent.[66] In 1769, the Pennsylvania House of Representatives took the first hesitant step toward a remedy. It formed a committee to investigate the possibility of making Middle Ferry over the Schuylkill free, but the proposal died in committee.[67] It appears that tampering with the traditional policy of granting exclusive rights to operate a ferry or

some, though not a great deal, of Northampton County trade went to New York. Theodore G. Thayer, *Pennsylvania Politics and the Growth of Democracy, 1740–1776* (Harrisburg, Pa.: Pennsylvania Historical and Museum Commission, 1953), p. 130, claims that "the farmers of Northampton County often sent his product to New York."

[61] Suggested by material presented earlier in the delineation of the western Pennsylvania and northern Maryland portions of the Philadelphia trading area.

[62] Petition to the House of Representatives of Pa., Dec. 23, 1774, *Votes*, 6:561; Johann D. Schoepf, *Travels in the Confederation, 1783–1784*, ed. and trans. A. J. Morrison, 2 vols. (Philadelphia: W. J. Campbell, 1911), 2:20. Schoepf, making this point as late as 1783, stressed danger and delay rather than cost. He said the main reasons why the inhabitants of York went to Baltimore was "not because that city is nearer to them or offers a better market for their flour, grain, cattle. . . ."

[63] Theodore B. Klein, *The Canals of Pennsylvania and the System of Internal Improvements* (Harrisburg, Pa.: William Stanley Ray, 1901), p. 4.

[64] The first road reform bill was passed in 1762, the next in 1765, the third in 1772, and another in 1779. "An act for opening and better amending and keeping in repair the publick roads and highways within this province," passed Feb. 17, 1762, James T. Mitchell and Henry Flanders, eds., *The Statutes at Large of Pennsylvania from 1682 to 1801*, 16 vols. (Harrisburg, Pa: C. E. Aughinbaugh, 1896–1911), 6:538ff.; "An act for opening . . . the public roads . . . ," passed May 21, 1772, Alexander J. Dallas, ed., *Laws of the Commonwealth of Penn-*

sylvania, From the Fourteenth Day of October, One Thousand Seven Hundred, to the First Day of October, One Thousand Seven Hundred and Eighty-One . . . (Philadelphia: Hall & Sellers, 1797), pp. 623–31; "An act to continue an act entitled an act for opening . . . the public roads," passed Sept. 30, 1779, Dallas, *Laws of the Commonwealth of Pennsylvania*, pp. 805–6.

[65] Petitions to House of Representatives of Pa., Jan. 9, 1767, *Votes*, 7:5950; Dec. 20, 1772, *Votes*, *1773–1774*, p. 69; two petitions, Jan. 13, 1772, *Votes*, *1771–1772*, p. 313; Jan. 20, 1772, *Votes*, *1771–1772*, p. 325.

[66] The charge to cross the Susquehanna in a loaded wagon was 7/6, see Harris Ledger, John Harris Collection, HSP. Theophile Cazenove claimed Harris was making a profit of £200 a year. Rayner W. Kelsey, ed., *Cazenove Journal, 1794; A Record of the Journey of Theophile Cazenove through New Jersey and Pennsylvania* (Haverford, Pa.: The Pennsylvania History Press, 1922), p. 54. The charge over the Schuylkill, fixed in 1723 and not changed during the colonial period, was much lower (one shilling for four horses and a loaded wagon). See an act for establishing a ferry over the Schuylkill, Dallas, *Laws of the Commonwealth of Pennsylvania*, p. 200; and the terms of the grant of ferry rights to John Harris, as contained in Egle, *History of the Counties*, p. 293. There were complaints of high profits on the Schuylkill ferries as early as 1750, see petition from inhabitants living west of Schuylkill, Nov. 30, 1750, *Votes*, 4:176.

[67] Resolution of the House of Representatives of Pa., Dec. 23, 1774, *Votes*, 8:7179; Jan. 6, 1769, *Votes*, 6:117; close scrutiny of House Journals until 1776 shows the committee never reported, or at least the House never acted.

with the rates fixed at the time of the grant was a more real and immediate danger than the supposed threat of a rival maritime entrepôt.[68]

Road reform was certainly much needed on the eve of the Revolution.[69] In 1762, the province began to move in this direction when it combined two or three townships into one road district for the sake of administrative efficiency.[70] Opposition was immediately forthcoming from each township that had spent more on roads than its partner in the new road district and now feared that it would have to help improve its neighbors' roads.[71] The pairing of Blockley and Kingsess townships, in Philadelphia County, provides a classic example of the problem. The Kingsess people had not only put their roads in order, as Blockley's settlers had not, but they were also outnumbered by the freeholders of Blockley. Thus, they complained that the people of Blockley "had it in their power to draw every penny of the [new road] tax" to their own use.[72]

By 1774, highway reform had become a provincial issue. Philadelphia County road supervisors complained that reform in the name of efficiency had gone so far that they were being denied their right to trial by jury in cases where they were accused of neglect of duty. At the same time, Lancaster petitioners complained that the stipulations of a newly proposed road reform bill, which provided penalties for road supervisors who neglected their duties, were not stringent enough.

Another unfortunate stipulation of the law, according to the Lancaster petitioners, was the provision that called for an examination of the accounts of the outgoing supervisors by four discreet freeholders, chosen by the freeholders of each district. The Lancaster County petitioners argued that this provision acted as a deterrent to "an active discharge" of the supervisors' duties, because the supervisors were afraid to proceed with boldness "lest their accounts should not be approved as just and reasonable."[73]

The question was then put to the House whether to proceed to a further consideration of the supplement to the act, already on the floor, for better opening and mending the public highway, without the amendments suggested by the Lancaster County petition or to wait until the alterations requested by the petitioners could be made. The members from Lancaster, naturally, voted to wait. They were joined by the representatives of York, Cumberland, Berks, and Northampton counties. But the representatives from Bucks, Chester, and Philadelphia (County and City) did not react kindly, with few exceptions, to the Lancaster suggestions.[74]

Bucks, Chester, and Philadelphia, with their roads somewhat in order, resembled Kingsess Township in this issue; they were unwilling to make concessions in the name of efficiency. The

---

[68] The charge at Harris Ferry was still 7/6, or the equivalent thereof in 1815, Myers, "River to be Crossed," p. 146. The demand that the ferry rates on the Schuylkill be lowered or a bridge built was opposed vigorously and effectively in 1749–1750 by the holders of the monopolies to operate ferries there; see petition to the House from James Coultas, June 8, 1749, *Votes*, 4:107; petition from Mrs. Mary Gray to the House, June 19, 1749, *Votes*, 4:108; petition from inhabitants on the west side of the Schuylkill to the House, Nov. 30, 1750, *Votes*, 4:176.

[69] In the 1740s, travel by wagon began rapidly increasing in the Philadelphia trading area. By 1750, the medieval system of relying on local governments and the statute labor, successful enough when heavy-wheeled vehicular traffic was minimal, was no longer adequately maintaining the roads. See report to the House of a committee appointed to inspect the laws relating to highways, Nov. 25, 1750, *Votes*, 4:175, and a petition from sundry overseers of the highways for the County of Philadelphia to the House, Nov. 18, 1750, *Votes*, 4:173.

[70] "An act for opening and better amending and keeping in repair the public roads and highways within this province," passed Feb. 17, 1762, Mitchell and Flanders, *Statutes*, 6:5382ff.

[71] For examples, see petition from the freemen and inhabitants of the townships of Plymouth, Whitpain, Worcester, and Norriton, Philadelphia County, to the House, Feb. 2, 1765, *Votes*, 7:5735; petition from the inhabitants of Dover Township, York County, to York County Court of Quarter Sessions, July, 1770, York County Quarter Sessions Docket, 10:71. There was "one long story of resistance to transfer of power from parish to county," in England, according to Sidney and Beatrice Webb, *The Story of the King's Highway* (1913; reprint ed., Hamden, Conn.: The Shoe String Press, 1963), introduction.

[72] Petition from the inhabitants of the Township of Kingsess, Philadelphia County, to the House, May 15, 1765, *Votes*, 7:5747–8; petition from the supervisor of the public roads and from diverse inhabitants of Blockley Township, Philadelphia County, to the House, Jan. 24, 1767, *Votes*, 7:5970–1.

[73] Petition from the Commissioners of the County of Philadelphia to the House, Dec. 13, 1774, *Votes, 1773–1774*, p. 63; petition from diverse freeholders and other inhabitants of Lancaster County to the House, Dec. 20, 1774, *Votes, 1773–1774*, p. 69.

[74] Record of voting concerning whether the House at that particular sitting should proceed to further consideration of the supplement to the act for better opening the public highways, Dec. 20, 1774, *Votes, 1773–1774*, p. 69. Merchants Michael Hillegas, for Philadelphia County, and Joseph Galloway, for Bucks, voted to proceed immediately without including the Lancaster suggestions to strengthen the supplement. Thomas Mifflin and Charles Thomson, representing the city of Philadelphia, cast similar votes. John Dickinson and one other Philadelphia County man voted no, as did one Chester County representative.

other counties resembled Blockley Township; they were less able to put their own roads in good order and were eager for a more general system of road repair, but in this case, although like Blockley the interior counties were more populous, they did not have it in their power to "draw every penny of the tax" to what purposes they desired.[75]

One might expect that the Lancaster members had even more trouble getting the House to appropriate a large sum of money to straighten and mend the King's Highway between Lancaster and Philadelphia, because on this project the westerners could not anticipate the support of Berks and Northampton. Yet the House had already approved, in 1772, a grant of £1,000 Pennsylvania currency for that purpose. Perhaps the westerners did receive support from Northampton and Bucks because the House agreed, at the same time, to appropriate a similar amount for the improvement of navigation on the first falls of the Delaware.[76] But there was a stipulation that the money for both projects would be paid only after it had been matched by private subscription. This was an opportunity for Philadelphia merchants to show their concern for better transportation to the west, but there are no records of individual contributions. The Delaware funds were matched and put to work; the King's Highway funds were not.[77] If wealthy citizens were pressed for contributions then, as they are now, it seems that Philadelphians favored the Delaware project over the Lancaster one, or none at all.

Philadelphia merchants were well aware that the threat of a major incursion into their inland trading preserve by merchants of a rival entrepôt could be met by lowering the cost of overland transportation from the Susquehanna and by lowering the cost of crossing the river. But awareness of something and the decisiveness necessary to set a high priority to deal with a threat are two different things. The merchants of Philadelphia, not understanding just how high the stakes were, were more interested in improving the passage over the falls on the upper Delaware than in improving the King's Highway from Lancaster to Philadelphia. Their gentlemen-farmer neighbors, representing Bucks, Philadelphia, and Chester counties, with their own roads already financed at the township level, were all too ready to agree with the merchants.[78] It took fifty years and the Erie Canal to alter this attitude in Pennsylvania. And then, in a desperate scramble, the backers of internal improvements nearly bankrupted the state.[79]

---

[75] A sectional interpretation of Pennsylvania politics is not offered here. The analysis and explanation is focused on "this issue" and "this case."

[76] Resolution of the House of Representatives of Pa., Mar. 20, 1772, *Votes, 1771–1772*, pp. 379–81.

[77] Report of the Committee of Assessors of the State of the Public Accounts, given to the House, Sept. 19, 1772, *Votes, 1771–1772*, pp. 394ff. Examination of subsequent annual reports until 1777 shows no account of the £1,000 for the Lancaster-Philadelphia highway project being paid out nor the surrender of the certificate upon the matching by private funds of the sum tentatively appropriated.

[78] At this same time, 1772, the assembly appropriated £1,500 "for the defense of the City of Philadelphia"; £3,000 was spent for materials and labor on the Philadelphia piers in the Delaware; and £8,000 was loaned to the City for paving its streets, Resolution of the House, Sept. 17, 1772, *Votes, 1771–1772*, p. 412, Accounts of the Wardens of the Port of Philadelphia, Dec. 29, 1775, *Votes and Proceedings of the House of Representatives . . . on the Fourteenth of October, Anno Domini 1774, and Continued by Adjournments* (Philadelphia: Henry Miller, 1775), p. 673; account, *Votes*, 6:406, 498.

[79] Avard L. Bishop, *The State Works of Pennsylvania* (New Haven, Conn.: Tuttle, Morehouse & Taylor, 1907), pp. 228–29. The original estimated cost of the Pennsylvania canal was $3 million but the total amount eventually spent by the state was $100 million.

A Historical Checklist of
the Pines of Eastern North America

Charles van Ravenswaay

AS THE age of craftsmanship recedes in time, the appeal of its products and our desire to learn about them increase. In this effort of rediscovery—for much that we seek was once part of the lore of early craftsmen—techniques of scientific analysis are becoming a significant aid in the identification and interpretation of examples of the American decorative arts. Wood, the most frequently used material, has received much attention through microscopic analysis, which can yield important information about early American wood objects. But the technique of microscopic identification still has shortcomings. Although many species can be identified by microscopic analysis, other woods are so similar in their cell structure, such as red pine (*Pinus resinosa* Ait.) and Scotch pine (*Pinus sylvestris* L.), that differentiation is sometimes impossible.

Further refinement of microscopic techniques may solve the problem of positively identifying all species of wood. In addition, the application of scientific analysis to subjects that have not yet been studied systematically could provide other useful information for students of the decorative arts. Lumbermen, carpenters, cabinetmakers, and botanists have long recognized that different growth conditions materially affect the texture and chemical composition of wood from trees of the same species. Soil experts have charted the distinctive regional soils of the continent and their localized variations. Perhaps scientists can develop techniques for identifying the type of soil in which a particular tree grew. Such a clue would narrow the area of speculation about where anonymous wooden objects were made.

But a complete answer to problems of identification can only emerge from a combination of historical and aesthetic judgment with the new information provided by scientific methods. Within recent years attention has focused on the significance of secondary woods used in furniture; subsequently, a popular myth has developed that secondary woods indicate the region or place in which a piece was made. This may be a convenient simplification, but it is not an accurate one. The scientific identification of these woods is only the first step in the involved process of determining what a particular kind of wood in a particular object really means.

The uninitiated, for example, may assume that eastern white pine (*Pinus strobus* L.) was limited in its growth to New England. Actually it grew far into the South along the Alleghenies, and some of its greatest stands were in the forests of western New York and Pennsylvania and in Michigan and Wisconsin. It does not necessarily follow that because a tree grew in a particular area it was always used there at an early period. White pine grew abundantly in the mountains of eastern Tennessee, but in such inaccessible areas that it was not economically exploited until the late nineteenth century. In South Carolina it was more accessible and may have had a limited use earlier, but it was not as available to the centers of population as were the southern hard pines whose greater permanence in the southern climate encouraged their use. Much lumber from within the present United States was shipped to Nova Scotia, to the West Indies, and to England before

It gives me particular pleasure to acknowledge the assistance of Harold Bruce, of the University of Delaware, for his critical reading of the manuscript during the preliminary stages of its compilation, and his many useful suggestions.

1800. Although most of it was used for the construction of houses and ships, some of it, other than the fine cabinet woods, was used in making furniture and other wares. For these reasons, in determining the significance of the use of a particular wood, students of early American wood technology must understand and assess a number of complex factors, factors which change with each generation—the availability of certain woods to the craftsman; regional and local preferences; and the internal, coastal, and foreign commerce in lumber. Unfortunately, much of the essential information is not readily available.

The following checklist is a limited and experimental effort to compile data useful to students of American furniture, buildings, ships, and other products in which wood is the essential raw material. The sources cited are only a sampling of the vast literature on the subject, but they include the more informative botanical works as well as travel books, government reports, and articles. It is hoped that this survey will encourage others to undertake more research on the subject.

In preparing the checklist, a particular effort was made to include all the common names used for the trees at various places and periods and to identify these names scientifically, so that students will not be confused by historical references. White pine, for example, is not necessarily *Pinus strobus* L. The name has been given to three species of eastern pines, not to mention a number of western pines. Similarly, many different species were called hard pine, yellow pine, and southern pine. The possible misunderstanding of references to the Canadian name of cypress for jack pine (*Pinus banksiana* Lamb.) is apparent.

Common names had various origins. Frequently settlers gave familiar names to American trees that resembled those they had known in their former homes, such as "walnut" for hickory in New England or "sycamore" for the American tree that has no relationship to the British sycamore. Sometimes they adopted Indian names or chose new ones, which were suggested by a characteristic feature of the tree or by the use that they made of it. Some names seem to be pure whimsy. Others that persisted are corruptions of names given by Swedish, Dutch, French, or Spanish settlers. This popular nomenclature was further enlarged by shipbuilders and those in the lumber industry, both in this country and abroad,

who often created their own names for American woods. As the nation moved west and new species were encountered, the vocabulary grew in size and complexity. By the early nineteenth century, botanists and laymen alike complained about the situation, echoing John Lowell's charge in 1817, that it "introduces a confusion into conversation and even into contracts, which is very inconvenient."[1]

With so much confusion in the meaning of the common names, one cannot fail to be sympathetic with the scientific problems of the pioneer botanists, as well as being impressed by the dedication of those who first explored the original forests of early America. Because of their sense of history and their insatiable curiosity, men like Michaux and George B. Emerson recorded not only scientific data but also the contemporary names of trees and their uses, information essential for the compilation of this study. Without their work these forests, whose immensity helped shape our national history and form the American character, might have disappeared leaving little record. The subject was generally ignored by others of the period who were more concerned with mundane or spiritual subjects, as it has been ignored by the historian. It is hoped that, from the following group of contemporary statements, the use and meaning of these names in different regions and periods, and the occasional false identification given them, will become apparent.

The pines of eastern North America were chosen for this study because they are a more manageable subject than the oaks, for example, and because of their wide distribution and economic usefulness since the beginning of European settlement. The thirteen species found in the region between the eastern slope of the Rocky Mountains and the Atlantic Ocean vary greatly in types of wood, and they were an essential resource in the "make-do" economy of North America's "age of wood." During that period, the technology of the continent was based upon wood, its most abundant raw material, and water for transportation and power. In evolving this wood-and-water technology, Americans combined the traditional lore of Europe with that of the Indians[2]

[1] John Lowell, "Remarks on the Gradual Diminution of the Forests of Massachusetts," *The Massachusetts Agricultural Repository and Journal* 5, no. 1 (Jan. 1818): 40.

[2] Mrs. [Anne MacVickar] Grant, in her *Memoirs of an American Lady* (New York: D. Appleton & Co., 1846), p.

and added to these from observation and experimentation. In time, Americans developed from necessity a great body of woodworking knowledge and skills, more complex than that of Western Europe where there was less reliance on wood and the varieties were more limited.[3] Unfortunately, much of the lore was not recorded and disappeared with the passing of the age of craftsmanship. Only a small part of the knowledge that once existed can be recaptured; nevertheless these clues to the historical uses of American woods, barks, roots, and resins can provide evidence for analyzing furniture and other wooden objects and for restoring and reconstructing early buildings and ships. Unfortunately, lack of space prevents the inclusion of references to the early use of wood products for dyes, foods, medicines, and similar purposes.

The following checklist is organized alphabetically, with dictionary-type entries. The major entries are headed by the scientific names of the species, while the minor entries are headed by the common names given to different species of pine. Scientific nomenclature, as established by Linnaeus in 1753, is based on the "binomial," which consists of two words, the first being the genus (generic name) and the second the species (the specific name). Following these two words is the abbreviated name of the botanist who named the plant, such as "L." for Linnaeus or "Michx." for Michaux.[4]

The entries headed by the scientific names include: a listing of the common names used for each species, the historical and twentieth-century distribution of each species, its growth characteristics, the qualities of wood,[5] its economic uses, the commerce in its lumber, and other information. Where applicable, resinous products have been included because of their relevance to the history of paints and varnishes in North America.

Entries under the common names include the scientific identifications established for the common names; the origin and meaning, if found, of the common name; and where and when it was used. It should be remembered that the common names of the more valuable and widespread species were used long before the first botanists recorded them, while some names were invented by botanists for convenience. In many instances, it has been difficult to identify the scientific species referred to by an obscure common name or by the vague descriptions given for various species in early works. Hopefully, informed readers will be able to correct any errors of attribution that may appear in the text.

The scientific and the common names are listed alphabetically. Scientific and French common names are alphabetized by the name of the species rather than under *"Pinus"* or *"Pin."* For example, *Pinus banksiana* Lamb. and *Pin blanc* both appear in the alphabetical order of their second names.

In order to simplify the checklist, an abbreviated method of citation has been used, and a key to the abbreviations is included in the bibliography. Citations precede the information to which they refer. The date given with each citation has often been difficult to establish. Whenever possible the date the information was recorded by the

---

48, spoke of the wood lore of the native Americans in the Albany, New York, area during the 1750s, "taught by their Indian friends, and the experimental knowledge of their fathers."

[3] "America is more favoured, says Monsieur Michaux, in the variety of her forest trees than France. The number of sorts of American forest trees, whose growth amounts to thirty feet at least, which Monsieur Michaux describes, is 137, of which ninety-five are employed in *the arts*. In France, there are only thirty-seven which grow to that size, of which eighteen only are found in their forests, and seven only of these are employed in civil and maritime architecture." Lowell, "Gradual Diminution of the Forests," p. 38. Wood technology was highly developed in western Europe, particularly in those areas in which native timber was abundant. Nevertheless, because of the general availability of common minerals and other raw materials and the production of glass and ceramics, Europeans were not forced to use wood as a substitute for these materials as frequently as settlers in North America, where the common metals were scarce and manufacturing was limited until the nineteenth century.

[4] The nomenclature and spelling of scientific names used in the checklist conforms to the usage adopted by Elbert L.

Little, Jr., of the U.S. Forest Service, in his valuable *Checklist of Native and Naturalized Trees of the United States (Including Alaska)*. During the past several centuries the scientific nomenclature of American plants has been constantly changed. Although Little's volume does not include all of the scientific names used by earlier writers, it is an essential aid for establishing modern usage, particularly when supplemented by the pioneering checklists compiled by George B. Sudworth while dendrologist of the Division of Forestry.

[5] All references to the specific gravity and the weight of the various woods have been taken from Charles Sprague Sargent's *The Silva of North America*, 14 vols. (Boston and New York: Houghton Mifflin Co., 1897).

author is used; otherwise, the date of publication or in the case of European visitors, such as François André Michaux, the last year of their residence or research in North America is used.

Alligator Pine   *P. virginiana* Mill.
1883 (P. M. Hale, *Woods and Timbers of North Carolina.* Raleigh: P. M. Hale, 1883, 211) : Caldwell County, North Carolina; a resident of that county reported the native woods included "Pine: Yellow, white, spruce or hemlock, black, alligator (?) ." Apparently the later name was unknown to the editor. 1951 (Schoonover, 50) : North Carolina.

Apple Pine   *P. strobus* L.
Before 1809 (Michaux, *Sylva,* 1859, 3:126) : "known in Canada and the United States by the name of *White Pine,* from the perfect whiteness of its wood when freshly exposed, and in New Hampshire and Maine, by the secondary denominations of *Pumpkin Pine, Apple Pine,* and *Sapling Pine,* which are derived from certain accidental peculiarities." 1951 (Schoonover, 34) : in current use.

Arkansas Pine
1. *P. echinata* Mill.
1953 (Little, 264) : the lumber trade.
2. *P. taeda* L.
1951 (Schoonover, 47) : the lumber trade.

Arkansas Shortleaf Pine   *P. echinata* Mill.
1951 (Schoonover, 51) : the lumber trade.

Arkansas Soft Pine   *P. echinata* Mill.
1951 (Schoonover, 51) : the lumber trade.

Balsam Pine   *P. strobus* L.
1951 (Schoonover, 34) : North Carolina.

Bank's [Banksian] Pine   *P. banksiana* Lamb.
1854 (Loudon, 4:2190): *P. banksiana,* "Bank's, *or the Labrador,* Pine." 1951 (Schoonover, 53) : "Banksian Pine (Lit.) ."

Pinus banksiana Lamb.   Jack Pine
Grows farther north than any other species of North American pine, extending from Nova Scotia to the Mackenzie River. Generally of low growth; wood brittle, light, soft, and close grained. Historically unimportant (Fig. 1) .

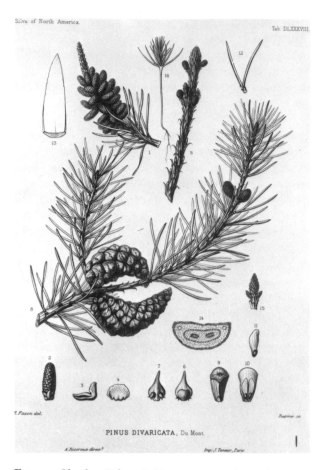

Fig. 1. Charles Edward Faxon, engraving of *Pinus divaricata* Du Mont. Modern identification *Pinus banksiana* Lamb. Plate 588 from Charles Sprague Sargent, *The Silva of North America,* vol. 11 (Boston: Houghton, Mifflin and Co., 1907) . H. 10¾″, W. 7¼″. (Photo, Winterthur.)

Common names. Bank's [Banksian] pine, black jack pine, black pine, Canada horn-cone pine, check pine, cypress, gray pine, Hudson's [Hudson] Bay pine, jack pine, juniper, Labrador pine, long-limbed Hudson's Bay pine, northern scrub pine, prince's [princess] pine, scrub pine, Sir Joseph Bank's pine.

Distribution. Before 1809 (Michaux, *Sylva,* 1859, 3:95) : André Michaux found it growing as far north as "the environs of Hudson's Bay," reported it rare in Nova Scotia and Maine. 1905 (Sargent, *Manual,* 1905, 28) : from Nova Scotia south to Nantucket; west to Minnesota, "most abundant and of its greatest size west of Lake Winnipeg and north of Saskatchewan."

Growth. Before 1822 (Loudon, 4:2190–92) : "a low scrubby, straggling tree, not rising higher in its native country . . . than from 5 ft. to 8 ft."

Reported André Michaux's description of mature, three-foot specimens in Labrador and of not having found specimens taller than ten feet. Cited Dr. Richardson, in Franklin's *Narr. of a Journey to the Shores of the Polar Seas in 1819 and 1822,* as having found forty-foot specimens; and Titus Smith, *Mag. Nat. Hist.,* 8:655, "On the shallow soils in the neighbourhood of Halifax, if not consumed by fires, it produces timber of a useful size." 1897 (Sargent, *Silva,* 11:147): often a "mere shrub" in eastern Canada and on the borders of the northeastern states; to the west where it "attains its greatest size and beauty" it frequently grows seventy feet, with a diameter of two feet.

Wood. Specific gravity, 0.4761; wt. per cu. ft., 29.67 lbs. 1897 (Sargent, *Silva,* 11:149): "light, soft, not strong and close-grained; it is clear pale brown or rarely orange-color, with thick nearly white sapwood, and contains broad conspicuous resinous bands of small summer cells, few small resin passages, and numerous obscure medullary rays."

Uses. Before 1809 (Michaux, *Sylva,* 1841, 3, pl. 136): "Canadians find a speedy cure for obstinate colds in a diet-drink made by boiling these cones in water . . . the only merit of a tree too diminutive to be of any other utility." 1822 (Loudon, 4:2192): citing Dr. Richardson, that the wood of this species, "from its lightness, and the straightness and toughness of its fibres, is much prized for canoe timbers." 1897 (Sargent, *Silva,* 11:149): "cut for fuel in the Province of Quebec, and sometimes is used for railway ties and posts; occasionally it is manufactured into lumber. By the Indians of Canada it is valued for the frames of canoes."

Commerce. No references found.

Folklore. 1897 (Sargent, *Silva,* 11:149, n. 4): "Curious fancies concerning this tree have taken possession of the popular mind in some parts of the country. It is considered dangerous to those who pass within ten feet of its limbs, the danger being greater for women than for men; it is believed to poison the soil in which it grows and to be fatal to cattle browsing near it; and if any misfortune comes to a man who has one of these trees on his land, or to his cattle, it must be burned down with wood, which is piled around it, for the prejudice against it is so strong that no one possessed of this belief would venture to cut down a Gray pine."

Bastard Pine

1. *P. echinata* Mill.

1884 (Sargent, *Forests,* 522): Florida, "The pine between Prairie and Peace creeks, which is sawed at the mill near Ogden . . . is quite shaky, [i.e. timber naturally full of slits or clefts] and . . . the yellow pine in Manatee, Orange, and Hillsborough counties is quite inferior, being mostly of the rough-barked, sappy variety called in this region *bastard pine.*"

2. *P. elliottii* Engelm.

1884 (Sargent, *Forests,* 292): "Bastard pine." 1951 (Schoonover, 56): Florida, Mississippi, and part of Alabama.

3. *P. pungens* Michx.

1770–1771 (Wm. Marshall, 290): quoting from Wm. Hanbury, *A Complete Body of Planting and Gardening* (London, 1770–71), " '*Bastard Pine* is another sort we receive from America. . . . The cones are rather long and slender, and the ends of the scales are so pointed, as to occasion its being called by some Prickly-coned Pine.' "

4. *P. serotina* Michx.

1898 (Sudworth, 18): South Carolina and Georgia.

5. *P. taeda* L.

Before 1822 (*Dict. Arts.,* "Pinus"): one of the varieties of this species. 1951 (Schoonover, 47): Virginia and North Carolina.

Birds-Nest Pine   [*Pinus glabra* Walt?]

1784 (Schoepf, 2:174): South Carolina, name suggested by the "number of small, round, bushy sprouts" along the trunk, "a great number of small twigs on the south side, and none or very few on the north side."

Black Fir   [*P. palustris* Mill?]

1748 (Kalm, 1:147): "Carolina," Kalm described the process for making tar from "only black firs, for the white firs will not serve their purpose."

Black Jack Pine   *P. banksiana* Lamb.

1951 (Schoonover, 53): Wisconsin.

Black Norway Pine   *P. rigida* Mill.

1951 (Schoonover, 49): New York State.

Black Pine

(Not to be confused with *P. thunbergii* Parl.,

Japanese black pine, now naturalized along much of the Atlantic coast.)

    1. *P. banksiana* Lamb.

        1951 (Schoonover, 53) : Minnesota.

    2. *P. rigida* Mill.

        Before 1809 (Michaux, *Sylva*, 1859, 3:118) : sometimes known in Virginia by this name. 1846 (Emerson, *Report*, 1846, 67) : "the bark of the tree is excessively rough, deeply cleft, and very dark colored, whence the tree is sometimes called black pine." 1860 (Hough, *Report*, 471) : Virginia, "called sometime in Virginia 'Black Pine.'" 1951 (Schoonover, 49) : North Carolina.

    3. *P. taeda* L.

        1681 (*Dict. Am.*, 122) : citing N. H. Probate Rec. 1, 47, "From that 48 Pole S. W. to a black Pine Stump on the West." 1809 (*Dict. Am.*, 122) : citing Kendall, *Travels*, 3:146, "The black pine or pitch pine (*pinus taeda*) grows in sands, has a very long leaf, and a bark in very large scales." 1951 (Schoonover, 47) : Virginia, North Carolina, and Georgia.

    4. *P. virginiana* Mill.

        1951 (Schoonover, 50) : Georgia.

Black Slash Pine   *P. taeda* L.

    1951 (Schoonover, 47) : South Carolina. See Slash Pine.

Pin Blanc   *P. strobus* L.

    1817 (Lowell, 43) : "*Pin Blanc,* or *White Pine,* by the Canadians."

Board Pine   *P. strobus* L.

    Before 1672 (Josselyn, 198, n. 3) : New England, "'Board-Pine, is a very large tree two or three fadom about.'"

Bog Pine   *P. taeda* L.
    1951 (Schoonover, 47) : North Carolina.

Broom Pine   *P. palustris* Mill.

    1773 (Bartram, *Travels*, 33) : Georgia, "the great long leaved Pitch-Pine, or Broom-Pine, *Pinus palustris.*" Before 1809 (Michaux, *Sylva*, 1859, 3:107) : one of the several names for this species in the South.

Brown Pine   *P. palustris* Mill.
    1898 (Sudworth, 19) : Tennessee.

Buckeye-Pine   (Unidentified)

    1876 (U.S. Department of Agriculture, "Statistics of Forestry," *Report of the Commissioner of Agriculture for the Year 1875.* Washington, D.C.: Government Printing Office, 1876, 267) : North Carolina. "*Yancey,* a mountainous country, reports . . . plenty of buckeye-pine."

Buckskin Pine   *P. taeda* L.

    1951 (Schoonover, 48) : Louisiana and Mississippi.

Bull Pine

    "Bull" is found used in the common names of various trees and appears to have a derogatory meaning, perhaps to express incongruity. 1884 (Sargent, *Forests*, 193) : first reference found and only for certain Western pitch pines: *jeffreyi, mitis, ponderosa,* and *sabiniana.* 1969 (Interview with Gordon Saltar, May, 1969) : Delaware and Maryland, a colloquism for the poorer grades of "sappy" eastern pitch (hard) pines, including the loblolly (*P. taeda* L.) , longleaf (*P. palustris* Mill.) , shortleaf (*P. echinata* Mill.) , slash (*P. elliottii* Engelm.) , pitch (*P. rigida* Mill.) , and pond (*P. serotina* Michx.) pines.

    1. *P. echinata* Mill.

        1897 (Sargent, *Silva*, 11:145, n. 2) : Arkansas, "*Pinus echinata.* . . . In Arkansas lumbermen recognize two varieties of the wood, yellow and bull, distinguishing them while the trees are still standing by cutting them with axes; the bull pine, which is from low ground, grows more rapidly, and is heavier with thicker sapwood." 1951 (Schoonover, 51) : Virginia.

    2. *P. serotina* Michx.

        1898 (Sudworth, 18) : South Carolina and Georgia.

    3. *P. taeda* L.

        1951 (Schoonover, 48) : Maryland, Arkansas, Texas, and the Gulf region.

Bull Sapling Pine   *P. strobus* L.

    1846 (Emerson, *Report*, 1846, 64) : Maine, not to be confused with "Sapling pine" (*P. strobus*) , for "Bull sapling resembles the pumpkin pine in all respects save the color of the wood, which is a clear white. These names are little used, except in Maine, and by persons who import wood from that State." See Sapling Pine (*P. strobus*) .

Canada Horn-Cone Pine   *P. banksiana* Lamb.
1951 (Schoonover, 53) : California and literature.

Canadian Pine   *P. resinosa* Ait.
1951 (Schoonover, 42) : English lumber trade.

Canadian Red Pine   *P. resinosa* Ait.
1951 (Schoonover, 42) : England.

Canadian White Pine   *P. strobus* L.
1951 (Schoonover, 34) : lumber trade.

Carolina Pine   *P. echinata* Mill.
1951 (Schoonover, 51) : North Carolina and part of Virginia.

Cedar Pine
1. *P. glabra* Walt.
1884 (Sargent, *Forests,* 201) ; 1905 (Sargent, *Manual,* 1905, 28) : both give this synonym.
2. *P. virginiana* Mill.
1860 (Hough, *Report,* 471) : North Carolina, "Often confounded with . . . [*P. echinata* Mill.] and bearing same names, as also of 'Cedar Pine.' " 1951 (Schoonover, 50) : North Carolina.

Check [Chek?] Pine   *P. banksiana* Lamb.
1898 (Sudworth, 19) : gave "Chek Pine" without indicating its area of use. 1951 (Schoonover, 53) : "Check Pine." Apparently taken from Sudworth's list and spelling changed; no area of use given.

Pinus clausa (Chapm.) Vasey.   Sand Pine
Distribution localized almost entirely within Florida. Wood light, soft, brittle. Historically unimportant (Fig. 2).

Common names. Florida spruce pine, oldfield pine, sand pine, scrub pine, spruce pine, upland spruce pine.

Distribution. 1897 (Sargent, *Silva,* 11:127–28) : southeastern Alabama along the coast of Peace Creek, Florida, generally within thirty miles of the coast; St. Augustine along the coast to Halifax River, southward to below Jupiter Inlet. Common in the vicinity of Pensacola Bay and reaches its greatest size near the head of Halifax River.

Growth. 1897 (Sargent, *Silva,* 11:127–28) : on the Florida dunes usually fifteen or twenty feet tall with a trunk rarely a foot in diameter. Maximum growth (near the head of Halifax River, Florida) from seventy to eighty feet with trunks two feet in diameter.

Wood. Specific gravity, 0.5576; wt. per cu. ft., 34.75 lbs. 1884 (Sargent, *Forests,* 199) : "Soft, light, not strong, brittle; . . . color, light orange or yellow, the thick sap-wood nearly white."

Uses. 1897 (Sargent, *Silva,* 11:128) : "stems are occasionally used for the masts of small vessels."

Commerce. No references found.

Folklore. No references found.

Cork Pine   *P. strobus* L.
1873 (*Dict. Am.,* 394) : the name was used in Michigan for white pine lumber which resembled "in softness and texture . . . the cork of commerce." 1884 (Sargent, *Forests,* 553, 557) : Michigan, "The belt of pine which ran through the center of the state . . . contained the best pine

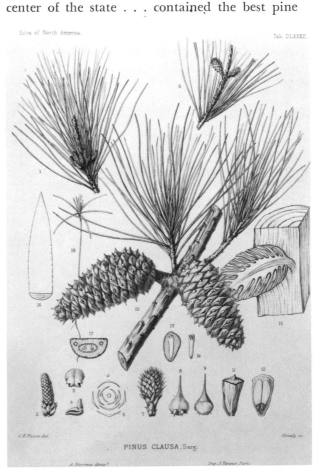

Fig. 2. Charles Edward Faxon, engraving of *Pinus clausa* Sarg. Modern identification *Pinus clausa* (Chapm.) Vasey. Plate 582 from Charles Sprague Sargent, *The Silva of North America,* vol. 11 (Boston: Houghton, Mifflin and Co., 1907). H. 10¾", W. 7¼". (Photo, Winterthur.)

in the northwest. This pine was what was called by lumbermen 'cork pine,' a soft white pine, large and sound, with a thick bark." Wisconsin, "On the Jump river are some fine bodies of pine, nearly approaching in quality Michigan cork pine." 1951 (Schoonover, 34) : Michigan.

Cornstalk Pine   *P. taeda* L.
     1951 (Schoonover, 48) : Virginia.

Cuban Pine   *P. elliottii* Engelm.
     1951 (Schoonover, 56) : area of use not given.

Cypress   *P. banksiana* Lamb.
     1951 (Schoonover, 53) : Quebec and Hudson Bay areas. (From *cyprès*, the French-Canadian name for *P. banksiana*. The Acadians used this name for eastern red cedar, *Juniperus virginiana* L.)

Dwarf Pine   *P. taeda* L.
     Before 1822 (*Dict. Arts*, "Pinus") : a variety of this species.

Eastern White Pine   *P. strobus* L.
     1951 (Schoonover, 34) : lumber trade. See White Pine.

Pinus echinata Mill.   Shortleaf Pine
     Widely distributed from southeastern New York to northern Florida. Tree suffers greatly from forest fire damage; is very susceptible to fungus diseases and insect attacks, but grows rapidly. Wood variable in quality; heavy, hard, and a source of resinous products. Historically important (Fig. 3) .
Common names. Arkansas pine, Arkansas shortleaf pine, Arkansas soft pine, bastard pine, bull pine, Carolina pine, forest pine, New York pine, North Carolina pine, North Carolina yellow pine, oldfield pine, pitch pine, poor pine, rosemary, rosemary pine, rosemary shortleaf, shortleaf [short-leaved] pine, short-leaved pitch pine, shortleaved [shortleaf] yellow pine, shortshat [shortschat?] pine, slash pine, southern pine, southern yellow pine, spruce pine, three-leaved prickly-coned bastard pine, Virginia yellow pine, yellow pine.
Distribution. 1785 (H. Marshall, 100) : "This grows naturally in Virginia." Before 1809 (Michaux, *Sylva*, 1841, pl. 137) : reported it abundant in the Middle States. Located from Connecticut and Massachusetts south through lower Jersey, the eastern shore of Maryland and lower Virginia to the Floridas; also on the Alleghenies in

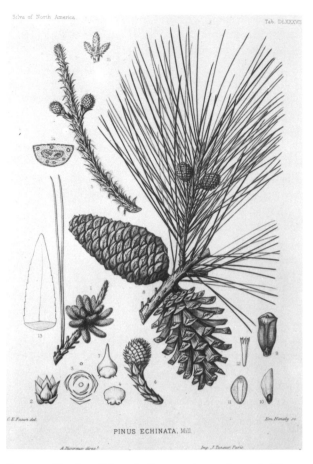

Fig. 3. Charles Edward Faxon, engraving of *Pinus echinata* Mill. Plate 587 from Charles Sprague Sargent, *The Silva of North America,* vol. 11 (Boston: Houghton, Mifflin and Co., 1907. H. 10¾", W. 7¼". (Photo, Winterthur.)

Tennessee and Kentucky. 1818 (Schoolcraft, 5) : near Meramec River, Missouri, "an elevated ridge of land, covered with yellow pine, . . . the soil being sterile, and the vegetation scanty." 1897 (Sargent, *Silva,* 11:145) : "One of most generally distributed and valuable timber-trees of eastern America." 1905 (Sargent, *Manual,* 1905, 39) : gave range from Long Island to northern Florida, westward through the Gulf states to eastern Texas, north to southern Missouri and Illinois, eastern Tennessee and West Virginia. Most abundant and largest growth west of the Mississippi River.
Growth. Before 1809 (Michaux, *Sylva,* 1841, pl. 137) : found the species grew fifty to sixty feet in New Jersey and Maryland; about the same height in Virginia and the upper part of the Carolinas but nearly twice the diameter. "I have measured several that were between five and six feet in cir-

cumference." 1905 (Sargent, *Manual*, 1905, 30): "usually eighty to one hundred, occasionally one hundred and twenty, feet high."

Wood. Specific gravity, 0.6104; wt. per cu. ft., 38.04 lbs. Before 1809 (Michaux, *Sylva*, 1841, pl. 137): "The heart is fine-grained and moderately resinous, which renders it compact without great weight"; an excellent wood "considered as next in durability to the Long-leaved Pine." 1821 (Loudon, 4:2197): England, in March, 1821, John White of Westbourne Green, "an extensive timber merchant," testified before a Parliamentary committee on the durability of different kinds of woods. He stated: " 'In general, Norway timber is the most durable of the fir timbers of Europe; because, after many years, it does not part with its resinous particles; but I consider,' he adds, 'that the American soft or yellow, pine (*P. mitis,* Michx.) is the most durable of the American firs. I have known it last, when exposed to the action of the sun and weather, for a long period, by the side of Norway timber, with equal effect, fully exposed to wind and rain; but, if painted, it does not stand at all so well.' " 1884 (Sargent, *Forests,* 200): "varying greatly in quality and amount of sap, heavy, hard, strong, generally coarse-grained, compact . . . very resinous, resin passages numerous, large; medullary rays numerous, conspicuous; color, orange, the sap-wood nearly white." 1897 (Sargent, *Silva,* 11:145, n. 2): "The sapwood varies greatly in thickness in trees of the same diameter, the variation being apparently dependent on situation, soil, exposure, and moisture. Trees on high ridges and in dry sterile soil have usually the thinnest sapwood, although on ridges it varies from two to six inches in thickness in trees growing side by side; and on lower land from three to twelve inches." See Bull Pine, *P. echinata* Mill. 1951 (Schoonover, 52): "It is one of the 'hard' pines and somewhat difficult to distinguish from other southern pines." It has "a rather exceptional pine figure depending upon the type of cut. . . . The wood holds nails and screws reasonably well, but shrinks a little more than the northern pines."

Uses. 1. Lumber. Before 1809 (Michaux, *Sylva,* 1859, 3:98): "In the Northern and Middle States, and in Virginia, to the distance of 150 miles from the sea, nine-tenths of the houses are built entirely of wood, and the floors, the casings of the doors and wainscots, the sashes of the windows, etc., are made of this species, as more solid and lasting than any other indigenous wood. In the upper part of the Carolinas, where the Cypress and White Cedar do not grow, the houses are constructed wholly of Yellow Pine, and are even covered with it. But, for whatever purpose it is employed, it should be completely freed from the sap [wood], which speedily decays. This precaution is sometimes neglected in order to procure wider boards, especially near the ports, where, from the constant consumption, the tree is becoming rare. Immense quantities are used in the dockyards of New York, Philadelphia, Baltimore, etc. for the decks, masts, yards, beams and cabins of vessels, and it is considered as next in durability with the Long-leaved Pine." 1812 (Stoddard, 217): Missouri, mentioned the yellow pine boards produced on the upper Meramec River, Missouri, "but the price of them are so exorbitant, that few only can afford to purchase them." 1819 (James, 1:79): Missouri, "Some saw-mills have already been erected, [on the Gasconade River] and from them, a supply of pine timber is brought to the settlements on the Missouri." 1897 (Sargent, *Silva,* 11:145–46): "Among the yellow pines it is only surpassed in quality by that of *Pinus palustris,* and being less resinous, softer, and more easily worked, it is often preferred to it for cabinet-making, for the interior finish of houses, and in the manufacture of sashes, doors, and blinds. It is largely used for these purposes, for the framework of buildings, weather-boards, and for flooring and shingles, in car-building, and for railway ties."

2. Resinous products. Before 1809 (Michaux, *Sylva,* 1859, 3:99): "Though this species yields turpentine and tar, their extraction demands too much labor, as it is always mingled in the forests with other trees." 1812 (Stoddard, 217): Missouri, "the pitch and tar" made at the yellow pine forests on the upper Meramec River is "nearly sufficient for the consumption of the country." 1897 (Sargent, *Silva,* 11:146): "It contains a large quantity of resin, and in North Carolina young trees, which are the most prolific, are worked for the production of turpentine."

Commerce. Before 1809 (Michaux, *Sylva,* 1859, 3:99): "The Yellow Pine, in boards from one inch to two and a half inches thick, forms a considerable article of exportation to the West Indies and Great Britain: in the advertisements of Liverpool it is designated by the name of *New York Pine,* and in those of Jamaica by that of *Yellow Pine;* in both places it is sold at a lower price than the Long-leaved Pine of the Southern States, but much higher than the White Pine." 1897 (Sargent, *Silva,* 11:145): "a considerable part of the hard pine lumber cut in the trans-Mississippi pineries used in the states of the central west" is of this species.

Folklore. No references found.

Pinus elliottii Engelm.   Slash Pine

Common in the coastal plain from southern South Carolina to central Florida and southeastern Louisiana; thrives in moist areas where it suffers little from forest fires; of rapid growth. Wood heaviest of all the pines; strong, hard,

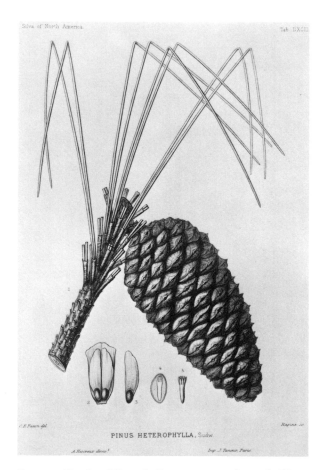

Fig. 4. Charles Edward Faxon, engraving of *Pinus heterophylla* Sudw. Modern identification *Pinus elliottii* Engelm. Plate 592 from Charles Sprague Sargent, *The Silva of North America,* vol. 11 (Boston: Houghton, Mifflin and Co., 1907). H. 10¾", W. 7¼". (Photo, Winterthur.)

straight grained, very resinous, not durable. Minor historical importance (Fig. 4).

Common names. Bastard pine, Cuban pine, meadow pine, pitch pine, saltwater pine, she pine, she pitch pine, slash pine, southern pine, spruce pine, swamp pine, yellow slash pine.

Distribution. 1967 (Mirov, 180): South Carolina southward along the coastal plain to central Florida. Along the Gulf coast to southeastern Louisiana.

Growth. 1897 (Sargent, *Silva,* 11:158): from one hundred to one hundred and fifteen feet in height; trunk from two and a half to three feet in diameter and "free of branches for sixty or seventy feet above the ground."

Wood. Specific gravity, 0.7504; wt. per cu. ft., 46.76 lbs. 1897 (Sargent, *Silva,* 11:158): the tree "produces straight sound spars of large dimensions, is little inferior to the Long-leaved Pine, the wood of the two trees being usually manufactured and sold indiscriminately. It is heavy, exceedingly hard, very strong, tough, durable, and coarse-grained; it is rich dark orange-color, with thick often nearly white sapwood, and contains broad resinous bands of small summer cells."

Uses. 1884 (Sargent, *Forests,* 202): "hardly inferior in value to that of *P. palustris,* although rarely manufactured into lumber. Turpentine is occasionally manufactured in southern Florida from this species." By 1897 (Sargent, *Silva,* 11: 158–59): the species had greater economic value. Sargent reported the more widespread use of its lumber (see above), and that the species was "now generally worked for turpentine in the south Atlantic and Gulf states, is rich in resinous products, yielding freely a limpid pale yellow turpentine, less viscoid and probably richer in volatile oil than that of the Long-leaved Pine." 1933 (Sargent, *Manual,* 1933, 16): "manufactured into lumber and used for construction and railway-ties. Naval stores are largely produced from this tree." 1951 (Schoonover, 56–57): "outranks all other southern pines in the production of naval stores, pine oils, etc. When treated with creosote it is used extensively for posts and poles. The wood is used for heavy general construction, ship building, sheathing and other common lumber uses where a high resin content is not objectionable."

Commerce. No references found before 1900.

Folklore. No references found.

Fat Pine   *P. palustris* Mill.
So named because of its high resinous content? 1951 (Schoonover, 54) : southern states.

Florida Longleaf Yellow Pine   *P. palustris* Mill.
1951 (Schoonover, 54) : lumber trade.

Florida Longleaved Pine   *P. palustris* Mill.
1951 (Schoonover, 54) : Atlantic region.

Florida Pine   *P. palustris* Mill.
1951 (Schoonover, 54) : Atlantic region.

Florida Spruce Pine   *P. clausa* (Chapm.) Vasey.
1898 (Sudworth, 18) : Alabama.

Florida Yellow Pine   *P. palustris* Mill.
1951 (Schoonover, 54) : Atlantic region.

Forest Pine   *P. echinata* Mill.
1951 (Schoonover, 51) : North Carolina.

Foxtail Pine   *P. taeda* L.
1951 (Schoonover, 47) : Maryland, Virginia.

Frankincense Pine   *P. taeda* L.
1770–1771 (Wm. Marshall, 291) : England, quoting from Wm. Hanbury, *A Complete Body of Planting and Gardening* (London, 1770–71), " 'Frankincense-Pine is another American sort, which we receive under that name.' " 1785 (H. Marshall, 102) : *"Virginian Swamp, or Frankincence Pine."* Before 1822 (*Dict. Arts,* "Pinus") : Considered a variety of this species. 1854 (Loudon, 4:2237) : England, "The Frankincense, *or Loblolly* pine." 1860 (Hough, *Report,* 471) : North Carolina, "An important variety [of *P. taeda* Mill.], known as 'Swamp Pine,' 'Slash Pine,' and about Wilmington [N.C.] as 'Rosemary Pine,' sometimes grows in low moist lands to a large size." Trees of this species, growing under swamp conditions, were reported as having heartwood "not very coarse."

Georgia Heart Pine   *P. palustris* Mill.
1951 (Schoonover, 54) : general use.

Georgia Longleaved Pine   *P. palustris* Mill.
1951 (Schoonover, 54) : Atlantic region.

Georgia Pine   *P. palustris* Mill.
1884 (Sargent, *Forests,* 202) : one of several common names for this species. 1951 (Schoonover, 54) : Delaware region.

Georgia Pitch Pine   *P. palustris* Mill.
Before 1809 (Michaux, *Sylva,* 1859, 3:106) : "This invaluable tree is known . . . in England and the West Indies, [as] Georgia Pitch Pine." 1951 (Schoonover, 54) : Atlantic region.

Georgia Yellow Pine   *P. palustris* Mill.
1951 (Schoonover, 54) : Atlantic region.

Pinus glabra Walt.   Spruce Pine
The least common pine of the southeast. Wood light, weak, and very close grained. Historically unimportant (Fig. 5) .
Common names. Birds-nest pine (?) , cedar pine, kingstree, lowland spruce pine, poor pine, smooth-barked pine (?) , spruce pine, Walter's pine, white pine.
Distribution. 1897 (Sargent, *Silva,* 11:131) : lower Santee River in South Carolina to middle and northwestern Florida and west to the Pearl River valley in eastern Louisiana, "being usually

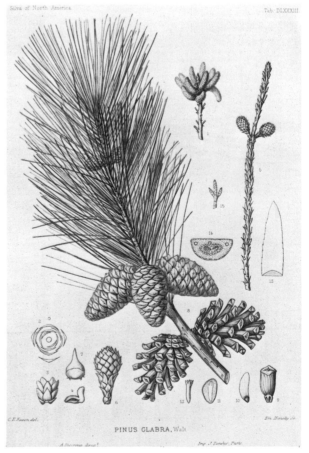

FIG. 5. Charles Edward Faxon, engraving of *Pinus glabra* Walt. Plate 583 from Charles Sprague Sargent, *The Silva of North America,* vol. 11 (Boston: Houghton, Mifflin and Co., 1907) . H. 10¾", W. 7¼". (Photo, Winterthur.)

found only in the neighborhood of the coast, where it grows, singly or in small colonies." Comparatively rare except in the region between the Chatahoochee and the Chockawhatchee rivers in northwestern Florida, where "it probably attains its greatest size and often covers areas of considerable extent, soon occupying abandoned clearings."

Growth. 1897 (Sargent, *Silva,* 11:131): usually eighty to one hundred feet, occasionally one hundred and twenty feet. Trunk from two to rarely three and a half feet diameter.

Wood. Specific gravity, 0.3931; wt. per cu. ft., 24.50 lbs. 1884 (Sargent, *Forests,* 201): "Light, soft, not strong, brittle, very coarse-grained, not durable; bands of small summer cells broad, not resinous, resin passages few, not large; medullary rays numerous, obscure; color, light brown, the sap-wood nearly white."

Uses. 1897 (Sargent, *Silva,* 11:131): "one of the largest of the Pine-trees of eastern North America, . . . has little economic value, although it is occasionally cut for fuel and the saw-mill."

Commerce. No references found.

Folklore. No references found.

Gray Pine   *P. banksiana* Lamb.
    Before 1809 (Michaux, *Sylva,* 1859, 3:95): in Canada called "Gray Pine." 1854 (Loudon, 4:2191): "The cones are . . . of a grey or ash colour (whence the American name of grey pine)." 1905 (Sargent, *Manual,* 1905, 27): "Gray Pine." 1951 (Schoonover, 53): Vermont, Minnesota, Michigan, Ontario.

Great Swamp Pine   *P. taeda* L.
    See Rosemary Pine, for which this is one of the synonyms used in eastern North Carolina.

Hard Pine
    Name commonly used for any one of various pine species that have hard wood.
    1. *P. palustris* Mill.
    1884 (Sargent, *Forests,* 202): "Hard Pine." 1951 (Schoonover, 54): Alabama, Mississippi, Louisiana.
    2. *P. resinosa* Ait.
    1951 (Schoonover, 42): Wisconsin, Maine, the lumber trade.

3. *P. rigida* Mill.
    1951 (Schoonover, 49): Massachusetts.

Heart Pine
    1. *P. palustris* Mill.
    1951 (Schoonover, 54): North Carolina and the south Atlantic region.
    2. *P. taeda* L.
    1951 (Schoonover, 47): North Carolina.

Hickory Pine
    1951 (*Dict. Am.,* 799): gave examples of combinations of "hickory" with names of various trees, i.e. hickory elm and hickory poplar. Reason not clear.

    1. *P. pungens* Lamb.
    1884 (Sargent, *Forests,* 199): "Hickory Pine."
    2. *P. virginiana* Mill.
    1951 (Schoonover, 50): North Carolina.

Horn Pine   *Nyssa sylvatica var. sylvatica.*
    Not a member of the pine family but black tupelo (*Nyssa sylvatica var. sylvatica.*). 1846 (Emerson, *Report,* 1846, 313): Massachusetts, "In Bristol County [Mass.], and the other southeastern counties, this is called the Snag Tree, and sometimes Horn Pine. . . ."

Hudson's Bay [Hudson Bay] Pine *P. banksiana*
                                              Lamb.
    1854 (Loudon, 4:2190): Britain, "Scrub Pine, Grey Pine, Hudson's Bay Pine." 1951 (Schoonover, 53): "Hudson Bay Pine," the lumber trade.

Huron Pine   *Tsuga canadensis* (L.) Carr.
    1951 (Schoonover, 64): Michigan and the lumber trade, for the eastern hemlock.

Indian Pine   *P. taeda* L.
    1951 (Schoonover, 47): Virginia, North Carolina.

Jack Pine   *P. banksiana* Lamb.
    "Jack" used in American colloquialisms in many combinations, often in a derogatory sense, to describe an inferior type. 1951 (*Dict. Am.,* 894): "Jack Pine, . . . any one of various North American pines, as *Pinus banksiana,* hickory pine, lodgepole pine, etc." However, the derogatory

term "scrub" or "scrubby" was more widely used for some of the pines than "jack."

Jack pine usually refers to *P. banksiana* Lamb.

1888 (*Dict. Am.*, 894) : citing Earl C. Beck, *Songs of Michigan Lumberjacks* (1941), 186, "We are swamping out in the jack pines, And I'll tell you it's no fun." 1897 (Sargent, *Silva*, 11:148, n. 9) : "in the upper part of the lower peninsula of Michigan numerous barrens, the largest with an area of several hundred square miles, are covered with this tree and are known as Jack Pine Plains from one of its common names." 1905 (Sargent, *Manual*, 1905, 27) : Sargent does not include "Jack Pine" in his *Forests*, but gives this synonym for the species in his *Silva* and *Manual*. 1951 (Schoonover, 53) : Michigan, Minnesota, Wisconsin, and the lumber trade.

Jersey Pine
  See New Jersey Pine.

Juniper   *P. banksiana* Lamb.
  1951 (Schoonover, 53) : Canada. Not to be confused with the true junipers or red-cedars, *Juniperus.*

Kingstree   *P. glabra* Walt.
  1898 (Sudworth, 19) : South Carolina.

Labrador Pine   *P. banksiana* Lamb.
  1854 (Loudon, 4:2190) : "Bank's, *or the Labrador,* Pine."

Lobby Pine
  1951 (Schoonover, 47) : Georgia. See Loblolly Pine.

Loblolly Pine
  "Loblolly" is an old seaman's term for "water-gruel or spoon-meat" and in this country was early used to describe a mudhole or puddle. In the South the word has been used in combination with the names of a number of trees growing in swampy places, e.g. "Loblolly-bay."
  1. *P. palustris* Mill.
  Before 1807 (Drayton, 99) : South Carolina, " 'American long leaved Swamp Pine.' Loblolly swamp pine."
  2. *P. serotina* Michx.
  1898 (Sudworth, 18) : North Carolina and Florida.

3. *P. taeda* L.
  1784 (Schoepf, 2:174) : South Carolina. Schoepf described "The Loblolly-pine" found near Charleston. Before 1809 (Michaux, *Sylva*, 1859, 3:123) : "Throughout the lower part of the Southern States this species is called *Loblolly Pine.*" 1898 (Sudworth, 17) : Delaware, Virginia, North Carolina, South Carolina, Georgia, Alabama, Florida, Mississippi, Louisiana, Texas, and Arkansas.

Long-Cone White Pine   *P. strobus* L.
  1738 (*Bartram's Am.*, 65) : cited Peter Collinson in London to John Bartram, April 6, 1738, "Send us some cones of the Long-cone White Pine." (Probably Collinson's own descriptive name; no other reference found) .

Longleaf [Long-Leaved] Pine
  1. *P. palustris* Mill.
  1773 (Bartram, *Travels,* 52) : Georgia, "a forest of the great long-leaved pine (*P. palustris* Linn.) ." Before 1809 (Michaux, *Sylva*, 1859, 3: 106) : One of several names for this species in the South. 1951 (Schoonover, 54) : "Longleaf Pine," in the lumber trade. Also "Longleaved Pine," in Virginia, North Carolina, Georgia, Alabama, Florida, Mississippi, Louisiana, and Tennessee.
  2. *P. rigida* Mill.
  1898 (Sudworth, 17) : "Longleaved Pine"; Delaware.
  3. *P. taeda* L.
  1951 (Schoonover, 47) : Delaware, Maryland, Virginia, and North Carolina.

Longleaf [Longleaved] Pitch Pine   *P. palustris* Mill.
  1773 (Bartram, *Travels,* 33) : Georgia, "the great long-leaved Pitch-Pine, . . . *Pinus palustris.*" 1951 (Schoonover, 54) : Atlantic region.

Longleaf [Longleaved] Yellow Pine   *P. palustris* Mill.
  1951 (Schoonover, 54) : Atlantic region and the lumber trade.

Long-Limbed Hudson's Bay Pine   *P. banksiana* Lamb.
  1854 (Loudon, 4:2191) : quoting from Titus Smith, *Mag. Nat. Hist.*, 8:655, that in " 'the neigh-

borhood of Halifax,' " the species is called " 'the long-limbed Hudson's Bay pine.' "

Longschat Pine

1951 (*Dict. Am.*, 1511): "Shats," origin obscure. An Eastern shore of Maryland "name for pine needles . . . meaning, presumably, things that are shattered down." 1898 (Sudworth, 17–18): reported that in Delaware *P. virginiana* Mill. and *P. echinata* Mill. were called "Shortshat Pine," and *P. taeda* L. and *P. rigida* Mill., "Longschat Pine." The length of needles on the four species and their other common names ("Longstraw Pine," "Longleaved Pine," "Short-leaved Pine," etc.) suggest that "schat," or "Shats," means pine needles.

   1. *P. rigida* Mill.
     1898 (Sudworth, 17): Delaware.
   2. *P. taeda* L.
     1898 (Sudworth, 17): Delaware.

Longshucks   *P. taeda* L.

1898 (Sudworth, 17): Maryland and Virginia. See Longschat Pine.

Longstraw Pine

The name may refer to the length of the needles, which on *P. taeda* L. measure from six to nine inches in length and on *P. palustris* Mill. are from eight to eighteen inches in length. However, among the other common names for *P. taeda* L., are Shortstraw Pine and Shortleaf Pine. In different areas "long" and "short" may refer to the comparative length of the needles of different species growing in proximity to each other. See Longschat Pine.

   1. *P. palustris* Mill.
     1898 (Sudworth, 19): Atlantic region.
   2. *P. taeda* L.
     1898 (Sudworth, 17): Virginia, part of North Carolina.

Lowland Spruce Pine   *P. glabra* Walt.
1898 (Sudworth, 19): Florida.

Maiden Pine   *P. taeda* L.
1951 (Schoonover, 48): North Carolina.

Marsh Pine   *P. serotina* Michx.
1897 (Sargent, *Silva*, 11:119): "Marsh Pine."

Mast Pine   *P. strobus* L.

Before 1809 (Michaux, *Sylva*, 1859, 3:130): "It serves exclusively for the masts of the numerous vessels constructed in the Northern and Middle States, and for this purpose it would be difficult to replace it in North America. Before the war of Independence, England is said to have furnished herself with masts from the United States; and she still completes from America the demand which cannot be fully supplied from the North of Europe. The finest timber of this species is brought from Maine, and particularly from the river Kennebeck." Michaux adds further information about the export of masts during the colonial period. For a more detailed history see Sargent, *Silva*, 11:20, n. 4; also, Lillian M. Willson, *Forest Conservation in Colonial Times* (St. Paul: The Forest Products History Foundation, 1948), 18–28.

Meadow Pine

   1. *P. elliottii* Engelm.
     1884 (Sargent, *Forests*, 202): "Meadow Pine." Spreads quickly onto abandoned fields and cutover forests. 1898 (Sudworth, 19): Florida and part of eastern Mississippi.
   2. *P. serotina* Michx.
     1898 (Sudworth, 18): North Carolina.
   3. *P. taeda* L.
     1898 (Sudworth, 17): Florida.

Minnesota White Pine   *P. strobus* L.
1951 (Schoonover, 34): the lumber trade.

Mountain Pine   *P. rigida* Mill.
1951 (Schoonover, 49): North Carolina.

Naval Timber Pine   *P. taeda* L.
See Rosemary Pine; eastern North Carolina.

New England Pine   *P. strobus* L.
1837 (Darlington, *Flora*, 549): "New England Pine."

New Jersey Pine [Jersey Pine] *P. virginiana* Mill.
Before 1809 (Michaux, *Sylva*, 1859, 3:103): "New Jersey Pine." 1818 (Barton, 2:183): "New Jersey Pine." "A . . . very common species, particularly in Jersey." 1898 (Sudworth, 18): "Jersey pine," New Jersey, Pennsylvania, Delaware, North Carolina, and South Carolina.

New York Pine — *P. echinata* Mill.
Before 1809 (Michaux, *Sylva,* 1859, 3:99):
Liverpool, England.

Nigger Pine — *P. virginiana* Mill.
1951 (Schoonover, 50): Tennessee and Georgia.

North Carolina Pine
1. *P. echinata* Mill.
1907 (Hough, *Handbook,* 14): "North Carolina Pine." 1951 (Schoonover, 51): North Carolina, part of Virginia, and the lumber trade.
2. *P. taeda* L.
1951 (Schoonover, 48): the lumber trade.
3. *P. virginiana* Mill.
1951 (Schoonover, 50): North Carolina.

North Carolina Pitch Pine — *P. palustris* Mill.
1951 (Schoonover, 54): Virginia and North Carolina.

North Carolina Yellow Pine — *P. echinata* Mill.
1898 (Sudworth, 18): North Carolina and part of Virginia.

Northern Pine
1. *P. resinosa* Ait.
1951 (Schoonover, 42): lumber trade.
2. *P. strobus* L.
1951 (Schoonover, 34): South Carolina and the lumber trade.

Northern Scrub Pine — *P. banksiana* Lamb.
1907 (Hough, *Handbook,* 13): "Northern Scrub Pine." See Scrub Pine.

Northern White Pine — *P. strobus* L.
1951 (Schoonover, 34): the lumber trade.

"Norway" — *P. resinosa* Ait.
1951 (Schoonover, 42): the lumber trade.

Norway Pine — *P. resinosa* Ait.
This, the American species, is quite different from the European tree often called Norway pine [*Picea abies* (L.) Karst], which is actually a spruce rather than a true pine. The American tree may have been given the name because of its similarity to the Norwegian species. 1854 (Loudon, 4:2293, 2295): "The lofty, or Norway, Spruce Fir, the loftiest of the European trees, attaining the height of 125 ft. to 150 ft.," used in

pine, southern pine, southern pitch pine, southern yellow pine, swamp pine, Texas longleaved
Britain for masts.
Before 1809 (Michaux, *Sylva,* 1859, 3:91): "In the northern parts of the United States it is called Norway Pine." 1817 (Lowell, 42): "Name . . . generally in use for this tree . . . in the District of Maine, New Hampshire, and Vermont." 1829 (*Dict. Am.,* 1141): citing Greenleaf, *Survey Maine,* 110, "Norway Pine is the common name in Maine, but improperly." 1846 (Emerson, *Report,* 1846, 74): "The Red or Norway Pine." 1890 (Newhall, 164): "Norway Pine." 1951 (Schoonover, 42): Maine, New Hampshire, Vermont, Massachusetts, New York, Wisconsin, Michigan, Minnesota, Ontario; in the lumber trade and in horticulture. See Red Pine.

Oldfield Pine
1. *P. clausa* (Chapm.) Vasey.
1898 (Sudworth, 18): "Oldfield Pine," Florida.
2. *P. echinata* Mill.
1951 (Schoonover, 51): North Carolina, Alabama, and Mississippi.
3. *P. taeda* L.
1865 (Darlington, *Weeds,* 335–36): "Loblolly or Old Field Pine. . . . According to Elliott, 'its seed is dispersed so easily and so universally over the country, that all lands which are thrown out of cultivation are immediately covered with this tree.'" 1951 (Schoonover, 48): "Oldfield Pine," Delaware, Virginia, North Carolina, South Carolina, Georgia, Alabama, Florida, Mississippi, Louisiana, Texas, and Arkansas.

Pinus palustris Mill. — Longleaf Pine
Comprises large forests from southeastern Virginia to central Florida. Wood very heavy, hard, one of the few pines having a pronounced figure, very resinous. Historically important (Fig. 6).
Common names. Broom pine, brown pine, fat pine, Florida longleaf yellow pine, Florida longleaved pine, Florida pine, Florida yellow pine, Georgia heart pine, Georgia longleaved pine, Georgia pine, Georgia pitch pine, Georgia yellow pine, hard pine, heart pine, longleaf [long-leaved] pine, longleaf [longleaved] pitch pine, longleaf [longleaved] yellow pine, longstraw pine, North Carolina pitch pine, pitch pine, red pine, rosemary pine, southern hard pine, southern heart

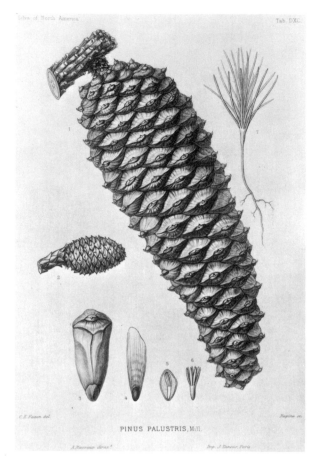

FIG. 6. Charles Edward Faxon, engraving of *Pinus palustris* Mill. Plate 590 from Charles Sprague Sargent, *The Silva of North America,* vol. 11 (Boston: Houghton, Mifflin and Co., 1907). H. 10¾″, W. 7¼″. (Photo, Winterthur.)

pine, Texas yellow pine, turpentine pine, yellow pine.

Distribution. 1783 (Schoepf, 2:41): near Fredericksburg, Virginia, "The pitch pine, . . . now appeared in quantity, composing whole forests." 1784 (Schoepf, 2:143): coastal North Carolina, "It grows here almost entirely on barren, sandy soils, and is found oftener towards the coast than farther inland." 1784 (Schoepf, 2:237): St. Augustine, Florida, common in that area. 1802 (Michaux, *Travels,* 285): the Carolinas; in the "low country of the two Carolinas, . . . Seventenths of the country are covered with . . . *pinus palustris.*" 1819 (Warden, 2:553): Louisiana; spoke of the pine, presumably this species, "to the east of Lake Ponchartrain." 1905 (Sargent, *Manual,* 1905, 15): southeastern Virginia to Florida, along the Gulf coast and inland to Texas.

Growth. 1784 (Schoepf, 2:143): North Carolina, "of tall comely growth." 1785 (H. Marshall, 100): South Carolina, "of a middling growth." 1832 (Browne, 229): gave average height as sixty to seventy feet, with a diameter of fifteen to twenty inches. 1905 (Sargent, *Manual,* 1905, 17): height one hundred to one hundred and twenty feet, "with a tall straight, slightly tapering trunk usually two to two and a half feet or occasionally three feet in diameter."

Wood. Specific gravity, 0.6999; wt. per cu. ft., 43.62 lbs. Before 1809 (Michaux, *Sylva,* 1859, 3:108–9): "The Long-leaved Pine contains but little sap [wood]; several trunks fifteen inches in diameter at the height of three feet, which I have myself measured, had ten inches of perfect wood. Many stocks of this size are felled for commerce, and none are received for exportation of which the heart is not ten inches in diameter when squared. The concentric circles in a trunk fully developed are close and at equal distances, and the resinous matter, which is abundant, is more uniformly distributed than in the other species; hence, the wood is stronger, more compact, and more durable: it is, besides, fine-grained, and susceptible of a bright polish. These advantages give it a preference over every other Pine." Michaux spoke of the different qualities of the wood of this species when grown on different types of soil: those grown in the poor soil near the coast are more resinous ["Pitch pine"], those on better soil are less resinous ["Yellow pine"]. "In certain soils its wood contracts a reddish hue" ["Red pine"]. 1860 (Hough, *Report,* 472): North Carolina, "In richer soil it is less resinous, and it is sometimes of a reddish hue, and hence is called 'Red Pine,' and is deemed better than other varieties. A tree with a small top is said to indicate the best heartwood." 1884 (Sargent, *Forests,* 202): "Wood heavy, exceedingly hard, very strong, tough, coarse-grained, compact, durable; . . . medullary rays numerous, conspicuous; color, light red or orange, the thin sapwood nearly white." 1951 (Schoonover, 54–55): "Straight but uneven-grained, . . . strong and durable. Care must be exercised in working with tools. . . . It nails hard but holds nails and screws satisfactorily. . . . It is one of the few pines having a pronounced figure."

Uses. 1. Lumber. 1784 (Schoepf, 2:140, 144): North Carolina, "excellent timber for building and other purposes. . . . The wood of these forests is made into boards, shingles, cask-staves &c., dressed and exported, and to this end there are already a good many saw-mills established in the country." 1784 (Schoepf, 2:237) : vicinity, St. Augustine, Florida, "The British colonists who came after [the Spanish] . . . by making use of the forests, especially the pine, . . . were able to repay themselves richly for their trouble. Boards, pitch, tar, all manner of ship-furnishings and building-materials were sold in great quantity and at a great profit to the near-by West Indies." 1794 (Coxe, 455) : "The southern pitch pine, and even the yellow pine have been supposed, of late years to be more suitable than white oak for beams, carlines, sills, and other straight timbers for ships and houses, in places liable to rapid decay." 1795 (Winterbotham, 3:383) : "The Pitch pine, . . . is the hardest and heaviest of all the pines, it is sometimes put to the same uses as the yellow pine; but at present the principal use of it is for fewel. When burnt in kilns, it makes the best kind of charcoal; the knots and roots being full of the terebinthine oil, afford a light surpassing candles; its soot is collected, and used for lamp black." 1802 (Michaux, *Travels,* 286) : the Carolinas, "These pines, encumbered with very few branches, and which split even, are preferred to other trees to form fences for plantations." Before 1807 (Drayton, 99) : South Carolina, "American Yellow Pine . . . ; 'from this tree, ship and other planks, flooring boards, feather edge boards, and house frames are sawed. It is used also for masts of vessels.' " Before 1809 (Michaux, *Sylva,* 1859, 3:109) : "This wood subserves a great variety of uses; in the Carolinas, Georgia, and the Floridas, four-fifths of the houses are built of it, except the roof, which is covered with shingles of Cypress; but in the country the roof is also of Pine, and is renewed after fifteen or eighteen years,—a considerable interval in a climate so warm and humid. A vast consumption takes place for the enclosure of cultivated fields. In naval architecture this is the most esteemed of the Pines; in the Southern States, the keel, the beams, the side-planks, and the pins by which they are attached to the ribs, are of this tree. For the deck it is preferred to the true Yellow Pine, and is exported for that purpose to Philadelphia, New York, etc., where it is in request also for the flooring of houses." In Northern dockyards the variety "Red Pine" was considered the best by shipwrights as being more

"durable on the sides of vessels, and less liable to injury from worms, than the Oak." 1897 (Sargent, *Silva,* 11:154) : "largely used for masts and spars, and in the building of bridges, viaducts, and trestle-work, in the construction of railway cars, for which it is preferred in the United States to any other wood, for railway ties, fencing, flooring, and the interior finish of buildings, and for fuel and charcoal."

2. Resinous products. 1670 (Sargent, *Silva,* 11:155, n. 3) : "That the production of tar and turpentine was an occupation of some importance on our southern coast in the seventeenth century appears from the following passage . . . of Samuel Clarke's *A True and Faithful Account of the Four Chiefest Plantations of England and America,* . . . published in London in 1670: *'Pot-ashes,* and *Soap-ashes; Pitch* and *Tar* for making whereof divers Polanders were sent over." 1748 (Kalm, 1:147) : Kalm learned from an unidentified informant that in the North American colonies two kinds of tars were made, one, "the common tar," which in "Carolina" was generally made from dead pine trees in the same manner as in Finland. The second, "Green Tar," was "made of green and fresh trees . . . They use only black firs, for the white firs will not serve their purpose . . . Green tar is dearer than common tar. It is already a pretty general complaint that the fir woods are almost wholly destroyed by this practice." 1784 (Schoepf, 2:140) : North Carolina, referred to the economic importance of "turpentine, tar, pitch, resin, and turpentine-oil," to the residents of North Carolina and described the processes used in their production. Before 1809 (Michaux, *Sylva,* 1859, 3:110–12) : mentioned that tar was formerly made in all the lower parts of the Carolinas and Georgia, and "throughout the Floridas vestiges are everywhere seen of kilns that have served in the combustion of resinous wood. At present, this branch of industry is confined to the lower districts of North Carolina, which furnish almost all the tar and turpentine exported from Wilmington and other ports." He gave six resinous products: turpentine, "scrapings," (coagulated sap), spirit of turpentine, rosin, tar, and pitch, and he described the processes used. "Throughout the United States it [turpentine] is used to make yellow soap of good quality." 1819 (Warden, 2:553) : Louisiana, "Pitch and tar are extracted from the pine to

the east of Lake Ponchartrain, and afford a very lucrative commerce." Warden also described the processes of production. 1884 (Sargent, *Forests,* 517): North Carolina, gave the following grades of resinous products recognized in the trade:

Turpentine. " 'Virginia dip,' or 'Soft white gum turpentine'—the product the first year the trees are worked; 'Yellow dip'—the product of the second and succeeding years, and becoming darker colored and less liquid every year; 'Scrape' or 'Hard turpentine'—the product of the scrapings of the boxes."

Rosin. "Is graded as follows: 'W'—Window-glass; 'N'—Extra pale; 'M'—Pale; 'K'—Low pale; 'I'—Good No. 1; 'H'—No. 1; 'G'—Low No. 1; 'F' —Good No. 2; 'E'—No. 2; 'D'—Good strain; 'C' —Strain; 'B'—Common strain; 'A'—Black."

Tar. "Produced by burning the dead wood and most resinous parts of the long-leaved pine in covered kilns, is graded as follows: 'Rope yellow,' or 'Ropemakers' tar—the highest grade, produced with a minimum of heat from the most resinous parts of the wood; 'Roany,' or 'Ship smearing'— the next running of the kiln; 'Black' or 'Thin'— the lowest grade, made from inferior wood, or the last running of the kiln, and therefore produced with the maximum of heat."

Commerce. 1. Lumber. 1785 (Schoepf, 2:237): vicinity, St. Augustine, Florida, "boards, pitch, tar, all manner of ship-furnishings and building-materials were sold in great quantity . . . to the near-by West Indies." Before 1809 (Michaux, *Sylva,* 1859, 3:109–10): the only species of pine exported from the Southern states to the West Indies. "A numerous fleet of small vessels is employed in this traffic," particularly from Wilmington, North Carolina, and Savannah, Georgia. "The stuff destined for the colonial market is cut into every form required in the construction of houses, and vessels; what is sent to England is in planks from fifteen to thirty feet long and ten or twelve inches broad; they are called *ranging timbers.* The vessels freighted with this timber repair chiefly to Liverpool, where it is said to be employed in the building of ships and of wet-docks: it is called Georgia Pitch Pine, and is sold twenty-five or thirty per cent higher than any other Pine imported from the United States." 1897 (Sargent, *Silva,* 11:154): "more valuable in their products and in their easy access than any other Pine forests in the world."

2. Resinous products. Before 1809 (Michaux, *Sylva,* 1859, 3:110–13): *P. palustris* "supplies nearly all the resinous matter used in the United States in ship-building, and a large residue for exportation to the West Indies and Great Britain." Michaux stated that in 1804 the southern states exported 77,827 barrels of turpentine to the western and northern states and to England and France (which in Paris was called "Boston turpentine"), where it was preferred, "as less odorous, to that made near Bordeaux."

Additions to this historical account are provided by Sargent. 1884 (Sargent, *Forests,* 516); 1897 (Sargent, *Silva,* 11:154, n. 3): Small quantities of crude turpentine were produced along the coast between Pamlico and Cape Fear rivers, North Carolina, soon after settlement. Before the Revolution, most of the crude turpentine was sent to England. "After the war it was distilled in clumsy iron retorts in North Carolina and in some of the northern cities, and as early as 1818 the demand had greatly increased the supply, although the field of operation was not extended south of Cape Fear River nor more than a hundred miles from the coast until 1836; but the introduction of the copper still in 1834 and the demand for spirits of turpentine in the manufacture of india rubber goods, and for illuminating purposes, rapidly developed this industry, which gradually spread farther inland and began to move southward." Production expanded into South Carolina in 1840 and after the Civil War into Mississippi and eastern Louisiana. In 1880, Wilmington, North Carolina, was "the most important distributing point for this industry in the United States," handling eighty percent of all the naval stores produced in North Carolina. Before 1870 Swansboro, Washington, and New Bern were also large shipping points. By 1897 Wilmington had been superseded by ports nearer the productive forests. In 1897 (Sargent, *Silva,* 11:154): *Pinus palustris* supplied "the world with a large part of its naval stores."

Folklore. No references found.

Pennsylvania Yellow Pine   *P. rigida* Mill.
    1951 (Schoonover, 49): Pennsylvania.

Pig Iron Norway   *P. resinosa* Ait.
    1951 (Schoonover, 42): Maine, Minnesota.

Pig Iron Pine   *P. resinosa* Ait.
    1951 (Schoonover, 42) : Minnesota.

Pitch Pine
    Sargent divided the American pines into two categories, soft pines and pitch pines. The latter have harder, more coarse grained woods, and some of these have been an important source of resinous products since the early period of settlement. This characteristic is the basis for their common name.
    1. *P. echinata* Mill.
        1951 (Schoonover, 51) : Missouri.
    2. *P. elliottii* Engelm.
        1884 (Sargent, *Forests,* 520, 522, 525, 531) : Sargent did not include this common name in his description of this species but quoted reports from Florida, Alabama, and southern Mississippi using this name. 1951 (Schoonover, 54) : Atlantic region.
    3. *P. palustris* Mill.
    The pitch pine of the South. Before 1809 (Michaux, *Sylva,* 1859, 3:106) : gave this as one of the several names used for this species in the South. The following gave only this name for the species. 1760s (Romans, 149) : Florida. 1783 (Schoepf, 2:41, 140, 143): near Fredericksburg, Virginia, and North Carolina. 1794 (Coxe, 455) : Philadelphia. Before 1807 (Drayton, 100) : South Carolina. 1951 (Schoonover, 54) : the Atlantic region.
    4. *P. resinosa* Ait.
        1806 (M'Mahon, 597): Philadelphia. 1951 (Schoonover, 42) : Canada.
    5. *P. rigida* Mill.
    The pitch pine of the Northern and Middle States. 1676 (*Dict. Am.,* 1255) : citing *Essex Inst. Coll.* 56:306, "4¾ acres of land . . . bounded by a pitch pine, small heap of rocks. . . ." 1743 (*Bartram's Am.,* 30) : western New York, "Some higher land affording . . . pitch pine." 1771 (*Dict. Am.,* 1255) : citing Copley-Pelham Lett. 138, "The floor of the Peazas except that next the kitchen should be Pitch Pine." 1806 (*Dict. Am.,* 1255) : citing *Ann. 9th Congress 2 Sess,* 1115, "The short-leaved, or pitch pine . . . is always found upon arid lands." Before 1809 (Michaux, *Sylva,* 1859, 3:120) : "on mountains and gravelly lands the wood is compact, heavy, and surcharged with resin, whence is derived the name of Pitch Pine." 1817 (Lowell, 43) : "*Pitch Pine,* general name in all the northern and middle states. This is the true pitch pine of New England, but very different from the pitch pine of the south." 1837 (Darlington, *Flora,* 549) : Chester County, Pennsylvania, "Pitch Pine." 1905 (Sargent, *Manual,* 1905, 20) : gave this as the only common name for this species. 1951 Schoonover, 49) : Vermont, New Hampshire, Massachusetts, Rhode Island, Connecticut, New York, New Jersey, Pennsylvania, Delaware, West Virginia, North Carolina, South Carolina, Georgia, Ohio, Maryland, Ontario, England.
    6. *P. virginiana* Mill.
        1818 (Barton, 2:183) : "Pitch Pine."

Pocosin Pine   *P. serotina* Michx.
    1965 (Fowells, 412) : North Carolina. The largest acreages of pure pond pine stands are found in upland bogs, named by the Indians " 'pocosin,' or 'swamp-on-a-hill,' and are so-called to this day."

Pond Pine   *P. serotina* Michx.
    Before 1809 (Michaux, *Sylva,* 1859, 3:117) : given this name by Michaux who reported it growing principally on the borders of ponds in the maritime parts of the Southern states. "It . . . has received no popular specific name; that which I have given it seems sufficiently appropriate."

Poor Pine
    1. *P. echinata* Mill.
        1898 (Sudworth, 18) : Florida.
    2. *P. glabra* Walt.
        1898 (Sudworth, 19) : Florida.

Poverty Pine   *P. virginiana* Mill.
    1951 (Schoonover, 50) : area of use not given.

Prickly-Coned Pine   *P. pungens* Lamb.
    1770–1771 (Wm. Marshall, 290) : England, quoting from Wm. Hanbury, *A Complete Body of Planting and Gardening* (London, 1770–71), " 'Bastard Pine* is another sort we receive from America . . . being called by some Prickly-coned Pine.' " 1854 (Loudon, 4:2197) : England, "The prickly-*coned, or Table Mountain,* Pine."

Prickly Pine   *P. pungens* Lamb.
    (Rees, *Dict.,* "Pinus") : named for its "cones . . . armed with extremely pungent incurved

spines." 1860 (Hough, *Report,* 471) : North Carolina, "Prickly Pine." See Prickly-Coned Pine.

Prince's [Princess] Pine   *P. banksiana* Lamb.
    The origin of this name not found. The herbaceous native wild flower Pipsissewa (*Chimaphila umbellata*) is also known as Prince's pine.
    1884 (Sargent, *Forests,* 201) : "Prince's Pine." 1898 (Sudworth, 19) : Ontario, "Princes Pine." 1965 (Fowells, 338) : in Canada, "princess pine."

Pumpkin Pine   *P. strobus* L.
    Before 1809 (Michaux, *Sylva,* 1859, 3:129) : "I have constantly observed the influence of soil to be greater upon resinous than upon leafy trees. The qualities of the White Pine, in particular, are strikingly affected by it. In loose, deep, humid soils, it unites in the highest degree all the valuable properties by which it is characterized, especially lightness and fineness of texture, so that it may be smoothly cut in every direction; and hence, perhaps, is derived the name of *Pumpkin Pine* . . . Sculptors employ it [White Pine] exclusively for the images that adorn the bows of vessels, for which they prefer the variety called *Pumpkin Pine.*" 1817 (Lowell, 43) : "*Pumpkin Pine* and *Sapling Pine,* names sometimes given to it [*P. strobus*] in Vermont, New Hampshire, and Maine, in reference to the quality of its wood." 1846 (Emerson, *Report,* 1846, 63) : "The white pines receive different names, according to their mode of growth and the appearance of the wood. When growing densely in deep and damp old forests, with only a few branches near the top, the slowly-grown wood is perfectly clear and soft, destitute of resin, and almost without sapwood, and has a yellowish color, like the flesh of the pumpkin. It is then called pumpkin pine." 1897 (Sargent, *Silva,* 11:19, n. 6) : "The so-called pumpkin pine is the close-grained satiny and very valuable wood of large trees which have grown to a great age in rich, well drained soil and have been favored with abundant air. Such trees are usually scattered singly through forests of deciduous-leaved trees, and are nowhere abundant." 1951 (Schoonover, 34) : Michigan and the lumber trade. See Apple Pine.

Pinus pungens Lamb.   Table Mountain Pine
    Found generally on the slopes of the central Alleghenies. Wood weak, brittle, and very coarse grained. Historically unimportant (Fig. 7).

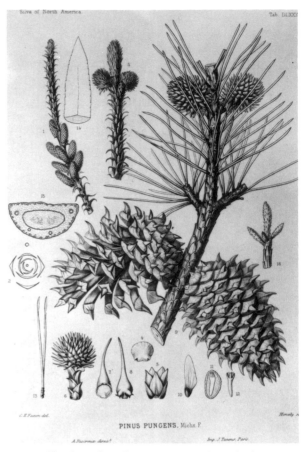

Fig. 7. Charles Edward Faxon, engraving of *Pinus pungens* Michx.F. Modern identification *Pinus pungens* Lamb. Plate 584 from Charles Sprague Sargent, *The Silva of North America,* vol. 11 (Boston: Houghton, Mifflin and Co., 1907). H. 10¾", W. 7¼". (Photo, Winterthur.)

Common names. Hickory pine, prickly-coned pine, prickly pine, southern mountain pine, Table-Mountain pine.

Distribution. 1897 (Sargent, *Silva,* 11:135) : on the slopes and ridges of the Alleghenies from Pennsylvania to North Carolina and eastern Tennessee, with isolated stands in Virginia, eastern Pennsylvania, and western New Jersey. "Toward the southern limits of its range it forms nearly pure forests of considerable extent."

Growth. Before 1809 (Michaux, *Sylva,* 1859, 3:105) : forty to fifty feet in height with proportionate diameter of trunk. 1897 (Sargent, *Silva,* 11:135) : in open ground usually twenty to thirty feet tall with a short, thick trunk. In the forest occasionally sixty feet in height, with a trunk two or three feet in diameter.

Wood. Specific gravity, 0.4935; wt. per cu. ft., 30.75 lbs. 1897 (Sargent, *Silva,* 11:135) : "Light, soft, not strong, brittle, and very coarse-grained. It is pale brown, with thick nearly white sapwood, and contains broad conspicuous resinous bands of small summer cells, numerous larger resin passages and many prominent medullary rays."

Uses. Before 1809 (Michaux, *Sylva,* 1859, 3:105): "It is appropriated to no particular use, but in the mountains of North Carolina its turpentine is preferred to every other as a dressing for wounds. I cannot discover the slightest difference between this resin and that of Pitch Pine." 1897 (Sargent, *Silva,* 11:135): "It is somewhat used for fuel, and in Pennsylvania is manufactured into charcoal."

Commerce. No references found.

Folklore. No references found.

Quebec Pine   *P. resinosa* Ait.
    1951 (Schoonover, 42): English lumber trade.

Red Deal   *P. resinosa* Ait.
    1951 (Schoonover, 42): English lumber trade.

Red Pine
    1. *P. palustris* Mill.
    Before 1809 (Michaux, *Sylva,* 1859, 3:106, 109): "this invaluable tree is known both in the countries which produce it, and in those to which it is exported, by different names: . . . in the Northern States, Southern Pine and Red Pine. . . . In certain soils its wood contracts a reddish hue, and it is for that reason known in the dockyards of the Northern States by the name of Red Pine. Wood of this tint is considered the best, and, in the opinion of some shipwrights it is more durable on the sides of vessels, and less liable to injury from worms, than the Oak."
    2. *P. resinosa* Ait.
    Before 1809 (Michaux, *Sylva,* 1859, 3:91–92): "called, by the French inhabitants of Canada, *Pin rouge,* Red Pine, and the name has been preserved by the English colonists. . . . The bark . . . is of a clearer red than upon that of any other species in the United States: hence is derived its popular name." 1817 (Lowell, 42): "Red Pine, only name given to this tree in Canada; often used in Nova Scotia and New Brunswick, and in Maine." 1828 (Cobbett, par. 263): "The Norway Red Pine, is that which produces the best timber; the same pine is found in abundance in America, and is there also called the Red Pine." 1846 (Emerson,

Report, 1846, 74): Massachusetts, "the Red or Norway Pine." 1951 (Schoonover, 42): Vermont, New Hampshire, New York, Wisconsin, Minnesota, Ontario, the lumber trade, and horticulture.
    3. *P. rigida* Mill.
    1951 (Schoonover, 49): New York.

Pinus resinosa Ait.   Red Pine
    Grows throughout the forests of the Northeast; disease resistant, of rapid growth. Wood heavier than white pine, straight grained, durable, with variations in color and texture because of growth conditions. Historically important (Fig. 8).

Common names. Canadian pine, Canadian red pine, hard pine, northern pine, Norway, Norway pine, pig iron Norway, pig iron pine, pitch pine, Quebec pine, red deal, red pine, *pin rouge,* shellbark Norway, yellow deal, yellow pine.

Distribution. Before 1809 (Michaux, *Sylva,* 1859,

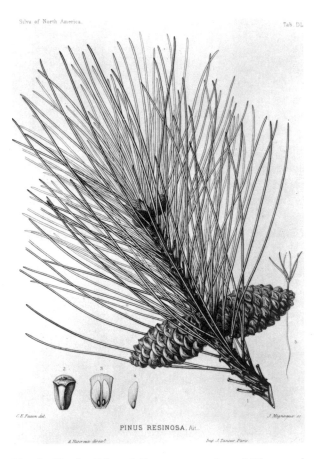

PINUS RESINOSA. Ait.

FIG. 8. Charles Edward Faxon, engraving of *Pinus resinosa* Ait. Plate 556 from Charles Sprague Sargent, *The Silva of North America,* vol. 11 (Boston: Houghton, Mifflin and Co., 1907). H. 10¾", W. 7¼". (Photo, Winterthur.)

3:91): reported the species from Lake St. John, Canada, south to Willkesbarre, Pennsylvania; reported rare south of the Hudson River and rare throughout the area, occupying "small tracts of a few hundred acres, alone or mingled only with the White Pine." 1829 (*Dict. Am.*, 1141): citing Greenleaf, *Survey Maine*, 110, "Norway Pine is the common name in Maine, but improperly." 1846 (Emerson, *Report*, 1846, 74): Massachusetts, "nowhere abundant in Massachusetts, but is found, as is usually the case elsewhere, in little detached clumps, in various parts of the State." 1884 (Sargent, *Forests*, 192): "common and reaching its greatest development through northern Wisconsin and Minnesota; rare in the eastern States, except in the extreme northern portions of New England."

Growth. Before 1809 (Michaux, *Sylva*, 1859, 3:91–92): "The Red Pine. . . . grows . . . seventy or eighty feet in height and two feet in diameter. It is chiefly remarkable for the uniform size of its trunk for two-thirds of its length." 1905 (Sargent, *Manual*, 1905, 25): "A tree, usually 70-80 feet or occasionally 150 feet high, with a tall, straight trunk 2-3 feet in diameter."

Wood. Specific gravity, 0.4854; wt. per cu. ft., 30.25 lbs. Before 1809 (Michaux, *Sylva*, 1859, 3:92): "It is rendered heavy by the resinous matter with which it is impregnated, and in Canada, Nova Scotia and the District of Maine, it is highly esteemed for strength and durability." Also, the tree is remarkable for the uniform size of its trunk for two-thirds of its length. 1846 (Emerson, *Report*, 1846, 75): "The wood is strong and somewhat durable, and much like that of pitch pine; but it is freer from resin, and softer, having qualities intermediate between it and that of white pine." 1890 (Newhall, 165): "hard and durable wood." 1951 (Schoonover, 42): "Red Pine heartwood is a pale very light red orange-brown or light pinkish tan, while the sapwood is moderately wide and creamy light yellow or nearly white color. The wood is straight-grained, medium-textured, moderately soft, non-porous, and heavier than White Pine."

Uses. Before 1809 (Michaux, *Sylva*, 1859, 3:92): "In Canada, Nova Scotia and the District of Maine, it is . . . frequently employed in naval architecture, especially for the deck of vessels, for which it furnishes planks forty feet long without knots. Stripped of the sap[wood], it makes very lasting pumps. The main mast of the St. Lawrence,

a ship of fifty guns, built by the French at Quebec, was of this Pine." He reported that the export of this pine to England had diminished "because the timber is said to consist in too great a proportion of sap[wood]; but the objection appears to me unfounded; several trunks a foot in diameter, that I have examined, contained only one inch of sap[wood]." 1846 (Emerson, *Report*, 1846, 75): "It was formerly employed, like that of the pitch pine, for the decks of vessels and sometimes for pumps and for masts; but it is found to be so much inferior in durability, that its use is almost entirely discontinued." 1884 (Sargent, *Forests*, 192): "largely manufactured into lumber and used for all purposes of construction, flooring, piles, etc." 1951 (Schoonover, 42): "commercially important for sash, doors, flooring, interior and exterior trim, cabin logs, hewed and sawed railroad ties, ship construction, general millwork and general construction, box car construction, agricultural implements, woodenware, toys and other uses similar to Eastern White Pine. It is also used for 'knotty pine' finishing and for paper pulp."

Commerce. See above, Uses.

Folklore. No references found.

Ridge Pine	*P. rigida* Mill.

1951 (Schoonover, 49): North Carolina.

Pinus rigida Mill.	Pitch Pine

Wide distribution from Ontario to northern Georgia. The tree is fire resistant because of its thick bark, although the wood is highly resinous. The wood is soft, coarse grained, very durable. Historically important (Fig. 9).

Common names. Black Norway pine, black pine, hard pine, longleaf [long-leaved] pine, longschat pine, mountain pine, Pennsylvania yellow pine, pitch pine, red pine, ridge pine, rigid pine, sap pine, shortleaf [short-leaved] pine, southern pine, southern yellow pine, split pine, torch pine, yellow pine.

Distribution. 1785 (H. Marshall, 101): "This grows common in many places throughout these states. . . . There are whole Forests of many hundred acres of these trees in some back parts of the country." Before 1809 (Michaux, *Sylva*, 1859, 3:118): "except the maritime part of the Atlantic States, and the fertile regions west of the Alleghany Mountains, it is found throughout the

United States, but most abundantly upon the Atlantic coast, where the soil is diversified but generally meagre." 1814 (Bigelow, 233) : Boston area, "The Pitch Pine is a very common inhabitant of barren, sandy tracts of land." 1817 (Lowell, 43) : "This is the true pitch pine of New England, but very different from the pitch pine of the south." 1837 (Darlington, *Flora*, 549) : Chester County, Pennsylvania, "not common." 1884 (Sargent, *Forests*, 506) : New Jersey, "The forests of pitch pine, which once covered large areas in the southern counties, have now generally been replaced by a stunted growth of oaks and other broad-leaved trees." 1884 (Sargent, *Forests*, 511) : Delaware, "In the sandy soil of the southern part of the state various pitch pines flourished, forming fully one-half of the forest growth. These pine forests were long ago consumed and are now replaced by a second growth, generally composed of the species

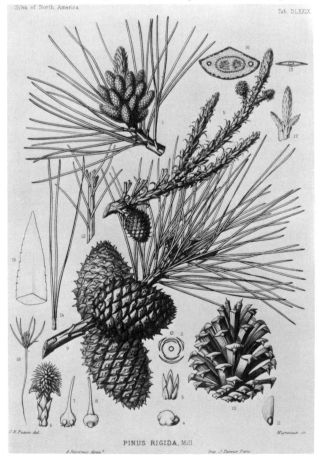

FIG. 9. Charles Edward Faxon, engraving of *Pinus rigida* Mill. Plate 579 from Charles Sprague Sargent, *The Silva of North America*, vol. 11 (Boston: Houghton, Mifflin and Co., 1907). H. 10¾″, W. 7¼″. (Photo, Winterthur.)

which originally occupied the ground." 1890 (Newhall, 166) : "Found, from New Brunswick to Lake Ontario, through the Atlantic States to Northern Georgia, and extending to the western slope of the Alleghany Mountains, in West Virginia and Kentucky. Usually in dry, sandy soil, sometimes in deep swamps. Very common."

Growth. Before 1809 (Michaux, *Sylva*, 1859, 3:119) : Michaux reported that this species did not "exceed twelve or fifteen feet" at the northern limit of its range in Maine and on Lake Champlain. In the Alleghenies of Pennsylvania and Virginia he found it growing thirty-five to forty feet, and twelve to thirteen inches in diameter. In lower New Jersey, Pennsylvania, and Maryland he frequently saw specimens in the large swamps from seventy to eighty feet high, and twenty to twenty-eight inches in diameter. 1846 (Emerson, *Report*, 1846, 66) : Massachusetts, "commonly forty or fifty feet high, and one or two feet in diameter at base. In the most favorable situations . . . it sometimes attains the height of seventy or eighty feet. . . . About the ponds in Plymouth, where these pines rise considerably above the uniform growth of oaks, they must be seventy feet high, and I found the average size of several of the largest to be five feet and seven inches in circumference. . . . In other parts of the lower counties, I have found the largest sometimes over six feet. . . . On the hills in the southwestern corner of the State, they are still found growing to the height of one hundred feet; and men are living in Massachusetts and Maine, who remember that it was not uncommon to find them of more than a hundred feet in height and four or five feet in diameter." 1894 (Emerson, *Report*, 1894, 1:83) : "On its northern borders it attains a height of only twelve or fifteen feet; on its southern, it is a large tree." 1905 (Sargent, *Manual*, 1905, 20) : "A tree, fifty-sixty feet or rarely eighty feet high, with a short trunk occasionally three feet in diameter."

Wood. Specific gravity, 0.5151; wt. per cu. ft., 32.10 lbs. Before 1809 (Michaux, *Sylva*, 1859, 120) : "The concentric circles are widely distant, and three-fourths of the larger stocks consist of sap[wood]. On mountains and gravelly lands the wood is compact, heavy, and surcharged with resin, whence is derived the name of *Pitch Pine*: in swamps, on the contrary, it is light, soft, and composed wholly of sap[wood]; it is then called *Sap Pine*." Michaux apparently considered the yellow pine of the north a different species whose "essential defects . . . place it below the Yellow Pine." (See Yellow pine, *P. rigida* Mill.) 1846 (Emerson, *Report,* 1846, 69): explained that different conditions of growth produced variations in the quality of lumber which lumbermen supposed represented different species. The yellow pine of New England "is an excellent substitute for white pine for any purpose to which the latter may be applied." 1860 (Hough, *Report,* 471): North Carolina, "Timber generally very knotty, heavy, and resinous, but in low grounds lighter, with more sapwood. It is used considerably, but is much inferior to yellow pine." 1890 (Newhall, 166): "The wood is hard and full of pitch, of slight value except for fuel and charcoal and coarse lumber." 1951 (Schoonover, 49): "It is somewhat 'gummy' to work with because of the heavy pitch content, but takes paint well."

Uses. 1. Lumber. 1771 (*Dict. Am.,* 1255): citing Copley-Pelham Lett. 138, "The floor of the Peazas except that next the kitchen should be Pitch Pine." Before 1809 (Michaux, *Sylva,* 1859, 3:120): "Yellow Pine . . . daily dwindling by the vast consumption in civil and naval architecture, it is partially replaced by the Pitch Pine, the poorer variety of which is used for the boxes employed in packing certain sorts of merchandise, such as soap, candles, etc. . . . On some parts of the Alleghanies, where this tree abounds, houses are built of it, and the wood, if it is not covered with paint, is recognized by its numerous knots. It is thought better than the Yellow Pine for floors that are frequently washed, as the resin with which it is impregnated renders it firmer and more durable. It serves perfectly well for ship-pumps, for which purpose trees with very little heart[wood] are preferred. The bakers of New York, Philadelphia and Baltimore, and the brick-makers in the vicinity of these cities, consume it in prodigious quantities." 1814 (Bigelow, 234): Boston area, "occasionally employed in building." 1846 (Emerson, *Report,* 1846, 69–70): Massachusetts, "pitch pine is of far more value than it has usually been considered. The variety called yellow pine is an excellent substitute for white pine for any purpose to which the latter may be applied. In Plymouth County, vessels have been made in many instances, for a considerable time past, almost entirely of pitch pine. For the upper floor, for the lower deck, and for the beams, the best oak only is superior. Its principal defect, as a

material for ship-building, is the comparatively insecure hold it gives to spikes; making it necessary to substitute, at certain points, pieces of oak timber. It is an excellent material for floors, not yielding to the Southern pine in durability and surpassing it in beauty. For water-wheels, it is preferred on account of its durability when exposed to alternations of wet and dry. For the same reason, it is selected for pumps, particularly ships' pumps, and also for aqueduct pipes, for which purposes pieces are chosen with little heart-wood. It is also an excellent material for the sills of houses and barns, . . . the sleepers of railroads and the stringers of bridges, . . . the frame of mills, and other structures in damp situations . . . staves for nail casks. It is preferred to any other wood in the Northern States as fuel for steam engines."

2. Resinous products. 1634 (Sargent, *Silva,* 11:117, n. 1): quoting William Wood, *New-England's Prospect,* pt. 1, 15, New England, " 'Out of these Pines is gotten the candle-wood that is so much spoken of, which may serve for a shift amongst the poore folkes; but I cannot commend it for singular good, because it is something sluttish, dropping a pitchie kinde of substance where it stands.' " 1679 (Sargent, *Silva,* 11:117, n. 1): quoting from Bliss, *Colonial Times on Buzzard's Bay,* 5, Buzzard's Bay, Massachusetts, "At the first meeting of a company, held in Plymouth, Massachusetts, on the 10th of March, 1679, which had recently acquired lands on Buzzard's Bay, where *Pinus rigida* is still common, it was agreed that those who 'first settell and are Livers shall be allowed to make ten Barrells of tarr a peice for a year.' " 1748 (Kalm, 1:28): New Jersey, Kalm stated that the forests in the province of New Jersey are "more ruined than any others" because of the manufacturing of tar. Before 1809 (Michaux, *Sylva,* 1859, 3:120–21): "The Pitch Pine seems to have formerly abounded in Connecticut, Massachusetts and New Hampshire; for, since the beginning of the seventeenth century till 1776, they have furnished a certain quantity of tar. About the year 1705, upon a misunderstanding with Sweden, whence she had drawn her supplies, Great Britain encouraged this branch of industry in the northern part of America by a premium of one pound sterling for eight barrels of tar made from dead wood, and of two pounds for the same quantity extracted from green trees . . . In consequence of this encouragement, or from other

causes, the destruction has been so rapid that the Northern States no longer furnish turpentine or tar for their own consumption. The little tar that is made on the shores of Lake Champlain is used for the small vessels that ply upon its surface, or is sent to Quebec. A few of the poorer inhabitants in the maritime part of New Jersey live by this resource, and the product of their industry is sent to Philadelphia, where it is less esteemed than the tar of the Southern States. What is required for the few vessels that are annually launched on the Ohio, is obtained at an exorbitant price from the Alleghany Mountains, and from the borders of Tar Creek, which empties into the Ohio 20 miles below Pittsburg. The essence of turpentine used in the Western Country in painting is brought from Philadelphia and Baltimore. . . . From the most resinous stocks is procured the lampblack of commerce." 1846 (Emerson, *Report,* 1846, 69): Massachusetts, *"Pitch wood.* . . . When a tree stands some time after its vigorous growth has ceased, the whole heart-wood, and even the whole wood, is filled with resin, and converted into what is called pitch wood. This is so incorruptible, that it is often dug up entire in old pine woods, where it has been exposed for scores of years to alternations of moisture and dryness."

Commerce. 1. Lumber. 1785 (H. Marshall, 101): from some of the forests in the back country, "great quantities of Boards are sawed and floated down some of our long rivers." 1794 (Cooper, 150): citing Philadelphia Prices Current, Jan. 11, 1794, included "Sap Pine" sold at the shallop price of $10.67 per thousand feet. The yard price was an additional $1.33 per thousand feet.

2. Resinous products. 1748 (Kalm, 1:28): Philadelphia, mentioned New Jersey tar being exported from Philadelphia to England.

Rigid Pine   *P. rigida* Mill.
    1898 (Sudworth, 17): English literature.

River Pine   *P. virginiana* Mill.
    1860 (Hough, *Report,* 471): North Carolina, " 'River Pine.' " 1898 (Sudworth, 18): North Carolina.

Rosemary   *P. echinata* Mill.
    1951 (Schoonover, 51): Louisiana and Texas.

Rosemary Pine
    1. *P. echinata* Mill.
       1898 (Sudworth, 18): North Carolina.
    2. *P. palustris* Mill.
       1898 (Sudworth, 19): North Carolina.
    3. *P. taeda* L.
       1784 (Schoepf, 2:143): North Carolina, "in greater plenty farther inland, grows the Rosemary-Pine so-called. . . . The name Yellow-Pine is given in this country for the most part to the rosemary-pine; but others hold that this is a particular variety of the pitch-pine, distinguished by . . . a softer, yellower wood . . . and that the variety . . . makes a better house-timber . . . It is difficult to get a clear notion of the many names, varieties, and sub-varieties of this region." 1884 (Sargent, *Forests,* 197): A variety of this species which, because of growth conditions, is "close-grained, less resinous, lighter, with much thinner sapwood," than the ordinary growth of this species. 1897 (Sargent, *Silva,* 11:113, n. 4): North Carolina, "These trees of eastern North Carolina, which vary remarkably from all others of the species in the character of their wood and especially in the thinness of the sapwood, were called Rosemary Pines, and also Great Swamp Pines, Naval Timber Pines, and Slash Pines. According to Edmund Ruffin, who in 1858 published the best account of them in volume iv., page 139, of *Russell's Magazine,* individuals from one hundred and fifty to one hundred and seventy feet in height, with trunk diameters of five feet, were not uncommon." 1898 (Sudworth, 17): Virginia and part of North Carolina.

Rosemary Shortleaf   *P. echinata* Mill.
    1951 (Schoonover, 51): North Carolina.

Pin Rouge   *P. resinosa* Ait.
    Before 1809 (Michaux, *Sylva,* 1859, 3:91): "by the French inhabitants of Canada, *Pin rouge,* Red Pine, and the name has been preserved by the English colonists." See Red Pine.

Saltwater Pine   *P. elliottii* Engelm.
    1951 (Schoonover, 56): Florida.

Sand Pine   *P. clausa* (Chapm.) Vasey.
    1884 (Sargent, *Forests,* 199): "Sand Pine," found on "barren, sandy dunes and ridges."

Sapling Pine   *P. strobus* L.

1795 (Winterbotham, 3:380) : "These trees have a very thin sap, and are distinguished by the name of mast pine from the succeeding growth of the same species, which are called saplings." Before 1809 (Michaux, *Sylva,* 3:126, 129) : [*P. strobus*] "known in Canada and the United States by the name of *White Pine,* . . . and in New Hampshire and Maine, by the secondary denominations of *Pumpkin Pine, Apple Pine,* and *Sapling Pine,* which are derived from certain accidental peculiarities. . . . On dry, elevated lands, its wood is firmer and more resinous, with a coarser grain and more distant concentric circles; and it is then called Sapling Pine. . . . In the district of Maine it is employed for barrels to contain salted fish, especially the variety called *Sapling Pine,* which is of a stronger consistence." 1809 (*Dict. Am.,* 1329) : citing Kendall, *Travels,* 3:53, "The yellow or red pine . . . . [is] called by the French colonists *sapin,* and by the English corruptly sapling." However, Kendall's explanation may have been incorrect. 1898 (Sudworth, 25) : reports that in Quebec *"Sapin"* was the name given the balsam fir, *Abies balsamea* (L.) Mill. 1846 (Emerson, *Report, 1846,* 63) : Massachusetts, "Standing nearly by itself, or surrounded by deciduous trees, especially on the boundaries between high lands and swamps, it grows rapidly, is usually full of knots and resin, has much sap-wood, and then receives the name of sapling pine." 1951 (Schoonover, 34) : area of use not given.

Sap Pine

1. *P. rigida* Mill.

Before 1809 (Michaux, *Sylva,* 1859, 3:120) : "In swamps . . . [the wood] is light, soft, and composed almost wholly of sap[wood]; it is then called *Sap Pine.*"

2. *P. taeda* L.

1898 (Sudworth, 17) : Virginia and North Carolina.

Savanna Pine   *P. serotina* Michx.

1860 (Hough, *Report,* 471) : North Carolina, "Common in small swamps and bays in the lower district, . . . and in some places is called 'Savanna Pine.' "

Scrubby Pine, Scrub Pine

"Scrub" or "Scrubby" often used to denote undersized or deformed trees; i.e., "Scrub Pine" or "Scrub Oak." 1777 (*Bartram's Am.,* 146) : Louisiana, William Bartram reported seeing near the Mississippi River "two or three scrubby pine trees, or rather dwarf bushes upon the highest ridge of these plains which are viewed here as a curiosity." 1816 (*Dict. Am.,* 894) : citing U. Brown, *Journal* 1, 266, "Ugly Hills . . . abounded with pines of a scrubby kind, Jack Oaks and other Scrub Wood." 1884 (Sargent, *Forests,* 240) lists two species of "scrub" oaks, and four species of "scrub" pines.

1. *P. banksiana* Lamb.

Before 1809 (Michaux, *Sylva,* 1859, 3:95) : "In Nova Scotia and the district of Maine, where it is rare, called *Scrub Pine,* . . ." 1907 (Hough, *Handbook,* 13) : gave the variant, "Northern Scrub Pine." 1898 (Sudworth, 19) : "Scrub Pine," in Maine, Vermont, New York, Wisconsin, Michigan, Minnesota, Ontario.

2. *P. clausa* (Chapm.) Vasey.

1884 (Sargent, *Forests,* 199) : "Scrub Pine," etc., but does not repeat the listing in his *Silva* (1897) or in his *Manual* (1905).

3. *P. virginiana* Mill.

Before 1809 (Michaux, *Sylva,* 1859, 3:103) : Pennsylvania, "On the scrubby ridges beyond Bedford . . . it is called *Scrub Pine.*" 1837 (Darlington, *Flora,* 548) : Chester County, Pennsylvania, "Scrubby Pine. Jersey Pine." 1860 (Hough, *Report,* 471) : North Carolina, "Scrub Pine." 1898 (Sudworth, 18) : "Scrub Pine," Rhode Island, New York, Pennsylvania, Delaware, North Carolina, South Carolina, Ohio.

Pinus serotina Michx.   Pond Pine

Widely distributed along the Atlantic and Gulf coasts. Wood heavy, coarse grained, very resinous. Historically unimportant (Fig. 10) .

Common names. Bastard pine, bull pine, loblolly pine, marsh pine, meadow pine, pocosin pine, pond pine, savanna pine, spruce pine.

Distribution. Before 1809 (Michaux, *Sylva,* 1859, 3:117) : reported it scattered throughout "the maritime parts of the Southern States, but is lost as it were among the Long-leaved Pines which cover these regions." 1860 (Hough, *Report,* 471) : North Carolina, "Common in small swamps and bays in

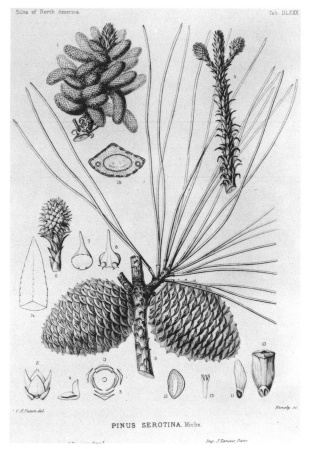

Silva of North America.   Tab. DLXXX.

C.E.Faxon del.   Himely sc.

PINUS SEROTINA. Michx.

Imp. J. Taneur, Paris.

FIG. 10. Charles Edward Faxon, engraving of *Pinus serotina* Michx. Plate 580 from Charles Sprague Sargent, *The Silva of North America,* vol. 11 (Boston: Houghton, Mifflin and Co., 1907). H. 10¾", W. 7¼". (Photo, Winterthur.)

the lower district. . . . It covers large tracts on rich, swampy, and peaty land, but not in extensive forests." 1884 (Sargent, *Forests,* 198) : "North Carolina, south near the coast to the head of the Saint John's river, Florida . . . not common." In 1933 (Sargent, *Manual,* 1933, 18) : gave a wider distribution, from southern New Jersey and southeastern Virginia along the coast to northern Florida and central Alabama.

Growth. Before 1809 (Michaux, *Sylva,* 1859, 3:117) : "The ordinary size of this tree, which it rarely exceeds, is thirty-five or forty feet in height and fifteen or eighteen inches in diameter." 1905 (Sargent, *Manual,* 1905, 21) : "occasionally seventy to eighty feet high, with a short trunk sometimes three feet but generally not more than two feet in diameter, stout, often contorted branches."

Wood. Specific gravity, 0.7942; wt. per cu. ft., 49.49 lbs. 1897 (Sargent, *Silva,* 11:119) : ". . . very

resinous, heavy, soft, brittle, and coarse-grained; it is dark orange color, with thick pale yellow sapwood, and contains broad bands of small summer cells."

Uses. Before 1809 (Michaux, *Sylva,* 1859, 3:117) : "appropriated to no use." 1860 (Hough, *Report,* 471) : North Carolina, "Wood occasionally used for masts of small vessels." 1897 (Sargent, *Silva,* 11:119) : "It is said to furnish now a considerable part of the lumber cut on the coast of North Carolina, where this tree is also tapped for the production of turpentine, and formerly was used for the masts of small vessels."

Commerce. No references found.

Folklore. No references found.

Shellbark Norway   *P. resinosa* Ait.
     1951 (Schoonover, 42) : Minnesota.

She Pine   *P. elliottii* Engelm.
     1898 (Sudworth, 19) : Georgia, Florida.

She Pitch Pine   *P. elliottii* Engelm.
     1898 (Sudworth, 19) : Georgia.

Shortleaf [short-leaved] Pine
     1. *P. echinata* Mill.
     Before 1809 (Michaux, *Sylva,* 1859, 3:96) : "in the Carolinas and Georgia [called], Spruce Pine, and more frequently Short-leaved Pine." 1897 (Sargent, *Silva,* 11:143) : "Short-leaved Pine." 1951 (Schoonover, 51) : "Shortleaf Pine," in Virginia, Maryland, Georgia, and the lumber trade; also, "Shortleaved Pine," in North Carolina, South Carolina, Georgia, Alabama, Mississippi, Florida, Louisiana, Texas, and Arkansas.
     2. *P. rigida* Mill.
     1951 (Schoonover, 49) : "Shortleaf Pine," in Georgia.
     3. *P. taeda* L.
     1898 (Sudworth, 17) : "Shortleaf Pine," in Virginia, North Carolina, South Carolina, Louisiana.

Shortleaved Pine   *P. virginiana* Mill.
     1898 (Sudworth, 18) : North Carolina.

Short-Leaved Pitch Pine   *P. echinata* Mill.
    1833 (Flint, 41) : "the common short leaved
pitch pine is abundant" in parts of Missouri and
Arkansas.

Shortleaved [Shortleaf] Yellow Pine
                                 P. echinata Mill.
    1951 (Schoonover, 51) : lumber trade.

Shortshat [Shortschat?] Pine
    1951 (Schoonover, 50–51) : only listing found
for "Shortschat." Schoonover apparently used
Sudworth's entries for "Shortshat" and changed
the spelling.
    1. *P. echinata* Mill.
        1898 (Sudworth, 18) : "Shortshat Pine," in
Delaware. See Longschat Pine.
    2. *P. virginiana* Mill.
        1898 (Sudworth, 18) : "Shortshat Pine," in
Delaware.

Short Shucks   *P. virginiana* Mill.
    1898 (Sudworth, 18) : Maryland and Vir-
ginia.

Shortstraw Pine   *P. taeda* L.
    1951 (Schoonover, 48) : area of use not given.
See Longstraw Pine.

Sir Joseph Bank's Pine   *P. banksiana* Lamb.
    1898 (Sudworth, 19) : England.

Slash Pine
    1816 (*Dict. Am.*, 1560) : citing D. Thomas,
Travels Western Country (1819), 230, "*Slashes*
means flat clayey land which retains water on the
surface after showers. From this comes the adjective, *slashy*." 1951 (*Dict. Am.*, "Slash," 1560) :
"Origin obscure. Perhaps suggested by *slashy*, wet,
miry." 1951 (*Dict. Am.*, "Slash pine," 1560) : "any
one of the various pines that grow in slashes, or
low coastal regions."
    1. *P. echinata* Mill.
        1898 (Sudworth, 18) : North Carolina and
part of Virginia.
    2. *P. elliottii* Engelm.
        1884 (Sargent, *Forests*, 202) : "Slash Pine."

1951 (Schoonover, 56) : Alabama, Mississippi,
Georgia, Florida.
    3. *P. taeda* L.
        1897 (Sargent, *Silva*, 11:113, n. 4) : explains
that in eastern North Carolina the names "Rosemary Pine," "Great Swamp Pine," "Naval Timber Pine," and "Slash Pine," were synonymous
and used to describe examples of this species,
which, because of growth conditions, varied "remarkably from all others of the species in the
character of their wood and especially in the thin-
ness of the sapwood." 1951 (Schoonover, 48) :
Virginia and part of North Carolina.

Smooth-Barked Pine   (*P. glabra* Walt.?)
    1784 (Schoepf, 2:175) : South Carolina, simi-
lar to "Birds-Nest Pine," but has pleasantly fra-
grant smooth cones and bark on the upper trunk,
"smooth and white, retaining this characteristic
and color . . . throughout all its limbs."

Soft Cork Pine   *P. strobus* L.
    1951 (Schoonover, 34) : lumber trade. See
Cork Pine.

Soft Cork White Pine   *P. strobus* L.
    1951 (Schoonover, 34) : lumber trade.

Soft Minnesota White Pine   *P. strobus* L.
    1951 (Schoonover, 34) : lumber trade.

Soft Pine   *P. strobus* L.
    1951 (Schoonover, 34) : Pennsylvania.

Soft White Pine   *P. strobus* L.
    1951 (Schoonover, 34) : lumber trade.

Southern Hard Pine   *P. palustris* Mill.
    1898 (Sudworth, 19) : in general use.

Southern Heart Pine   *P. palustris* Mill.
    1898 (Sudworth, 19) : in general use.

Southern Mountain Pine   *P. pungens* Lamb.
    1898 (Sudworth, 18) : Tennessee.

Southern Pine
    1. *P. echinata* Mill.
        1953 (Little, 264) : "southern pine."
    2. *P. elliottii* Engelm.
        1951 (Schoonover, 56) : lumber trade.
    3. *P. palustris* Mill.
    Historically this name seems to have been

limited to this species; in this century it has been given to various species within the *Taeda* group. Before 1809 (Michaux, *Sylva,* 1859, 3:106): "This invaluable tree is known both in the countries which produce it, and in those to which it is exported, by different names; . . . in the Northern States, Southern Pine and Red Pine." 1898 (Sudworth, 19): North Carolina, Alabama, Mississippi, Louisiana, and the lumber trade. 1905 (Sargent, *Manual,* 1905, 17): "Long-leaved Pine, Southern Pine."

   4. *P. rigida* Mill.
     1951 (Schoonover, 49): lumber trade.
   5. *P. taeda* L.
     1951 (Schoonover, 48): lumber trade.

Southern Pitch Pine   *P. palustris* Mill.
   1951 (Schoonover, 54): in general use.

Southern Yellow Pine
   1. *P. echinata* Mill.
     1898 (Sudworth, 19): in general use. 1951 (Schoonover, 51): lumber trade.
   2. *P. palustris* Mill.
     1898 (Sudworth, 19): in general use.
   3. *P. rigida* Mill.
     1951 (Schoonover, 51): area of use not given.

Split Pine   *P. rigida* Mill.
   1814 (Bigelow, 233): Boston area, *"Pinus rigida.* L." "Pitch Pine . . . occasionally employed in building, but is chiefly used as a light fuel, under the form of 'split pine.' "

Spruce   *P. virginiana* Mill.
   1951 (Schoonover, 50): Georgia.

Spruce Pine
   The bog spruce, *Picea mariana* Mill.; also any one of the various American pines or hemlocks having light, soft wood. The eastern pines for which this synonym has been used are all "pitch pines," except *P. strobus* L., and are the eastern pines with the shortest needles. 1684 *(Dict. Am.,* 1622): quotes I. Mather, *Providences* (1856), 10:223, " 'Passing through a thick swamp of spruse pine . . .' " and 1765, J. Bartram, Diary, 25 Sept. "Ye 2 leaved or spruice pine grows very large in swamps.' "
   1. *P. clausa* (Chapm.) Vasey.
     1884 (Sargent, *Forests,* 199): Florida, "Spruce

Pine." 1898 (Sudworth, 18): Florida.
   2. *P. echinata* Mill.
     Before 1809 (Michaux, *Sylva,* 1859, 3:96): the Carolinas and Georgia, "called . . . in the Carolinas and Georgia, Spruce Pine, and more frequently Short-leaved Pine." 1890 (Newhall, 165): "Spruce Pine." 1898 (Sudworth, 18): Delaware, Mississippi, and Arkansas.
   3. *P. elliottii* Engelm.
     1898 (Sudworth, 19): southern Alabama.
   4. *P. glabra* Walt.
     1884 (Sargent, *Forests,* 201): "Spruce Pine." 1898 (Sudworth, 19): South Carolina, Alabama, and Florida.
   5. *P. serotina* Michx.
     1898 (Sudworth, 18): South Carolina and Georgia.
   6. *P. strobus* L.
     1898 (Sudworth, 13): Tennessee.
   7. *P. taeda* L.
     1898 (Sudworth, 17): part of Virginia.
   8. *P. virginiana* Mill.
     1785 (H. Marshall, 102): *"Pinus virginiana. Two-leaved Virginian, or Jersey Pine* . . . This is called, in some places, Spruce Pine." 1951 (Schoonover, 50): New Jersey, Maryland, Virginia, North Carolina, South Carolina, Tennessee, Alabama. See Spruce.

Pinus strobus L.   Eastern White Pine
   A tall forest tree growing from Newfoundland to southern Georgia and west beyond the Great Lakes. Wood light, straight grained, and soft, with variations in color and texture because of growth conditions. The only five-needled pine native in the East. Historically important (Fig. 11).
   Common names. Apple pine, balsam pine, *Pin blanc,* board pine, bull sapling pine, Canadian white pine, cork pine, eastern white pine, long-cone white pine, mast pine, Minnesota white pine, New England pine, northern pine, northern white pine, pumpkin pine, sapling pine, soft cork white pine, soft Minnesota white pine, soft pine, soft white pine, spruce pine, Weymouth pine, white fir, white pine, Wisconsin white pine.
   Distribution. 1749 (Kalm, 1:336): Albany, New York, "The White Pine is found abundant here." Before 1807 (Drayton, 100): South Carolina, "White Pine, 'New England Pine,' grows near the mountains." Before 1809 (Michaux, *Sylva,* 1859,

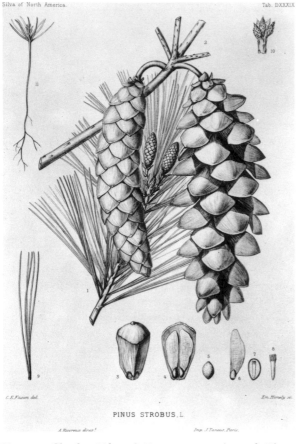

FIG. 11. Charles Edward Faxon, engraving of *Pinus strobus* L. Plate 539 from Charles Sprague Sargent, *The Silva of North America,* vol. 11 (Boston: Houghton, Mifflin and Co., 1907). H. 10¾", W. 7¼". (Photo, Winterthur.)

3:126) : "diffused, though not uniformly, over a vast extent of country: it is incapable of supporting intense cold, and still less of extreme heat." André Michaux found it in Canada as far north as latitude 48 degrees 50 minutes. "It is found in the valleys and on the declivities of the Alleghanies to their termination, but at a distance from the mountains on either side its growth is forbidden by the warmth of the climate." The species reached its greatest size in Maine, the upper part of New Hampshire, Vermont, and near the mouth of the St. Lawrence. 1819 (James, 1:14–15) : "About the sources of the Alleghany are extensive forest of pine . . . This tree [White pine] though not exclusively confined to the northern parts of our continent, attains there its greatest magnitude and perfection. It forms a striking feature in the forest scenery of Vermont, New Hampshire, and some parts of Canada, and New York." 1833 (Flint, 40–41) : "On the Alleghany, on the waters of the

Upper Mississippi, between Rock River and the falls of St. Anthony, and in some places on the Illinois, the Weymouth, or Norwegian Pine—the white pine of New England—is found in all its beauty and perfection. It nowhere had a larger and taller shaft, or a more beautiful verdure of foliage, than on the Alleghany." 1837 (Darlington, *Flora,* 549) : Chester County, Pennsylvania, "Rich woodlands; old fields, &c. not common." 1846 (Emerson, *Report,* 1846, 64) : Massachusetts, "It is every year becoming more scarce." Before 1878 (Hough, *Report,* 485) : Tennessee, "The white pine is less abundant [than *P. echinata*], but is found on the slopes of the Unaka Mountains and locally on the Cumberland table-lands." Before 1878 (Hough, *Report,* 490) : West Virginia, "Not very prevalent." 1881 (Gilmore, 112) : Tennessee, "It is the universal impression that no white pine grows in this State, but that only shows the almost universal ignorance prevailing in regard to this region. In altitudes 2,000 feet or more above the sea it grows here in great abundance." 1884 (Sargent, *Forests,* 496) : New Hampshire, "The original white-pine forests of New Hampshire are practically exhausted, although in the northern counties of the state there still remain a few scattered bodies remote from streams and of small size." 1884 (Sargent, *Forests,* 498) : Vermont, "A forest of white pine once stretched along the banks of the Connecticut, and great bodies of this tree occurred in the northwestern part of the state, adjacent to Lake Champlain. The original white pine forests of the state are now practically exhausted." 1884 (Sargent, *Forests,* 553) : Michigan, "The belt of pine which ran through the center of the state . . . contained the best pine in the northwest. This pine was what was called by lumbermen 'cork pine,' a soft white pine, large and sound, with a thick bark." 1884 (Sargent, *Forests,* 557) : Wisconsin, "On the Jump river are some fine bodies of pine, nearly approaching in quality Michigan cork pine." 1890 (Newhall, 168) : "Its finest growth is in the region of the Great Lakes." 1905 (Sargent, *Manual,* 1905, 4) : Newfoundland to Manitoba, south to Pennsylvania, portions of Ohio, Indiana, Illinois, Iowa, and along the Alleghenies to eastern Kentucky and Tennessee and northern Georgia.

Growth. 1785 (H. Marshall, 101) : "This is allowed to out top in growth most of our other trees, rising with a large erect trunk, to the height of an hundred feet or more, covered with a smooth bark and sending off many long branches." 1795 (Winterbotham, 3:380): "undoubtedly the prince of the American forest in size, age, and majesty of appearance." Before 1809 (Michaux, *Sylva*, 1859, 3:127): gave the maximum height for this species at about 180 feet. On the Kennebeck River he measured the trunks of two felled trees, "of which one was 154 feet long and fifty-four inches in diameter, and the other 142 feet long and forty-four inches in diameter." 1819 (James, 1:14–15): "Its trunk often attains the diameter of five or six feet, rising smooth and straight from sixty to eighty feet, and terminated by a dense, conical top. This tree . . . forms a striking feature in the forest scenery . . . rising by nearly half its elevation above the summits of the other trees, and resembling, like the palms of the tropics . . . 'a forest planted upon another forest.' "

Wood. Specific gravity, 0.3854; wt. per cu. ft., 24.02 lbs. 1748 (Kalm, 1:132): New York City, the residents considered shingles "made of the white fir tree, or *Pinus strobus* L. . . . as durable as one made in Pennsylvania of the white cedar, or *Cupressus thyoides* L." 1795 (Winterbotham, 3:383): "of smooth grain and when free from knots, does no injury to the tools of the workmen; but the softness of its texture subjects it to shrink and swell with the weather. The sapling pine, though of the same species, is not so firm and smooth as the veteran pine of the forest, and is more sensibly affected by the weather. . . . The stumps and roots of the mast pine are very durable. It is a common saying, that 'no man ever cut down a pine, and lived to see the stump rotten.' " Before 1809 (Michaux, *Sylva*, 1859, 3:128): "it has little strength, gives a feeble hold to nails, and sometimes swells by the humidity of the atmosphere." However, "it is soft, light, free from knots and easily wrought; is more durable, and less liable to split when exposed to the sun; furnishes boards of a great width, and timber of large dimensions: in fine, it is still abundant and cheap." (See Pumpkin Pine and Sapling Pine for a description of the different qualities of wood found in individual trees of this species.) 1881 (Gilmore, 112): Tennessee, "The wood [of the White Pine in eastern Tennessee] is not so light nor fine grained as the cork pines in Michigan, but it is fully equal in size and quality to the white pine of the Susquehanna region of Pennsylvania." 1905

(Sargent, *Manual*, 1905, 4): wood "light, not strong, straight-grained, easily worked, light brown often slightly tinged with red."

Uses. Before 1663 (Josselyn, 198, n. 3): *"Pinus Strobus*, L. . . . 'Of the body the English make large canows of 20 foot long, and two feet and half over; hollowing of them with an adds, and shaping of the outside like a boat.' " 1748 (Kalm, 1:132): New York City, "The roofs are commonly covered with tiles or shingles, the latter of which are made of white fir tree, or *Pinus strobus* L." 1795 (Winterbotham, 3:382–83): "The best white pine trees are sold for masts, bowsprits and yards, for large ships. Those of an inferior size, partly unsound, crooked or broken in falling, are either sawn into planks and boards, or formed into canoes, or cut into bolts for the use of coopers, or split and shaved into clapboards and shingles. Boards of this wood are much used for wainscoting and cabinet work. . . . The stumps and roots of the mast pine are very durable. . . . After many years, when the roots have been loosened by the frost, they are, with much labour, cut and dug out of the ground, and being turned up edgeway, are set for fences to fields, in which state they have been known to remain sound for half a century." 1802 (Michaux, *Travels*, 82): Wheeling, West Virginia, "We purchased a canoe, twenty-four feet long, eighteen inches wide, and about as many in depth. These canoes are always made with a single trunk of a tree; the pine and tulip tree are preferred for that purpose, the wood being very soft." Before 1809 (Michaux, *Sylva*, 1859, 3:128–30): used "in greater quantities and far more diversified uses than that of any other American Pine." Throughout the northern states, "except in the larger capitals, seven-tenths of the houses are of wood, of which three-quarters, estimated at about 500,000, are almost wholly of White Pine: even the suburbs of the cities are built of wood. The principal beams of churches and the other large edifices are of White Pine.

"The ornamental work of outer doors, the cornices and friezes of apartments, and the mouldings of fireplaces, which in America are elegantly wrought, are of this wood. It receives gilding well, and is therefore selected for looking-glass and picture-frames. Sculptors employ it exclusively for the images that adorn the bows of vessels, for which they prefer the variety called *Pumpkin Pine.*

"At Boston, and in other towns of the Northern

States, the inside of mahogany furniture and of trunks, the bottom of windsor chairs of an inferior quality, water-pails, a great part of the boxes used for packing goods, the shelves of shops, and an endless variety of other objects, are made of White Pine.

"In the district of Maine it is employed for barrels to contain salted fish, expecially the variety called *Sapling Pine,* which is of a stronger consistence. For the magnificent wooden bridges over the Schuylkill at Philadelphia, and the Delaware at Trenton, and for those which unite Cambridge and Charlestown with Boston, of which the first is 1500 and the second 3000 feet in length, the White Pine has been chosen for its durability. It serves exclusively for the masts of the numerous vessels constructed in the Northern and Middle States, and for this purpose it would be difficult to replace it in North America. Before the war of Independence, England is said to have furnished herself with masts from the United States; and she still completes from America the demand which cannot be fully supplied from the North of Europe. The finest timber of this species is brought from Maine, and particularly from the river Kennebeck.

"Soon after the establishment of the Colonies, England became sensible of the value of this resource, and solicitous for its preservation. In 1711 and 1721, severe ordinances were enacted, prohibiting the cutting of any trees proper for masts on the possessions of the crown. The order comprised the vast countries bounded on the south by New Jersey and on the north by the upper limit of Nova Scotia." See Mast Pine. 1837 (Darlington, *Flora,* 549): Chester County, Pennsylvania, "The value of its *wood,* in affording boards, shingles, and other lumber, is well known." 1846 (Emerson, *Report,* 1846, 64): Massachusetts, "As it receives paint perfectly, it is employed for floors which are to be painted. For such as are exposed to much wear, as those of kitchens and back entries and stairs, the woods of the pitch pine and the southern pine are preferred, on account of their superior hardness.

"Everything made of white pine is usually painted. Doors, panels, and tables of this wood are sometimes only varnished, so as to exhibit the wood itself. In this state, it gradually takes a yellowish or light reddish color, and has considerable beauty. Stained and varnished, it is a beautiful

material for wainscoting, window frames, and the other internal finishing of a house." 1854 (Loudon, 4:2284): England, at a parliamentary inquiry, Mr. Copland, "An extensive builder and timber-merchant," testified that American White Pine was inferior in quality, much softer, and not so durable, in comparison with Baltic pine, " 'and very liable to dry rot: indeed, it is not allowed by any professional man under government to be used; nor is it ever employed in the best buildings in London: it is only speculators that are induced to use it, from the price of it being much lower (in consequence of its exemption from duty) than the Baltic timber': . . . The wood of Weymouth Pines grown in England has been used for floors, and by cabinet-makers; but, as the species is generally valued as an ornamental tree, it is seldom cut down for timber." 1860 (Hough, *Report,* 472): North Carolina, "It grows on mountains, and not accessible to markets. Its timber . . . has a local use." Before 1878 (Hough, *Report,* 485): Tennessee, "The supply is limited, and much of it is inaccessible." 1884 (Sargent, *Forests,* 501): Winchendon, Worcester County, Massachusetts, "Winchendon, the most important point in the United States for the manufacture of woodenware, small cooperage, etc., is supplied with material from the young forests of this and the neighboring counties. Timber is reported to have deteriorated. The supply of pine is not equal to the demand." 1884 (Sargent, *Forests,* 187): In speaking of the use of White Pine throughout the United States, Sargent commented, "more largely manufactured into lumber, shingles, laths, etc., than that of any other North American tree; the common and most valuable building material of the northern states; largely used in cabinet-making, for interior finish, and in the manufacture of matches, woodenware, and for many domestic purposes."

Commerce. 1749 (Kalm, 1:336): Albany, "A vast quantity of lumber from the white pine is prepared annually on this side of Albany, which is brought down to New York and exported." 1785 (H. Marshall, 101): "This also grows in great plenty towards the heads of some of our rivers, from whence great quantities are rafted down, affording excellent masts, yards, spars, &c. &c. for ship building." Before 1809 (Michaux, *Sylva,* 1859, 3:131–35): "The vast consumption of this tree for domestic use, and for exportation to the West Indies and to Europe, renders it necessary every year to penetrate farther into the country. . . . Next to the district of Maine, which furnishes three-quarters of the White Pine exported from the United States, including what comes from New Hampshire by the Merrimack and is brought to Boston, the shores of Lake Champlain appeared to be the most abundantly peopled with this species, and to be not unfavorably situated for its transportation. All that is cut beyond Ticonderoga, comprising about three-fourths of the length of the lake, which is one hundred and sixty miles from north to south, is carried to Quebec, two hundred and seventy miles distant, by the Sorel and the St. Lawrence. What is furnished by the southern part of the Lake is sawn at Skeesborough, transported seventy miles in the winter on sledges to Albany, and, with all the lumber of the North River, brought down in the spring to New York in sloops of eighty or one hundred tons, to be afterwards exported in great part to Europe, the West Indies, and the Southern States. . . .

"The upper part of Pennsylvania, near the source of the Delaware and Susquehanna, which is mountainous and cold, possesses large forests of this Pine, and in the spring the timber floats down these streams for the internal consumption of the State. It enters into the construction of houses both in the country and in the towns, and is sawn into planks for exportation from Philadelphia to the West Indies. The masts of vessels built at Philadelphia are also obtained from the Delaware.

"Beyond the mountains, near the springs of the river Alleghany, from 150 to 180 miles from its junction with the Ohio, is cut all the White Pine destined for the market of New Orleans, which is 2900 miles distant. In the spring, immense quantities descend the river for the consumption of the country. Three-quarters of the houses of Wheeling, Marietta, and Pittsburg, and of Washington, in Kentucky, are built with White Pine boards.

"Boston is the principal emporium of this commerce in the Northern States. The White Pine is found there in the following forms: —In square pieces from twelve to twenty-five feet long, and of different diameters; in *scantling,* or square pieces six inches in diameter, for the lighter part of frames; and in boards, which are divided into *merchantable* or *common,* and into *clear* or *picked* boards," (the latter also called *"panel* boards"). "The merchantable boards are three-fourths of an inch thick, from ten to fifteen inches wide, from ten to fifteen feet long, and frequently deformed with knots; at New York they are called Albany boards, and are sold at the same price as at Boston. The clear boards, formed from the largest stocks of the Pumpkin Pines, are of the same length and thickness as the first, and twenty, twenty-four, and thirty inches wide. They should be perfectly *clear;* but they are admitted if they have only two knots small enough to be covered with the thumb: they are employed for all light and delicate works of joinery, particularly for the panels of doors and the mouldings of apartments; at Philadelphia they are called *White Pine panels.* . . .

"Clapboards are of an indeterminate length, six inches wide, three lines thick at one edge, and thinner at the other; they form the exterior covering of houses, and are placed horizontally, lapping one upon another, so that the thinner edge is covered. The shingles are commonly eighteen inches long, from three to six inches wide, three lines thick at one end, and one line at the other; they should be free from knots, and made only of the perfect wood. They are packed in square bundles, and sustained by the two cross-pieces of wood confined by withes. The bundles sometimes consist of five hundred, but oftener of two hundred and fifty shingles; the price at Hallowel, in 1807, was three dollars a thousand: two men can make sixteen or eighteen hundred in a day.

"East of the river Hudson, the houses are almost invariably covered with these shingles, which last only twelve or fifteen years. They are exported in great quantities to the West Indies, and in the French islands they are called *essentes blanches."*

Great Britain in 1807 imported from the United States timber "reckoned at $1,302,980, of which I suppose the White Pine to have formed a fifth. In 1808, it was sold at Liverpool at about sixty cents the cubic foot. Planks two inches thick and twelve wide were worth four cents a foot, and common planks six cents."

1819 (James, 1:14): Pittsburg area, "About the sources of the Alleghany are extensive forests of pine, whence are drawn great supplies of lumber, for the country below as far as New Orleans." 1829 (Atwater, 215): St. Louis, "All the boards and scantling used in building here, that I inquired where they were brought from, came from Pittsburgh, and were brought down the Alleghany river from the pine groves at the heads of that river and its branches. Though these boards were dearer, of course, than the same articles were at Cincinnati and Louisville, they were much cheaper than I would have supposed, considering the great distance they had been transported from their native forests, and the mills where they had been manufactured." 1833 (Flint, 40–41): Pittsburg area, "The White, or Norwegian pine. . . . From the banks of this distant stream [the Allegheny], and from its waters in the state of New York, that New Orleans is supplied with white pine plank of the greatest clearness and beauty." 1846 (Emerson, *Report*, 1846, 64–65): New England, White Pine "is every year becoming more scarce. The exportation from the growth of this State [Massachusetts] has almost ceased, and from New Hampshire and the southern parts of Maine it has much diminished, and the lumber has become of inferior quality." Although the export of lumber from the Penobscot and other northern rivers in Maine "is still immense," each year the lumbermen have to go deeper into the back country to obtain wood. "The same thing is happening in New York." 1884 (Sargent, *Forests*, 501): New York State, "fifty or seventy-five years have passed since the pine of the Champlain valley was harvested and shipped to England by way of the Saint Lawrence." 1884 (Sargent, *Forests*, 503): Albany, New York, "As a lumber market Albany ranks second in the United States, or next to Chicago. White pine is the variety of lumber most largely handled here, and two-thirds of it comes from Michigan by way of the Erie canal, the remaining one-third coming from Canada through Lake Champlain, the white pine contributed by New York being an inappreciable quantity."

Folklore. No references found.

Swamp Pine

   1. *P. elliottii* Engelm.

     1884 (Sargent, *Forests*, 202): one of several names given for this species. Customarily found "along the dunes and marshes of the coast, or wet clay borders of ponds, abandoned fields, etc." 1898 (Sudworth, 19): Florida, Mississippi, and part of Alabama.

   2. *P. palustris* Mill.

     1806 (M'Mahon, 597): Philadelphia, "*P. palustris.* Swamp Pine."

   3. *P. taeda* L.

     1760 (*Dict. Am.*, 985): citing *Ga. Gen. Ass.*

Acts, 219; Georgia, "squared Timber . . . made of swamp or loblolly pine and Shipped or offered to sale." 1898 (Sudworth, 17): Virginia and North Carolina.

Table Mountain Pine   *P. pungens* Lamb.

     Before 1809 (Michaux, *Sylva*, 1859, 3:105): Michaux named it for Table Mountain, North Carolina, on which he found this species. 1854 (Loudon, 4:2197): Britain, "the *prickly-coned, or Table-Mountain,* Pine." 1884 (Sargent, *Forests*, 199): "Table-Mountain Pine. Hickory Pine."

Pinus taeda L.   Loblolly Pine

   Grows from southern New Jersey to central Florida and the Gulf coast. Tree resistant to forest fires because of its thick bark and location in swampy areas; is subject to insect damage. Wood brittle, coarse grained, not durable; a source of resinous products. Historically important (Fig. 12).

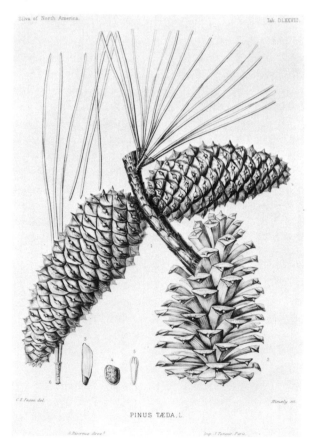

FIG. 12. Charles Edward Faxon, engraving of *Pinus taeda* L. Plate 578 from Charles Sprague Sargent, *The Silva of North America*, vol. 11 (Boston: Houghton, Mifflin and Co., 1907). H. 10¾", W. 7¼". (Photo, Winterthur.)

Common names. Arkansas pine, bastard pine, black pine, black slash pine, bog pine, buckskin pine, bull pine, cornstalk pine, dwarf pine, foxtail pine, frankincense pine, great swamp pine, heart pine, Indian pine, lobby pine, loblolly pine, longleaf [long-leaved] pine, longschat pine, longschucks, longstraw pine, maiden pine, meadow pine, naval timber pine, North Carolina pine, oldfield pine, rosemary pine, sap pine, shortleaf [short-leaved] pine, shortstraw pine, slash pine, southern pine, spruce pine, swamp pine, three-leaved American swamp-pine, three-leaved Virginian pine, torch pine, tough pine of the plains, two-leaved American pine, Virginian swamp pine, Virginia pine, Virginia sap pine, white pine, yellow American pine, yellow pine, yellow tough pine.

Distribution. Before 1809 (Michaux, *Sylva*, 1859, 3:123): Michaux thought its northern limit was around Fredericksburg, Virginia. In the lower part of Virginia and in parts of North Carolina, he found it growing on dry and sandy soil and on lands exhausted by cultivation. "In the more Southern States it is the most common species after the Long-leaved Pine, but it grows only in the branch-swamps, or long narrow marshes that intersect the pine-barrens, and near the creeks and rivers, where the soil is of middling fertility . . . such as the vicinity of Charleston, S. C." 1865 (Darlington, *Weeds*, 336): "According to Elliott, 'its seed is dispersed so easily and so universally over the country, that all lands which are thrown out of cultivation are immediately covered with this tree.'" 1884 (Sargent, *Forests*, 197): "Southern Delaware, south to cape Malabar and Tampa bay, Florida, generally near the coast, through the Gulf states to the valley of the Colorado river, Texas, and north through southern Arkansas to the valley of the Arkansas river . . . springing up on all abandoned lands from Virginia southward, and now often replacing in the southern pine belt the original forest of *Pinus Palustris*."

Growth. Before 1809 (Michaux, *Sylva*, 1859, 3:124-25): the tree exceeds eighty feet in height with a diameter of two or three feet; the tallest trees he saw in relation to their diameter were near Richmond, Virginia. "Next to the White Pine, the tallest tree of its genus in the United States." 1860 (Hough, *Report*, 471): North Carolina, on abandoned fields the trees reach a height of "50 to 70 feet, with a diameter of 2 to 3 feet,"

but in swampy areas, such as the West Roanoke Swamps, "it has been found 5 feet in diameter and 150 to 170 feet high." 1897 (Sargent, *Silva*, 11:113): "In southeastern Arkansas and the Indian Territory it is one of the most important timber-trees, growing in great nearly pure forests on rolling uplands and low tertiary plains; and in western Louisiana and eastern Texas it forms considerable forests north of the region occupied by the Long-leaved Pine, and is scattered through the low woods which border the marshes of the coast."

Wood. Specific gravity, 0.5441; wt. per cu. ft., 33.91 lbs. Before 1809 (Michaux, *Sylva*, 1859, 3:124-25): Virginia, comments on "its spongy consistence. . . . This species . . . decays rapidly when exposed to the air, and is regarded as one of the least valuable of the species." 1860 (Hough, *Report*, 471): North Carolina, the trees which grew to immense size in the swamps were considered "an important variety" of the species, and were variously designated "Swamp Pine," "Slash Pine," and "Rosemary Pine. . . . The grain of this heartwood is generally not very coarse, but more so than the long-leaf, and still more than the yellow pine." 1897 (Sargent, *Silva*, 11:114): "The wood of the *Pinus Taeda*, which usually grows very rapidly, varies much in quality in the different regions which it occupies and under differing conditions of growth. That of the great trees which once grew on Pamlico Sound and were valued in naval construction, and especially for the masts of large vessels, is said to have been very close-grained and durable, with thin sapwood. A large part of the trees of original growth and the oldest and best matured second-growth trees now produce coarse-grained wood, nearly one half the diameter of the trunk being sapwood, while the wood of trees which have grown rapidly on abandoned fields and now supply an important part of the timber cut on the south Atlantic coast . . . is very coarse-grained and still more largely composed of sapwood. In the forests west of the Mississippi River it is of better quality."

Uses. 1. Lumber. 1785 (H. Marshall, 102): "This is useful for boards." Before 1809 (Michaux, *Sylva*, 1859, 3:124-25): Virginia, "Three-fourths of the houses in this part of Virginia [Petersburg] are built of the Loblolly Pine, which is even used in the absence of the Yellow Pine for the ground-floors; but the boards, though only four inches wide, and strongly nailed, shrink, and become uneven. . . . In the ports of the Southern States this species is used, like the Pitch Pine in those of the North, for the pumps of ships; at Charleston the wharves are built with logs of Loblolly Pine, consolidated with earth; bakers consume it in their ovens, and it is sold a third cheaper than the more resinous wood of the Long-leaved Pine." 1840s (Sargent, *Silva,* 11:113, n. 4) : Bastrop and adjoining counties, Texas, large forests of *P. taeda* supplied the construction needs of "all the towns of the central and western parts of the state, before the building of the Texas railroads." 1884 (Sargent, *Forests,* 197) : "Largely used for fuel and manufactured into lumber of inferior quality."

2. Resinous products. 1785 (H. Marshall, 102) : "This is useful for . . . producing turpentine and tar." Before 1809 (Michaux, *Sylva,* 1859, 3:125) : "It affords turpentine in abundance, but in a less fluid state than that of the Long-leaved pine; as it contains more alburnum, from which the turpentine distils." 1884 (Sargent, *Forests,* 197) : "Turpentine is occasionally manufactured from this species." 1897 (Sargent, *Silva,* 11:114) : the resin "does not flow rapidly when the trees are boxed and soon hardens on exposure to the air, and this species is probably not much worked commercially for the production of turpentine."

Commerce. 1760 (*Dict. Am.,* 985) : citing *Ga. Gen. Ass. Acts,* 219, "squared Timber . . . made of swamp or loblolly pine and Shipped or offered to sale." 1884 (Sargent, *Forests,* 512) : "A large amount of second-growth pine (*Pinus taeda*) is shipped from the different Virginia ports by schooner to New York for fuel, and this second-growth pine furnishes the principal building material used throughout the state." 1897 (Sargent, *Silva,* 11:114) : "In the forests west of the Mississippi River it is of better quality, a considerable part of the Yellow Pine lumber shipped from southern Arkansas and western Louisiana to northern markets being of this species."

Folklore. No references found.

Texas Longleaved Pine   *P. palustris* Mill.
    1898 (Sudworth, 19) : Atlantic coast.

Texas Yellow Pine   *P. palustris* Mill.
    1898 (Sudworth, 19) : Atlantic coast.

Three-Leaved American Swamp-Pine   *P. taeda* L.
    Before 1822 (*Dict. Arts,* "Pinus") : considered a variety, with slight distinctions, of this species.

Three-Leaved Prickly-Coned Bastard Pine
                                                    P. echinata Mill.
    1785 (H. Marshall, 100) : "This grows naturally in Virginia."

Three-Leaved Virginian Pine   (*P. taeda* L.?)
    1806 (M'Mahon, 597) : Philadelphia, "*P. taeda v. Rigida.* Three-leaved Virginian Pine."

Torch Pine
    1. *P. rigida* Mill.
    Although the high resinous content of the wood of this species made it useful for illumination from the earliest period of settlement, no reference to the early use of this synonym has been found. 1900 (Keeler, 454) : "Torch Pine." See Split Pine, Pitch Pine.
    2. *P. taeda* L.
    1898 (Sudworth, 17) : "English literature."

Tough Pine of the Plains   *P. taeda* L.
    Before 1822 (*Dict. Arts,* "Pinus") : considered a variety, with slight distinctions, of this species. See Yellow Pine, *P. palustris* Mill.

Turpentine Pine   *P. palustris* Mill.
    1898 (Sudworth, 19) : North Carolina.

Two-Leaved American Pine   *P. taeda* L.
    Before 1822 (*Dict. Arts,* "Pinus") : considered a variety, with slight distinctions, of this species.

Upland Spruce Pine   *P. clausa* (Chapm.) Vasey.
    1898 (Sudworth, 18) : Florida.

Pinus virginiana Mill.   Virginia Pine
    A small, short-leaved pine found usually in sterile soil; widely distributed from Long Island to central Georgia. The wood is light, brittle, coarse grained. Historically unimportant (Fig. 13) .
Common names. Alligator pine, black pine, cedar pine, hickory pine, Jersey pine, New Jersey pine, nigger pine, North Carolina pine, pitch pine, poverty pine, river pine, scrubby pine, scrub pine, shortleaved, shortshat [shortschat] pine, short schucks, spruce, spruce pine, Virginia pine.
Distribution. Before 1809 (Michaux, *Sylva,* 1859,

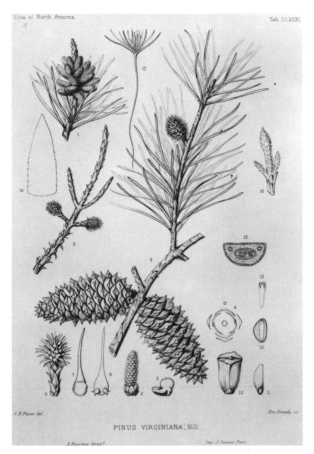

FIG. 13. Charles Edward Faxon, engraving of *Pinus virginiana* Mill. Plate 581 from Charles Sprague Sargent, *The Silva of North America,* vol. 11 (Boston: Houghton, Mifflin and Co., 1907). H. 10¾", W. 7¼". (Photo, Winterthur.)

3:103) : reported common in the lower part of New Jersey; also found in Maryland, Virginia, Kentucky, Pennsylvania beyond Chambersburg; no specimens found north of the Hudson River, or in the Carolinas and Georgia. 1818 (Barton, 2:183) : Philadelphia area, "very common species, particularly in Jersey." 1837 (Darlington, *Flora,* 548) : Chester County, Pennsylvania, "Sterile hills: not common." 1897 (Sargent, *Silva,* 11:123) : Long Island southward, generally near the coast, to central Georgia and northeastern Alabama through eastern and middle Tennessee and Kentucky to southeastern Indiana.

Growth. Before 1809 (Michaux, *Sylva,* 1859, 3:103–4) : "sometimes thirty or forty feet high and twelve or fifteen inches in diameter, but it rarely attains these dimensions. . . . Next to the Gray Pine, this is the most uninteresting species of the United States." Too small to be useful. 1818 (Barton, 2:183) : Philadelphia area, "low, strag-

gling." 1860 (Hough, *Report,* 471) : North Carolina, "Too small and often too crooked for use." 1897 (Sargent, *Silva,* 11:123) : usually small in the Atlantic states, thirty to forty feet in height. Attains greatest height west of the Allegheny Mountains, "frequently rising on the low hills or knobs of southern Indiana to the height of over one hundred feet."

Wood. Specific gravity, 0.5309; wt. per cu. ft., 33.09 lbs. 1897 (Sargent, *Silva,* 11:123) : "light, soft, not strong, brittle, close-grained, and durable in contact with the soil; it is light orange-color, with thick nearly white sapwood, and contains broad conspicuous resinous bands of small summer cells, few resin passages, and many thin medullary rays." 1951 (Schoonover, 50) : "The heartwood . . . generally quite knotty. It is nonporous and considerably resinous."

Uses. 1884 (Sargent, *Forests,* 199) : "largely used for fuel." 1884 (Sargent, *Forests,* 546) : Louisville, Kentucky, "The manufacture of pumps and water-pipes from logs of the Jersey pine . . . at one time an important industry at Louisville, has, since the general introduction of city and town water-works, become unremunerative and unimportant." 1897 (Sargent, *Silva,* 11:123) : in Kentucky and Indiana sometimes used for lumber; "in Indiana tar was formerly obtained by burning the wood of this tree."

Commerce. No references found prior to 1900.

Folklore. 1749 (Rees, *Dict.,* "Pinus") : "Kalm has remarked that cattle in hot weather studiously single out this tree for shade in preference to all others. Its effluvia are supposed to be agreeable to them; or rather perhaps hostile to some insects which persecute them."

Virginian Swamp Pine   *P. taeda* L.
    1785 (H. Marshall, 102) : *"Virginian Swamp, or Frankincence Pine."*

Virginia Pine
  1. *P. taeda* L.
    1898 (Sudworth, 17) : Virginia, North Carolina. 1951 (Schoonover, 48) : lumber trade.
  2. *P. virginiana* Mill.
    1951 (Schoonover, 50) : Maryland, Virginia, North Carolina, and the lumber trade

Virginia Sap Pine   *P. taeda* L.
    1951 (Schoonover, 48) : eastern lumber trade.

Virginia Yellow Pine   *P. echinata* Mill.
    1951 (Schoonover, 51) : used in part of Virginia.

Walter's Pine   *P. glabra* Walt.
    1898 (Sudworth, 19) : South Carolina. (Named for Thomas Walter [1740–1788], a South Carolina planter and botanist.)

Weymouth Pine   *P. strobus* L.
    1854 (Loudon, 4:2282–83) ; 1933 (*Ox. Dict.,* "Weymouth," 12:334) : English name for this species since early in the eighteenth century; came into common use in New England early in the nineteenth century. The species is reported to have been first cultivated in England in 1705 by the Duchess of Beaufort. Soon after, large quantities were planted at Longleat, Wiltshire, the seat of Lord Weymouth, whose interest in the species caused it to be called "Lord Weymouth's Pine," or "Weymouth Pine." 1731 (*Ox. Dict.,* 12:334) : citing Philip Miller, *Gard. Dict.,* England, "Lord Weymouth's Pine."
    Before 1809 (Michaux, *Sylva,* 1859, 3:135) : "In England this tree is called the Weymouth Pine,—a name which is gradually becoming common in America." 1833 (Flint, 40) : "On the Alleghany, on the waters of the Upper Mississippi, . . . and in some places on the Illinois, the Weymouth, or Norwegian pine—the white pine of New England—is found in all its beauty and perfection." 1837 (Darlington, *Flora,* 549) : Chester County, Pennsylvania, "White Pine. Weymouth Pine. New England Pine." 1846 (Emerson, *Report,* 1846, 60) : Massachusetts, "known throughout New England by the name of white pine. . . . In England, it is called the Weymouth Pine." 1884 (Sargent, *Forests,* 187) : "White Pine. Weymouth Pine." 1898 (Sudworth, 13) : Massachusetts and South Carolina.

White Fir   *P. strobus* L.
    1748 (Kalm, 1:132) : New York City, "The white fir tree, or *Pinus strobus* L." 1748 (Kalm, 1:147) : "Carolina," making tar; "They use only black firs, for the white firs will not serve their purpose."

White Pine
    1. *P. glabra,* Walt.
        1884 (Sargent, *Forests,* 200) : "White Pine."

1898 (Sudworth, 19) : South Carolina and Florida.
    2. *P. strobus* L.
        1738 (*Bartram's Am.,* 65) : citing Peter Collinson in London to John Bartram, April 6, 1738, "Try what thee canst do to send us some cones of the Longcone White Pine." 1795 (Winterbotham, 3:380) : "The White Pine . . . is undoubtedly the prince of the American forest." Before 1809 (Michaux, *Sylva,* 1859, 3:126) : "known in Canada and the United States by the name of *White Pine,* from the perfect whiteness of its wood when freshly exposed." 1817 (Lowell, 43) : "*White Pine,* only name given to this tree in the greater part of the United States, and in Nova Scotia and New Brunswick . . . *Pin Blanc,* or White Pine, by the Canadians." 1951 (Schoonover, 34) : throughout the northeastern and north central states, and Ontario, Canada.
    3. *P. taeda* L.
        Before 1809 (Michaux, *Sylva,* 1859, 3:123) : Virginia, sometimes called "*White Pine* about Petersburg and Richmond, in Virginia."

Wisconsin White Pine   *P. strobus* L.
    1951 (Schoonover, 34) : lumber trade.

Yellow American Pine   *P. taeda* L.
    Before 1822 (*Dict. Arts,* "Pinus") : considered a variety, with slight distinctions, of this species.

Yellow Deal   *P. resinosa* Ait.
    1951 (Schoonover, 42) : English lumber trade.

Yellow Pine
    1. *P. echinata* Mill.
        Before 1809 (Michaux, *Sylva,* 1859, 3:96) : "in the Middle States, where it is abundant and in common use, it is called Yellow Pine; in the Carolinas and Georgia, Spruce Pine, and more frequently Short-leaved Pine." 1884 (Sargent, *Forests,* 200) : "Yellow Pine." 1951 (Schoonover, 51) : New York, New Jersey, Pennsylvania, Delaware, Virginia, North Carolina, Alabama, Mississippi, Louisiana, Arkansas, Missouri, Illinois, Indiana.
    2. *P. palustris* Mill.
        The yellow pine of the South. 1770–1771 (Wm. Marshall, 290) : quoting from Wm. Han-

bury, *A Complete Body of Planting and Gardening,* (London, 1770–1771), American name used in England, *"'The Yellow American Pine,* and the *Yellow Tough Pine,* and the *Tough Pine of the Plains,* I received by those names: There is some difference in the size and shape of the cones, though that seems inconsiderable.'" 1802 (Michaux, *Sylva,* 1859, 3:110): east Tennessee, "Since the year 1804, extensive tracts of the finest Pines are seen covered only with dead trees. In 1802, I remarked a similar phenomenon among the Yellow Pines, in East Tennessee." Before 1809 (Michaux, *Sylva,* 1859, 3:106–7): "This invaluable tree is known both in the countries which produce it, and in those to which it is exported, by different names; in the first it is called Long-leaved Pine, Yellow Pine, Pitch Pine and Broom Pine. . . ." 1819 (Warden, 2:449): South Carolina, "The pitch and yellow pine serve for masts, yards, and planks." 1951 (Schoonover, 54): Delaware, North Carolina, South Carolina, Alabama, Florida, Louisiana, Texas, and the lumber trade.

3. *P. resinosa* Ait.

1817 (Lowell, 42): *"Pinus rubra—Yellow Pine,* name sometimes given to it in Nova Scotia."

4. *P. rigida* Mill.

Before 1809 (Michaux, *Sylva,* 1859, 3:120):

apparently considered yellow pine a different species from the Pitch pine (*P. rigida*); he says: "essential defects place it [Pitch Pine] below the Yellow Pine; but, as that species is daily dwindling by the vast consumption . . . it is partially replaced by the Pitch Pine." The confusion is explained 1846 (Emerson, *Report,* 1846, 67): "The Yellow Pine." Those trees which have a trunk free of branches "to a great height, and the wood is clear, and soft, free from knots, and almost free from resin, and, from the slow growth, the bark is less rough than usual. Such trees are called yellow pines, and are supposed by lumber-men to be of a different species." 1951 (Schoonover, 49): Pennsylvania and Georgia.

5. *P. taeda* L.

1951 (Schoonover, 48): northern Alabama, North Carolina, and Arkansas.

Yellow Slash Pine   *P. elliottii* Engelm.

1951 (Schoonover, 56): area of use not given. See Slash Pine.

Yellow Tough Pine   *P. taeda* L.

Before 1822 (*Dict. Arts,* "Pinus"): considered a variety, with slight distinctions, of this species.

Bibliography

ATWATER   Atwater, Caleb. *The Writings of Caleb Atwater.* Columbus, Ohio: The author, 1833.

BARTON   Barton, Dr. William P. C. *Compendium Florae Philadelphicae.* 2 vols. Philadelphia: M. Carey and Son, 1818.

BARTRAM'S AM.   Cruickshank, Helen Gere, ed. *John and William Bartram's America.* Garden City, N.Y.: Doubleday & Co., The Natural History Library Anchor Books, 1961.

BARTRAM, *DIARY*   Bartram, John. "Diary of a Journey Through the Carolinas, Georgia, and Florida from July 1, 1765, to April 10, 1766." Annotated by Francis Harper. *Transactions of the American Philosophical Society* 33, pts. 1–2 (1942): 1–242.

BARTRAM, *TRAVELS*   Bartram, William. *Travels through North & South Carolina, Georgia, East & West Florida, . . . Together with Observations on the Manners of the Indians.* Edited by Mark van Doren. New York: Dover Publications, 1928.

BIGELOW   Bigelow, Jacob, M. D. *Florula Boston-iensis: A Collection of Plants of Boston and its Environs.* Boston: Cummings and Hilliard; Cambridge: Hilliard & Metcalf, 1814.

BROWNE   Browne, D. J. *The Sylva Americana.* Boston: William Hyde & Co., 1832.

COBBETT   Cobbett, William. *The Woodlands.* London: The author, [1826–1828].

COOPER   Cooper, Thomas. *Some Information Respecting America.* London: J. Johnson, 1794.

COXE   Coxe, Tench. *A View of the United States of America.* Philadelphia: William Hall and Wrigley & Berriman, 1794.

DARLINGTON, *FLORA*   Darlington, Dr. William. *Flora Cestrica: An Attempt to Enumerate and Describe the Flowering and Filicoid Plants of Chester County, in the State of Pennsylvania.* 2d ed. West Chester, Pa.: The author, 1837.

DARLINGTON, *WEEDS*   Darlington, Dr. William. *American Weeds and Useful Plants.* Revised, with additions by George Thurber. New York: Orange Judd, 1865.

DICT. AM.   *A Dictionary of Americanisms on Historical Principles.* Edited by Mitford M. Mathews. Chicago: Chicago University Press, 1951.

DICT. ARTS   *A Dictionary of Arts & Sciences.* Edited by D. D. Gregory. 2d Am. ed. New York: William T. Robinson, 1822.

DRAYTON   Drayton, John. *The Carolinian Florist of Governor John Drayton of South Carolina 1766–1822.* Edited by Margaret Babcock Meriwether. Columbia, S.C.: The South Caroliniana Library of the University of South Carolina, 1943.

EMERSON, *REPORT*, 1846   Emerson, George B. *A Report on the Trees and Shrubs Growing Naturally in the Forests of Massachusetts.* Boston: The Commissioners on the Zoological and Botanical Survey of the State, 1846.

EMERSON, *REPORT*, 1894   Emerson, George B. *A Report on the Trees and Shrubs Growing Naturally in the Forests of Massachusetts.* 2 vols. 5th ed. Boston: Little, Brown, and Company, 1894.

FLINT   Flint, Timothy. *The History and Geography of the Mississippi Valley.* 2 vols. 3d ed. Cincinnati: E. H. Flint; Boston: Carter, Hendee, and Co., 1833.

FOWELLS   Fowells, H. A., comp. and ed. *Silvics of Forest Trees of the United States.* Agriculture Handbook no. 271. U.S. Department of Agriculture, Forest Service, Division of Timber Management Research. Washington, D.C.: Government Printing Office, 1965.

GILMORE   Gilmore, James R. "The Timber Resources of Tennessee." *American Architect and Building News* 10 (1881): 111–13.

HODGES   Hodges, Leonard B. *The Forest Tree Planters' Manual.* St. Paul: Minnesota State Forestry Association, 1879.

HOUGH, *HANDBOOK*   Hough, Romeyn Beck. *Handbook of the Trees of the Northern States and Canada East of the Rocky Mountains.* Lowville, N.Y.: The author, 1907.

HOUGH, *REPORT*   Hough, Franklin B. *Report Upon Forestry.* Vol. 1. U.S. Department of Agriculture. Washington, D.C.: Government Printing Office, 1878.

JAMES   James, Edwin, comp. *Account of an Expedition from Pittsburgh to the Rocky Mountains, performed in the years 1819 and '20.* 2 vols. Philadelphia: H. C. Carey and I. Lea, 1823.

JOSSELYN   Josselyn, John. *New-Englands Rarities Discovered.* London, 1672. Reprint. *American Antiquarian Society Transactions* 4 (1860): 105–238.

KALM   Benson, Adolph B., ed. *The America of 1750; Peter Kalm's Travels in North America.* 2 vols. New York: Wilson-Erickson, 1937.

KEELER   Keeler, Harriet L. *Our Native Trees.* 9th ed. New York: Charles Scribner's Sons, 1917.

LITTLE   Little, Elbert L., Jr. *Check List of Native and Naturalized Trees of the United States (Including Alaska).* Agriculture Handbook no. 41. U.S. Department of Agriculture, Forest Service, Tree and Range Plant Name Committee. Washington, D.C.: Government Printing Office, 1953.

LOUDON   Loudon, J. C. *Arboretum et Fruticetum Britannicum.* 8 vols. 2d ed. London: Henry G. Bohn, 1854.

LOWELL   Lowell, John. "Remarks on the Gradual Diminution of the Forests of Massachusetts." *The Massachusetts Agriculture Repository and Journal* 5, no. 1 (June 1818): 32–61.

M'MAHON   M'Mahon. Bernard. *The American Gardener's Calendar.* Philadelphia: The author, 1806.

H. MARSHALL   Marshall, Humphry. *Arbustrum Americanum: The American Grove.* Philadelphia: J. Crukshank, 1785.

WM. MARSHALL   [Marshall, William]. *Planting and Ornamental Gardening; a Practical Treatise.* London: J. Dodsley, 1785.

MICHAUX, *SYLVA*, 1841   Michaux, F. A. *The North American Sylva.* 3 vols. Philadelphia: J. Dobson, 1841–1842.

MICHAUX, *SYLVA*, 1859   Michaux, F. A. *The North American Sylva.* 3 vols. Philadelphia: D. Rice & A. N. Hart, 1859.

MICHAUX, *TRAVELS*   Michaux, F. A. *Travels to the West of the Alleghany Mountains.* London: B. Crosby and Co.; J. P. Hughes, 1805.

MIROV   Mirov, N. T. *The Genus Pinus.* New York: The Ronald Press, 1967.

NEWHALL   Newhall, Charles S. *The Trees of Northeastern America.* New York and London: G. P. Putnam's Sons, The Knickerbocker Press, 1890.

OX. DICT.   *The Oxford English Dictionary.* Oxford, 1933.

REES, *DICT.*   Rees, Abraham, ed. *The Cyclopaedia; or, Universal Dictionary of Arts, Sciences, and Literature.* 1st. Am. ed. Philadelphia: Samuel F. Bradford, and Murray, Fairman and Co., [1802–1819].

ROMANS   Romans, Bernard. *A Concise Natural History of East and West Florida.* 1775. Facsimile reproduction. Introduction by Rembert W. Patrick. ·Gainesville: University of Florida Press, Floridiana Facsimile & Reprint Series, 1962.

SARGENT, *FORESTS*   Sargent, Charles Sprague, *Report on the Forests of North America (Exclusive of Mexico).* Vol. 9, *U.S. Tenth Census: 1880.* Washington, D.C.: Government Printing Office, 1884.

SARGENT, *MANUAL,* 1905   Sargent, Charles Sprague. *Manual of the Trees of North America (Exclusive of Mexico).* Boston and New York: Houghton Mifflin Co., 1905.

SARGENT, *MANUAL,* 1933   Sargent, Charles Sprague. *Manual of the Trees of North America (Exclusive of Mexico).* 2d rev. ed. Boston and New York: Houghton Mifflin Co., 1933.

SARGENT, *SILVA*   Sargent, Charles Sprague. *The Silva of North America.* 14 vols. Boston and New York: Houghton Mifflin Co., 1897.

SCHOEPF   Schoepf, Johann David. *Travels in the Confederation (1783–1784).* Translated and edited by Alfred J. Morrison. 2 vols. Philadelphia: William J. Campbell, 1911.

SCHOOLCRAFT   Schoolcraft, Henry R. *Journal of a Tour into the Interior of Missouri and Arkansaw.* London: Sir Richard Phillips and Co., 1821.

SCHOONOVER   Schoonover, Shelley E. *American Woods.* Santa Monica, Calif.: Watling & Co., 1951.

STODDARD   Stoddard, Major Amos. *Sketches, Historical and Descriptive, of Louisiana.* Philadelphia: Mathew Carey, 1812.

SUDWORTH   Sudworth, George B. *Check List of the Forest Trees of the United States, Their Names and Ranges.* Bulletin no. 17. U.S. Department of Agriculture, Division of Forestry, Washington, D.C.: Government Printing Office, 1898.

WARDEN   Warden, D. B. *A Statistical, Political, and Historical Account of the United States.* 3 vols. Edinburgh: Archibald Constable and Co., 1819.

WINTERBOTHAM   Winterbotham, W. *An Historical, Geographical, Commercial, and Philosophical View of the United States.* 4 vols. New York: John Reid, 1796.

Ott & Brewer: Etruria in America

James Mitchell

THE state of New Jersey and especially the city of Trenton have a long tradition of importance in the manufacture of American pottery. In colonial times New Jersey was already noted for its pottery products, and by the mid-nineteenth century Trenton was one of the largest pottery centers in the nation. The eighteenth-century Trenton potteries of Morton and Wimer, Shepherd and Campbell, and John McCully made lead-glazed redware thrown on the wheel, but unfortunately no marked examples of this early ware survive.[1]

In the nineteenth century, the range of pottery types produced in New Jersey expanded considerably. The McCully pottery made trailed slip-decorated, lead-glazed plates and platters as well as glazed and bisque jars from the last years of the eighteenth century to the mid-nineteenth (Fig. 1). The manufacture of Rockingham-glazed earthenware was centered in Jersey City between 1828 and 1845.[2] By the 1850s, this utilitarian brown, green, blue, and yellow-glazed ware was also made in East Liverpool, Ohio; Bennington, Vermont; and South Amboy, Woodbridge, and Trenton, New Jersey. Some of the Trenton potteries making Rockingham earthenware were: Young, Taylor and Speeler, Millington and Astbury, Charles Hattersley, Rhodes and Yates, and James and Thomas Lynch.[3] Later in the decade William Young began

making whiteware, and other potteries followed his lead (Fig. 2).[4]

The typical products of Trenton potteries in the 1860s included the new white graniteware, cream-colored ware, and ironstone china. A partial roster of Trenton firms in the 1860s includes the names Millington, Astbury and Poulson; Glasgow Pottery; William Young and Sons; Tams, Stephens and Company; Mercer Pottery Company; New Jersey Pottery Company; Coxon and Company; Taylor and Company; and the Etruria Pottery.[5] Not surprisingly, Trenton continued to be a center for innovation in American pottery throughout the last half of the century. The name of the Etruria Pottery is linked with some of the most important artistic and technical developments in American pottery production.

William Bloor, Joseph Ott, and Thomas Booth combined in 1863 to form a company that would become a success in the burgeoning field of American ceramics. Their factory, built in May of 1863, was named Etruria Pottery, presumably after

---

[1] Henry J. Podmore, "Early Trenton Potteries," *Ceramic Age* (July 1948): 332.

[2] Lura Woodside Watkins, "Henderson of Jersey City and His Pitchers," *Antiques* 50, no. 1 (Dec. 1946): 388–92.

[3] Archibald M. Maddock II, *The Polished Earth, A History of the Pottery Plumbing Fixture Industry in the United States* (Trenton, N.J.: Estate of Archibald M. Maddock II, 1962), p. 51.

[4] John Hart Brewer, Manuscript note on white pottery pitcher 354.1, Brewer Collection, New Jersey State Museum (hereafter NJSM).

[5] Maddock, *Polished Earth*, p. 53. Whiteware is a generic term that encompasses many types of white earthenware and stoneware. Graniteware, cream-colored ware, queensware, and ironstone are among the types of pottery included under the rubric whiteware. Specific types of whiteware are often difficult to distinguish from each other, and, in general, the designation of specific types of ware in this paper, i.e. graniteware, creamware, ironstone, etc., is based on advertisements by Trenton potteries stating which particular types of whiteware they manufactured, rather than on technical differences in the objects. In addition many individual pieces bear a mark that aids in identifying the particular type of ware. For example, the plate illustrated in Fig. 5 is marked "ironstone."

FIG. 1. J. McCully, Trailed slip-decorated redware. Trenton, New Jersey, 1799–1852. Redware: Jar; H. 11″, Jar; H. 11″, Platter; L. 18″, Plate; Diam. 10″. (New Jersey State Museum 264, 68.180, 70.212, 70.244.)

FIG. 2. William Young, White pitcher. Trenton, New Jersey, 1852. Porcelain; H. 11″. (New Jersey State Museum, Brewer Collection 354.1.)

FIG. 3. Taylor and Speeler, Blue and brown pitcher. Trenton, New Jersey, 1852–1859. Rockingham-glazed yellowware; H. 11″. (New Jersey State Museum 68. 161.)

Wedgwood's famous pottery.[6] Bloor had come to Trenton from East Liverpool, Ohio, in 1854. At first he worked with Henry Speeler and James Taylor. By 1856, the firm was known as Speeler, Taylor and Bloor, and it manufactured colored Rockingham-glazed earthenware (Fig. 3). In 1859, Bloor left Speeler and Taylor and returned to Ohio where he started his own firm, which he later sold to William Brunt, Jr.[7] Bloor returned to Trenton in 1863 and formed a new partnership with Ott and Booth. At the time neither Ott nor Booth was in the pottery business. Ott had owned a livery stable with William P. Brewer, and Booth had been in the stationery business. Bloor may have known Ott and Booth during his previous residence in Trenton. Apparently the combination of Ott and Booth provided the financial resources necessary to erect a new pottery. In 1860, Ott's livery stable had been valued at $9,900 and Booth's business had been valued at $10,000.[8] Ott's and Booth's financial capabilities combined with Bloor's practical knowledge of pottery production allowed the new firm to build a factory and start production. They made cream-colored ware and white graniteware.[9]

Within a year the ownership of the new business altered. In 1864, Booth retired and sold his interest to Garret Schenck Burroughs. One year later, ill health forced Burroughs to sell his share to John Hart Brewer.[10] John Hart Brewer was the son of William P. Brewer, Ott's former partner in the livery business, and Brewer was also the nephew of Ott.[11] He was only twenty-one when he bought Burroughs's interest in the Etruria Pottery and became associated with his uncle and Bloor.

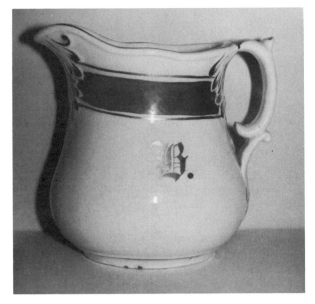

FIG. 4. Bloor, Ott and Brewer, White, green, and gold pitcher. Trenton, New Jersey, 1866. Graniteware; H. 6½″. (New Jersey State Museum, Brewer Collection 354.6.)

At this time, the firm advertised in the Trenton directories that they were making ironstone and queensware. Unfortunately, they never employed a mark that would have identified any of their surviving queensware, although they did mark their ironstone.

From the outset, the pottery presumably produced ware of a utilitarian nature, but even in their early products Bloor, Ott and Brewer showed a tendency toward innovation through their interest in decoration and their efforts to solve technical problems. White graniteware was made by Bloor, Ott and Brewer and decorated by Herman Roledge in 1866 (Fig. 4). At that time, Roledge was the only decorator in Trenton.[12] One of the problems nineteenth-century potters faced was the checking or crazing of glazes on pottery bodies. Although some potteries had solved the problem of crazing by a process of trial and error, a scientific technique for making a glaze and a body with the same coefficient of expansion had not yet been developed. Bloor, Ott and Brewer made a white plate decorated with a network of blue lines that hopefully anticipated the pattern in which the

[6] Edwin Atlee Barber, *The Pottery and Porcelain of the United States* (New York: G. P. Putnam's Sons, 1909), p. 214.

[7] Maddock, *Polished Earth*, p. 53.

[8] Manuscript Returns, Trenton, Mercer County, New Jersey, U.S. Census of Population, 1860, Bureau of Archives and State History, New Jersey State Library, Trenton.

[9] John O. Raum, *History of the City of Trenton, New Jersey* (Trenton: W. T. Nicholson & Co., 1871), p. 254.

[10] Raum, *History of Trenton*, p. 255.

[11] Manuscript Returns, Trenton, Mercer County, New Jersey, U.S. Census of Population, 1860, Bureau of Archives and State History, New Jersey State Library, Trenton. John Hart Brewer went into the pottery business immediately after he was discharged from his service as a seaman aboard the U.S.S. *Huntsville* in the union navy during the Civil War. William S. Stryker, *Record of Officers and Men of New Jersey in the Civil War* (Trenton: John L. Murphy, 1876), p. 1607.

[12] John Hart Brewer, Manuscript note on white graniteware pitcher 354.6, Brewer Collection, NJSM.

FIG. 5. Bloor, Ott and Brewer, Plate. Trenton, New Jersey, 1865–1871. Pottery; Diam. 9″. (New Jersey State Museum, Brewer Collection 354.10.)

glaze would check (Fig. 5). But over the years the glaze not only crazed in a pattern as large as the blue lines but also in an intricate web of much smaller lines.

Some time after President Lincoln appointed General Ulysses S. Grant to command the Army of the Potomac, the firm produced a parian porcelain bust of Grant clearly marked "B.O. & B." (Fig. 6). Authors in the past have felt that wares such as parian porcelain, which is a type of unglazed and undecorated white porcelain often used for statuary, were made after, not prior to, the excitement of the 1876 centennial, but the impressed block-letter mark "B.O. & B." on the bust of Grant shows that the firm made the unglazed body prior to 1871. The bust portrays Grant in military uniform, while a later Ott and Brewer bust of Grant as President shows him in civilian garb (Fig. 7). Only one other parian porcelain bust, that of Abraham Lincoln, can be attributed definitely to Bloor and Ott, with Booth, Burroughs, or Brewer, based on the "B.O. & B." mark (Fig. 8).

In 1871, Bloor left the partnership, and Ott and Brewer carried on the Etruria works.[13] Between 1871 and 1876, they produced both cream-colored earthenware and white graniteware. Parian porce-

[13] Maddock, *Polished Earth,* p. 54.

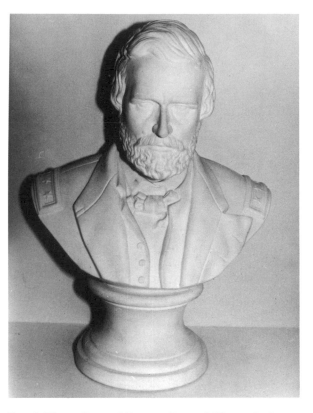

FIG. 6. Bloor, Ott and Brewer, Bust of Ulysses S. Grant. Trenton, New Jersey, 1865–1871. Parian porcelain; H. 12″. (New Jersey State Museum, Brewer Collection 354.31.)

FIG. 7. Ott and Brewer, Bust of Ulysses S. Grant. Trenton, New Jersey, 1876. Parian porcelain; H. 8″. (New Jersey State Museum 69.222.)

FIG. 8. Bloor, Ott and Brewer, Bust of Abraham Lincoln. Trenton, New Jersey, 1865–1871. Parian porcelain; H. 12½″. (New Jersey State Museum, Brewer Collection 354.33.)

lain might also have been made during this period. A profusion of busts were made for the 1876 centennial, culminating in Ott and Brewer's parian porcelain baseball vase (Fig. 9) and the life-sized bust of Cleopatra in a new metallic blue body decorated with gold and silver (Fig. 10).

In 1873, Ott and Brewer employed Isaac Broome to create porcelain sculpture for the centennial. Broome was the designer of the famous baseball vase and the Cleopatra bust, and his employment by a pottery was an unusual undertaking as the models for pottery and porcelain were usually created by unnamed artisan modelers who never signed their work. At the same time that he was creating porcelain sculpture for Ott and Brewer, he was also designing lithographs for the first lithographic printing on pottery in America. Prior to this time American pottery decoration consisted of hand painting, gold striping, molded relief, and applied ornament. In 1876, Ott and Brewer produced a pitcher ornamented with the head of George Washington by a process of litho-

FIG. 9. Ott and Brewer, Baseball vase. Trenton, New Jersey, 1876. Parian porcelain; H. 34″. (New Jersey State Museum, Brewer Collection 354.22.)

FIG. 10. Ott and Brewer, Bust of Cleopatra. Trenton, New Jersey, 1876. Colored bisque porcelain; H. 22″. (New Jersey State Museum, Brewer Collection 354.24.)

graphic transfer printing (Fig. 11).[14] Broome's employment by Ott and Brewer, in the 1870s, emphasized their desire to experiment in the production of artistically eminent porcelain objects.

Broome had had extensive experience in many aspects of the fine arts, and after his work for Ott and Brewer he went on to achieve even greater prominence, especially in the field of ceramic arts. He had studied at the Pennsylvania Academy of the Fine Arts, and he later traveled extensively in Italy, France, and England between 1855 and 1860. After work on the statues for the north pediment of the United States Capitol and a statue for W. W. Corcoran's mausoleum, he was elected, in 1860, Academician of the Pennsylvania Academy of the Fine Arts to fill a vacancy created by the death of Rembrandt Peale. About 1866, he established a short-lived terra-cotta factory at Pittsburgh, which made vases, fountains, and architectural designs, and after a period of painting portraits and creating sculptures, he established an architectural terra-cotta works in Brooklyn, New

[14] John Hart Brewer, Manuscript note on ivory porcelain pitcher 354.4, Brewer Collection, NJSM.

York, in 1871. Broome won awards for his ceramic art from the Centennial Exposition in 1876 and the Paris Exposition in 1878, and after his association with Ott and Brewer, he continued to work as a designer for various pottery firms while carrying on an active career as a teacher, lecturer, and author.[15]

At the same time that Ott & Brewer produced parian wares and developed the process of lithographic printing, they were experimenting with body materials. Over the years potters have tried to develop bodies made from single substances that would not require combination with other substances to achieve desired results. In 1876, Ott and Brewer attempted to make a body using only one clay. One pitcher was made from clay found at Asbury, New Jersey (Fig. 12), and a second pitcher was made from clay found at the farm of

[15] *Who Was Who in America* (Chicago: Marquis' Who's Who, 1943), 1:144. In 1883, Broome worked for the Trent Tile Company, in 1885, for the Providential Tile Works, and in 1890, for the Beaver Falls Art Tile Company. He made an extensive survey of European ceramic art and published articles, poetry, and two books.

FIG. 11. Ott and Brewer, Pitcher. Trenton, New Jersey, 1876. Ivory porcelain; H. 8″. (New Jersey State Museum, Brewer Collection 354.4.)

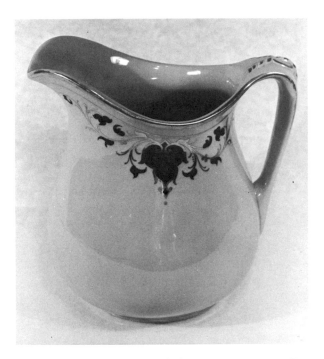

FIG. 12. Ott and Brewer, Pitcher. Trenton, New Jersey, 1876. Pottery; H. 8″. (New Jersey State Museum, Brewer Collection 354.3.)

FIG. 13. Ott and Brewer, Pitcher. Trenton, New Jersey, 1876. Pottery; H. 9″. (New Jersey State Museum, Brewer Collection 354.48.)

John P. Wene in Warren County, New Jersey (Fig. 13).[16] Both pieces are gray and covered with clear glaze. They have survived with Brewer's hand-written notes pasted to their bases attesting to their composition. In 1877, a metallic green body was used to make a bisque bust of George Washington (Fig. 14).[17] Probably the same body was used for a glazed egg-shaped vase with the head of a clown jutting out at one side (Fig. 15). It is marked with a longhand, scratched mark that is only found on one other piece, a parian porcelain plaque picturing Robert Fulton.

Throughout its ceramic history, America has been an English province, and the late nineteenth century was no exception especially in the area of high quality porcelain ware, the acme of the potter's art. In the 1870s, America produced little true glazed porcelain. England, Ireland, and the continent monopolized the manufacture of glazed translucent ware, and Americans purchased it. American potteries had long tried to produce a ware that would simulate the qualities of European porcelain, including its commercial success,

and Ott and Brewer certainly wanted to share the market. Even when porcelain was made in America, some ingredients for the body formula had to be imported from Europe, although there were known deposits of china clay, or kaolin, in America.

In 1876, when Ott and Brewer perfected a body that they called ivory porcelain, they made a new departure in the history of American ceramics (Fig. 16). A body such as ivory porcelain was a mixture of ingredients including kaolin and feldspar as well as small quantities of frit and ball clay. Other chemical ingredients were added to vary the color and plasticity of the unfired ware. Ott and Brewer's new body was made entirely from American materials. When they displayed the new ware at the Centennial Exposition in Philadelphia, Ott and Brewer were well aware of the obvious economic advantages as well as the patriotic implications of an entirely American porcelain.[18]

Ott and Brewer's ivory procelain was an attempt to copy porcelain made in Ireland at Belleek. Belleek porcelain, as made in Ireland and later in America, was a thin porcelain body of cream color

---

[16] John Hart Brewer, Manuscript note on pottery pitcher 354.3; Manuscript note on pottery pitcher 354.48, Brewer Collection, NJSM.

[17] John Hart Brewer, Manuscript note on Washington bust 354.28, Brewer Collection, NJSM.

[18] John Hart Brewer, Manuscript note on ivory porcelain column vase 354.19, Brewer Collection, NJSM.

FIG. 14. Ott and Brewer, Bust of George Washington. Trenton, New Jersey, 1877. Bisque metallic green porcelain; H. 8". (New Jersey State Museum, Brewer Collection 354.28.)

FIG. 15. Ott and Brewer, Vase. Trenton, New Jersey, 1876. Glazed green porcelain; H. 8". (New Jersey State Museum, Brewer Collection 354.26.)

FIG. 16. Ott and Brewer, Vase. Trenton, New Jersey, 1876. Ivory porcelain; H. 6¾". (New Jersey State Museum, Brewer Collection 354.19.)

covered with an iridescent glaze that was labeled "nacreous," because it looked like the seashell nacre found on the south shore of France in the Mediterranean Sea. The body was a true porcelain made of china clay and feldspar and cast as thin as possible. Porcelain was not thrown on the wheel in America. The objects were made by pouring slip, i.e. pulverized body materials and water, into porous plaster of paris molds. The molds extracted water from the slip. After a suitable length of time, the casting workman poured the slip out of the mold leaving a thin residue covering the entire interior of the mold. The residue continued to dry and contracted slowly pulling away from the walls of the mold. Part of the mold was removed very quickly so that the ware was not torn apart. The ware continued to dry and shrink, and it was soon removed from the mold in its entirety. After drying sufficiently, the mold lines were sponged off and the clay object was fired. The success of the casting technique depended as much on the skill of the man at the casting bench as on the composition of the body itself.

Possibly the ware was glazed before firing, but it

might have been glazed after it was fired and then refired. Any painted decoration was fired in a successive firing. Gold decoration was fired in a third or fourth firing. Each firing was set at a lower temperature, for a shorter time.

Ott and Brewer continued their efforts to imitate Belleek porcelain in 1882. Brewer was aided by William Bromley, Jr., and in 1883, William Bromley, Sr., and William Jr.'s brother, John, were brought to Trenton from Belleek, County Fermanaugh, Ireland, to make true Belleek porcelain.[19] Ott and Brewer's ivory porcelain body when glazed but undecorated had an essentially colorless cast. The pieces looked like twentieth-century plastic. True Belleek ware, on the other hand, had a body with an orange cast. With the aid of the Bromleys, Ott and Brewer perfected the details of body composition necessary to change their ivory porcelain body to a facsimile of the Irish product.

During this period, Ott and Brewer marked undecorated objects made in an ivory porcelain body "O. & B." usually in brown. On decorated ware, they also used a mark consisting of a crown with a sword running through it from lower right to upper left. The letters "O&B" were placed underneath, and the word "BELLEEK" usually appeared above. The crown and sword mark is often found on objects with the ivory porcelain mark "O. & B." (Fig. 17). Ware with the crown and sword mark alone or with the crown and sword mark combined with the ivory porcelain mark should be

[19] Barber, *Pottery and Porcelain of the United States,* p. 215.

FIG. 17. Ott and Brewer, Crown and sword mark. Trenton, New Jersey, 1876–1882. Belleek decorated ivory porcelain; H. 7/16″, W. 9/16″. (New Jersey State Museum 70.22.18b.)

called Belleek decorated ivory porcelain rather than simply Belleek porcelain as has been the custom (Fig. 18).

After 1883, Ott and Brewer used a mark consisting of a crescent with the horns up, containing the word "TRENTON" with "N. J." below. Superimposed on the crescent were the letters "O & B," and over it was the single word "BELLEEK" (Fig. 19). The ware marked with the crescent was often decorated with an iridescent nacreous glaze. The crescent mark was also combined with retailers' names, such as "Tiffany & Co." (Fig. 20), and "Shreve, Crump & Low," and in the case of a cup and saucer for chocolate, with the Southern Art Union's name and the date 1884 (Fig. 21).[20]

Ott and Brewer continued their policy of advertising their wares by exhibits at expositions throughout the 1870s and 1880s. In 1878, Isaac Broome was appointed U.S. Commissioner of Ceramics to the Paris Exposition, held in that year. Apparently he took the blue-bodied bust of Cleopatra, which had won a medal at the Philadelphia Centennial, with him to Paris where it won a second medal. Two nacreous-glazed Belleek porcelain mirror frames made by Ott and Brewer were exhibited at the New Orleans Exposition in 1884.[21]

In 1878, the Etruria Pottery Company was incorporated to make earthenware, crockery, porcelain ware, and other articles. It was capitalized at $50,000 and 500 shares of stock were issued. Ott held 243 shares; Brewer owned 242; John H. Hartpence, the business manager, held 5 shares; Charles H. Cook, the secretary, held 5 shares; and Timothy H. Hunt also owned 5 shares. For an unknown reason the corporation was dissolved on December 12, 1881, although the firm continued to manufacture ware.[22]

In fact, business was good in the late 1880s, and in this period Ott and Brewer probably produced the great quantity of Belleek porcelain with their mark that has survived to the present. At the same

[20] In 1887 a few of the retailers selling Ott and Brewer's wares were Galt's, in Washington, D.C., Bailey, Banks and Biddle, and Caldwell & Co., both in Philadelphia. International Publishing Company, *Quarter-Century's Progress of New Jersey's Leading Manufacturing Centres* (New York: International Publishing Co., 1887), p. 267; NJSM 70.22.19.

[21] The mirror frames were marked with Ott and Brewer's crescent and the name of the exposition. NJSM 70.62.2.

[22] Corporate Records A4448, Department of State, State House, Trenton.

FIG. 18. Ott and Brewer, Two open salts, a pepper shaker, and a salt shaker. Trenton, New Jersey, 1876–1892. Belleek decorated ivory porcelain and Belleek porcelain; H. 1⅛″, Diam. 2½″; H. ¾″, L. 2½″; H. 1¾″; H. 2″. (New Jersey State Museum 70.22.20, 65.5.4c, 65.5, salt shaker, Brewer Collection 354.39.)

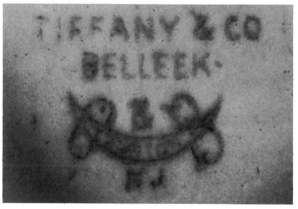

FIG. 20. Ott and Brewer, Tiffany & Co. mark. Trenton, New Jersey, 1883–1892. Belleek porcelain; H. ⅝″, W. 1⅛″. (New Jersey State Museum 68.123.7a.)

FIG. 21. Ott and Brewer, Southern Art Union mark. Trenton, New Jersey, 1884. Belleek porcelain; Diam. 11⁄16″. (New Jersey State Museum 70.22.19.)

FIG. 19. Ott and Brewer, Crescent mark. Trenton, New Jersey, 1883–1892. Belleek porcelain; H. 7⁄16″, W. ½″. (New Jersey State Museum, Brewer Collection 354.41.)

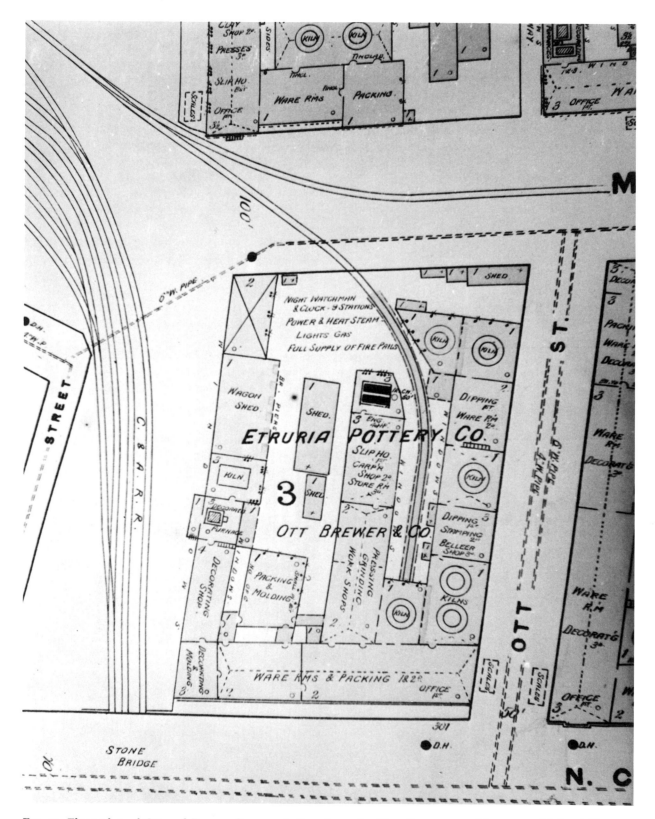

Fig. 22. Floor plan of Ott and Brewer Company's Etruria works. Plate from p. 15 of *Insurance Maps of Trenton, New Jersey* (New York: Sanborn-Perris Company, 1890). H. 5⅞″, W. 4⅛″. (Photo, New Jersey State Museum.)

time they continued to make the staples of the pottery industry: white graniteware and cream-colored ware. One mark used by Ott and Brewer in the late 1880s shows a sun rising over a body of water beneath the words "OTT AND BREWER Co." The mark reflects the second incorporation of the firm in 1888.[23]

The Etruria works in 1887 employed 250 workers, and its machinery was driven by a fifty horsepower steam engine. Six decorating and six white kilns on the premises were in active operation. The factory was a three-story brick building.[24] The 1890 Sanborn maps for the city of Trenton show the floor plan of the Etruria Pottery works in that year. The color coding of the maps indicates that although the building was mainly brick it had various small frame sheds. There was a railroad siding running into the factory, and it also contained six bottle or periodic kilns and one unusual rectangular kiln (Fig. 22). The rectangular kiln was invented by Broome in 1876 for the firing of parian and decorated porcelain.

Machinery was used for working the body materials. Ball mills, utilizing a tumbling process, pulverized clay and spar and glazing materials. Other machinery used included presses for forming objects under pressure in steel dies. Objects formed by this process were solid, such as doorknobs and tile. The potter took a handful of clay and put it into a stationary lower die with one hand. With his other hand, he reached above his head and rotated a cross arm attached to a twist screw that drove the upper die into the lower one. He then backed the screw off and removed the finished object, which was ready to be cleaned, glazed, and fired.

Ware such as plates, cups, saucers, and bowls were made on a jiggering machine. The jigger was a plaster mold that had on its top surface the exact contours of the inside of a plate or small object. The jigger was placed on top of a vertical rotating spindle, and a bat of solid clay, in the shape of a disc, was positioned on the jigger. The jigger was then rotated, and a cutter template, with the shape of the bottom contours of the plate, was used to cut away excess clay, making the jiggered bat into a finished, unfired object. A pug mill, which contained a rotating set of knives and allowed water to drain off, was used to prepare the bats for jiggering.[25]

In 1887, Ott retired, and on January 30, 1888, the Ott and Brewer Company was again incorporated. It was capitalized at $120,000. Of the 1200 shares of stock issued, John Hart Brewer held 1198 shares, Albert Brewer held one share, and Jonathan Coxon held one share.[26] Although Ott retired in 1887, from 1890 to 1892 he was listed as the president of the company in the city directories. In 1892, general financial discomfort and a damaging potters' strike in Trenton resulted in the suspension of production and the sale of the factory to Charles H. Cook. In later years Brewer reflected that, although the Etruria works had not been a great financial success, the firm had made a definite contribution to the history of ceramics.[27]

[23] One example of the Ott and Brewer mark used in the late 1880s is a porcelain pitcher. NJSM 70.146.

[24] International Publishing Company, *New Jersey's Leading Manufacturing Centres*, p. 267.

[25] Jennie Young, *The Ceramic Art: A Compendium of the History and Manufacture of Pottery and Porcelain* (New York: Harper & Bros., 1878), p. 79, fig. 29, and chap. 4 for illustrations and descriptions of machinery used in potteries of the period.

[26] Corporate Records A7137, Department of State, State House, Trenton.

[27] Maddock, *Polished Earth*, p.57.

Carpentry in the Southern Colonies during the Eighteenth Century with Emphasis on Maryland and Virginia

Peter C. Marzio

I. Defining the Colonial Carpenter

AS EUROPEANS began colonizing the North American continent they attempted to transfer ideas and institutions from the Old World to the New. These transplants often failed, and few cases of failure are more evident than that of the system of building trades, particularly carpentry, in the southern colonies. In eighteenth-century Europe, carpentry was an exclusive profession bound to tradition. The carpenter was recognized by his leather apron, his heavy iron hammer, and his wooden ruler. In most cases his father had been a carpenter, and there was a good chance that his sons would follow in his footsteps. The guild system provided the aspiring artisan with an education and insured society that homes would be built by time-honored methods.[1]

R. Campbell's *The London Tradesmen,* a book published in 1747 for "the Information of Parents, and Instruction of Youth in their Choice of Business," described the carpenter's trade in full. "The carpenter is the next Person of Consequence in the Employ of the Architect," noted Campbell; "[he] is employed in the Woodenwork, from the Foundation to the Top." In addition to laying the "Joists, Girders, and Rafters," the carpenter was expected to put on the roof and prepare it for the slater. *The London Tradesmen* also emphasized that "Strength is the chief of his study," and instructed the carpenter "to dispose his work in such

a Manner as that which is designed for the Support of a Building may not by its Weight, overturn it." Perhaps most important was Campbell's insistence that the carpenter "ought to have a solid Judgement . . . , to be able to act not only by the common Mechanical Principles of his Art, but to strike out of the common Road when the Case requires it." In addition to hand skills, the carpenter was also expected to be able to "read English, write a tolerable Hand and know how to Design his Work. He must understand as much Geometry as relates to Mensuration of Solids."[2]

The *Encyclopaedia Britannica* of 1791 defined "carpentry" more succinctly as the "art of cutting, framing, and joining large pieces of wood, for the uses of building. . . . [It involves] raising, roofing, [and] flooring of houses."[3] The carpenter erected the superstructure of a building, and various European encyclopedias were at pains to emphasize that he must not be confused with a joiner. The joiner, noted Denis Diderot, the French encyclopedist, followed many of the same procedures as the carpenter, but his work was concentrated on the inside of a building and on de-

---

[1] John Sumerson, *Georgian London* (London: Plelades Books, 1945), p. 53. There is no equivalent in English to either Antoine Moles, *Histoire des Charpentiers* (Paris: Librairie Grund, 1949), or Paul Lacroix, *Histoire de la Charpenterie et des Anciennes Communautes . . .* (Paris: A. Delahays, 1851). Both works give the deep sense of tradition in carpentry.

[2] R. Campbell, *The London Tradesmen* (London: T. Gardner, 1747), pp. 160–61.

[3] "Carpentry," *Encyclopaedia Britannica* (1791), vol. 4. Thomas Dyche and William Pardon, *A New General English Dictionary* (9th ed.; London: C. Ware, 1758), give a similar definition, "an artificer that works in wood, and particularly in the rough, large, or strongest parts of house or ship-building." See also "Carpentry," *The Builder's Magazine* (London: F. Newbery, 1779). Other dictionaries, like Samuel Johnson, *A Dictionary of the English Language* (2nd ed.; London: J. Knapton et al., 1760), give a more general definition. The dictionaries also mention carpenters as shipbuilders, but I have omitted this dimension from my study.

tails such as staircases and wall paneling.[4] This formal definition was exemplified in the urban centers of England where the building trade was composed of numerous exclusive crafts, and carpenters were as distinct from joiners as glaziers were from masons.[5]

In France and England, where much of the land was settled or owned, men were often born and buried in the same village. During their lifetimes, they worked at a particular skill and served the village in this capacity exclusively. One such skill was carpentry, the practice of which was characterized by stability and entrenched in tradition.[6]

The wilderness of the southern American colonies during the eighteenth century defied tradition and made new demands on those men who dared to emigrate from the Old World. In Maryland, Virginia, and the less populous colonies in the South, it was not enough for a carpenter to be a carpenter. If he used a hammer and ruler to build a house one day, he might use a scythe and seed-hole drill to raise his food the next. The American carpenter in the southern colonies (particularly those who lived in rural areas) had to be skilled not only with wood, but also with crops, horseshoes, and even firearms. He differed not only from his London counterpart but also from those carpenters who worked in tiny English villages. Even in these hamlets, where a carpenter was less specialized and might do the work of a joiner or coffin maker, he seldom worked at a task that did not involve wood, a saw, and a ruler.

The abundance of cheap, fertile, and unoccupied land, as well as numerous navigable rivers, broke the patterns of life established in the Old World. Unlike their deeply rooted European contemporaries, many southern colonial settlers were on the move—continually searching for new and better lands on the frontier. Much of the South was a farming community without villages where a man and his family performed all those tasks previously assigned to specially trained professionals. A few farmers were actually carpenters by trade, but the rural environment and the great distances between houses forced most farmers to become their own carpenters. The professional carpenter, a product of a stable civilization, was seldom found in this fluid society.

In 1711, the Reverend John Urmstone of North Carolina observed the hostility of the American environment—especially in the South—toward the European craft system when he described the American pioneer as "generally of all trades . . . carpenters, joiners, wheelwrights, coopers, butchers, tanners, shoemakers, tallow-chandlers, watermen, and whatnot. . . . He . . . that cannot do all these things . . . will have but a bad time of it; for help is not to be had at any rate, every one having business enough of his own. This makes tradesmen turn planters, and these become tradesmen."[7] Therefore, the formal definition of a carpenter seemed irrelevant in the rural South. A man might be skilled (or semiskilled) in a variety of trades, and it was impossible, at times, to determine when he was working as a carpenter or as another type of craftsman.

The vast, almost unlimited, scope of activities of the southern craftsman presents the historian with a serious problem. Traditionally, historians have used occupations as indicators of social class, political attitudes, and religious beliefs. In discussing the causes of revolutions, historians have examined the ideas and actions of artisans, factory workers, farmers, businessmen, intellectuals, and aristocrats. Each group supposedly had distinctive ideas and goals that affected its role in a political movement. But how does one classify a carpenter-farmer or a farmer-lawyer? Did the artisan's values override those of the farmer? Or suppose the farmer was also a lawyer?

The fact that any one man performed a variety of occupational tasks makes it difficult, or even impossible, for one to learn about any specific trade in detail. While a full-time carpenter might have recorded his activities, a man who built his own house seldom kept a carpenter's account book. Because so many colonial Americans practiced carpentry sporadically, it is difficult to learn about the colonial carpenter. Carl Bridenbaugh, in his unique book, *The Colonial Craftsman*, has documented the activities of some colonial car-

---

[4] "Charpente," *L'encyclopédie ou Dictionaire Raisonné des Sciences, des Arts et des Métiers* (Paris: Briasson, 1751–65), vol. 3.

[5] Summerson, *Georgian London*, p. 53.

[6] Peasant stability is discussed in Peter N. Stearns, *European Society in Upheaval* (New York: Macmillan Co., 1967), pp. 22–30.

[7] Ulrich B. Phillips, *Plantation and Frontier*, vol. 2 of the *Documentary History of American Industrial Society*, ed. John R. Commons et al. (Cleveland, Ohio: Arthur H. Clark Co., 1910), pp. 271–72.

FIG. 1. Unearthed masonry foundation, Williamsburg, Va., eighteenth century. (Photo, Colonial Williamsburg.)

penters in the South, but most of Bridenbaugh's evidence comes from towns and cities, where professional and semiprofessional carpenters practiced their craft. The carpenter of the rural South remains a mystery. He is a vague, shadowy figure who left few buildings and still fewer plans or account books, and all too often his existence can be proven only by the evidence of masonry foundations (Fig. 1). He is indistinct and ephemeral to historians today because his special character was obscure even in his own day.

Deterioration of the European craft system was not endemic exclusively to the South. Research in the rural areas of Long Island, for example, has uncovered similar unsystematic practices by carpenters there.[8] Probably this was true also in western Pennsylvania, upper New York, and northern New England. What makes the South an important area for study is its style of agriculture and the fact that it remained rural up to and through the Civil War. Moreover, while some studies concerning building technology and carpenters in the northern colonies have been done, the South, with the exception of Colonial Williamsburg and Historic Annapolis, has been all but ignored.

This article is intended to suggest some ideas and concepts about southern carpenters from 1700 to 1780. The majority of evidence comes from Maryland and Virginia, but one can assume that similar conditions in Georgia, South Carolina, and North Carolina created comparable situations. There has been little study of individual carpenters in the South. Therefore, sketches of the different kinds of carpenters and their work should be taken at best as generic types. It is very possible that no one carpenter fits precisely these descriptions. It is known that, despite the rural environment of the southern colonies and the lack of a concentration of people to serve as a profitable market, a few colonists were able to secure a livelihood by working with wood. These men were professional carpenters, but not in the exclusive English definition of the trade; they were less specialized and more open to a variety of jobs.

In general, the carpenters in the southern colonies from 1700 to 1780 were either (1) independent, itinerant craftsmen with only their labor to offer or (2) master builders who provided their own materials and a number of workmen besides themselves. With few exceptions, little is known about these artisans. Generalizations must be based upon fragmentary evidence.

II. The Independent, Itinerant Artisan

The itinerant carpenters are especially difficult to document, because they seldom advertised in the local newspapers. The advertisements that did appear indicate that wandering workmen hardly expected to earn a living as carpenters. They took pains to advertise their versatility. The *Maryland Journal* of June 4, 1774, noted, "There is arrived in this town, a person well recommended as a house carpenter and Joiner, and in drawing plans and elevations of houses, and in mensuration."[9] After working in the colonies for a number of years, Thomas Lamb, who had been a millwright in Newcastle, England, advertised his competence as a millwright, engineer, and joiner. He also proposed to carry on "the House Carpenter's branch" as he had been employed in the line "since his arrival . . . by Messrs. Winthrop, Todd & Co.," for whom he had erected a crane that could "lift goods of the weight of two tons,

---

[8] See the study by Charles F. Hummel, *With Hammer in Hand: The Dominy Craftsmen of East Hampton, New York* (Charlottesville: University Press of Virginia, 1968), pp. 3–27, 354–406.

[9] Quoted in Alfred C. Prime, *The Arts and Crafts in Philadelphia, Maryland, and South Carolina 1721–1785, Gleanings from Newspapers* (Topsfield, Mass.: Walpole Society, 1929), p. 298.

by only one man."[10] Lamb was seeking work in three other trades as well as in carpentry, and he was by no means the exception. Carpenters worked as coffin makers, coopers, shipbuilders, timber salesmen, merchants, architects, and at other trades, but the combination of skills most frequently offered was that of "carpenter-joiner."[11] Yet, there were few men who could eke out a living even in this dual capacity. To augment their incomes many of them turned to farming.[12] From the scraps of available evidence, it appears that when a journeyman carpenter arrived in the New World he found work scarce and prospective clients separated by vast distances. To earn his expenses, he probably found it necessary to purchase land on the frontier so that he could farm while working occasionally in his trade. After planting his crop in the spring, the carpenter might have left his farm and searched for work with a master builder on a daily wage basis. In this way, the carpenter-farmer would not be under contract to complete a building, and he could return to his land at harvest time. One "farmer" advertised in the *Maryland Gazette* of March 14, 1765, that in addition to his knowledge of farm implements and crops, he could "do Carpenter's or Joiner's Business." Other carpenters apparently practiced their skills until they could acquire land and become farmers. Sometime before the fall of 1750, for example, Low Todd, a carpenter, moved into the frontier of Augusta County, Virginia. He purchased 251 acres of land along Whistle Creek and, apparently, began to farm while keeping the title of carpenter. He probably worked on the small

county church in Forks Community near his home and assisted other settlers in erecting farm buildings. Todd quickly discovered a generally accepted notion that in the southern colonies "tillage is the more Proffitable emploiment."[13] By 1752 he had become a planter and a lieutenant in the county militia, and he found it convenient to withdraw his title of "carpenter."[14] Many others found the frontier as inviting as did Lieutenant Todd. There, English-made hammers were often replaced by hoes, and leather aprons were discarded.[15]

In the more established sections of the Tidewater, there was greater opportunity for the carpenter-farmer. Roving carpenters often worked on the large plantations, which were in constant need of repair. Most jobs on these sprawling estates required little skill but were long and tedious. To build a full-sized gate, for example, took one man an entire day.[16] Since many colonies had fencing ordinances, a plantation needed a great number of "hedge-carpenters."[17] Tobacco houses, windmills, and bridges were also erected throughout the eighteenth century.[18]

Unfortunately for the free artisan, slaves also served as carpenters and frequently cut into the carpenter-farmer's work.[19] The inventories and ac-

---

[10] Charleston *Evening Gazette*, Aug. 1, 1785, quoted in Phillips, *Plantation*, p. 351.

[11] For shipbuilding, see Howard I. Chapelle, *The History of American Sailing Ships* (New York: W. W. Norton & Co., 1935), pp. 6–44. According to Walter Rose, *The Village Carpenter* (New York: Macmillan Co., 1937), p. 121, the English carpenter was often an undertaker. Rose notes that so far as the carpenter was concerned, "a corpse aroused no more emotion in him than a plank of wood." The practice was probably brought to America.

[12] Carl Bridenbaugh, *The Colonial Craftsman* (Chicago: University of Chicago Press, 1961), pp. 4–5; Philip Alexander Bruce, *Economic History of Virginia in the Seventeenth Century*, 2 vols. (New York: Peter Smith, 1935), 2:400, 422–25. Bruce names some of the carpenter-farmers. Free Negro carpenters often had great economic difficulty; see Susie M. Ames, *Studies of the Virginia Eastern Shore in the Seventeenth Century* (Richmond, Va.: Dietz Press, 1940), p. 106. John R. Commons et al., *History of Labour in the United States*, 4 vols. (New York: Macmillan Co., 1936), 1:66, mentions the itinerant carpenter.

[13] David John Mays, ed., *The Letters and Papers of Edmund Pendelton, 1734–1803*, 2 vols. (Charlottesville: University Press of Virginia, 1967), 2:493.

[14] F. B. Kegley, *Kegley's Virginia Frontier* (Roanoke, Va.: Southwest Virginia Historical Society, 1938), pp. 73, 142.

[15] Many of the carpenters' tools were imported from England. For example, most saw blades came from Sheffield and were fitted with handles in the colonies. Peter Jones and E. N. Simons, *Story of the Saw 1760–1960* (London: Newman Neame, 1961), p. 32. For a typical advertisement, see *Virginia Gazette*, Mar. 21, 1755.

[16] Rose, *Village Carpenter*, p. 72.

[17] William Waller Hening, ed., *The Statutes at Large of all the Laws of Virginia*, 13 vols. (Richmond, Va.: Franklin Press, 1809–23), 6:38–40; Francois Xavier Martin, ed., *The Public Acts of the General Assembly of North Carolina*, 2 vols. (Newbern, N.C.: Martin and Ogden, 1804), 1:21; 2:72; Horatio Marbury and William H. Crawford, *Digest of the Laws of the State of Georgia* (Savannah, Ga.: Seymour, Woolhopter, and Stebbins, 1802), p. 235; Bruce, *Economic History*, 1:313.

[18] Advertisements like the following appeared continually in southern newspapers: "WANTED / A MAN that understands building a mill and mill house. Such a one may hear of encouragement by applying to Robert Nicolson"; *Virginia Gazette*, Jan. 12, 1769. See also Jack P. Greene, ed., *The Diary of Colonel Landon Carter of Sabine Hall, 1752–1778*, 2 vols. (Charlottesville: University Press of Virginia, 1965), 1:445.

[19] Raymond B. Pinchbeck, *The Virginia Negro Artisan*

count books of most plantations reveal the presence of carpenter's tools. Planters could not wait for the unpredictable, itinerant carpenter to appear, so they often conducted their own building operations without the aid of a professional artisan. Landon Carter, the self-styled aristocrat of Sabine Hall, was proud of his Negro carpenters, and, from the entries in his diary, he provided them with plenty of work.[20] Occasionally, a talented Negro could be purchased in Virginia from slave importers like Captain Colin Somervell,[21] but slaves usually acquired a knowledge of carpentry while living on the plantation. Often plantations hired a "knowledgeable white carpenter" to supervise the slaves and to instruct them in the mysteries of the woodworking craft. In fact, some pioneer carpenters advertised themselves as "capable of superintending a few Negro Carpenters, either in Town or Country."[22] Thomas Jefferson, who was continually erecting new buildings, hired many white carpenters to teach their trade to his slaves. James Oldham, James Densmore, John Nielson, Hugh Chrisholm, and John Perry were among Jefferson's more talented artisans.[23] In addition to working on buildings, they served as tutors—not like Philip Fithian who taught drawing and dancing at the Carter plantation—but as master carpenters, demonstrating the proper use of rulers, hammers, and chisels.

III. Master Builders

The practices of established master builders contrasted to those of itinerant carpenters. The term *master builder* did not refer to a position in the hierarchy of the guild system but was a generic name for prosperous carpenters working in the southern colonies. As a carpenter's business grew, he automatically became a master. These master builders, such as John Wheatly and Benjamin

Powell (both from Williamsburg), hired free white carpenters, sponsored several apprentices, or even owned a few Negro slaves.[24] In some cases, the slave holdings of carpenters were quite large. For example, three master builders residing in Richmond, Virginia, in 1750 owned twenty-three slaves.[25] Most master builders lived in towns where they maintained permanent residences and worked in the vicinity of their homes.[26] Their residences usually served as their offices, while outbuildings provided storage areas for the builders' tools.[27]

Some master builders lived outside the towns. Captain Joseph Harrison, the "Undertaker," or general contractor, in charge of rebuilding the Gate House in Annapolis during the mid-1720s, lived in the rural area of Charles County, Maryland. He owned sizeable tracts of land, one of which he named "Carpenters Square," and his will and inventory list indicate that he was a gentleman of more than moderate means. In addition to being a master builder, his title of captain suggests either a position in the colonial militia or a preoccupation with the sea. He also served as a prominent member of the lower house in Maryland's colonial assembly during the 1720s and practiced a fair amount of farming. Even a master builder was by no means exclusively a craftsman.[28]

[24] Marcus Whiffen, *The Eighteenth Century Houses of Williamsburg* (Williamsburg: Colonial Williamsburg, 1960), pp. 23–24.

[25] Pinchbeck, *Virginia Negro*, p. 40.

[26] The names of some master builders are given in T. E. Campbell, *Colonial Caroline* (Richmond, Va.: Dietz Press, Inc., 1954), pp. 406, 444–48; Hugh Morrison, *Early American Architecture, from the First Colonial Settlements to the National Period* (New York: Oxford University Press, 1952), pp. 289–91; Sidney Fiske Kimball, *Domestic Architecture of the American Colonies and of the Early Republic* (New York: Charles Scribner's Sons, 1927), p. 55; and Marcus Whiffen, *The Public Buildings of Williamsburg* (Williamsburg: Colonial Williamsburg, 1958), pp. 15–17.

[27] The *South Carolina Gazette*, Feb. 9, 1765: "Robert Kirkwood, Carpenter, Carries on his business at his house in Tradd Street." Quoted in Prime, *Arts and Crafts*, p. 296.

[28] Clayton Colman Hall, ed., *Proceedings and Acts of the General Assembly of Maryland* (Baltimore: Maryland Historical Society, 1914), Oct. 1724–July 1726, pp. 10 and throughout the subsequent proceedings (hereafter cited as *PAGAM*); Wills, Liber CC., No. 2, 1726–1730, pp. 151–55, Hall of Records, Annapolis, Md.; Inventories, No. 12, 1727, pp. 207–13, Hall of Records, Annapolis, Md. For information about the land holdings of some carpenters in Anne Arundel County, Md., see Anne Arundel County Deeds, BB., No. 2, 1760, pp. 350, 353, 371–73; BB., No. 3, 1765, pp. 441–42, 477–78; IB., No. 2, 1770, pp. 163–65; IB., No. 3, 1771–1773, pp. 218, 232–33; IB., No. 5, 1774, p. 1; IB., No. 5, 1774–1778, pp. 118–19, 238–39, Hall of Records, Annapolis, Md.

and Tradesman (Richmond, Va.: William Byrd Press, 1926), pp. 25–44; Bridenbaugh, *Colonial Craftsman*, pp. 15–16, 138, 140–41; Louis B. Wright, *The Cultural Life of the American Colonies 1607 to 1763* (New York: Harper & Brothers, 1957), p. 28. The Negro carpenter also offered a variety of skills. See the advertisement in the *Maryland Gazette*, May 7, 1752.

[20] Greene, *Landon Carter*, 1:414, 483, 522.

[21] *Virginia Gazette*, Dec. 22, 1768.

[22] *Charleston Gazette of the State of South Carolina*, July 8, 1784.

[23] Edwin Morris Betts, ed., *Thomas Jefferson's Farm Book* (Princeton, N.J.: American Philosophical Society, 1953), pp. 456–58.

The tendency to practice several professions was not limited to the rural carpenter. From the account book kept between 1765 and 1789 by the Annapolis carpenter, William Monroe, versatility appeared in villages and towns. Among other crafts, "carpenter" Monroe worked as a coffin maker, a joiner, a ship's carpenter, a supplier of cut timber, a cabinetmaker, and a tavern owner. His account book is a unique document for between its covers are orders for locks, boards, barrels of rum, and boxes for corpses. Such a conglomeration of enterprises would have bewildered his European counterpart.[29]

Like the ideal builder described in *The London Craftsman*, some master carpenters were competent draftsmen, capable of making "designs of houses according to the modern taste," but it was unusual for any structure to be preceded by detailed drawings.[30] The carpenter also provided cost estimates derived from carpentry manuals, which showed "how to measure Carpenters . . . Work: How to undertake . . . [that] work, and at what Price; the Rates of each Commodity, and the common Wages of Journeymen."[31] Preliminary negotiations between builders and their employers also included a contract that stipulated the size of the building, the types of material to be used, and sometimes the cost.[32]

The relationship between client and contractor

varied with each job. The carpenter might be responsible for an entire building, much as a general contractor is today, or he might be hired for his skilled labor and nothing else. George Washington, for example, while remodeling Mount Vernon, acted as his own general overseer and assumed the responsibility of coordinating the numerous aspects of his building projects.[33]

In some contracts, the master builder was responsible for supplying lumber and nails. He either purchased these materials from a lumber yard or maintained a timbering operation of his own. In urban areas, lumber yards were owned and operated by men interested exclusively in buying and selling building materials. Thomas Wright's yard in Charleston, South Carolina, for instance, advertised a wide range of items: "Cypress boards of different thicknesses and breadth, Pine inch edge and two inch planks, Pine laths for Shingling, plastering laths, and slabbs, pine joists, pine timber and scantling, pine shingles, and cypress shingles, by the thousand . . . and lightwood post for gardens."[34] Many businesses in southern towns were unable to offer such an impressive variety of materials. The owner of the yard in Williamsburg, Virginia, notified his neighbors that any person "in Want of an Pine Plank for House Building . . . may be supplied by the Subscriber in a short Time." Business in Williamsburg must have been slow, because the yard owner also offered to "undertake small Buildings."[35] In

[29] Account book of William Monroe, 1765–1789, Hall of Records, Annapolis, Md. The versatility of carpenters residing in towns is discussed also in Whiffen, *Eighteenth Century Houses of Williamsburg*, pp. 23–24.

[30] *Maryland Journal*, June 4, 1774, quoted in Prime, *Arts and Crafts*, pp. 296, 298; Harold Donaldson Eberlein, *The Architecture of Colonial America* (Boston: Little, Brown, and Co., 1915), p. 259. Although I disagree completely with Mr. Eberlein about the talents of most colonial carpenters in the South, I do agree with his idea that only "rough sketches" were used by colonial builders. See also Whiffen, *Public Buildings of Williamsburg*, p. 19, which shows a very sketchy drawing.

[31] Quoted from an advertisement for *The American Instructor* in the *Virginia Gazette*, Sept. 26, 1751.

[32] A sample contract, Phillips, *Plantation*, pp. 275–76, reads:

Memorandum of an agreement made between John Johnson of the one Part and Col. James Patton of the other Part both of Augusta County Witnesseth that the sd. Johnson is to build a Framed House for the sd. Patton on Mark James Place on James river, the house to be thirty two feet long and eighteen feet wide from outside to be eight feet from floor to floor to be convered and weatherboarded with clapboards two Tire of joists to be laid and the whole jobb to be finished in a workmanlike manner against

ye first day of July next, for which the sd. Patton is to pay the sd. Johnson seven Pistoles and a half as soon as the work is finished and to find him Diet and Lodging Hawling and help to Raise the Frame and Nails for the whole Jobb To the true performance of the above agreement—Each party do hereby bind themselves to each other in the Penal Sum of fifteen Pistoles to paid to the Party observing by the Party failing for witness whereof both parties have hereunto set their hands and seals this 26th Feby 1775.

his
John X. Johnson
mark
James Patton

Witness Present,
Wm. Preston

See also the contracts in C. G. Chamberlaye, ed., *The Vestry Book of Christ Church Parish Middlesex County, Virginia 1663–1761* (Richmond, Va.: privately printed, 1927), pp. 120–31; *PAGAM*, Oct. 1723, pp. 558–59.

[33] Edwin Tunis, *Colonial Craftsmen* (Cleveland, Ohio: World Publishing Co., 1965), p. 85.

[34] *South Carolina Gazette*, July 2, 1763, quoted in Prime, *Arts and Crafts*, p. 292.

[35] *Virginia Gazette*, Feb. 27, 1772.

rural areas, a timber yard even the size of Williamsburg's was rare. Most planks were cut from trees on the location where the building was to be erected. Wood, a bulky product, defied long-distance, overland transportation, so timber yards served only areas of high population density or plantations located on navigable rivers. It was easier to ship a load of planks to England by sea (as the southern colonies did) than it was to send a shipment overland to the southern frontier.[36]

If the master carpenter had to make his own planks, he and his workers were faced with a strenuous, back-breaking task. When the sap was down, trees were felled and trimmed immediately. The bare logs were then dragged to a saw pit where two men cut the tree into planks.[37] The arduous task was often done by Negroes or apprentices, but occasionally even the sophisticated joiner must have assumed the chores of a sawyer.[38] To transform a good-sized tree into a pile of one-half inch planks took two men one week. Once the planks were cut, they were stacked and lathed for drying. A plank one inch thick, for example, was supposed to season for one year.[39] During the seventeenth and eighteenth centuries, in both the North and the South, many colonists were in desperate need of housing, and they could not allow the planks sufficient time to season. As a result, most of the buildings were unstable and served only as temporary shelters. This situation recurred many times on the frontier, and it was not until the appearance of the balloon frame house that solid buildings appeared on virgin soil.

IV. The Level of Building Technology and Education

The basic principles of building differed little from those employed by medieval craftsmen, and many carpenters had only a vague idea of the fundamentals. A properly constructed building had wooden sills placed upon a stone or brick foundation, each piece being mortised and tenoned to provide a secure fit (Fig. 2). The sides were framed

Fig. 2. Large timbers from Ewing House, Williamsburg, Va., ca. 1780. (Photo, Colonial Williamsburg.)

with heavy timber beams, posts, and braces. Each frame was assembled flat on the ground, and when two sides were completed, they were lifted into place on top of the sills. Clapboard sheathing covered the exterior, and all cracks or spaces were filled with mud and rubble to seal the buildings against wind and rain. All pieces of wood over two inches thick were mortised and tenoned, while the rest were joined by handmade nails.[40]

Contrary to popular belief, most colonial buildings were crude and uncomfortable, and it has been estimated that in the rural areas few of them lasted longer than twenty years.[41] For example, in 1750, the citizens of newly established Frederick County, Maryland, hired Joseph Hardman, bricklayer, and John Shelman, carpenter, to erect a

[36] Tench Coxe, *View of the United States of America* (Philadelphia: William Hall et al., 1794), pp. 130–31.

[37] Rose, *Village Carpenter*, pp. 24–34. Rose's account is about nineteenth-century English carpentry, but this process must have been practiced for centuries.

[38] Pinchbeck, *Virginia Negro*, p. 33; *Virginia Gazette*, Jan. 24, 1750.

[39] Rose, *Village Carpenter*, pp. 32, 124.

[40] Carl W. Condit, *American Building Art, the Nineteenth Century* (New York: Oxford University Press, 1960), pp. 10–16. Nails were used widely in colonial buildings. See Coxe, *View of the U.S.*, p. 144.

[41] Anthony N. B. Garvan, *Architecture and Town Planning in Colonial Connecticut* (New Haven: Yale University Press, 1951), p. 143. Garvan's account is of seventeenth-century Connecticut, but the frontier conditions he writes of remained throughout much of the South in the eighteenth century.

suitable courthouse. Because of various delays, the building was not completed until 1756. Very soon thereafter, the courthouse began to deteriorate, and by 1784 it was uninhabitable. The "Justices and sundry Inhabitants of Frederick County" provided a poignant description of the twenty-eight year old building.

The public papers and Records are not only exposed to be purloined and taken out of the office above Stairs, but to be damaged and defaced by every driving rain and Snow that may happen by penetrating into the Office among the said Records and papers, that the Walls of the said Court House are giving away being Cracked and Chasms made from the foundation to the roof thereof that the Gaol is likewise in a very decayed State and will be insufficient with all the repairs that can be given to secure criminals.[42]

Structures of this type were seen by many travelers who provided their own graphic descriptions (Fig. 3). John F. D. Smyth, a loyalist who enjoyed

[42] Morris L. Radoff, *The County Courthouses and Records of Maryland, Part One* (Annapolis: Hall of Records Commission of the State of Maryland, 1960), pp. 81–83.

FIG. 3. Typical colonial building displays extra "legs" or posts used for support, Wetherburn Tavern, Williamsburg, Va., 1738-60. (Photo, Colonial Williamsburg.)

debunking the New World in his travel account, *Tour in the United States of America,* observed that as late as 1780 the houses in the area of Richmond, Virginia:

are almost all of wood, covered with the same; the roof with shingles, the sides and ends with thin boards, and not always lathed and plaistered within; only those of the better sort are finished in that manner, and painted on the outside. The chimneys are sometimes of brick, but more commonly of wood, coated on the inside with clay. The windows of the best sort have glass in them; the rest have none, and only wooden shutters.[43]

Other observers concurred. In 1756, Henry Laurens noted that in South Carolina "none but the better class glaze their houses"; and the loyalist William Eddis, in his *Letters,* emphasized that a two room house—one for animals and one for people—was deemed a luxury by even the most ambitious pioneer. Bishop Reichel and his wife, representatives of the Moravian church at Barby, Saxony, while traveling from Lititz, Pennsylvania, to Salem, North Carolina, in 1780, noted: "Here and there in the woods, we saw Virginia cabins, built of unhewn logs and without windows. Kitchen, living room, bed room and hall are all in one room into which one enters when the house door opens. The Chimney is built at the gable end, of unhewn logs looking like trees, or it is omitted altogether."[44]

Many of the buildings in the southern colonies

FIG. 4. Uneven timber, Mount Vernon, Va., ca. 1774. (Photo, The Smithsonian Institution.)

were by no means the pride of the carpentry trade. Faulty construction was due, in part, to the colonists' use of unseasoned timber. This was unavoidable on the frontier where housing was an immediate necessity. Only in the older settlements of the Tidewater was dried lumber readily available. The lack of straight planks and wood of standard sizes must also have plagued the carpenter (Fig. 4). The main ridge beams and posts in many colonial houses were surely bowed and twisted, defying the use of a straight-edge or plumb bob (Figs. 5, 6). Such poor practices were due to the lack of proper milling techniques and, probably, to the carpenter's inclination to use

[43] John F. D. Smyth, *A Tour in the United States of America,* 2 vols. (London: Robinson, Robson, and Sewell, 1784), 1:49. Hugh Jones gives an account that contradicts the thesis of this paper and the observations of Smyth. He says that the houses of Williamsburg "are justly reputed the best in all the English America, and are exceeded by few of their kind in England." Hugh Jones, *Present State of Virginia* (London: J. Clarke, 1724, reprinted for J. Sabin, 1865), p. 70. Jones's enthusiasm for America must be taken into consideration, and it should be noted that Williamsburg was the economic and cultural center of Virginia. The best the southern colonies had to offer would be located there; James H. Soltow, "The Role of Williamsburg in the Virginia Economy, 1750–1775," *William and Mary Quarterly,* 3rd ser. 15, no. 4 (Oct. 1958): 467–82. The same criticism must be made of Robert Beverley's glorified account in his *History and Present State of Virginia,* ed. Louis B. Wright (Chapel Hill: University of North Carolina Press, 1947), pp. 289–90. See also Douglas Southall Freeman, *George Washington, A Biography,* 7 vols. (New York: Charles Scribner's Sons, 1948), 1:90–96.

[44] Quoted in Charles M. Andrews, *Colonial Folkways* (New Haven: Yale University Press, 1919), pp. 54–55; Newton D. Mereness, *Travels in the American Colonies* (New York: Antiquarian Press, 1961), p. 590. See also Charles C. Jones, *The Dead Towns of Georgia* (Savannah, Ga.: Morning News Steam Printing House, 1878), for numerous accounts of poor building construction in the ill-fated colony of Georgia.

Fig. 5. Floor joists of rough timber from Cheswell House, Williamsburg, Va., eighteenth century. (Photo, Colonial Williamsburg.)

those trees nearest the building site. In addition, apparently there was no general system of standardized sizes in the home lumber industry, although some colonies, like Virginia, passed laws standardizing the size of wood for export.[45] Many carpenters were faced with the chore of using crooked planks of various sizes, in a vain attempt to erect a structure that measured straight and true.

Poor construction resulted not only from inadequate materials but also from the carpenter's ignorance of his craft. Tench Coxe, an astute observer writing about American carpenters as late

as 1794, noted a condition that appears to have been especially acute in the South: "The mechanic branches have been, till this time, on [a] . . . good footing; but those employed in the erection of buildings ought now to seek the aid of such parts of science as have relation to their calling. Rural and city architecture has been too little studied. It ought not to be forgotten, that a competent knowledge of it is no less conducive to ECONOMY and CONVENIENCE, than to elegance and splendour."[46] It would be interesting to know how often colonial houses were destroyed by wind or washed away by sudden floods. There are accounts of houses on the banks of the Roanoke being carried downstream in the rainy season.[47] The justices of Prince Georges County, Maryland, complained in the winter of 1747 that the wooden courthouse

[45] Hening, *Statutes at Large*, 6:233–35; William Winterbotham, *An Historical, Geographical, Commercial and Philosophical View of the United States*, 4 vols. (London: J. Ridgeway, 1795), 3:112. Within some local area carpenters did use wood of standard sizes. A survey of the buildings in Colonial Williamsburg will reveal the use of posts, beams, joists, and rafters that were cut according to a system of sizes.

[46] Coxe, *View of the U.S.*, p. 357.
[47] Smyth, *Tour in the U.S.*, 1:85–86.

Fɪɢ. 6. Variety of timber sizes and crooked plumblines in construction from Mr. Page's room of Wetherburn Tavern, Williamsburg, Va., 1738–60. (Photo, Colonial Williamsburg.)

was in such a delapidated condition "that in driving rains and snows, the records get wet; by which the Properties of all those concerned in the said records are endangered."[48] The *Maryland Gazette,* September 4, 1766, informed its readers that the roof fell in on the house that was finished only nineteen years earlier for Governor Bladen, "the Tenons being all Rotten in the Mortoises" (Fig. 7).

The difficulty in the southern colonies was compounded because skilled carpenters were not willing to leave England. The lack of numerous villages and towns, as well as the self-sufficiency of the large plantations, must have discouraged any carpenter sailing to America. Many of those who arrived were either convicts, indentured servants, or young carpenters who were probably discour-

aged by the restrictive guild system of England and fearful that they might remain journeymen for most of their lives.[49] American wages were high

[48] *Maryland Gazette,* Dec. 16, 1747, quoted in Prime, *Arts and Crafts,* p. 283. In 1748, John Mercer of Marlborough, Va., reluctantly paid carpenter William Monday £126.16.2½ for "work done about my House which is not near the value as by Maj^r Walker's Estimate below, yet to avoid Disputes & as he is worth nothing I give him Credit to make a full Ballance." Quoted in C. Malcolm Watkins, *The Cultural History of Marlborough, Virginia* (Washington, D.C.: Smithsonian Institution Press, 1968), p. 36.

[49] On the ship *Elizabeth,* for example, 124 passengers left from England sometime between Dec. 11 and 18, 1773, bound for Virginia. There were 26 farmers and only 8 carpenters. Of the 8, most were between 19 and 25 years of age: see George Sherwood, *American Colonists in English Records* (Baltimore, Md.: Genealogical Publishing Co., 1961), pp. 197–200. In the seventeenth century, Parliament began the practice of shipping felons to America in order to rid England of undesirable elements. At first the government paid merchants £0.40.0 per convict for transportation to the colonies, but this stipend barely covered expenses. The bounty was raised, however, and by 1740 numerous rival petitions appeared before Parliament in search of this trade. The success of the British policy was reported in 1765 by an anonymous French traveler who stated that "the number of Convicts and indented servants imported to virginia [is] amazing." The southern colonies received a majority of the "undesirables": see Edward Channing, *A History of the United States of America,* 6 vols. (New York: Macmillan Co., 1927), 2:370–76; Leo Francis Stock, ed., *Proceedings and Debates of the British Parliaments Respecting North America,* 5 vols. to date (Washington: Carnegie Institution of Washington, 1941), 5:xx–xxi; "Journal of a French Traveller in the Colonies, 1765," *American Historical Review* 26, no. 4 (July 1921): 744; Marcus Wilson Jernegan, *Laboring and Dependent Classes in Colonial America,* 1607–1783 (Chicago: University of Chicago Press, 1931), p. 135.

Fig. 7. Skeleton from smokehouse shows wood decayed by time and usage, Williamsburg, Va., ca. 1760. (Photo, Colonial Williamsburg.)

in comparison to English wages,[50] and almost anyone could claim the title of master without fear of reprisal. Unfortunately for America, these young craftsmen seldom were well-versed in their trade. Doubtless, the carpenters who left England were infrequently men who had been declared competent by Old World masters. Yet, there was only a vague, uncertain standard of quality in America to which they could compare their work, and, since guilds did not exist in the southern colonies, there was no organization to inspect the craftsman's talents and to insure the community of his competence. The colonial South, especially those areas west of the Tidewater, was, indeed, a haven for the inept carpenter.

The southern colonies attempted to establish a viable apprenticeship system. Throughout the seventeenth and eighteenth centuries, colonial assemblies passed apprenticeship laws designed to relieve state responsibility for the poor and orphans and to increase the number of skilled artisans in the New World. These laws bound out poor or orphaned boys and girls to experienced craftsmen who taught them a trade.[51]

The master carpenter served as both a surrogate father and a practical teacher. When a child was apprenticed, he, or his guardian, signed a contract called an indenture, which was applicable for a given period of time. In America, the apprenticeship was seldom more than four or five years, while in England a minimum of seven years was mandatory. The apprentice pledged to obey the master and to keep the secrets of his trade. In return, the master agreed to teach the apprentice the mysteries of carpentry, to provide room and board, and to assure a minimum education in reading and writing. Little else is known about the system. It is not known whether apprentices were required to pass examinations attesting to

[50] Tunis, *Colonial Craftsmen,* p. 15.

[51] See Hening, *Statutes at Large,* 4:212, 482; 5:452, 558; 6:32, 368.

their skill. It appears likely that a final test of skill was required, but its exact nature has not been discovered.[52]

Knowledge of the relationship between master and apprentice in America is also inadequate, but, from the number of runaways, many apprentices appear to have been dissatisfied with the system.[53] Samuel Duval, a master carpenter in Caroline County, Virginia, placed this notice in the *Virginia Gazette*, February 14, 1750.

Ran away from the subscriber . . . on Saturday Night, being the 9th Instant, an Apprentice, about 20 Years of Age, named *Richard Green*, a House Carpenter and Joiner by Trade, about 5 feet 9 inches high, slim-made, tin Visage, freckled, and very talkative . . . [He wore] a Pair of new tann'd Sheep Skin Breeches with a Bawdy-house flap, with carv'd white Metal Buttons, a Pair of blue Worsted Stockings, two Pair of blue Yarn ditto, *Virginia*-made shoes, with carv'd Silver Shoe Buckles . . . [He] stole from the Subscriber a hunting Saddle with Hog-skin Seat, green Cloth Housing with green and white strip'd Worsted Lace . . . also stole two horses.

The very young apprentice, dressed in leather pants stained with tree sap, fleeing from an irate master upon the master's horse was a sight often recorded in the newspapers of the southern colonies.[54] Whether lured by the vast unoccupied land to the west, by the glory of the colonial militia,[55] or by the idea of freedom, it appears that the budding carpenter often left his master before the termination of the indenture. The innumerable, varied, and novel opportunities in the colonies and the open, fluid society were not conducive to

the maintenance of a feudal institution or to the education of a knowledgeable carpenter.

While some colonists learned carpentry from masters as apprentices, others tried to teach themselves from English carpentry manuals.[56] Although these works contained information for "masons, carpenters, and carvers," many were esoteric in character, concentrating on principles of baroque or classical architecture. James Gibbs's *A Book of Architecture* (1728) was addressed to gentlemen "in the remote parts of the Country, where little or no assistance for Designs can be procured."[57] While some of these books were advertised as practical or simple, most provided an academic, rather than a craftsman's, approach to construction. Design and style as well as abstract engineering principles were emphasized (Figs. 8, 9, 10, 11, 12, 13). The young carpenter could learn about Doric and Ionic columns, but basic structural information, such as proper nailing and joining techniques, was not included. The dubious value of such treatises and the failure of the apprenticeship system meant that carpenters who were trained in the southern colonies received at best a rudimentary education. Most learning resulted from trial and error, and the short lives of many colonial buildings attest to the weaknesses of this system.

Not only the carpenter's inexperience, but the demand of the colonists for cheap living quarters further promoted the tradition of crude and primitive building practices. The quality of construction was dictated by a client's personal judgment as the public planning codes that existed in the South pertained only to fire prevention, building location, and sanitation.[58] In sparsely populated

---

[52] See contracts of indentures for Anne Arundel County, Hall of Records, Annapolis, Md., for the eighteenth century. In William Monroe's account book, Hall of Records, Annapolis, Md., it is noted that Thomas Baley was bound as a servant for only three and one-half years.

[53] Abbot Emerson Smith, *Colonists in Bondage* (Gloucester, Mass.: Peter Smith, 1965), pp. 264–70; Eugene Irving McCormac, *White Servitude in Maryland* (Baltimore: Johns Hopkins Press, 1904), pp. 48–59; Warren B. Smith, *White Servitude in Colonial South Carolina* (Columbia: University of South Carolina Press, 1961), pp. 22–26.

[54] See examples in *Virginia Gazette*, Nov. 21, 1751; Apr. 16, 1767; *Maryland Gazette*, Aug. 28, Nov. 13, 1775; Jan. 15, 1756; Apr. 16, 1764; Nov. 16, 1769; June 20, 1776; Mar. 20, 1788.

[55] An extreme example is that of apprentice Samuel Duval, who, at the age of twelve and one-half years, ran away from carpenter Gabriel Mitchell and was enlisted into the colonial militia. T. E. Campbell, *Colonial Caroline*, p. 151.

[56] Ernest Allen Connally, *Printed Books on Architecture 1485–1805* (Champaign, Ill.: The Adah Patton Memorial Fund of the University of Illinois, 1960), p. 38; Whiffen, *Eighteenth Century Houses of Williamsburg*, pp. 39–43; Morrison, *Early American Architecture*, pp. 287–88. Batty Langley, *The Builder's Jewel; or the Youth's instructor, and workman's remembrancer* (first published in London in 1746, with ten subsequent English editions by 1768); Joseph Moxon, *Mechanick Exercises* (London: J. Moxon, 1683); Francis Price, *The British Carpenter* (3rd ed.; London: C. and J. Ackers, 1753) were popular English handbooks in America.

[57] Connally, *Printed Books*, p. 36. Both Gibbs and Langley were widely used in colonial America. For a list of manuals, see Helen Park, "A List of Architectural Books Available in America before the Revolution," *Journal of the Society of Architectural Historians* 20, no. 3 (Oct. 1961): 115–130.

[58] Whiffen, *Eighteenth Century Houses of Williamsburg*, pp. 53–56.

FIG. 8. Complex roof structure from Benjamin Waller House, Williamsburg, Va., prior to 1749. (Photo, Colonial Williamsburg.)

FIG. 9. "North Elevation" showing Palladian window at right, Peyton-Randolph House, Williamsburg, Va., 1715–83. (Photo, Colonial Williamsburg.)

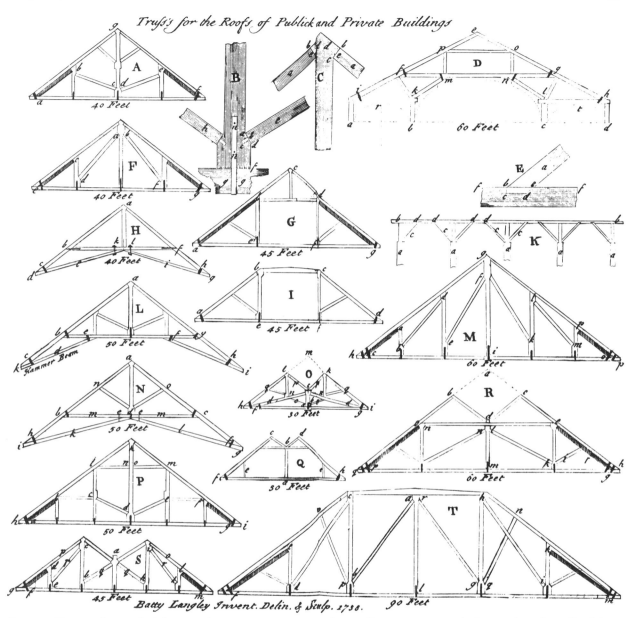

FIG. 10. Trusses for roofs. Plate 54 from Batty Langley, *The Builders Compleat Assistant* (London: R. Ware, 1738). (Photo, The Smithsonian Institution.)

areas the colonial carpenter was at his worst. Because tobacco was "the great dependence of Every Inhabitant of this Province," Southerners structured their living patterns according to the requirements of the sacred broad leaf.[59] On the tobacco plantations, where the soil was exhausted every six or seven years and farmers were continually forced to seek new lands, buildings were characterized by their small size, crude finish, and weak construction.[60] Since most farmers moved with

their entire families, buildings were totally abandoned when the soil was depleted. Constant mobility led to the hasty construction of residences and outbuildings, with the roughly hewn wooden sills placed directly on the rich earth without benefit of a brick foundation. One traveler described the humble abode of a Maryland planter

[59] Hall, *PAGAM*, p. 485.

[60] Lewis Cecil Gray, *History of Agriculture in the Southern United States to 1860*, 2 vols. (Washington: Carnegie

Institution of Washington, 1933), 1:217; Harry J. Carman, ed., *American Husbandry* (New York: Columbia University Press, 1939), p. 187; Joseph C. Robert, *The Story of Tobacco in America* (New York: Alfred A. Knopf, 1952), pp. 18–19.

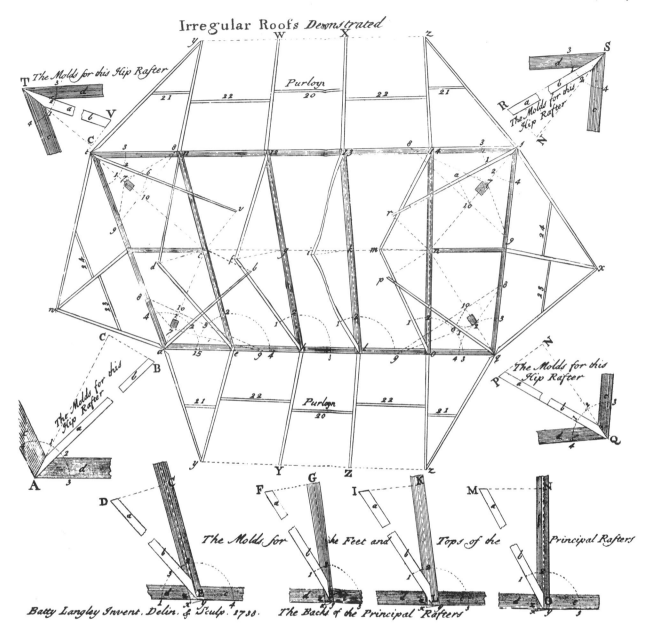

Fig. 11. Irregular roofs. Plate 58 from Batty Langley, *The Builders Compleat Assistant* (London: R. Ware, 1738). (Photo, The Smithsonian Institution.)

as "very bad, and ill-contrived."[61] Dirt floors, unfinished interiors, and oiled-paper windows made housecleaning difficult, and many farmers' wives must have wondered whether or not their houses would outlive the harvest (Fig. 14).

The great Southern manses and plantation houses that survive today were not the first buildings erected on their sites. Mount Vernon was pre-ceded by several modest structures, and Thomas Jefferson's famous Monticello occupies ground that earlier had seen shacks and lean-tos.[62] Until a farmer became a planter-aristocrat, he was compelled to move periodically from one crude home to another.

Even in urban areas there were no laws regulating building quality. When colonial legislatures

[61] James Birket, *Some Cursory Remarks* (New Haven: Yale University Press, 1915), quoted in Andrews, *Colonial Folkways*, p. 55.

[62] Freeman, George Washington, 1:n53, 90–95; Dumas Malone, *Jefferson and His Time*, 2 vols. (Boston: Little, Brown, & Co., 1948), 1:27.

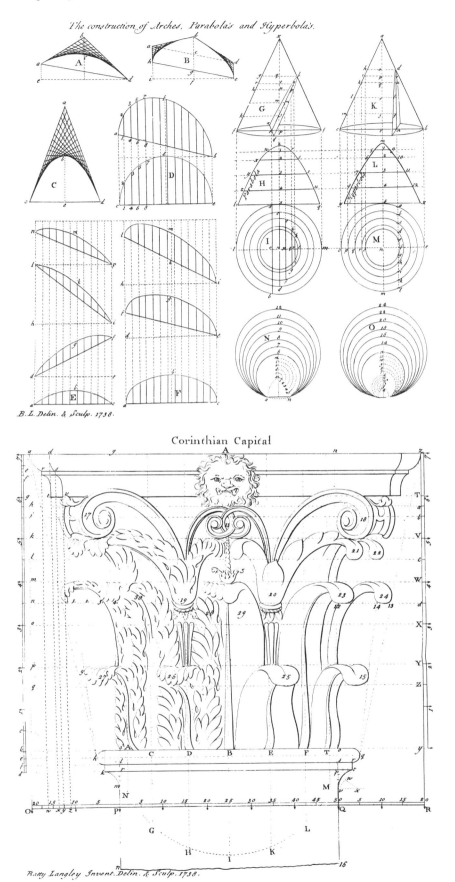

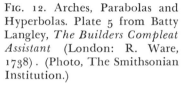

FIG. 12. Arches, Parabolas and Hyperbolas. Plate 5 from Batty Langley, *The Builders Compleat Assistant* (London: R. Ware, 1738). (Photo, The Smithsonian Institution.)

FIG. 13. Corinthian Capital. Plate 35 from Batty Langley, *The Builders Compleat Assistant* (London: R. Ware, 1738). (Photo, The Smithsonian Institution.)

issued charters for the building of new towns, the problem of quality was left to a special committee of citizens or "town properties" responsible for each village.[63] The closest the colony of Virginia came to legislating the quality of buildings (with the exception of fire prevention laws) was in 1758, when the House of Burgesses gave the trustees of Stephensburg, Winchester, and Leesburg power "to settle and establish such rules and orders for the more regular and orderly building of . . . houses . . . as to them shall seem best and most convenient."[64] Even in older urban areas, many structures, especially outbuildings like necessaries and storage sheds, were poorly made and often became permanent eyesores. The account book of Humphrey Harwood, a bricklayer and building contractor in Williamsburg, contains references to these "temporary" structures. He often contracted to make these shanties into

more substantial buildings by jacking them up and placing a foundation under them.[65] Thus, a temporary building often became a permanent fixture (Fig. 15).

The need for versatile craftsmen was also a cause of the decline in the quality of workmanship. Men who were compelled to perform a variety of tasks seldom enjoyed the luxury of learning the principles of each craft. In the South, which remained rural until after the Civil War, most men worked with wood, and many men claimed to be skilled carpenters. Thomas Lamb called himself a carpenter after working on one job. He was not trained by the apprenticeship system; yet he claimed skills reserved for a master craftsman. Rural America was hostile to tradition, and titles used in professions were easily appropriated.[66] Men who were properly qualified carpenters (by English standards) worked in areas

[63] Thomas Cooper, *The Statutes at Large of South Carolina*, 5 vols. (Columbia, S.C.: A. S. Johnston, 1837), 5:218; Hening, *Statutes at Large*, 3:419–32; Martin, *Public Acts*, 2:72.

[64] Hening, *Statutes at Large*, 7:236.

[65] This account book is at Colonial Williamsburg.

[66] This fluidity of profession was not relegated to carpentry alone. See Daniel J. Boorstin, *The Americans, The Colonial Experience* (New York: Random House, 1958), pp. 191–95.

FIG. 14. Brick nogging characteristic of more substantial homes, Peyton-Randolph House, Williamsburg, Va., 1715–83. (Photo, Colonial Williamsburg.)

Fig. 15. Outbuilding placed on new foundation, Williamsburg, Va., ca. 1800. (Photo, Colonial Williamsburg.)

like Williamsburg and, of course, emphasized their English training and their knowledge of English methods.[67] England, not the southern colonies, was the cradle of quality and the symbol of tradition. When Governor Tryon of North Carolina wanted to erect his sumptuous "Palace," he was unable to find a properly skilled artisan in America. Thus, he and numerous southern aristocrats contracted with English carpenters to come to the New World to erect their homes.[68]

V. Immigration and Society

It is not surprising that the southern colonies

made repeated efforts to lure trained carpenters to America. Advertisements to entice "useful mechanics" to the "Land of Promise" where "freedom, peace, and plenty" could be secured were distributed from Ireland to Germany.[69] "Labouring people," wrote one enthusiast shortly after the Revolution, "can have constant employment . . . because we have . . . so many new dwelling houses, workshops, barns, and other buildings to erect."[70] These advertisements reflected a common belief that the southern colonies needed skilled hands to build homes and repair fences. Yet, in the agrarian communities a skilled artisan was

[67] See Dudley Inman's advertisement in Prime, *Arts and Crafts*, p. 296.

[68] Alonzo T. Dill, "Tryon's Palace," *North Carolina Historical Review* 20, no. 2 (Apr. 1942): 119–67. Emphasis upon the shoddy work of America's carpenters should not blur the fact that a few master builders were capable men. They could write a decent letter and read a book, and many were competent draftsmen who rose to become architects, for example, William Buckland, Samuel Rhoads, John Ariss, and Joseph Brown.

[69] R. J. Dickson, *Ulster Emigration to Colonial America 1718–1775* (London: Routledge and Kegan Paul, 1966), pp. 16–18, 39, 44–45, 60–61, 89, 139. Some colonies like South Carolina offered bounties to attract immigrants. See Bruce, *Economic History*, pp. 401, 620–21; Bridenbaugh, *Colonial Craftsman*, p. 11; Phillips, *Plantation*, pp. 169–76.

[70] Coxe, *View of the U.S.*, p. 95.

unable to find uninterrupted, lucrative employment.

The apparent lack of carpenters was most obvious when new building contracts were offered for a church or a large plantation house. Colonial legislatures, church groups, and individual planters advertised in local newspapers for bids from craftsmen or master builders.[71] Despite numerous attempts and wide coverage, many advertisements received little, if any, response. After failing to attract workmen, colonists denounced England's mercantile policy as a restrictive measure, especially regarding the immigration of skilled laborers to America. In the *Virginia Gazette,* September 15, 1768, the colonists were notified that the House of Burgesses was prepared to debate the question of "how far the Americans may be permitted to engage British artificers to quit the Kingdom." The Navigation Acts, which implemented mercantile ideas, were a curse to those colonials seeking economic self-sufficiency. These acts specified that all manufacturing was to be carried on in England and that artisans such as iron workers, silversmiths, and hat makers were not to leave the mother country.[72] Colonial boosters and emigration agents had grounds for holding English policy responsible for some of America's technical backwardness, but they overstated their case when they included carpentry. No law forbidding the emigration of carpenters from England has been found.[73] The colonists did not import houses from Great Britain, and the settlers needed protection from the elements. If carpenters did not rush to the southern colonies, it was because they did not see a haven there for sophisticated craftsmen. Many who came were sponsored by gentlemen for a specific project; otherwise, it was better to remain in England where carpentry work was readily available.

The colonial legislatures and gentlemen planters who continually debated this issue neglected the true cause. The South had few professional carpenters because few were needed. The rural environment, the constant mobility of the tobacco farmers, and the presence of Negro slaves almost eliminated the need for an English-trained carpenter. The needs of the southern colonies differed from those of England, and the unanswered call for a too infrequent building contract was no proof of a great demand for skilled labor.

In addition to the fact that the southern colonies did not need an army of specialized craftsmen, some evidence suggests that those skilled craftsmen who were available were reluctant to accept employment from public bodies for fear of not being paid. Although the evidence is not abundant, it seems likely that a more detailed examination of public building contracts in the southern colonies would reveal that many of the carpenters employed in those projects actually failed to receive the agreed compensation for their work. As early as 1678 when the Pamunkey and Mattaponi valleys in Virginia were opened for settlement, the colonial council commissioned William Meridaye to build a fort for protection. Upon completion of the structure, the council declared that Meridaye had failed to follow its instructions, and they refused to appropriate any funds to pay him.[74] Another instance occurred in 1769, when the Wiccomico parish in Northumberland County contracted John Wiley to erect a new church. Edmund Pendleton, the general overseer, became displeased with Wiley and charged him with failing "to finish the Church . . . according to agreement."[75] In all probability Wiley was not paid. The story was repeated all too often, and numerous private contractors, as well as various public bodies, refused to pay their just debts to artisans.[76]

This is not to say that the carpenters were always trustworthy and upstanding. In some contracts, master builders were obliged to "give good

[71] *Virginia Gazette,* Dec. 12–19, 1745; Apr. 17–24, 1746; Feb. 28, 1750; Dec. 15, 1768. Advertisements usually ran for a number of issues and indicated that "committees" were in charge of building contracts. One should not be led to believe that these contracts abounded. Williamsburg, for example, did not build a substantial courthouse until the 1770s.

[72] Carroll W. Pursell, Jr., "Thomas Digges and William Pearce: An Example of the Transit of Technology," *The William and Mary Quarterly,* 3rd ser. 21, no. 4 (Oct. 1964): 551–52; *Statutes at Large* (London: Mark Basket, 1763), 3:230–34, 267–71.

[73] Leonard Woods Labaree, ed., *Royal Instructions to British Colonial Governors, 1670–1776* (New York: D. Appleton-Century Co., 1935), mentioned nothing about restricting carpenters.

[74] T. E. Campbell, *Colonial Caroline,* p. 10.

[75] Mays, *Letters and Papers,* 1:42.

[76] Bruce, *Economic History,* 2:416, notes that planters were often in debt to artisans; Will of Captain Joseph Robinson, Hall of Records, Annapolis, Md.; Account book of William Monroe, Hall of Records, Annapolis, Md.

Security for *ye* finishing" of a building under penalty of forfeiture.[77] Carpenters were probably as fickle as their patrons, and many must have failed to complete their work.

Some breaches of contracts were probably the result of misunderstandings. Detailed architectural plans were seldom drawn for colonial buildings.[78] The carpenter, working from a simple drawing or a model in his building manual, would begin erecting the structure, consulting the owner periodically. Fine details, such as handrailing designs and moldings, were chosen from pattern books, and rough sketches of specific parts of a building were drawn on an odd scrap of wood at the job site.[79] Thus, a building was often the spontaneous product of a carpenter's mind and experience, rather than the result of a concrete plan agreed upon in advance.

This method of building was especially troublesome when more than one supervisor or owner examined the construction. In the case of public buildings, the colonial carpenter had to proceed in a manner pleasing to the majority of a legislative assembly. Moreover, in southern colonies assemblies were likely to be composed of "gentlemen" who believed themselves to be knowledgeable about architecture. Architecture was one of the primary elements in the proper education of a gentleman. The planter's library commonly contained a copy of Vitruvius or Langley, and while an ability to define various styles was a mark of culture, a knowledge of engineering principles was considered elementary science.[80] Planters often boasted of the bridges or mills they had designed. Landon Carter emphasized in his diary that the bridge he had built on his planation was "taken from Vitruviusi's bridge over the Rhine in Julius Ceasar's days."[81]

Usually, a legislature or church vestry would designate a few of its members as the inspection committee.[82] When confusion or disagreement occurred, the carpenter would be torn between opposing factions. Even when he collected his fees, the extra time and energy expended in securing payment must have given him second thoughts about future work for such an employer.

A classic example of building procedures in the southern colonies occurred between 1742 and 1747, when Governor Bladen of Maryland commenced the erection of a suitable residence. On the approval of the Maryland assembly, Bladen commissioned Patrick Creagh of Annapolis, a master builder (who also was known as a "painter, merchant, shipbuilder, farmer, mariner, contractor for the maintenance of His Majesty's forces, and . . . gentleman"), to supply materials and labor. Creagh's work was obviously less than satisfactory because the inspection committee complained that some bricks were "moulter'd and Decayed." The committee was also dismayed by the fact that "there is a Crack in the wall of said House from the Bottom almost to the Top . . . there is a large Quantity of plank and scantling lying in great Danger of being spoiled, occasioned by the Rains coming through the Roof of the House; and that part of the sommers of the said House appears to be upon decay; Jews-Ears growing now out of the side thereof." Shoddy craftsmanship was only one cause of trouble, however, because Bladen exceeded his budget in an attempt to build an edifice on too grand a scale. His extravagance earned him a reprimand from the assembly which concluded that the governor "hath not complied with the Directions of the Act . . . to build . . . a Dwelling House and other Conveniences for the Residence of the Governor of Maryland." In typical fashion, Creagh was caught between an irate assembly, which was extremely budget conscious, and a governor whose mind was filled with visions of architectural grandeur. Creagh apparently suffered economic hardship and was forced to rely upon his other financial ventures.[83]

Other master builders also encountered the

---

[77] Chamberlaye, *Vestry Book*, pp. 126–31; see also Hall, *PAGAM*, Oct. 1723, p. 558.

[78] Very few plans from colonial America have been found. It has been suggested that the plans that were used in America were drawn in England. This does not mean that plans were totally absent. Men such as Peter Harrison and Thomas Jefferson were competent draftsmen, but they were the exception. Sometimes the plan of a building was written out and accompanied by a crude sketch. For example, see Greene, *Landon Carter*, 1:86–87; Hall, *PAGAM*, Oct. 1723, pp. 558–59.

[79] Such a scrap of wood has been found; see Whiffen, *Eighteenth Century Houses of Williamsburg*, pp. 29–30.

[80] Louis B. Wright, *The First Gentlemen of Virginia* (San Marino, Calif.: Huntington Library, 1940), pp. 117–54.

[81] Greene, *Landon Carter*, 1:457.

[82] Whiffen, *Public Buildings of Williamsburg*, p. 21, and every building project noted in Hall, *PAGAM*, Oct. 1720–Oct. 1723 and Oct. 1724–July 1726.

[83] Joy Gary, "Patrick Creagh of Annapolis," *Maryland Historical Magazine* 48, no. 4 (Dec. 1953): 310–26.

wrath of gentlemen's building committees. Upon finishing the Gate House in Annapolis in 1724, Captain Joseph Robinson was informed that before he received full payment he must complete several details and repair defective work: "The Under pinning to be finished The turning the Arch of the Chimney above Stairs to be made a Brick thicker. The plaistering above the Stairs to have the Cracks and Breakers filled up and to give it a white washing. To make the Chimney at the Gable End tight and workmanlike To Shift all the bad plank in the weather boarding."[84]

In addition to being told that their work was "indifferently done," carpenters faced the sluggish machinery of every legislative body. On January 23, 1710/11, for instance, the vestry of Christ Church in Middlesex County, Virginia, ordered a church to be built. The structure was to be "Sixty foot long and five and twenty foot wide . . . the Sills of the said Church the Sumers and Girders be of the best White Oake to be of quartered Stuff and A foot Square att least." After dealing with the builder or timber salesman, the vestry was forced to change its plans. On February 5, 1710/11, the parishioners were notified that "the Sills of *ye* aforesaid Church, which were Ordered to be of quartered Stuff being too difficult to be gott, Itt is now Ordered That the said peices be of *ye* best Ring Oake Squared with *ye* Saw of the Same Demencons."[85] Dealing with a church vestry or legislative assembly must have been a cumbersome and laborious undertaking. If carpenters began to steer clear of public contracts, it was in part because of unhappy experiences in the past.

In addition to all these difficulties, the carpenter's talent, social standing, and working habits were also ridiculed by southern gentlemen. One observer characterized the colonial artisan as the "very scum and offscouring" of England who were nothing but "vagrant or condemned persons" renowned for the "Looseness or viciousness of their lives."[86] In Virginia, a group of citizens categorically denounced all artisans for their cunning and laziness, while in South Carolina, the legislature ruled that a craftsman could not use his account book in a court of law as proof that money was owed to him by another party.[87] These gentlemen made life difficult for the carpenter, but they continued to insist that the South needed his skills.

VI. Summary

This was the carpenter's dilemma throughout the southern colonies: he was called to America because, according to the propaganda of the emigration agents, people were in desperate need of him; yet, when he arrived he was apt to find personal abuse and unemployment. The vastness of the land, the farmers' self-sufficiency, the system of slavery, and the pedantry of gentlemen combined to make most areas of the eighteenth-century South hostile toward sophisticated craftsmen. As a result, the men who worked as carpenters were not trained or skilled according to European standards, and most buildings reflected shoddy workmanship. In fact, it is difficult to prove the existence of carpenters in many sections of the rural South, because the buildings they constructed have long since collapsed.

Even the trained carpenters who lived in the southern colonies were likely to discover that traditional building techniques were unsuited to the demands of a mobile population. Americans needed light, simple buildings that were easy to assemble. Portable houses would have been ideal. To the carpenter who was educated in traditional principles these demands were absurd, for they violated the commonly accepted definition of a house. In the tobacco-growing areas of the colonial South, a house meant shelter; in the northern cities of America, it symbolized permanence. These conflicting notions caused a confusing period in the history of building technology in the southern colonies, and it was not until the nineteenth century that the profession regained a semblance of order.

[84] Hall, *PAGAM*, Oct. 1724–July 1726, proceedings for Oct. 16, 1724.

[85] Chamberlaye, *Vestry Book*, pp. 122–23, 126–31.

[86] Quoted in Marcus Wilson Jernegan, *The American Colonies, 1492–1750* (New York: Frederick Ungar Co., 1959), p. 96.

[87] *Virginia Gazette*, Oct. 1, 1772; Cooper, *Statutes at Large*, 2:511.

Index

Notes on Contributors

Jay E. Cantor is an author, lecturer, and researcher in American art and architecture.

Henry H. Glassie is assistant professor, Folklore Institute, Indiana University.

Maureen O'Brien Quimby is curator of decorative arts, Eleutherian Mills-Hagley Foundation.

The late Edward Deming Andrews was a student of Shaker history and collector of Shaker materials.

Suzanne C. Hamilton is research assistant, Bicentennial Project, National Portrait Gallery.

John F. Walzer is associate professor, Department of History, California State College at Long Beach.

Charles van Ravenswaay is director, Winterthur Museum.

James Mitchell is assistant curator of Americana, New Jersey State Museum.

Peter C. Marzio is historian, Museum of History and Technology, United States National Museum.

Portfolio 7

was composed, printed, and bound by Kingsport Press, Inc., Kingsport, Tennessee. The types are Baskerville and Bulmer, and the paper is Mohawk Superfine. Design is by Edward G. Foss.